INTRODUCTION TO
TERRORISM

Copyright © 2010 by
K & M Publishers, Inc.
Post Office Box 701083
Tulsa, OK 74170-1083
www.kmpublishers.com

Reprinted in 2010 by CRC Press

Introduction to Terrorism

by David H. McElreath, Chester L. Quarles, Carl J. Jensen, Stephen L. Mallory & Michael P. Wigginton

ISBN: 978-0-9823658-1-6

Production by

Multiprint
4606 E. 11th
Tulsa, OK 74112
918-832-0300
www.MultiprintTulsa.com

Cover Design by

Whitney Coleman
www.africangreydesigns.com

INTRODUCTION TO TERRORISM

by

David H. McElreath, Michael Wigginton, Carl J. Jensen, Chester L. Quarles and Stephen Mallory (The University of Mississippi)

I.   Authors' Credentials:

David H. McElreath, PhD: Dr. McElreath's background includes Professor and Chair, Department of Legal Studies, University of Mississippi; Professor and Chair, Department of Criminal Justice, Washburn University; Associate Professor, Southeast Missouri State University; Colonel, United States Marine Corps; and Law Enforcement and Corrections positions with the Oxford (Mississippi) Police and Forrest County (Mississippi) Sheriff's Department. His education and training include a Ph.D. in Adult Education and Criminal Justice, University of Southern Mississippi; M.S.S., United States Army War College; M.C.J., University of Mississippi; B.P.A., University of Mississippi; graduate of the United States Army War College. He is also the author of numerous publications on the criminal justice system.

Michael Wigginton, PhD: Dr. Wigginton's background includes Assistant Professor of Criminal Justice and Director of the University of Mississippi Master of Criminal Justice Executive Cohort Program, Department of Legal Studies, with the University of Mississippi, former Assistant Professor, Southeast Louisiana University and an adjunct professor with Tulane University, Senior Special Agent, United States Customs Service, Special Agent, United States Drug Enforcement Administration, detective and State Trooper, Louisiana State Police, police officer, New Orleans Police Department and an United States Air Force Security Police Dog Handler with service in Vietnam. His education and training include a Ph.D. in Criminal Justice, University of Southern Mississippi; M.S. The University of New Orleans; M.S. The University of Alabama; B.A. Loyola University of New Orleans. He is also the author of numerous publications on the criminal justice system.

Carl J. Jensen, PhD: Dr. Jensen's background includes Assistant Professor, Department of Legal Studies, University of Mississippi and Senior Behavioral Scientist at the RAND Corporation. He served as a Special Agent with the Federal Bureau of Investigation (FBI) for 22 years; his FBI career included service as a field agent, a Forensic Examiner in the FBI Laboratory, and an Instructor and Assistant Chief of the Behavioral Science Unit. Prior to that, he served as a Naval Officer aboard a nuclear fleet ballistic missile submarine. He received a B.S. degree from the U.S. Naval Academy, an M.A. from Kent State University and a Ph.D. from the University of Maryland. He has published extensively and has lectured throughout the world. Dr. Jensen and his family reside in Oxford, Mississippi.

Chester L. Quarles, Ph.D., CPP: Dr. Quarles' background includes Professor of Criminal Justice at the University of Mississippi; Director of the Mississippi Bureau of Narcotics; CEO of his own private security company; Director, Mississippi Crime Lab;

Criminal Investigator of the Mississippi Department of Public Safety; Criminal Investigator (Certified) of the United States Army; and Military Policeman, United States Army. His education and training includes a Ph.D. in Criminal Justice from Sam Houston State University; M.A. in Sociology/Criminology from the University of Mississippi; and B.S. Degree in Criminology from Florida State University. He is also a graduate of the Mississippi Highway Patrol Academy, the U.S. Army Criminal Investigation Course and the U.S. Army Military Police Academy. He has been recognized as a Certified Protection Professional, a Certified International Investigator and as a Fellow in the Institute of Professional Investigators. He has written six books, coauthored seven books, and has published some seventy plus articles during his career. He and his family reside in Tula, Mississippi.

Stephen Mallory, PhD: Dr. Mallory's background includes Professor, Department of Legal Studies, University of Mississippi, Professor and former chair, Department of Criminal Justice, University of Southern Mississippi, senior agent, Mississippi Bureau of Narcotics. His education and training include a Ph.D., University of Mississippi; M.S. The University of Southern Mississippi; B.S. Mississippi State University and the FBI National Academy. He is also the author of numerous publications on the criminal justice system to include Understanding Organized Crime (2007).

INTRODUCTION TO TERRORISM

Table of Contents

Chapter	Title	Page
	FOUNDATIONS OF TERRORISM	
1	THE EVER CHANGING WORLD	1
2	HISTORY OF TERRORISM	17
3	THE STRUCTURE AND PSYCHOLOGY OF TERRORIST GROUPS	49
4	TERRORISM AS A WEAPON OF CHANGE	77
	TERRORISM TODAY	
5	TRANSITIONAL THREATS: ORGANIZED CRIME AND TERRORISM	99
6	INTERNATIONAL TERRORISM: STATE SPONSORS OF TERRORISM	127
7	INTERNATIONAL TERRORISM: GROUPS AND MOVEMENTS	147
8	DOMESTIC TERRORISM	179
	COMBATING TERRORISM	
9	COMBATING TERRORISM: THE UNITED STATES	213
10	COUNTERING INTERNATIONAL TERRORISM	249
11	DISASTER AND TERRORISM EVENT RECOVERY	287
12	THE ROLE OF INTELLIGENCE IN THE WAR ON TERROR	315
13	KEY INTERNATIONAL PARTNERS IN THE WAR ON TERROR	345
14	FUTURE OF TERRORISM	375

CHAPTER 1
THE EVER CHANGING WORLD

From Stettin in the Baltic to Trieste in the Adriatic, an iron curtain has descended across the Continent. *Winston Churchill* (1946)

Introduction

Since the earliest days of mankind, the world has been in a state of globalization: economically, socially, diplomatically and militarily. Countless cultures have merged, dominated and disappeared. Trade routes have developed, explorers have sought new discoveries and the globe has become a much smaller place. Today, few parts of the world are inaccessible.

Advances in communication and transportation technology, combined with free-market ideology, have given goods, services, and capital unprecedented mobility. The vast majority of countries want to open world markets to their goods and take advantage of abundant, cheap labor in other parts of the world.

Beginning in the latter half of the 20th century, international financial institutions and regional trade agreements reduced tariffs, in some cases privatizing state enterprises and relaxing environmental and labor standards. Transnational corporations have become some of the largest economic entities in the world, surpassing many states. Their continuous push for liberalization has driven globalization while challenging environmental, health, and labor standards in many countries. In many countries, the US dollar became the national currency. In others, the national currency has been pegged to the US dollar.

Prior to the 20th Century

It is unfair to history to lump centuries of social, economic and political evolution into a few paragraphs, but for the purpose of this text, human history is divided in the pre and post 20th century. In the history of human civilization prior to 1900, various nations rose to great power. China, ancient and medieval Japan, Egypt, the powers of the Middle East, the Turks, pre-Latin Central and South America, Greeks, Romans, Spanish, French and British all gained great power during our global history. Each of these nations saw its power and influence rise and then decline as the result to social, political, and economic forces.

The 20th Century

The 20th Century proved to be a period of scientific and social advancement unparallel in human history. As the century dawned, the major world powers were concentrated in Europe and operated predominately under various forms of monarchies. By the end of the 20th century, the old monarchies had ceased to exist or had witnessed their powers dramatically reduced. The United States and the Soviet Union had emerged as global superpowers during the 2nd half of the century in a struggle for power and influence that would end with the collapse of the Soviet Union.

Globalization

The world is in a dynamic time of change, a time of globalization unseen in the past. Today, we are witnessing a globalization encompassing a wide range of social, political and economic changes. A revolution in technology, science, industry, agriculture, environmental and social issues. A time of cultural classes, many linked to religious differences. A time of internal conflicts in which nations reexamined their vital national interests. A time in which the developed nations looked at the dangers posed by undeveloped, transitional and failed nations.

With the end of World War II, the United States and the Soviet Union emerged as global superpowers. Under their influence, the world would be divided for the next four decades in what became known as "the bi-polar" world. During those four decades, economic, social, political and military power was used globally as the two superpowers continually tested themselves in a dangerous game to achieve the international advantage.

During the late 1980s, the long struggle between the United States and the Soviet Union came to an end with the fall of the Soviet Union. As the bi-polar world dissolved, the United States emerged as the world's only remaining economic and military superpower. For a time, there was great optimism that stability had finally come to the world; scholar Francis Fukuyama went so far as to assert that we had witnessed "the end of history." He predicted that liberal democracy (as practiced in the West) had so demonstrably shown itself to be the "one, true way" that all other forms of government would inevitably fall away (Fukuyama, 1992). This proved to be untrue. From the bi-polar world emerged a multi-polar world and the multi-polar would prove to be a world full of its own unique challenges and dangers.

The forces that would help shape the new world were in play long before the Cold War ended. As early as 1979, two seemingly unrelated events unfolded whose wide-ranging ramifications would not be understood for a long time to come: the Shah of Iran, a staunch ally of the United States was deposed and the Soviet Union invaded Afghanistan.

The Rise of a Theocratic Iran

Mohammed Reza Shah Pahlavi came to power as the Shah of Iran in classic Cold War style. In 1951, the Iranian people had elected Mohammed Mosaddeq as the Prime Minister of Iran. However, his threat to nationalize the massive Iranian oil industry and his friendship with the Soviet Union concerned the United States and Britain. In 1953, with substantial assistance from the CIA, the popular Mosaddeq was deposed in a coup and Pahlavi, thereafter often just referred to as the Shah, was installed as the leader of Iran.

The Shah would prove a great friend to the United States. He supported the modernization of his country, maintained cordial relations with the West, and was the first leader of a Muslim nation to recognize the state of Israel. These attributes, however, did not endear him to many of his subjects. As well, the wealth in Iran was not evenly distributed. Those close to the Shah enjoyed great prosperity while most received little. In order to maintain control, the Shah employed a brutal secret police called the SAVAK which imprisoned and tortured several thousand political prisoners during his reign.

By 1979, the people of Iran had suffered enough. The Shah was convinced to leave the country for his own safety; suffering from cancer, he stayed for short periods of time in several different countries before succumbing to the disease in 1980 in the United States. The fact that he had been strongly supported by the United States and was allowed to die there infuriated many Iranians.

In his place, the people installed the Grand Ayatollah Seyyed Ruhollah Musavi Khomeini as the first Supreme Leader of Iran. Khomeini had served all his life as a religious leader; for his opposition to the Shah, he had been exiled to Paris. Upon his triumphant return and appointment as leader, he declared Iran to be an Islamic Republic, with all facets of government guided by his very conservative Shi'a interpretation of Islam. Unlike the Shah, Khomeini was no friend of the United States. When several of his followers took over the U.S. embassy in Teheran in 1979 and held its occupants hostage for 444 days, Khomeini at first did nothing; later, he gave the hostage takers his support.

The Ayatollah continued to rule Iran until his death in 1989. After he died, the country continued as a theocracy, with power primarily invested in Iran's Shi'a leadership.

Soviet Invasion of Afghanistan

The installation of the Ayatollah Khomeini in Iran was not the only watershed event to occur in 1979. That same year, the Soviet Union invaded Afghanistan, its neighbor to the south, to prop up an allied government that was wildly unpopular with the Afghan people. The Soviets were confident that, with the world's largest land army, they would make quick work of the Afghan rebellion. However, ten years later, a humiliated Soviet army retreated in defeat.

This shocking turn of events came about for several reasons. Chief among these was the fierce resistance put up by the mujahedeen, a group of devout Muslim fighters who came from throughout the world to expel the "infidel" Soviet army from a Muslim country. Initially, the mujahedeen met with little success—they were no match for the well trained, technologically superior Soviets. However, once U.S. aid was funneled through the CIA, such as Stinger missiles that proved deadly to Soviet helicopters, the mujahedeen staged a stunning comeback. The resistance of these fighters, the generally inhospitable conditions of Afghanistan, the unpopularity of the war in the Soviet Union and the demoralized state of the Soviet troops all conspired to hasten the Soviet Union's defeat. While it wasn't recognized at the time, the victory of the mujahedeen would have profound effects later for the United States.

Victory also had profound and, at the time, little recognized ramifications for the mujahedeen. Many of these fighters returned to their native countries. However, some stayed behind in Afghanistan. Energized by their victory over the Soviets, these former fighters were convinced that God had not only engineered the Soviet defeat, but that He had greater plans for them. One of those who stayed behind was a rich expatriate from Saudi Arabia named Osama bin Laden. Raised in an ultra wealthy family whose patriarch owned a construction company, bin Laden embraced a conservative, austere form of Islam named Wahhabism. Soon after the Soviet invasion, he traveled to Afghanistan and served in the resistance until the end of the war. With the defeat of the Soviet Union complete, the United States paid little further attention to Afghanistan and, initially, to bin Laden. This would prove to be a stunningly bad decision.

The ramifications of the war for the Soviets were immediate and extreme. For years, the weak Soviet economy had struggled to support the massive Soviet bureaucracy, military, and surrogate countries such as Cuba. The Afghan War proved to be the final nail in the Soviet Union's coffin. Victory over the Soviets by the Mujahedeen only bolstered confidence that "with Allah, all things are possible." With breathtaking speed after the fall of the Berlin Wall on November 9, 1989, the Soviet Union ceased to exist. Instead, Russia and a host of new countries emerged from its ashes.

Globalization: The Fall of the Soviet Union and the Rise of an Islamic Theocracy in Iran; Prelude to the 21st Century

The fall of the Soviet Union and the rise of a theocracy in Iran helped set the stage for the emerging concept of globalization. Iran became a model for political Islam. This is a model that would be emulated by countries (e.g., Sudan, Afghanistan) as well as by groups that sought to expand political control (e.g., Hizbollah, Hamas, al Qaeda) in the early part of the 21st century.

For a time after the end of the Cold War, U.S. domination on the world stage seemed all but assured. In all arenas—military, cultural, and economic—America reigned supreme. However, that dominance proved short-lived. Another phenomenon termed "globalization" began to take hold. In short, globalization refers to the coming together of people and economic markets. It lessens the significance of countries and increases the importance of individuals and companies. That could not have been possible in a bi-polar world in which economies were guarded and protected and the movement of people and communications were tightly regulated. When the Soviet Union dissolved, markets opened, economic barriers disappeared, and people began to move about freely.

What has changed? A confluence of factors has worked together to create a phenomenon known as **globalization,** which Bhagwati defines as:

> [The] integration of national economies into the international economy through trade, direct foreign investment…short-term capital flows, international flows of workers and humanity generally, and flows of technology…" (Bhagwati, p. 3)

Consider the General Motors (GM) example. Charles Wilson, President of GM and a future Secretary of Defense in the 1950s made this statement, *What is good for the country is good for General Motors and vice versa.* His point was that the success of the United States and its large corporations were inexorably linked. If GM did well, it would increase America's wealth, employ many citizens and pay large taxes. Likewise, as long as the United States prospered, GM would have a steady supply of customers eager for its products. While that statement may have made sense when he made it, consider the situation today: GM products are manufactured in 33 different countries (General Motors, n.d.). There is no longer any brand of automobile that is exclusively manufactured in the United States. The phrase "buy American," which was popular in the 1970s, is becoming increasingly irrelevant. At the time of the Wilson statement GM products were made exclusively in the United States, all of GM's revenues benefited the American economy. Today, GM's revenues benefit the economies of the 33 countries in which its products are manufactured. In essence, the world is moving toward a global economy.

There are many reasons this is occurring. One big one is the proliferation and development of new technologies, especially with regard to computers. Consider how personal computers and the Internet have changed the world in a few, short years. Instantaneous, global, cheap, and dependable forms of communication are the norm today. Retrieval of vast amounts of information is at one's fingertips.

One of the realities of the globalized world is the speed at which technology changes. Author and inventor Ray Kurzweil has developed the "Law of Accelerating Returns," in which he suggests that the rate of technological change is itself increasing. He predicts that, in the next several years, we may witness technological growth unfathomable today. Such things as artificial intelligence, nano-engineering, robotic humans, and vastly extended human life-spans may become reality rather than the stuff of science fiction. To that end, we should be prepared for the global world to change rapidly around us (Kurzweil, 2000).

Businesses today are already taking advantage of the leaps and bounds that have been made in recent technological advancement. Many are completely automated with billing, ordering, and mailing all accomplished online. When you pick up the phone to call technical services for a computer problem, the chances are great that the person who helps you will be overseas. That is because technology has allowed American companies to outsource various services to take advantage of the cheap labor found in foreign countries.

It's not just services, either. The inexpensive shirt that you purchase at the local department store may very well have been manufactured in Asia. Companies have found that many products can be made more cheaply overseas and shipped to America.

While technology is certainly essential in this process, it is not the only important factor. Globalization on the scale that we are seeing it could not have occurred in a bi-polar world. The markets of unfriendly nations were either closed to one another or high tariffs were placed on imported and exported items, making them very expensive to purchase. However, when the bi-polar world ceased to be, many countries made the political decision to open their markets. Alliances such as the European Union (EU), the North Atlantic Free Trade Agreement (NAFTA) and the World Trade Organization (WTO) were crafted to facilitate freer markets.

The opening of markets has produced a global supply chain in which raw materials and finished goods routinely travel between countries. This has produced a record number of imports coming into the United States. In fact, so much is brought through American ports that only a small percentage is ever examined by Customs officials. As a result, experts have opined that terrorists could exploit this weakness by introducing a weapon of mass destruction through a U.S. port that would easily avoid detection.

Globalization, however, is not only an economic phenomenon; it is a social one as well. Today, people move across borders as they never have before. Immigrants and visitors come into the United States in unprecedented numbers. While America has always prided itself on integrating newcomers into its "melting pot" society, the sheer number of new arrivals severely challenges homeland security and law enforcement officials. While the overwhelming majority of immigrants are law-abiding citizens looking for a better life, criminal organizations from foreign lands have also found their way into the United States (see the case study of Mara Salvatrucha). Moreover, many immigrants enter the United States illegally, generally through Mexico. Many officials are concerned that weak border security could be exploited by terrorists entering the United States undetected.

Ramifications of Globalization for Homeland Security

Globalization has had an overall positive effect on the world and United States' economies. However, it has also redefined the way we conceptualize "security." What benefits us also benefits those who would do us harm.

The advent of globalization has shifted the balance of power in the world today. While the United States has enjoyed the financial benefits of outsourcing services and purchasing cheap imports, the big winners have actually been the countries engaged in these activities. Many experts predict that the emerging superpowers in the world will be China and India, whose economies and influence on the world stage are expected to continue to increase, even as those of the U.S. decline (National Intelligence Council, 2004).

China, for one, does not appear content to confine its growth only to the economic arena. It has also increased its military reach accordingly; for example, the discovery of a secret Chinese nuclear submarine base in 2008 has raised concerns that China may attempt to challenge United States maritime dominance in the Pacific (Harding, 2008).

Another obvious concern in a world of ubiquitous communications and easy travel is the spread of dangerous technologies. Perhaps nothing worries homeland security officials more than the possibility that either a nuclear weapon or nuclear technology will fall into the wrong hands. When the Soviet Union dissolved, there was great concern that some of its nuclear arsenal would make its way to terrorist groups. This was not an unreasonable worry: in the days following the collapse of its economy, Soviet nuclear facilities were often poorly guarded. Further, those entrusted with the care of nuclear weapons were poorly paid, if at all. This led to speculation that someone might try to sell a nuclear weapon or nuclear material on the black market. In fact, al Qaeda's number two leader, Ayman al-Zawahri, has claimed that the group has already purchased a number of "suitcase nukes" from disgruntled Russian scientists, a claim Russia has officially denied (Badkhen, 2004).

Countries That Possess Nuclear Weapons		
Members of the Nuclear Proliferation Treaty Known to Possess Nuclear Weapons	**Other Known Nuclear Powers (Countries That Have Detonated Nuclear Weapons)**	**Undeclared Nuclear Weapons States**
United States Russia United Kingdom France China	India Pakistan North Korea	Israel

Perhaps a more likely and imminent threat concerns the continued development of nuclear technology on the part of nation-states. As of the writing of this book, Iran is suspected by many of being on the threshold of developing its own nuclear weapon. This would not only lead to the further destabilization of an already volatile Middle East, it would also raise the unpalatable possibility that such a weapon would fall into the hands of an Iranian terrorist surrogate, such as Hezbollah.

As the 9-11 attacks made clear, it is not just nation-states that have the ability to wreak havoc on the United States. Today, technology allows even little groups to act "big." If the Internet has been a blessing for the average citizen, it has proven to be a godsend for international and domestic terrorists and criminals, allowing them to spread their ideology and communicate with one another easily and cheaply. Individuals no longer need to meet physically to swap ideas and plan activities; much if not all of that can be carried on in cyberspace. Additionally, sociologists and social psychologists have long recognized the dynamics that occur within groups. Group members can encourage one another and build cohesion, especially if there is a perceived threat from an outsider. Historically, individuals have had to meet face-to-face for this to emerge; however, with the advent of the Internet, the notion of the "cyber sense of group" can promote a similar phenomenon. What's more, before the Internet, individuals had to seek out others of a like mind to establish a meaningful group. This could be a laborious process and people with radical or "different" ideas were often unsuccessful in finding others who shared their beliefs. That is no longer the case. With the advent of chat rooms, social networking sites and electronic bulletin boards, groups can be quickly and easily assembled in cyberspace.

The Internet also allows for the rapid dissemination of information of all types. Compared to other forms of deadly technology, information about developing nuclear weapons remains generally secure, at least for the present. That is certainly not the case with chemical, biological or radiological weapons, however. For example, documents seized in Afghanistan reveal that al Qaeda possessed crude procedures for producing VX nerve agent, sarin and mustard gas. As well, recipes for deadly substances like ricin and procedures for making radiological "dirty" bombs circulate freely on the Internet (Stratfor, 2004).

Instructions for making poisons and bombs are not the only advantage the Internet offers terrorist groups. Today, a single individual has the ability to gather and analyze information in a way that only sophisticated intelligence agencies once could. Consider the numerous maps, satellite photos, and information about America's critical infrastructure that currently appears online. The intelligence community recognizes the considerable value of this "open source" intelligence: recently, the CIA opened its Open Source Center to gather and analyze the vast amount of information that gets released to the public daily (CIA, 2005).

Ironically, it's not just the information on the Internet that has made us more vulnerable, it's the Internet itself. The original concept for the Internet was developed as far back as Russia's launch of the Sputnik satellite in 1957. Worried about losing its technological dominance over the Soviet Union, the United States government opened the Advanced Research Projects Agency (ARPA) in the late 1950s. One of ARPA's projects was the development of a robust network of computers that could survive major losses to the underlying network. This system, dubbed the ARPANET, was the predecessor to today's Internet (Defense Advanced Research Projects Agency, 1981).

Today, many systems in the United States, such as those that control utilities and dams, are run through the Internet. Hackers have already demonstrated the ability to break into these vulnerable systems, worrying officials who fear that terrorists or extortionists may do the same (Baschuk, n.d.).

Another major concern that officials in the globalized world have is the occurrence of a "Cyber Pearl Harbor," an attack of epic proportions which could disable major parts of the Internet. Such an attack could have enormous ramifications for business, government, and the average citizen (Miller, 2007).

Advanced technologies and open borders don't only benefit nations and terrorist groups. They have also made America increasingly vulnerable to transnational criminal organizations. Organized crime groups and individuals from as far away as Russia, Asia, Africa and South America increasingly victimize U.S. citizens and companies. As well, the revolution in communications and technology has created whole new types of criminal activity, such as identity theft, the fastest growing crime in the United States. American law enforcement agencies by and large have proven incapable of stopping this crime and arresting perpetrators, many of whom operate with impunity beyond U.S. borders. Today, because of the power they wield and the sophisticated tactics they can employ, some criminal organizations are even considered threats to American national security (FBI, 2005).

A major theme of globalization is the increasing empowerment of even small groups. Consider the case of al Qaeda, a relatively small organization. In the wake of the 9-11 attacks, the United States has been forced to respond to its activities the way it historically reacted to foreign enemy states. Technology and the unrestricted movement of personnel have proven to be force multipliers for al Qaeda, allowing it to wield a level of influence on the world stage unthinkable years ago.

Perhaps the greatest challenge facing homeland security officials comes not from outside the organization but from inside. Those who study globalization note that, in a world of speedy computers and ever-changing cultural and social networks, it is the swift and flexible, and not the big, who usually survive. Many criminal and terrorist organizations understand this; they have "flattened" their organizational structures, thereby exploiting the power of the computer age. Not all agree that the United States government has done the same. For example, the Department of Homeland Security was created after the attacks of 9-11 to allow for better sharing of information and resources across agencies. Some critics contend, however, that this has just produced an even more bloated bureaucracy, slow and fundamentally incapable of keeping up with a rapidly evolving enemy (Paul, 2007).

The Global World: Demographics

Globalization is not just about technology and business, it is about people as well. World population is expected to increase significantly in the next several years. Population growth, however, will not occur uniformly. Some countries, such as the United States, have low rates of birth which produces an "aging" population (one in which the average age is increasing). Still other areas of the world, such as the Middle East and Africa, are experiencing "youth bulges" with large numbers of children being born (CIA, 2004). Unfortunately, many of the countries experiencing youth bulges also suffer from failed or failing economies. This volatile combination—large numbers of poor and unemployed youth fueled by rage and humiliation—could provide a fertile recruiting ground for criminal and terrorist organizations.

Terrorism: A Backlash to Globalization?

Whenever there is a rapid change in the social order, there are often groups or individuals who oppose it. For example, in the early part of the nineteenth century, a group of British textile workers protested against changes brought about by the industrial revolution by destroying mechanized weaving looms. This group, dubbed the Luddites, felt their livelihoods were threatened by new technology.

Like the anti-technology stance of the Luddites, much of today's terrorism can be seen as a response against globalization. Certainly, most terrorist groups embrace and readily use new technologies, such as the Internet.[1] However, many object to other aspects of globalization, particularly the increasing power of international business and the movement of people and culture throughout the world. For example, in the 1990s, many militia groups spoke against the "New World Order" that they thought was secretly being installed. They believed that the new order consisted of a one-world government along the lines of a dictatorship of the wealthy over all others; they viewed globalized business as a particular enemy. Al Qaeda can also be seen as having a similar anti-globalization agenda. Osama bin

---

[1] A notable exception to this was Theodore Kaczynski, dubbed "The UNABOMBER" by the FBI. To protest what he thought was the erosion of human freedom by modern technology, Kaczynski carried out a deadly series of bombings over the course of seventeen years. Kaczynski was fiercely against modern technology, going so far as to craft nails and hinges used in the bombs. Although diagnosed as suffering from paranoid schizophrenia, Kaczynski is widely admired by some anarchist groups today who support both his theories and tactics (Corey, 1998).

Laden is clear in his desire to remove representatives of foreign governments and un-Islamic leadership from Muslim lands and in his disdain for the "decadent" culture of the West. Instead, he favors a return to the "perfect" times of the 7th century, when the Prophet Mohammed lived. Finally, environmental and anarchist groups direct much of their anger against international business concerns, which are viewed as polluters of the earth and exploiters of poor and indigenous people.

Barring some unforeseen economic or other catastrophe, globalization is likely to continue and may well increase. As it expands, the response against it will likely intensify as well. Viewed in this context, we can expect little relief from terrorism and other forms of pushback, at least in the near term.

Clash of Civilizations

In some ways, the whole of human history can be viewed as a series of conflicts. From all-out, bloody struggles, such as World War II, to more subtle affairs like the Cold War, humankind fights with itself with depressing regularity. Many wonder, what will prove to be the defining struggle of the global age? One scholar, Samuel Huntington, has produced a provocative body of research that suggests the struggle will not involve countries as much as it will involve cultures and religions. Huntington's premise has generated much debate. To many, it appears consistent with the current fight between the al Qaeda movement and the West and its tenets fit nicely with the realities of the globalized world. Huntington is not, however, without critics. Because of the large debate and discussion his work has generated, we consider it here.

Huntington calls his theory the "Clash of Civilizations." He wrote it in response to a 1992 book by former RAND Corporation social scientist Francis Fukuyama titled *The End of History and the Last Man*. Fukuyama's premise was that, with the end of the Cold War, liberal democracy had "triumphed" over all other forms of government and would forever reign as the final form of governance (Fukuyama, 1992).

Huntington disagreed. In a 1993 article in the journal *Foreign Affairs*, he declared:

> It is my hypothesis that the fundamental source of conflict in this new world will not be primarily ideological or primarily economic. The great divisions among humankind and the dominating source of conflict will be cultural. Nation states will remain the most powerful actors in world affairs, but the principal conflicts of global politics will occur between nations and groups of different civilizations. The clash of civilizations will dominate global politics. The fault lines between civilizations will be the battle lines of the future (Huntington, 1993, pp. 45-57).

According to Huntington, several civilizations currently exist in the world. He identified them as

o   The West
o   The Orthodox World (including Russia and many of its former satellites)
o   Latin America
o   The Muslim World
o   The Hindu World
o   The Sinic Civilization (including China, Korea, and other Asian countries)
o   Japan
o   Sub-Saharan Africa
o   Buddhist Areas
o   Various "Lone States" (Ethiopia, Haiti, and Turkey)

Huntington was especially concerned about potential conflicts between the West and Islam. According to him, each was based on an "absolutist" religious tradition which viewed itself as the one, true way. The root of the conflict between the two civilizations ran deep—all the way back to the Crusades and the Muslim conquest and occupation of Europe. More recently, Western imperialism in the Middle East and "universalism" (the view that all civilizations should adopt western values) has enraged Muslim populations; according to Huntington, this combined with the "youth bulges" and economic troubles present in the Middle East will inevitably lead to conflict (Huntington 1993, 1998).

The rise of al Qaeda in the 1990s and the attacks of 9-11 proved to many that Huntington was prescient in his analysis. However, not everyone agreed. Some claim that Huntington has mis-identified the cultures that exist in the world. Still others argue that, in a globalized society, people may embrace many identities simultaneously (e.g., religious, national, ethnic). These may co-exist or clash, even at the individual level. Finally, some question whether conflict is inevitable—will different groups be forever consigned to fighting or can some lasting peace emerge across cultures?

Despite these criticisms, Huntington's view has proven resilient. It has provided those involved in homeland security with a theoretical template to consider the present and near-term future. Other paradigms will no doubt emerge; they should be considered with equal seriousness.

Conclusion

After the end of the Cold War, American military, cultural, and economic domination of the world seemed complete. However, even as the United States enjoyed the illusion of dominance, other forces were at work that would change the world radically. The installation of a strict Islamic theocracy in Iran set the stage for other countries and groups to follow. The mujahedeen, who defeated the Soviet Union in Afghanistan with the help of the United States, were energized by this defeat and encouraged by the existence of an Islamic state run by clerics. They would soon emerge as al Qaeda, the number one terrorist threat faced by the United States today.

The dissolution of the Soviet Union destroyed the bi-polar world. As enemies became friends, economic markets were opened and new alliances were formed. Assisted by new technologies such as the Internet, this process became known as "globalization." In short, globalization represented the integration of national economies into one international one and the rapid, easy movement of people, goods, culture, and ideas.

While globalization is generally viewed as an economic construct, it produces many challenges for homeland security. The Internet allows terrorist groups to communicate and share ideas, such as recipes for weapons of mass destruction. Open borders provide opportunities for terrorists and criminals to travel internationally with little difficulty. The very concept of globalization has spurred the formation of new terrorist groups who object to international economies as well as the dispersion of people and culture into previously closed societies.

Finally, the globalized world has caused us look differently at conflict and the behavior of societies. Samuel Huntington has developed a theory he calls "the clash of civilizations" which divides the world into different clusters and argues that conflict between certain "civilizations" is all but inevitable. Although Huntington is not without his critics, his innovative style of examining the world is one that will likely be emulated in the formation of other paradigms.

The world continues to change around us—future challenges to homeland security will come from a variety of sources, some of which we presently recognize--such rogue states, transnational criminal organizations, natural disasters and terrorist groups--and others which have yet to emerge. It is therefore incumbent upon those entrusted with the protection of our homeland to remain ever vigilant to the dynamic threats we face. Otherwise, we are doomed to repeat the mistakes of our past.

Case Study: Mara Salvatrucha

For many, the word "gang" conjures up an image of a group of disaffected young people engaged in criminality to gain identity, raise money, and acquire and maintain "turf." However, many of the gangs of today are better described as true transnational criminal organizations. Consider the case of Mara Salvatrucha, also known as MS-13, which the FBI describes as "one of the greatest threats to the safety and security of all Americans" (FBI, 2005).

MS-13, which originated in Los Angeles in the 1980s, was started by El Salvadorian immigrants, many of whom had participated in or been victimized by that country's bloody civil war. Unusually violent, MS-13 members engage in drug distribution, murder, rape, prostitution, robbery, home invasions, immigration offenses, kidnapping, carjackings/auto thefts, and vandalism.. They have also been known to violently assault law enforcement officers.

With an estimated 10,000 members currently located throughout the UNITED STATES and an estimated 100,000 members worldwide, they are truly a transnational entity, with members traveling freely between the UNITED STATES, Canada, Mexico, Guatemala, Colombia, Spain, Great Britain and Germany.

Their ability to travel freely and the level of fear and intimidation they bring to their communities has proved a difficult challenge for security officials, who most recently have set up extensive international task forces to deal with the threat. There has also been concern registered by UNITED STATES officials that international terrorist groups like al Qaeda may attempt to establish alliances with MS-13 to facilitate the movement of terrorists into the United States.

Sources: FBI, 2005, 2008; ABC 5, 2006; MSNBC, 2006

References

ABC 5 (2006). *MS-13/Al-Qaeda connection*. Retrieved August 15, 2008, from
http://www.newschannel5.tv/2005/2/28/1671/MS-13-Al-Qaeda-Connection

Badkhen, A. (2004). Al Qaeda bluffing about having suitcase nukes, experts say. *San Francisco Chronicle*. Retrieved August 15, 2008, from http://www.sfgate.com/cgi-in/article.cgi?file=/chronicle/archive/2004/03/23/MNG8D5PM7L1.DTL

Baschuk, B. (n.d.). Hackers can use Internet search to take down utilities, other companies *Washington Internet Daily*. Retrieve August 15, 2008, from http://www.infragardmembers.org/modules/articles/article.php?id=33

Bhagwati, J. (2004). *In defense of globalization*. New York: Oxford University Press, USA

CIA. (2005). Establishment *of the DNI Open Source Center: DNI and D/CIA announce establishment of the DNI Open Source Center*. Retrieved August 15, 2008, from https://www.cia.gov/news-information/press-releases-statements/press-release-archive-2005/pr11082005.html

Corey, S. (1998) Revolutionary suicide. *Salon*. Retrieved September 10, 2008, from http://www.salon.com/news/1998/01/21news.html

Defense Advanced Research Projects Agency. (1981). *A History of the ARPANET: The first decade*, (prepared by Bolt, Beranek and Newman). Washington, D.C.: Defense Tech. Info.

FBI. (2005). *Statement of Chris Swecker, Assistant Director, Criminal Investigative Division, Federal Bureau of Investigation, before the Subcommittee on the Western Hemisphere House International Relations Committee, April 20, 2005*. Retrieved August 15, 2008, from http://www.fbi.gov/congress/congress05/swecker042005.htm

Friedman, T. (2007). The *World is Flat: A Brief History of the Twenty-First Century (3rd release)*. New York: Macmillan (Farrar, Straus and Giroux).

Fukuyama, F. (1992). *The end of history and the last man*. New York: Free Press.

General Motors. (n.d.). *About GM*. Retrieved August 15, 2008, from http://www.gm.com/corporate/about/

Harding, T. (2008). *Chinese nuclear submarines prompt 'new Cold War' warning*. Retrieved August 15, 2008, from http://www.telegraph.co.uk/news/newstopics/uselection2008/1920917/Chinese-nuclear-submarines-prompt-'new-Cold-War'-warning.html

Huntington, S. (1993). The clash of civilizations? *Foreign Affairs* 72(3): 44-57 Excerpt retrieved from http://www.foreignaffairs.org/19930601faessay5188/samuel-p-huntington/the-clash-of-civilizations.html.

Huntington, S. (1998). *The clash of civilizations and the remaking of world order.* New York: Simon and Shuster.

Kurzweil, R. (2000). *The age of spiritual machines: When computers exceed human intelligence.* New York: Penguin.

Miller, J. (2007). *Feds take 'cyber Pearl Harbor' seriously.* Retrieved August 15, 2008, from http://www.fcw.com/print/13_17/news/102825-1.html

MSNBC. (2006). *MS-13' is one of nation's most dangerous gangs.* Retrieved August 14, 2008, from http://www.msnbc.msn.com/id/11240718/

National Intelligence Council. (2004). *Mapping the global future: Report of the National Intelligence Council's 2020 project.* Washington, DC:

9-11 Commission. (2004). *Final report of the National Commission on terrorist attacks upon the United States.* Washington, D.C.: National Commission on Terrorist Attacks Upon the United States/Government Printing Office.

Paul, R. (2007). *Security, Washington-style.* Retrieved August 15, 2008, from http://www.lewrockwell.com/paul/paul386.html

Stratfor. (2004). *Al Qaeda and the threat of chemical and biological weapons.* Retrieved August 15, 2008 from http://www.stratfor.com/al_qaeda_and_threat_chemical_and_biological_weapons

Wilson, C. (n.d.) *What's good for the country is good for General Motors, and vice versa.* Retrieved August 15, 2008, from http://www.answers.com/topic/what-s-good-for-the-country-is-good-for-general-motors-and-vice-versa

16

CHAPTER 2
THE HISTORY OF TERRORISM

While we must remain determined to defeat terrorism, it isn't only terrorism we are fighting. It's the beliefs that motivate terrorists. A new ideology of hatred and intolerance has arisen to challenge America and liberal democracy.
Senator John Kerry

Introduction

Throughout world history, government entities have dealt with terrorism and the fear, panic, and chaos it produces. As this text book will illustrate, acts of terrorism are motivated by secular and religious beliefs. Secular terrorist organizations such as the Sicarri perpetrated acts of terrorism to drive the occupying Roman forces out of Judea. The Assassins were an Islamic religious terrorist group who engaged in acts of terrorism to cleanse the Islamic faith.

The French Revolution has been described as the birth of modern era terrorism. The term "terrorism" originated during the reign of terror in which the Republic executed thousands of French citizens. Moreover, the French Revolution is a prime example of state sponsored terrorism because of the atrocities that were committed by the French Republic against its own people.

The 19th century gave rise to anarchism and nationalism. During this period in world history, Nobel invented dynamite and the use of explosives revolutionized the tactics employed by terrorist organizations. Bombings by anarchist and nationalist terrorist organizations increased the amount death and carnage which increased a deep rooted sense of fear for their intended victims. These horrific acts were designed to demoralize government officials and have governments capitulate to their demands.

After World War II, many ethno-nationalist groups committed acts of terrorism in order to have the right of self-determination. Their main objective was to receive their independence from their European colonial rulers. During this period in the history of terrorism, revolutionaries were labeled as terrorists while those who sought the right of self-determination considered themselves to be freedom fighters. In order to understand the terrorist threat we must have an understanding of the origins of terrorism.

Ancient Acts of Terrorism

Tyrannicide

Terrorism is not a new phenomenon. The origins of terrorism can be traced back to the Ancient Greeks who believed in the act of tyrannicide or the killing of a tyrant. According to Harty (1912), "Tyrannicide literally is the killing of a tyrant, and usually is taken to mean the killing of a tyrant by a private person for the common good" (p.1). The term does not apply to tyrants killed in battle or killed by an enemy in an armed conflict (Harty,1912).

Moreover, tyrannicide can be considered a form of political assassination. The ancient Greeks believed that it was their civic duty and not a crime toassassinatea "despotic ruler" (Griset & Mahan, 2003). Catholic theologians of the Middle Ages claimed that tyrannicide was permissible when tyranny became extreme and no other means of safety was available.

Many scholars claim that the assassination of Julius Caesar on the Ides of March in 44 B.C., by Marcus Julius Brutus, Gaius Cassius Longinus and a host of other Roman

Senators, was an act of tyrannicide. Many historians contend that Julius Caesar was assassinated because he deviated from the founding principles of the Republic. Shortly after Caesar's death, Brutus yelled in the streets of the capitol "People of Rome, we are once again free."

Political assassinations have been a common occurrence throughout world history and have been an important instrument of terrorist organizations. The United States was not immune from tyrannicide; for example, the assassination of President Abraham Lincoln in 1865 by John Wilkes Booth is considered to be such an act.

President Woodrow Wilson stated "America is the place where you cannot kill your government by killing men who conduct it." After the assassinations of Presidents Lincoln, McKinley and Garfield, the American government remained functional due to the organizational structure of the executive branch of the United States government. This is what President Wilson was referring to when he stated that one cannot kill a government.

One of the world's most famous acts of tyrannicide occurred in 1914 when Archduke Ferdinand was assassinated by a Bosnian anarchist. Historians credit this assassination as the spark that ignited World War I.

McCann (2006) states "The assassination of a political leader is a favored form of violence among terrorist groups because the death of a single individual can often bring about dramatic and profound changes in government" (p.24). Moreover, McCann (2006) adds that the assassination of a significant political leader has international ramifications as well as national implications.

Zealot-Sicarii

In the first century B.C., Judea (now modern day Israel) was occupied by the Romans. The Roman occupation gave birth to an ancient Jewish terrorist group known as the **Sicarii** or the "daggermen". They were named after the dagger (sicae) which was their weapon of choice that was used to murder Roman leaders and Jewish collaborators. Their goal was to oust the Roman occupiers from their homeland.

In Latin the word "sicarii" is a common term for an assassin. As part of their methodology, members of the Sicarii would conceal their daggers under their clothing and perpetrate their brazenly murderous acts in broad daylight usually in town squares, markets or in and other popular meetings areas located in and around a city. The numerous assassinations that were perpetrated by the Sicarii instilled a deep psychological fear in their potential victims. As a result of their murderous acts, Roman officials were extremely fearful to congregate in public during daylight hours.

Tactically speaking, the Sicarri was different from many other terrorist organizations because they would occasionally engage the Roman army on the open battlefield. This was extremely unusual because many armies were far superior to most terrorist groups. Historically, terrorist groups, because of their lack of weapons and manpower, usually relied upon asymmetric warfare (guerilla tactics) to accomplish their political objectives. Second, on two occasions the Sicarri attempted to initiate an uprising against Roman occupation. The Romans were fearful that the Sicarii would inflame the population and the rebellion would spread throughout the entire eastern region of the

Roman Empire. Thus, the Romans felt compelled to crush the rebellion as expeditiously as possible.

The Sicarri was a short lived terrorist organization that lasted for approximately twenty-five years. They met their demise at their mountain stronghold of Masada which was located just west of the Dead Sea. This mountain fortress was considered to be inaccessible and impregnable; however, in 74 A.D., the Romans laid siege to the fortress, and the leader of the Sicarii was able to convince his followers to commit suicide instead of being subjugated by the Romans. The mass suicide at Masada for all practical purposes ended the Sicarii reign of terrorism.

The Assassins

The Assassins were a sect within Shi'a Islam (also known as the Ismailis) during the period from the 11th to the 13th century. The Assassins were noted for their murderous acts, most notably during the Crusades. "They viewed themselves as enforcers of proper Islamic conduct, which included killing public officials and other prominent individuals who were deemed to have strayed from the right path of Islam" (Yungher, 2008 p. 71).

They were also referred to as the "*Hashishin*" because they performed their murders while allegedly under the influence of hashish, a cannabis derivative.
In some languages, the term assassins means "murderers." According to Chaliand and Blin (2007), there is no corroborating evidence that the assassins engaged in the consumption of hashish prior to going to battle. Some scholars suggest that the legend of the assassins was promulgated by the manner in which they fought. The assassins were

described by their enemies as being tenacious fighters who conducted themselves on the battlefield in such a manner in which they appeared to be in a crazed, intoxicated state.

The assumption that the assassins fought under the influence of hashish is contradictory to their doctrine. The assassins were a well disciplined fighting organization which adopted a rigorous physical training program. The consumption of cannabis and alcohol was strictly prohibited.

However, many scholars believe that the entomology of the idiom *"Hashishin"* was used to identify the followers of Hazssan E Sabbah who was the leader of this Islamic sect. Hazssan was a charismatic leader who was able to persuade the inhabitants of the mountainous region of northern Persia (present day Iran) to follow him and his Islamic sect. As a result of his persuasiveness, Hassan and his assassins were able to occupy several mountain strongholds located in Northern Persia and Syria as their base of operations which was used to terrorize the entire Middle East.

The methodology of the Assassins was similar to those utilized by the Sicarii. They carried out their murderous acts at religious locations, especially on holy days. Their acts of terror created a deep psychological message and were intended to publicize their cause. The Assassins were conditioned by their leaders never to be caught alive. This mindset was quite obvious because the weapon of choice for the Assassins was a dagger which would make it almost impossible for the attacker to escape. The dagger is a short bladed weapon which required the user to position himself in close proximity to the target as opposed to a bow which could be fatal from a distance.

Hoffman (2006) claims that "violence for the Assassins was a sacramental act, a divine duty, commanded by religious text and communicated by clerical authorities "(p.84). Similar to many other religious inspired terrorist organizations, the Assassins believed that if they perished while perpetrating their acts of terrorism, they were guaranteed that they would ascend to heaven or paradise. This same ethos of self-sacrifice and suicidal martyrdom can be seen in many modern day Islamic terrorist organizations (Hoffman, 2006).

The Assassins' mountain stronghold of Alamut was destroyed by the Mongol invasion of Persia in 1256, thus reducing them as a formidable terrorist organization. However, the legacy of the Assassins is that they were a much feared organization throughout the Middle East. Saladin, the great Muslim warrior who denied King Richard the Lion Heart entry into Jerusalem was fearful of the assassins and virtually left them alone. During their campaigns of terror, the Assassins were often referred to as the *fedayeen.* The term often refers to an Arabic commando in the Middle East. The reader should be mindful of the fact that the insurgents who fought against the coalition forces during the second Iraqi war were called fedayeen. The legends of the Assassins have continued to inspire many modern day radical Islamic terrorist organizations.

Thugees or Thugs

According to Yungher (2008), the Thugs or the Thugees were worshipers of the Hindu goddess Kali. They were an Indian religious cult who strangled their victims, usually with a scarf or noose, as a sacrifice to their goddess Kali who was directly associated with death and destruction. While the objectives of this group were obscure, it is clear that their acts of terror were undertaken for personal and ritualistic reasons rather than political aims (Flood, 191, p.57). The word "thug" is English slang for a gangster, a petty thief, or a minor villain, deriving from the above mentioned cult. The Thugees were an active terrorist group from the seventh until the mid nineteenth centuries. Their modus operandi was to ingratiate themselves with merchants who traveled throughout India and, when the moment was right, they would strangle their victim with a yellow scarf or a noose (called a *phansi),* mutilate and then ritually bury them with a pickaxe. It is believed that the thugs received their commands from the goddess Kali through a series of omens; part of the Thugee's proceeds from the murders were reserved for her.

Membership into the Thugees was usually passed on from father to son. However, on occasion the children of the slain travelers were recruited into their ranks. In addition, many Indians joined their ranksas a means to escape poverty.

According to Rappoport (1984), the thug was obligated to supply Kali with blood that was required to keep the world in equilibrium. His mission was to stay alive as long as he could so that he could continue to kill. It is estimated that the average thug perpetrated approximately three murders annually (Rappoport, 1984).

During the 1830s, the British government initiated a campaign to eradicate the thugs. Their campaign consisted of a sophisticated intelligence network and the utilization of informants to assist in the identification of the cult members. These were the same sort of tactics which were used by the United Kingdom intelligence services to disrupt and dismantle the Irish Republican Army during the 1980s. In 1852, Historical reports claim that the thugs religious sect had been officially eradicated.

The thugs have been described as the most prolific terrorist organization in history. They lasted for approximately one hundred and fifty years, and have been allegedly responsible for killing approximately two million people.

Gunpowder Plot 1605

The Gunpowder Plot occurred in England in 1605 when a number of Catholics conspired to blow up British Parliament while King James I attended the opening ceremony. During this era of English history, the British government was intolerant of Catholicism and King James, under severe pressure from the Puritans, issued a proclamation during the Hampton Conference of 1604 calling the expulsion of all Catholic priests and the reintroduction of recusancy fines. Needless to say, this proclamation infuriated many Catholics and led Guy Fawkes and his conspirators to plot to blow up Parliament and kill the king.

During this time in England, Catholic citizens were persecuted after Queen Elizabeth was excommunicated from the Catholic Church in 1587. During the reign of Elizabeth she mandated that all of her subjects swear an oath attesting that she was the Supreme Governor of the Church (Greist & Mahan, 2003). Catholics who refused to submit to the Church of England were known as *recusants.* The Catholics were hopeful that King James I, who succeeded Queen Elizabeth I and who was a Catholic, would restore the Catholic Church to its original prominence in England. However, they were greatly disappointed by his anti-Catholic actions. As a result, several English Catholics conspired to commit treason by plotting the death of the king. This conspiracy became known as the "Gunpowder Plot."

Fawkes and his followers managed to smuggle approximately thirty-six barrels of gunpowder over a period of time into a cellar which was located below the House of Lords. The opening day of Parliament was scheduled to convene on November 5, 1605. According to their plan, Fawkes would ignite the fuse and then flee. According to Griest and Mahan (2003), on the morning of November 5, 1605, Fawkes was arrested while guarding the gunpowder by guards who were making their last minute rounds. Upon being apprehended, Fawkes was sent to the Tower of London where he was tortured until he identified his accomplices. The remaining conspirators were either shot attempting to flee or were located and apprehended. The remaining conspirators were paraded through the streets of London, where they were hung and then drawn and quartered.

The Gunpowder Plot provides a good example of religious terrorism. While the motivation of the confederates was to install the Pope as the head of England, they grossly misjudged their fellow Catholics. Fawkes and his band of followers strongly believed that after they blew up Parliament and King James I was killed, the English Catholic population would rise up against the anti-Catholic monarchy. Fawkes and his band of followers grossly misjudged their fellow Catholics because the rebellion they sought to achieve never came about.

Following the thwarted plot to kill him, King James I ordered the people of England to build a great bonfire on the night of November 5 to celebrate the thwarting of the gunpowder plot (www,historylearning.site.com). This particular fire was accompanied by the burning of an effigy of the pope, a ritual that continues to this day.

Modern Terrorism

The French Revolution

The eighteenth century was considered to be the *"Age of Enlightenment," A period in which the divine right* of European monarchies was challenged. The European monarchs believed that their crown was a God given right. During this period, theories of *natural law and natural rights* were espoused by political theorists such as John Locke and Rousseau. Natural law and natural rights claimed that man has an inherent right to life, liberty and the ownership of property. In this era, there was a vast disparity between the social classes of France. The wealthy aristocrats maintained a lavish lifestyle while the ordinary citizens were poverty stricken and lived in squalorous conditions.

Locke was the author of the *Social Contract Theory,* which held that man is a social being and, as a result, is compelled to create a social order. Societies establish governments for the purpose of protection from other societies. In essence, citizens make a contract with the government and relinquish some of their civil liberties for the greater good of defending society. If members of that society violate any laws, the government has the authority to punish the offender. Moreover, if the government violates any provisions of the contract, society has the right to replace that government, even by force if necessary.

John Locke's Social Contract Theory served as the framework of the United States Declaration of Independence which was authored by Thomas Jefferson. The founding fathers strongly felt that the British Crown treated the American colonies unfairly especially when it came to "taxation without representation." During the American Revolution, the French government provided the colonies with military assistance and the Marquis de Lafayette and his troops assisted the Americans in defeating the British. While serving in the American colonies, the French troops were exposed to the concepts of liberty and democracy; when they returned to France they brought these ideas with them.

During the 1790s, times were hard in France. Poverty was widespread and several European monarchs had declared war on France. French people became unruly and began to demand a better quality of life for themselves and their families. Citizens who were outspoken about the political and economic oppression they suffered at the hands of the king often found themselves thrown into the Bastille prison.

The French fortress *Bastille* was constructed in Paris as part of the defense system that protected the eastern wall of Paris. However, the Bastille became a political prison and was a symbol of royal tyranny. Historically, prisoners were arrested as a result of secret warrants signed by the king, and prisoners were kept surreptitiously in the Bastille without being formally charged with a crime. The mystique of secrecy and terror made the Bastille a focus of anger for the people of France.

On July 14, 1789, an unruly mob stormed the Bastille which was weakly guarded; the mob killedthe prison guards and released all of the prisoners. The storming of the Bastille is a national holiday in France and marks the official beginning of the French Revolution. Even though only seven prisoners were released from the prison, the storming of the Bastille was a symbolic message that the king's power was no longer absolute. The tricolor flag flown by the rebellious mob represented the Republic's three ideals: Liberty, Equality and Fraternity. The mob was supported by a group of radical revolutionaries along with French soldiers who joined their cause and eventually took control of the government. King Louis XVI was tried and convicted for crimes committed against the citizens of France by the revolutionary government and on January 21, 1793, was executed.

The French Revolution gave birth to the term "terrorism." The etymology of the term terrorism was attributed to revolutionary Maximilien Robespierre. Robespierre created the *Committee of Public Safety and the Revolutionary Tribunal,* and under his leadership, the *regime de la terreur* began (Griest & Mahan, 2003). From September 1793 through July 1794, the "revolutionary government" of the Reign of Terror overwhelmed its enemies and affected nearly all aspects of life in France. The new Republic engaged in widespread fear by searching for alleged enemies of the state. The chief target of the Committee of Public Safety were French nobels who sought to resist the revolutionary government's authority within France.

Prior to the French Revolution, the preferred method of execution in France was beheading. In 1791, the French General Assembly debated this method of execution. Dr. Joseph Guillotine proposed a more "humane" and less painful form of execution, the *"guillotine."* The guillotine was a machine that was designed to administer a fast and painless death to anyone regardless of age, sex or wealth (Wilde, 2009). According to Griest & Mahan (2003) the "guillotine was the perfect fit for France's ruthless state sponsored terrorism" (p. 5).

During the Reign of Terror, in its effort to establish a "new society," the Committee of Public Safety was responsible for executing approximately 40,000 French citizens. It is estimated that 200, 000 citizens might have died in prison as the result of either starvation or brutal treatment (Crenshaw & Pimlott, 1997).

By the summer of 1794, it appeared that the reign of terror had come to an end. The Republic became a reality, the aristocratic resistance had subsided and the will to punish traitors had decreased. Robespierre announced to his followers that he had compiled a new list of traitors. Members of the Committee of Public Safety, fearing that their names might be included on the list, ordered the arrest of Robespierre; he was arrested on July 27, 1794 and on the next day, he was guillotined (Kreis, 2004). After the execution of Robespierre, the leadership of the Republic was passed on to the property owning bourgeoisie (middle class). The term *bourgeois* refers to trades people, merchants, artisans and other non-peasants who were excluded from the upper class (White, 2009).

The French Revolution is considered to be *state-sponsored terrorism* because of the atrocities committed by the Republic against its citizens during the Reign of Terror. By 1799, France remained in political turmoil and was being militarily confronted by several European countries. Consequently, the leadership of the country passed into the hands of generals. In November 1799, Napoleon Bonaparte took advantage of the unsettling times and seized control of the government. According to Kreis (2004), "In 1789, the French had created a Republic, under the name of a monarchy. Ten years later, they created a monarchy, under the name of a Republic" (p.4).

Anarchists and Nationalism   (19th Century)

During the late 19th century, radical political theories such as the *Propaganda of Deed and the Catechism of the Revolutionary,* along with the invention of dynamite, helped propel anarchist groups to strike against numerous European countries and even the United States. *Anarchists* believed in the total rejection or destruction of all forms of government so that the people could live and network together without government interference.

Carlos Piscane was an Italian aristocrat who abrogated his nobility to participate in an unsuccessful revolution against the Bourbon monarchy. Piscane is credited with advancing the theory *propaganda of the deed,* which advocated the use of physical violence against political enemies which would rally the masses towards revolution. Piscane's theory served as the framework for the anarchist's movement of the 19th century.

The Russian anarchist group *Narodnaya Volya* (People's Will), founded in 1878, was the first terrorist organization to put the propaganda of the deed into practice(Hoffman, 2006).   The primary objective of the Narodnaya Volya was to overthrow the regime of the Tsars. They were inspired by the ideals of the American and French Revolutions which encouraged them to seek democratic and social reform within Russia (Zalman, 2009). Members of the Narodnaya Volya were self- proclaimed terrorists who strongly believed that terrorism was a just means to achieve their political goals.

The People's Will employed the tactic of selective assassination to create a sense of fear and to disrupt the ruling class of Russia. The group targeted the Tsar, the Royal family, police officials, and high ranking government and military leaders in an attempt to topple the Tsarist government.

Tsar Alexander II was a reform minded monarch. He abolished serfdom and relaxed government control over freedom of speech and assembly. According to Greist and Mahan (2003), the progressive actions of Alexander II were influenced by the European Age of Enlightenment which led to his undoing and ultimately his assassination. The Narodanya Volya was greatly influenced by the publication *Catechism of the Revolutionary* co-authored by Sergey Nechaev in 1869. Nechaev was a Russian revolutionary anarchist who espoused the pursuit of revolution through any means possible, to include political violence.

In the first few lines of his manifesto, Nechaev believed that the true revolutionary must always be prepared to face torture or death, and must give up love, friendship, and gratitude in the single minded pursuit of his mission. Furthermore, Nechayev added that he knew only one science, the science of destruction and for that reason he should study mechanics, physics, chemistry and perhaps medicine. He claimed that the only objective of the revolutionary is the destruction of the "filthy order."

The People's Will was committed to the destruction of the Tsarist government of Russia. Their organization was comprised of five hundred members of whom twenty-five percent were women. The group began a campaign of selective assassination to include Tsar Alexander II. They believed that assassination of the Tsar would rally the citizens of Russia and propel the country into revolution and the people would take control of the nation. The Narodnya Volya was one of the first terrorist organizations to employ the use of dynamite in their acts of terrorism, and they developed a bomb that could be thrown at its target, similar to today's hand grenade.

During the winter and fall months of 1881, the People's Will plotted the assassination of the tsar. On March 1, 1881; members of the Narodnya Volya awaited the arrival of Tsar Alexander II along one of the central streets of St. Petersburg, near the Winter Palace and a bomb detonated injuring several civilians (New World Encyclopedia, 2006). Shortly after the explosion Tsar Alexander II exited his bullet proof sleigh to check on the injured bystander wounded by the explosion. "Thank God, I am safe," the Tsar reportedly declared –just as the second bomber emerged from the crowd and detonated his weapon, killing both himself and his target" (Hoffman, 2003, pp. 18-19).

After numerous attempts to assassinate Tsar Alexander II, the Narodnaya Volya was finally successful. However, their success not long lived. The Russian authorities were quick to respond to the death of the Tsar and members of the Narodonya Volya were arrested and hanged.

Months following the assassination of Tsar Alexander II, a group of radical anarchists in London convened an "anarchist conference" which publicly applauded the assassination and extolled tyrannicide as a means to achieve revolutionary change. The conference decided to establish an "Anarchist International" or Black International in an attempt to coordinate worldwide anarchist activities.

Anarchists' acts of terrorism were not restricted to foreign lands. The United States was also victimized on several occasions at the hands of anarchists.

On September 6, 1901, U.S. President William McKinley was assassinated while attending the Pan American Exhibition in Buffalo, New York. The assassin was identified as Leon Czolgosz, a young Hungarian refugee, who confessed to being an anarchist. However, a follow-up investigation revealed that many anarchist organizations refused to enlist him because they feared that he was a government informant. It was never proven that Czolgsoz was a true anarchist, even though it was learned that he attended many anarchist meetings and read many anarchist texts. Czolgosz was tried and convicted and was executed on October 29, 1901. Two years following the assassination of President McKinley, the U.S. Congress enacted legislation that made presidential protection a permanent Secret Service responsibility (Kingseed, 2001).

Moreover, Congress swiftly enacted legislation barring known anarchists or anyone who believed in or was opposed to all organized government from entering the United States. During the mid-nineteenth century, anarchists were responsible for an impressive string of assassinations of heads of state and a number of bombings until the second decade of the twentieth century.

Nationalism

The term nationalism commonly refers to devotion to one's nation or patriotism or the attitude that one has about their national identify. The term can also mean the actions taken when people are seeking to achieve ***"self-determination"*** or the ability or desire for people of a geographical area to govern themselves.

The 19th century gave rise to the birth of anarchism. The propaganda of the deed motivated anarchists to rebel against European governments through the use of violent means. Their actions were widely regarded as acts of terrorism. Conversely, nationalists fought for the right to govern themselves as opposed to anarchists who desired to remove all forms of government.

Terrorism in the 20th Century

Terrorism Prior to World War I

In the months preceding the Great War, terrorism still maintained a revolutionary connotation. The Ottoman and Hapsburg (Austria-Hungary) empires were eroding and beginning to decay. However, the Turks still possessed a formable military force that could harshly and swiftly crush any rebellion orchestrated by their historic fors, the Armenians. Armenia is a predominately Christian country located in Western Asia.

For centuries the Armenian people were subjugated to Ottoman (Muslim) rule. The occupying Muslims believed that the Christian Armenians were inferior to members of the Islamic faith, and were considered second class citizens. Consequently, Armenian civil liberties were severely restricted. For example, Armenians were prohibited from riding atop horses and were banned from residing in homes that were constructed above the homes of Muslims. Because of their plight, the Armenians desperately sought intervention for their cause from many Western countries.

During the 1880s and 1890s, an Armenian nationalist movement began to rise and pursue a terrorist strategy against their Ottoman occupiers in an attempt to solicit Western sympathy. The Armenian terrorist tactics would later be adopted by most of the post World War II ethno-nationalists/separatist movements. They utilized many tactics associated with the Peoples Will with an impetus on selective assassination.

According to Hoffman (2003), the Armenians culminated their revolt in 1896 with the ill-fated seizure of the Ottoman Bank, which was the Turkish financial center, located in Constantinople. The botched bank seizure was followed by several days of rioting which led to the deaths of numerous Armenians.

In 1915, the Turkish government ordered the deportation and the elimination of approximately one million Armenians. Armenian people were physically removed from their homes and were forced to march hundreds of miles without food and water; the march was designed to lead to the death of the deportees. Many social scientists have described this event as the first modern systematic genocide of the 20th century. Noam Chomsky (2002) argues that governments describe acts of terrorism as being immoral but governments often react outside the bounds of morality. Chomsky further contends that responses to terrorist attacks cannot be an act of terrorism.

The Armenian genocide perpetrated by the Turks was clearly an act of terrorism that exceededthe boundaries of morality. Unfortunately, history reveals that numerous governments have acted outside or moral boundaries when they reacted to acts of terrorism. Governments must be mindful of the fact that overreacting to acts of terrorism can serve as a major recruiting tool for terrorist organizations.

Bosnia

In 1908, Austria annexed Bosnia and Herzegovina, which caused great concern for the people who were about to be occupied by the Hapsburg monarchy. Several days following the annexation of their country, many high ranking men met to create a semi-secret society known as the *Narodna Odbrana* (translation: National Defense or People's Defense). The purpose of this organization was to recruit and train partisans for a possible war between Serbia and Austria (Shackelford, 2007). Members of the *Narodona Odbrana* engaged in anti-Austrian propaganda and established a network of spies and saboteurs who operated within the Austrian empire.

The National Defense had many satellite groups. The Bosnian spinoff was named the "Young Bosnians" And was comprised of disaffected nationalists, Bosnia-Serb intellectuals, and university students. This group rose up against the Hapsburg monarchy which governed their country.

In 1911, the *Black Hand* (also known as Unification of Death) was a secret society that was established to unite all of the territories that were annexed by the Austrian-Hungarian Empire through violent means. They were formed by former members of the *Narodna Odbrana* and took over their terrorist actions (Shackelford, 2007). Many members of this secret society were Serbian military officers who conspired to overthrow the Hapsburg monarchy. The *Black Hand* began to organize a plot to assassinate Arch Duke Ferdinand, the heir apparent to the Austrian-Hungarian crown. In particular, it recruited and trained three members in the techniques of bomb throwing and marksmanship to carry out the plan to assassinate the Arch Duke.

On June 28, 1914, Gavrilo Princip, a Bosnian-Serb, shot and killed Arch Duke Ferdinand. This assassination has been credited with catapulting the world into World War I.

Anti-colonialism Terrorism

The Stanford Encyclopedia of Philosophy (2006) defines colonialism as "a practice which involves the subjugation of one people to another" (p.1). Moreover, colonialism involves the political and economic control of one country over another. In particular, , starting especially in the 19th century, European countries colonized countries in the Middle East, Africa and Asia and the Americas.

At the outbreak of World War II (WWII), European empires like England and France petitioned their colonies for military assistance to help them defeat the Axis powers. Many of these colonies were promised independence once the allies were victorious. Upon the defeat of Germany and Japan, however, the colonial empires reneged on their promises. As a result of these failed promises, nationalism began to rise and the colonies demanded their right of self-determination or the right to rule themselves. In essence, ***nationalism*** during this era began to mean *"resistance to foreign domination."*

In post-World War II, the term anti-colonialism was employed to describe and explain the struggle for, and attainment of freedom from colonial rule in Asia and Africa. During the era of anti-colonialism, many countries obtained their independence from their colonial rulers. The tactics utilized by both the occupying governments and the revolutionary colonies have been described as being terrorist in nature. Two of the most important conflicts during the anti-colonialism period were the Jewish struggle for the creation of the state of Israel and the fight for independence by the people of Algeria against the French.

Irgun and Zionism

The Irgun was a Jewish terrorist organization that sought to establish the state of Israel in Palestine, which was controlled by the British following World War I. Their group was considered to be a *Zionist* organization which meant that Jews throughout Europe had a yearning desire to return to the birthplace of the Jewish people the land of Israel and Jerusalem.

Modern Zionism emerged in the late 19th century in response to the violent persecution of Jews in Eastern Europe and ant-Semitism in Western Europe (Anti-Defamation League, 2009). The *Irgun* or the *National Military Organization in the Land of Israel* was formed during the 1930s in response to the Arab Rebellion (1936-39). The Arab Rebellion was an organized terrorist campaign directed against the Jews who were residing in Palestine and to counter the large wave of Jewish immigration into the Arab land.

In 1939, WWII had begun and members of the Irgun decided to cease all attacks on the English because they felt that their terrorist campaign would stifle the Allies chances of winning the war. Furthermore, many Irgun members joined the English army and participated in many military campaigns against Germany and Italy in the Middle

East. The Irgun members who fought alongside the British during WWII strongly believed that their participation in the war would lead to the British granting their freedom and Israel would become an independent nation. However, the United Kingdom was not prepared to relinquish control over Palestine.

In 1943, Menachem Begin assumed command of the Irgun and a decision was made to resume their terrorist campaign against the British because it appeared that the Allies were assured victory in Europe. In the years following WWII, the Irgun initiated a clandestine military campaign against the occupying English military forces. Western news agencies including the *New York Times* described these attacks as acts of terrorism.

Begin's strategy was to target British symbolic targets, demoralize the occupying government and wear down the British resolve to occupy Palestine. The most infamous attack conducted by the Irgun was the bombing of the King David Hotel located in Jerusalem, which served as the civilian and military headquarters for the occupying British government. On July 22, 1946, a bomb went off in the hotel, killing ninety-one and injuring forty-five (Hoffman, 2003). According to their ideology, the Irgun historically did not intentionally target innocent civilians. The bombing of the King David hotel resulted in the death and injury of British subjects, Arabs and, for that matter, Jews. Shortly after this terrorist attack, the Irgun made an apology for injuring innocent civilians. Begin insisted that prior to the bombing of the hotel, his organization warned hotel employees and British officials of the impending attack. Needless to say, there was a public denunciation of this wanton act of terrorism.

Begin believed that if his organization could cause massive disruption of the daily operations of the occupying forces, the British would resort to harsh and repressive countermeasures (Hoffman, 2003). These suppressive countermeasures would result in a public relations nightmare for the British government and that the English would be regarded as oppressors rather than protectors. Begin's strategy to wear down the British government began to succeed. Public opinion shifted in favor of the Jewish cause and the British resolve to remain in Palestine began to dwindle. Moreover, political pressure from the United States for Britain to withdraw from Palestine led to Israel becoming an independent state. "On May 15, 1948, the United Kingdom's rule over Palestine had concluded and the establishment of the State of Israel was proclaimed" (Hoffman, 2003 p. 53).

Front de Liberation Nationale (FLN): The National Liberation Front

In the years following World War II, the idea of anti-colonialism or decolonialism had spread throughout the world. The British were battling rebellions in Palestine, Cyprus, Malaya and Kenya, while the Dutch were countering revolts in Indonesia. The French were attempting to maintain control of Indochina but were defeated at the battle of Diem Bien Phu, thus loosing Indochina as a French colony.

French Algerians, like their Palestinian counterparts, volunteered to assist France in its war against the Axis powers. In lieu of their participation in the war, they sought their independence from France but once again they were disappointed. On November 1, 1954, the National Liberation Front launched armed attacks in the French colony of Algeria, igniting a brutal conflict that would continue for eight years and claim approximately one million lives (Grose, 2007). This date became known as the *Toussaint Rouge* (Red All Saints Day).

Subsequent to the Algerian insurrection, French security forces were able to successfully curtail the FLN resistance in the outlaying areas of Algeria, forcing the group to redirect its terrorist campaign to the urban environment of Algiers. The FLN leadership was predisposed to the use of violence to gain full independence from France, and adopted the philosophy of Carlos Marighela who wrote the famous *Minimanual of the Urban Guerrilla.* In this manual, Marighela introduced tactics and organizational methods specifically designed for use in an urban environment. This was in direct opposition to the prevailing doctrine that guerilla warfare should be conducted in the countryside. According to Towers (2002), the leaders of the FLN were young, well-educated and sincere admirers of Ho Chi Minh, who had led the Viet-Minh to victory against the French in Indochina.

The FLN began a terrorist campaign of bombing and political assassinations. Prior to the Battle of Algiers, the FLN did not selectively target innocent civilians; however, during the Algiers campaign, they began to target civilian meeting locations such as restaurants, cafes and amusement parks, resulting in the deaths of innocent Europeans who resided in Algiers. Many of the bombings perpetuated by the FLN were conducted by attractive FLN female members. During the Battle of Algiers, the French restricted the movement of Arabs throughout the city in an attempt to control the travel of possible insurgents. The leaders of the FLN believed that by using attractive women with European physical features, they would not encounter any difficulty in negotiating security check points. In December 1956, the mayor of Algiers was assassinated. The

FLN orchestrated a campaign of organized demonstrations, labor strikes and work stoppages. It became apparent that the French were losing control of Algiers. As a result of the insurrection and increased incidents of violence, the French Colonial Governor of Algeria requested military assistance.

The elite 10th Paratrooper Regiment was dispatched to Algeria; the majority of the *"paras"* were veterans of the French-Indochina war and accustomed to counter insurgency operations and tactics that the Algerians were learning from Vietnamese communists (Tower, 2002).

The command staff of the airborne troops was instructed to use whatever methods were necessary to crush the Algerian revolution and were given absolute power without regard to civil liberties. Thus began an unprecedented operation of harsh and brutal repression by the French paratroopers. During the beginning phase of their counterinsurgency strategy, the paratroopers confiscated police records on any Algerian who was suspected of collaborating or sympathizing with the FLN. Thousands of Algerians were incarcerated; during this period, it was rumored that the French were torturing Algerians to extract information.

The FLN countered the French offensive by orchestrating labor strikes, work stoppages and massive demonstrations. The French paratroopers were instructed to "break the strike" at all costs. In an attempt to break the strike, the French paratroops forcibly opened shops that were closed during the work stoppage. The merchants had a choice either to open or face arrest; even worse, many feared that their businesses would be torched. Second, the army physically removed laborers from their homes and delivered them to the appropriate workplace (Tower, 2002). After several days of employing these tactics, the strike was over.

Additionally, the command staff of the paratroopers believed in establishing a strong intelligence network which included the use of many informants to dismantle the FLN. The objective of using informants and intense interrogation was to identify and locate ranking members of the FLN, thereby slowly but surely dismantling the terrorist organization. During the height of the Algerian War for Independence, the interrogation methods of the French army became extremely controversial. According to Talbot (1980), the army utilized brutal and harsh interrogation techniques such as water deprivation, beatings, and splinters pushed under the nails of fingers and toes and lighted cigarettes pushed against the flesh. A favorite interrogation method was the use of the *"magneto,"* which was a hand cranked generator that was used to torture terrorist suspects through the use of electrical shock (Talbot, 2002). This shock created intense pain but did not leave any marks that would indicate that a person was tortured. Many French army personnel objected to this sort of behavior and even a high ranking French general resigned in protest of the interrogation techniques.

This violent oppression of the FLN backfired on the French. Grose (2007) states "The FLN and its modern progeny count on heavy-handed reprisals to feed propaganda campaigns that generate public support and recruits. After a harsh French counter attack, one FLN member told a western journalist; "The stupid bastards are winning the war for us."

Militarily, the French won the Battle of Algiers but they lost the war. Their counterterrorism measures were successful in dismantling the National Liberation Front and forced them to flee to Tunisia. In June 1962, France capitulated and Algeria became an independent nation. The Algerian War of Independence witnessed horrific atrocities committed by both the French Army as well as the FLN from 1954 to 1962.

Conclusion

Terrorism and the use of the tactics of terrorism have captured the attention of the world. As the world enters the second decade of the 21st century, the world appears be have become an even more dangerous place than before the attacks of 911. In reality, the world has remained dangerous, but with the attacks, the attention of the world has focused upon the use and impact of what we call terrorism.

This chapter has traced the beginning of terrorism with the origin of the ancient Sicarii to the rise of nationalism in post World War Two where terrorists waged their campaign against their colonial occupiers. Moreover, we have learned that governments can be guilty in conducting acts of terrorism against their own people. State sponsored terrorism can best be exemplified by Maximilien Robespierre's Committee of Public Safety during the reign of terror during the French Revolution where thousands of the French nobility were executed and incarcerated.

During the 1880's. the Russian anarchist group, Narodnya Volya, was the first terrorist organization to utilize the bomb as their weapon of choice. Currently, the weapon of choice remains to be the bomb and especially the car bomb or the suicide bomber.

Terrorist organizations have often been described as "copycats" due to the fact that they often copy the successful tactics used by other terrorist groups. For an example, the FLN targeted civilian targets during their campaign for independence against the

French in Algeria. During the 1960s and 1970s Palestinian terrorist groups adopted the same tactics. Menachem Begin the leader of the Irgun, a Jewish terrorist organization, studied the tactics of the ancient Sicarii to aid them during their terrorist campaign against the Arabs and the British colonial rulers.

The history of terrorism provides us not only with an understanding of their tactics and ideology but it gives us an insight into the causes of terrorism as well.

References

Chaliand, G. & Blin, A. (2007). *The History of Terrorism From Antiquity To Al Qaeda.*

Chomsky, N. (2002). *"Who Are The Global Terrorists?"* http://secondpress.ca/articles/151-may25-chomsly.pdf

Greist, P. & Mahan, S. (2003). *Terrorism in Perspective.* Thousand Oaks, CA: Sage Publications.

Grose, T. (2007, August 5). The Terrorist Playbook Contemporary lessons from the bloody Battle of Algiers. U.S. News and World Report

Harty, J. (1912). Tyrannicide. In The Catholic Encyclopedia. New York: Robert Appleton Company. Retrieved January 3, 2009 from New Advent: http://www.newadvent.org/cathen/15108a.htm

Hoffman, Bruce. (2003). *Inside Terrorism.* New York, NY: Columbia University Press.

McCann, J. (2006). *Terrorism on American Soil A Concise History of Plots and Perpetrators from the Famous to the Forgotten.* Boulder, CO: Sentient Publications.

Rapoport, D. (1984). *"Fear and Trembling: Terrorism in Three Religious Traditions.* In Political Science Review 78(3).

Shackelford, M. (2007). *The Black Hand The Secret Serbian Terrorist Society.* Retrieved from http://net.lib.byu.edu/~rdh7/wwi/comment/blk-hand.html

Talbot, J. (1980). *The War Without a Name France in Algeria 1954-1962.* New York, NY: AlfredA. Knopf, Inc.

Towers, J. (2002). The French In Algeria, 1954-1962 Military Successes Failure Of Grand Strategy. (Strategy Research Project). U.S. Army War College, Carlisle Barracks, PA.

Trueman, C. (2000). *The Gunpowder Plot of 1605.* Retrieved from http://www.historylearningsite.co.uk/gunpowder_plot_of_1605.htm

Zalman, A. (2009). *Terrorism Issues: Narodnaya Volya (The People's Will, Russia).* Retrieved from http://terrorism.about.com/od/groupsleader1/p/NarodnayaVolya.htm?p=1

CHAPTER 3
THE PSYCHOLOGY AND STRUCTURE OF TERRORIST GROUPS

He who knows the enemy and himself will never in a hundred battles be at risk; He who does not know the enemy but knows himself will sometimes win and sometimes lose Sun-Tzu (Ames, 1993:113)

Introduction

There are many theories that try to explain the behavior of terrorists; the fact that none has emerged as dominant underscores the complexity and breadth of the issue. Perhaps the most vexing question is whether terrorists are rational actors, weighing the potential costs and benefits of their actions or whether they have some sort of psychological "need" to do what they do.

Even this seemingly fundamental question has produced no end of debate. For example, psychologist Charles Ruby states unequivocally:

> ..terrorism is basically another form of politically motivated violence that is perpetrated by rational, lucid people who have valid motives. The only real difference between terrorism and military action is one of strategy. Terrorists lack the necessary resources to wage war in furtherance of their political goals (Ruby, 2002:15).

Former CIA psychiatrist Jerrold Post sees the matter differently. To him, the primary reason for joining a terrorist group is not the achievement of a particular goal. Rather, it is the psychological fulfillment (e.g., camaraderie, sense of adventure) one feels through membership itself:

> ...the cause is not the cause. The cause, as codified in the group's ideology, according to this line of reasoning, becomes the rationale for acts the terrorists are driven to commit. Indeed, the central argument of this position is that individuals become terrorists in order to join terrorist groups and commit acts of terrorism (Post, 1990:35).

It is not the goal of this text to attempt to solve a debate that will no doubt rage for many years to come. Rather, readers should be aware that disagreement exists and that most researchers fall somewhere between these two extremes. Most groups and movements do have goals that, at least for the membership, make sense. While it is often easy to dismiss or trivialize these goals, we do so at our own risk. It is generally more difficult, but significantly more productive, to understand the ideologies and desires of people motivated enough to engage in extreme behaviors. At the same time, Post is no doubt correct that personality and social factors play a role. For example, Americans generally support the U.S. military and admire the men and women who put themselves in harms way to protect their countrymen. However, many of these ardent and sincere supporters refrain from joining the armed forces, claiming "it's just not for me."

A second, but related, question is whether terrorism is sufficiently distinct from other human activity that it deserves its own brand of psychological/sociological discourse. Judging by the amount of scholarship that has emerged in recent years dealing with the sociology and psychology of terrorism, one would certainly think it deserves its own seat at the academic table. However, consider the admonition of Randy Borum, who has studied the issue at length:

> No single theory has gained ascendance as an explanatory model for all types of violence. Perhaps the diversity in behaviors regarded as violent poses an inherent barrier to such a global theory...Terrorist violence most often is deliberate (not impulsive), strategic, and instrumental; it is linked to and justified by ideological (e.g., political, religious) objectives and almost always involves a group or multiple actors/supporters. These issues all add complexity to the construction of terrorism as a form of violence and challenge the emergence of a unifying explanatory theory (Borum, 2004: 17).

In this chapter, we will review some of the dominant psychological and sociological theories that seek to explain why individuals join terrorist groups, how they can justify attacking often unprotected and civilian targets, why some choose to leave these groups, and how psychological constructs can be used to understand and mitigate the actions of terrorists. Because there is no invisible line separating "terrorist" from "conventional" psychology, theories not exclusive to terrorism will also be presented.

Behavior in General

Those who have spent any time in psychology classrooms are no doubt familiar with the most basic of questions: What is the primary force directing human behavior, genetics or the environment? In other words, which carries more weight, nature or nurture?

Recent scholarship suggests that biological, psychological, and social factors all combine to influence behavior, albeit in different ways for each individual (Pinizzotto, personal communication with the author, 2004). To that end, each will be considered in the following analysis.

Biological Factors

A starting point for many first-year Criminology texts is Lombroso and his theory of the "atavist," the born criminal.[1] With his protruding forehead and other unique physical characteristics, the atavist was easy to spot. He was basically "born" into crime and could not be changed. Conveniently for the upper class, rehabilitation was out of the question.

With the ascension of social and environmental theories of crime in the 20th century, Lombroso and other biologically-based Criminologists fell into disfavor. However, while few would suggest that atavism has a place in modern Criminology, biological theories of behavior are nevertheless reappearing. Indeed, given the advances in genetics that have been witnessed in recent years, it would be seem foolish to think that biology has no influence in the manner in which individuals behave and interact.

For example, Oots and Wiegle (1985) propose that frustration of political goals can lead to continual states of arousal. Acts of terrorism achieve the twin goals of allowing for relief from

---

[1]However, Lombroso did not originate biological theorizing in the social sciences. See, for example, Pfohl (1994) for a discussion of the ancient Greek humoral explanation of behavior.

this arousal as well as removal of the initial cause of the actor's frustration.

Some researchers report that an overabundance or lack of certain brain chemicals, such as norepinephrine, acetylcholine, endorphins and serotonin, interact to produce higher levels of aggression (see .Hubbard 1983 and Borum 2004).

In studies that would no doubt have pleased Lombroso, Raine (1997) proposes that dysfunction in the front part of the brain may be related to aggressive behavior. In particular, those whose frontal lobes display abnormalities are more likely to experience low levels of arousal, low reactivity, and fearlessness. Each of these has been shown to be related to aggression and anti-social behavior.

While biology and physiology may ultimately play some role in determining who is attracted to terrorism, they will not likely serve as the dominant factors. Given the political dimensions of most groups and the general need for the terrorist to sublimate his own desires for the good of the movement (in contrast to the self-interested focus of most "normal" criminals), it is difficult to imagine that a purely biological/physiological explanation of terrorism will gain wide acceptance, at least in the near future. Rather, both biology and psychology provide a great deal of explanatory power for a small number of terrorists, such as the Unabomber, and will provide a more limited, but nevertheless potentially important, explanation for a wide range of terrorist activity.

Psychological Factors

In contrast to biology, quite a bit has been written with regard to psychological factors affecting terrorist behavior.[2] A popular, if not empirically supported, position is that terrorists are mentally ill. The polar opposite to that maintains that terrorism is nothing more than a normal reaction to an extraordinary circumstance. What follows is a brief summary of many of the better known psychological perspectives on terrorism.

Mental Illness and Terrorism

[There is] no such thing as an isolated terrorist: that's a mental case.
Criminologist Franco Ferracuti (Hudson, 1999: 23)

An easy, and perhaps reassuring, explanation for terrorist behavior is that it has to be the work of someone who is mentally ill.[3] In the case of the 9-11 hijackers, how could 19 young men readily fly airplanes into buildings, killing themselves along with innocent men, women, and children? In at least some cases, that logic fits. For example, Theodore Kaczinski, the UNABOMBER, was diagnosed as being a paranoid schizophrenic (Ruby, 2002).

To properly determine whether someone actually has a mental illness, however, requires going beyond mere rules-of-thumb or popular definitions. Professionals utilize the *Diagnostic and Statistical Manual of Mental Disorders*, more popularly known as the DSM, as a guide for

---

[2]Works on terrorism often assume that readers fully understand the differences between biological and psychological explanations. For the sake of this book, biology refers to immutable features of an individual, those that he or she is born with and that can not be changed without a physical intervention. Psychology, on the other hand, is a broader term that refers to one's mind, personality, and/or behavior. Historically, psychology has tended to focus on those areas that can be understood or altered through counseling or some form of social intervention. In reality, with the increasing popularity of neuropsychology, the boundaries between these two arenas are blurring. For the sake of simplicity and congruity with past works, the authors have chosen to adopt the old demarcations. Readers are reminded that, in the real world, these divisions are not clear and, at times, downright arbitrary.

[3]These claims are not limited to lay persons or students. One early treatise on the causes of terrorism was titled *Crusaders, Criminals, Crazies: Terror and Terrorism in Our Time* (Hacker, 1976)

diagnosing mental illness.[4] Numbering several hundred pages, the DSM utilizes strict guidelines for each illness it describes. In order to meet the DSM criteria for various diagnoses, particular symptoms must manifest themselves over a designated period of time. The DSM also makes specific reference to politically or religiously motivated behavior:

> Neither deviant behavior (e.g., political, religious, or sexual) nor conflicts that are primarily between the individual and society are mental disorders unless the deviance or conflict is a symptom of a dysfunction in the individual...(American Psychological Association, 1994: xxii).

Strictly adhering to the DSM criteria makes it less likely that one can make sweeping generalizations regarding the presence or absence of illness, especially at the group level. Every person, after all, is unique and whether he/she possesses some form of psychopathology must be judged on its own merits.

On the far end of the mental health spectrum, it is unlikely that terrorist groups will want to recruit, train, and utilize operatives who are severely mentally ill. Those individuals cannot be counted upon to maintain operational secrecy or contribute in some meaningful way to advancing the group's mission. Even in the utilization of such tactics as suicide bombings, groups want to have some assurance that their operations will be carried out successfully. While it may make sense from time to time to employ individuals who have mental challenges, it is not something that most groups pursue as a general policy.

That said, many researchers claim that there are psychological characteristics or histories that terrorists possess, setting them apart from the general population.

Perhaps no one has written more extensively on terrorist psychology than former CIA

---

[4]The current edition of the DSM is the 4th edition, published in 1994, with a text revision added in 2000. Hence, the shorthand version currently used is DSM-IV or DSM-IV-TR.

psychiatrist Jerrold Post. It is his view that psychology can explain many facets of terrorist motivation and behavior, just as it explains normal behavior.[5] Post does not claim that a generalized terrorist "profile" exists; rather, if one looks closely enough, both individual and group motivations and behaviors can be discerned

Post (1984) describes two very different types of terrorists: one, which he names the "anarchic-ideologue," is intent on destroying the world of her father. An example of this type of group would include the Weather Underground, a violent, 1970s U.S.-based terrorist organization, many of whose members were the sons and daughters of wealthy, industrialist parents. They rejected the world their parents had created and were willing to use violence to overthrow the existing order. The other type of group, the "nationalist-separatist," is entirely different. Using the IRA and ETA as examples, individual members are often second and third generation terrorists, carrying on their parents' work. Rather than rejecting their fathers' and mothers' goals, they embrace them. In one case, you have an example of the "good child"; in the other, the "bad child." The psychological forces that produce these two extremes differ radically.

A central theme in much of the current literature concerns the concept of **narcissism**, or extreme self-interest to the exclusion of others. In a review of several studies, Borum (2004: 19) explains:

> Indeed, "narcissistic rage" has been posed by more than one observer as the primary psychological precipitant of terrorist aggression. In developmental context the way in which this evolves is that as children the nascent terrorists are deeply traumatized, suffering chronic physical abuse and emotional humiliation. This creates a profound sense of fear and personal vulnerability that becomes central to their life concept. To eliminate this fear and create a more tolerable self-image, such individuals feel the need

---

[5]Post (1990) describes terrorist behavior in terms of "psycho-logic," which replaces rationality; "psycho-logic" both motivates an individual to commit acts of terrorism and allows him to rationalize such behavior as justified.

to "kill off" their view of themselves as victims. They buttress their own self-esteem by devaluing others. The result of this devaluation of others -- what some have termed "malignant narcissism"-- muffles their internal voice of reason and morality.

Another popular explanation for terrorist behavior is that those who engage in such activity are sociopaths/psychopaths. The DSM uses the term antisocial personality disorder (ASD) when referring to psychopathy and outlines precise diagnostic criteria. In general, those with ASD lack empathy and are totally self-involved. They are not averse to hurting others; indeed, they derive pleasure from watching others suffer. While true psychopaths make up a small percentage of the population at-large, they are over-represented in prisons, given their natural predisposition to engage in criminal behavior. However, not all psychopaths become criminals. Consider unscrupulous businesspeople, lawyers, or government officials; many of them possess psychopathic traits and tendencies.

There is great debate about whether ASD is a good predictor of future terrorist behavior (Corrado, 1981). Nevertheless, terrorists often display many of the same characteristics as psychopaths, such as shame, fear, aggression, arrogance, hostility, and an indifference to the suffering of others (Martens, 2004). At least one researcher has proposed that a variety of factors can come together to produce "situational psychopaths" who then engage in acts of terror (Gilmartin 1996).

Individual-level explanations of terrorism, whether bio-genetic or psychological, appear to be small, albeit important, pieces of the puzzle. In general, most researchers cite social or environmental characteristics as more important that individual ones in understanding terrorist behavior.

Terrorism and Social Factors

Relative Deprivation and Frustration Aggression

There is a wide range of opinion with regard to the effects of social factors on terrorist behavior. Some see environmental variables as important while others eschew psychological theorizing altogether and maintain that terrorists are rational actors who, because of limited resources, are forced to engage in asymmetrical warfare to achieve political ends (Ruby, 2002).

Over the past fifty years, perhaps no single theory has received greater attention than Ted Gurr's relative deprivation hypothesis. Simply put, Gurr believes that individuals judge their status not in absolute terms, but as compared to others around them. The greater the gap between an individual's perceived well-being and that of his neighbors, the greater his level of frustration. This frustration in turn produces anger which often leads to violence. When groups share this sense of frustration, they may band together to engage in revolutionary violence (Gurr, 1970).

Recently, Mark Sageman wrote about al Qai'da members in a way that sounds much like Gurr's hypothesis. In particular, Sageman noted that most al Qai'da soldiers did not match the common suicide-terrorist stereotype (young, single, poorly educated, unemployed male). Rather, many were raised in secular homes, were well-educated, had wives, held good jobs and/or had excellent prospects for employment. What seemed to link many of them together was their perceived status as "international citizens" who were treated badly in western society. Many left their native countries to pursue good jobs in the west and, upon relocating, felt lonely, mistreated, and marginalized in their new surroundings. They viewed western culture as decadent and, in an attempt to remedy their loneliness and frustration, drifted in to radical mosques. There, they became radicalized (Sageman, 2004).

Social Learning Theory

As far back as the 1930s, Criminologists theorized that criminal behavior and deviance is learned from observing and modeling the behaviors of others (Sutherland, 1939). As explained by Bandura (1977: 22):

> (M)ost human behavior is learned observationally through modeling: from observing others one forms an idea of how new behaviors are performed, and on later occasions this coded information serves as a guide for action.

More recently, social learning theory has been applied to terrorism. Reasoning that terrorist violence is a subset of violence in general, Oots & Wiegele (1985) state that it can be, and generally is, a learned behavior.

Terrorism as a Rational Choice

Many researchers, including several psychologists, dismiss the idea that terrorism is primarily a psychological construct. Instead, they view it as a strategic and political choice: those with grievances who lack resources find themselves forced to engage in low intensity warfare. Some who argue for the terrorism-as-rational choice model also assert that, under certain circumstances, terrorism can be justified. Using the rationale that "one man's terrorist is another man's freedom fighter," they point to many accepted examples where they say terrorism has been used: the American Revolution or the establishment of the state of Israel, for example.[6]

---

[6]See Valls (2000) who argues that terrorism can, in certain circumstances, be justified under the Just War doctrine. "Just War" is a moral doctrine first articulated by Augustine and refined by Thomas Aquinas that discusses the conditions under which war is morally justifiable. Among other things, it requires that: a) one's cause is "just"; b) that the articulated cause is, in fact, the reason for going to war; c) that violence be confined to that which is necessary (i.e., not excessive and not intentionally directed at non-combatants) (Lowe, 2003).

Concluding that terrorism can be morally justified is not a prerequisite for accepting the notion that it represents a choice, however. Choice implies that a calculation of costs versus benefits has been made; when an actor concludes that the benefits of terrorism outweigh its costs, he/she will choose to engage in it.

Perhaps the most well-known proponent of the terrorism-as-a-choice model is Wesleyan University Professor of Government Martha Crenshaw. Since the 1980s, she has examined various groups and movements and has concluded that most terrorists do not suffer from psychological defects. Rather, they weigh the likely costs and benefits of their actions and proceed in a manner that they think will maximize reward. Many people have difficulty understanding how, for example, suicide bombing provides a reward sufficient to justify its almost contagious current use. Crenshaw notes, however, that benefits are not merely material. Rather, they can be psychological (e.g., being held in high esteem by one's family, tribe, or allies) or spiritual (the knowledge that one will ascend to heaven) (Crenshaw (1988, 1992, 2000)).

Another proponent of the rational actor theory is retired Army psychologist Charles Ruby. In a review of what he calls the "personality defect" model of terrorism, Ruby concludes that there is little empirical support for the notion that terrorists are significantly psychologically different than non-terrorists. He notes that in some ways, terrorists appear to cope with stressors such as having to kill people in the same manner that professional soldiers do. Ultimately, Ruby concludes that terrorists as a whole are not deranged; rather they are similar to soldiers, only they lack the resources to engage in conventional warfare (Ruby, 2002).

Group Dynamics

The dynamics that occur within a group, regardless of whether it is a terrorist group or not, have a powerful influence on its membership. Consider, for example, the changes that one goes through upon entering the military. What may have once been a largely individualistic and self-directed lifestyle suddenly becomes one of intense discipline, mission focus, and loyalty to the group instead of oneself. While terrorist groups have their own unique attributes that are generally not found in other types of organizations, they are nevertheless not immune from the dynamics that occur everywhere.

Social Facilitation

Individuals often form groups to accomplish a goal. By utilizing the unique talents and skills of members, groups are able to accomplish what even disparate individuals working together cannot. Consider a football team; not everyone can be the quarterback. For that matter, not everyone can be a successful offensive tackle. Indeed, it is likely that many quarterbacks would make downright lousy offensive tackles.

Groups provide both material and psychological benefits to members. As far back as 1898, psychologist Norman Triplett noted that bicycle racers performed better in competition than when riding by themselves (Davis, Huss & Becker, 1995). More recent experiments have found that those who are skilled at a particular task get better when individuals watch; those who are novices get worse (Michaels, Blommel, Brocato, Linkous, and Rowe, 1982). Clearly, individuals want to do well when viewed by their peers. As discussed in the next section, no one wants to let down the team, either.

Social and Task Cohesion

Four brave men who do not know each other will not dare to attack a lion. Four less brave, but knowing each other well, sure of their reliability and consequently of mutual aid, will attack resolutely. -- Ardant du Picq, 1870, quoted in Wong, Kolditz, Millen and Potter (2003)

It is axiomatic in military circles that soldiers fight for their comrades, not for the cause. Put another way, no one wants to let a comrade down. History is replete with examples of squad mates sacrificing themselves to save the life of a fellow soldier. Sociologists call this "social cohesion," where individuals put the good of their friends ahead of the good of a cause or mission. This stands in contrast to "task cohesion," where only the accomplishment of a goal is considered.

In a myriad of studies examining World War II through Vietnam, it has generally been found that social cohesion is more powerful than task cohesion (see Stouffer, et al. 1947 and Moskos, 1970, among others). However, most recently, other studies suggest that both social and task cohesion play a significant role in why individuals are willing to kill and die (Wong et al., 2003).

One can expect to find both task and social cohesion at play in terrorist groups, or any group with a high degree of cohesion, for that matter. Both forces can produce a tremendous willingness for self-sacrifice. To that end, we must be careful not to underestimate the commitment of terrorists to kill and die.

Obedience[7]

Why are seemingly normal, intelligent people willing to follow the orders of those in authority, even when it leads to violent or self-destructive consequences? In the late 1960s, Yale psychologist Stanley Milgram set out to examine that question. In particular, he wanted to understand the Nazi phenomenon: how could so many civilized individuals follow the brutal orders of those in authority to put millions of innocents to death? Milgram believed that there was a small percentage of the population that would carry out any order, even a blatantly

---

[7] The description of the Milgram experiments in this section is taken from Milgram (1974).

immoral one, without question. He devised a now classic experiment to identify what he thought would be a small group of people and intended to study what made them different from the majority population.

Milgram told his volunteers that he was studying operant conditioning and memorization. In each round of the study, two subjects were required. The first would be isolated in a room and hooked up to a machine that would allegedly provide him with electrical shocks. The second subject would be in a separate room before a console, accompanied by the study administrator. Subject number 2 was instructed to read a series of words to the first subject, who was required to repeat them verbatim. Whenever the first subject was incorrect, the study administrator ordered the second subject to apply an electrical shock.

The console was supposedly rigged with a dial that could adjust the voltage of the shocks -- at the far end of the dial, there was a well-marked warning that the voltage in that area could be fatal. As the first subject continued to answer incorrectly, the administrator ordered the "shocker" to increase the voltage, even into the area that was clearly marked as being potentially fatal.

What the second subject did not realize was that the first subject, the "learner," was actually a confederate and that he/she was not hooked up to any electricity. As the imaginary shocks proceeded at correspondingly higher voltage levels, the "learner" would scream in pain and request to be released from the experiment. The administrator, however, would order the shocker to ignore the protests and continue at all costs. At one point in the experiment, the person being "shocked" stopped answering; the implication was that he/she had passed out, or worse. Nevertheless, the administrator continued to insist that the experiment continue, with progressively higher levels of voltage being administered.

Milgram believed that this experiment would allow him to identify the small portion of the population, perhaps 10%, who would obey an authority figure under all circumstances, even when common sense and decency told him to stop. Much to Milgram's amazement, however, 65% of his subjects continued to provide shocks, even into the fatal area. Only 35% defied the orders of the administrator. So the real "deviants," at least numerically, appear not to be those who follow authority -- rather, it is those who are willing to stand up and question it. The key to the experiment seemed to be the presence of the authority figure: when he left the room, compliance dropped.

Milgram carried out his studies in America, a country that values rugged individualism and the rights and needs of the individual above the state. One wonders what his findings would have been in a society in which group, family, and state is considered more important than the individual.

Those terrorist leaders that are able to maximize their credibility and authority, whether through the persuasiveness of their personalities or through the cloak of the legitimacy of their title, will be ale to demand, and receive, increased levels of obedience. As a result, leaders spend a great deal of time attempting to solidify and enhance their status.

Putting It All Together: The Lethal Triad[8]

Former police officer and current police psychologist Kevin Gilmartin has constructed what he calls the "Lethal Triad," a model that explains under what conditions isolated extremist

---

[8]Except where noted, the following section is taken from Gilmartin (1996).

groups can turn violent. While Dr. Gilmartin established this model to deal with domestic terrorism in the United States,[9] the Lethal Triad nevertheless offers insights into all types of extremist groups.

Specifically, Gilmartin maintains that three social-psychological variables--isolation, projection, and pathological anger--work together to enhance and nurture a group's cohesion and reinforce its belief system. As well, Gilmartin claims that the Lethal Triad can help predict under what circumstances groups will turn deadly.

The first branch of the triad, isolation, occurs when group members sequester themselves from the society at large. This isolation is both physical, with members often going to private camps or retreats, and psychological, through the taking on new names and severing relations with family members and friends. As individualism gives way to group identity, critical thinking begins to diminish. The group can enhance this conversion through restricting one's access to books, newspapers, or television, instead providing only that information it wishes the member to receive. The ultimate goal is to have a person committed to the group's goals and ideas, not her own.

The isolation process depends upon the groupthink phenomenon. Groupthink, first described by Irving Janis, refers to the dynamic where groups under pressure discourage individual dissent. Members are directly and indirectly encouraged to "go along with the program." Indeed, for most groups, a great deal of time is spent on this phase. Communal prayer meetings and indoctrination sessions regularly reinforce the "rightness" of the group's goals and encourage members' commitment to the larger mission.

---

[9]The FBI classifies terrorist groups as either "domestic" or "international." According to the Bureau, the Ku Klux Klan is a domestic group while al Qai'da is an international one.

While Gilmartin looked primarily at physical isolation, consider how the Internet provides many of the same benefits that physical groups could once exclusively provide. Members who communicate virtually may be subjected to many of the same psychological and social forces found in the physical world. For example, one who sits in front a computer for most of his day, accessing only those sites and individuals who reinforce a specific line of thought, is for all intents and purposes isolated from the world around him, immune from critical thinking in a way similar to one who resides in an isolated terrorist compound.

Once critical thinking skills are diminished and group cohesion enhanced, the second leg of Gilmartin's triad, projection, emerges. Projection is a psychological term that refers to transferring feelings or thoughts from yourself to another. With regard to the Lethal Triad, projection takes on two dimensions. In the first, group members, devoid of critical thinking skills, project all decision-making onto the group's leader(s). To that end, the role of the follower is not to think, but to obey. As the Milgram experiment above demonstrated, many individuals have a strong capacity to obey. To that end, both isolation and projection are symbiotic: group leaders need to demonstrate their authority by breaking down critical thinking and installing themselves as supreme. It is therefore no coincidence that many groups today justify their actions through religion -- after all, what higher authority is there than God, speaking through His representative?

The second role of projection is that of projecting all evil onto the enemy. Terrorist groups have a strong capacity to engage in "splitting," in which the world is split into two distinct camps: absolute good and absolute evil. As a natural consequence of this split, those things that impact negatively on the group, regardless of their cause, are seen as large conspiracies. Some groups construct very complex and intricate histories, tracing what they believe to be modern conspiracies back to the Knights Templar of the Middle Ages and beyond.

The final leg of the triad is pathological anger. Building upon their isolation and projection, group members become increasingly hostile to the "other" who they blame for their problems. If this anger becomes intense enough, group members can become what Gilmartin terms "situational sociopaths," individuals who for a time lose any feelings of remorse or empathy and who are able to engage in acts of incredible brutality and violence.

The Special Case of Religion

Terrorists want a lot of people watching, not a lot of people dead.
Brian Jenkins (Jenkins, 1975:15)

Brian Jenkins was probably correct when he made that pronouncement in 1975. Most terrorist groups in the 1970s were secular, political constructions.[10] They followed Crenshaw's (1988, 1992) model of the rational actor, seeking to find the most effective and efficient means of accomplishing their goals. That included a constraint on bloodshed: enough to be noticed, but not enough to alienate the population. Yet today, there is little doubt that if al Qai'da were able to get its hands on a nuclear weapon, it would use it without a moment's hesitation. What has changed? One crucial factor: today's groups increasingly use religion to justify their activities.

When one thinks of the modern religiously-motivated terrorist, the image that emerges is probably that of Osama bin Laden, the wealthy son of a Saudi businessman who eschewed a comfortable, secular lifestyle to first join the Afghan resistance against the Soviet Union in the late 1970s and subsequently went on to found al Qaeda. While that is not incorrect, it is certainly

---

[10]While some groups, such as the Irish Republican Army, had religious links, their goals and motivations were primarily secular.

incomplete. In the first place, religious terrorism has been around for some time. The word "zealot" comes from a Jewish sect that fought against the Romans in the first century, A.D. As well, an "assassin" in the 12th century A.D. was one who ingested hashish before engaging in religiously motivated murder (Hoffman, 1999).

Those who practice radical Islam are not the only ones engaged in religiously-motivated violence. The Ku Klux Klan has historically viewed itself as a Christian organization and Tim McVeigh, the Oklahoma City bomber, may have had ties to a group that views white supremacy as biblically-inspired. Many well-publicized recent extremist events, such as the release of sarin nerve gas in the Tokyo subway system by the Aum Shinrikyo sect and the standoff/suicide of Branch Davidians in Waco, Texas, both of which occurred in 1995, were carried out by those with strong religious beliefs.

How is it that religion can be such a strong motivator to violence? After all, most think of religion as promoting peace and harmony and, indeed, most religions do. There are those individuals, however, who interpret religious tracts in a way that not only allows, but commands, violence.

The Millennial Connection

Many religions incorporate a millennial component, that is, one that speaks to the transformation and purification of society (Jensen and Hsieh, 1999). Oftentimes, this takes the form of an apocalyptic battle between good and evil (see Inset 1). When one sees himself as an extension of a divine force, several factors come into play: a) The normal constraints society imposes on individuals to refrain from deviant or violent behavior no longer apply; in some cases violence is commanded if one wishes to work himself/herself into heaven; b) Political goals are less important than being a "good soldier." Since one's reward will be in heaven, achieving a particular short term political outcome no longer matters and Jenkin's admonition does not apply. Since God has already ordained the battle, killing as many of the enemy as possible is one's mission; c) Martyrdom becomes not only understandable, it becomes desirable. Whether one straps on a suicide belt, drinks poison-laced Kool Aid, or restrains one's children as the fires of a religious compound rage, giving one's life for his/her religion is the ultimate form of devotion. While many of us have trouble understanding the motivations of the 9-11 hijackers, far fewer would question the dedication, devotion, and even saintliness of Joan of Arc.

Given that as background, consider the words of Hassan Salame, who orchestrated a series of suicide bombings in Israel in 1996:

> A suicide bombing is the highest level of jihad, and highlights the depth of our faith. The bombers are holy fighters who carry out one of the more important articles of faith (Salame, quoted in Post, 2003: 19).

A Model for Understanding Terrorist Groups: The Terrorist Organizational Profile

Some years ago, Tom Strentz of the FBI's Special Operations and Research Unit, formulated an organizational model of the "typical" terrorist organization. Strentz based his model on studies he conducted involving the Symbionese Liberation Army (SLA), a left-wing radical group that kidnapped heiress Patty Hearst in 1974. Strentz's approach at the time was unique: he put together a terrorist group model based upon the roles that individuals played within that group. Rather than looking at individual psychology, Strentz argued that there are certain functions and roles that are common to all groups. These roles require certain personality attributes if the group is to succeed. As such, those individuals who initially possess these attributes are naturally drawn to the corresponding role within the group. Alternatively, those who find themselves filling a particular role either possess or begin to develop the necessary attributes, or they vacate the role. In spite of its age, the Strentz model still provides a useful means to examine and understand a particular group (Strentz, 1981).

According to the model, there are 3 primary roles or functions that exist in every terrorist organization: leader, activist-operator, and idealist. The role of leader is, of course, a crucial one. It is he or she who sets the entire tone of the organization and is ultimately responsible for its operations. If there is any single characteristic that seems to hold true across different types of groups, it is the notion on the part of the leader of the rightness of the cause, and by extension, the rightness of the leader. Most terrorist leaders are either by temperament or training loathe to compromise or back away from a position. This all-consuming sense of "rightness" causes the leader, and hence the group, to see the world in a very black-and-white manner. Often, this is articulated in very apocalyptic terms. It is not uncommon to hear groups from al Qai'da to the Aryan Nations describe the "final battle" between good and evil that is usually just around the corner. Of course, the group is on the side of ultimate good while the enemy is cast in the most demonic terms possible. It is important to stress that the thinking here is of absolute good versus absolute evil. The enemy can do no good, the group can do no wrong. For example, some criminal white supremacist gangs refer to Jewish people not just as the enemy, but as the "spawn of Satan."

Along with this sense of rightness there usually follows a good dose of non-delusional paranoia. While a certain amount of paranoia makes sense in a group that is likely being investigated or hunted, the level that exists is often way beyond what one would expect. Indeed, while often fatal in the long run, paranoia can provide benefit to the group in the short term. For example, members can "project" their feelings of inadequacy and failure onto the enemy, explaining away shortcomings as the result of the "conspiracy" that is working against them.

The leader can also posses some engaging qualities. For example, he may be charismatic and charming. When dealing with authority figures, while he will likely try to not reveal information of value, he may be more than willing to talk about his beliefs, in the hope of recruiting the interviewer. The leader will often have the ability to manipulate: after all, she is responsible in some cases for convincing individuals to engage in dangerous or even suicidal behavior.

The next role that Strentz says occurs in groups is that of the activist-operator. In some ways, this is the most significant individual in the group from the perspective of law enforcement, because it is he who is generally responsible for planning and carrying out criminal activity. This is the operational "muscle" of the group, the one who is called upon to handle the "heavy-duty" assignments. Strentz also termed this individual the "opportunist," because when examining the SLA, he noted that many of the individuals who held this position were former prison inmates. According to him, these actors showed little actual loyalty to the group; in fact, they were too self-interested to offer loyalty to anyone but themselves. That being the case, the opportunist may be in an ideal position to assist law enforcement. His role and personality allow him to turn on former comrades with little hesitation when it serves his purpose.

While Strentz was likely correct with regard to the SLA, it is unclear that the role of activist-operator necessarily goes to someone who possesses sociopathic impulses. For example, Mohammed Atta, who was the ground commander for the September 11th terror strikes, filled the role of activist-operator. And yet, he willingly sacrificed his life in furtherance of the cause, something that a true sociopath would likely never do.

Finally, Strentz characterizes the rank-and-file as idealists, individuals who are drawn to the group and willingly serve as its "cannon fodder." While not generally held in the same high esteem as the activist-operator, the idealist is nevertheless absolutely crucial to the stability of the group. In many cases, she is a "true believer," one who accepts the goals of the group and the rules of the leader without question. In fact, the leader - idealist relationship is completely symbiotic; while the idealist provides the leader with the adoration she craves, the leader gives the idealist the meaning and direction he needs.

As with any model, the neat distinctions that Strentz lays out may not apply quite so nicely in the real world. To date, the model has not undergone rigorous empirical testing, so its efficacy is as yet unknown. Nevertheless, it offers an organizing structure that analysts and law enforcement officers may find quite useful when examining terrorist groups.

Conclusion

Human behavior is a complex subject, regardless of whether it refers to terrorism or more "normal" pursuits. To that end, no single terrorist profile has emerged that contains sufficient explanatory and predictive power. Some theorists maintain that terrorist behavior is best explained as a rational pursuit of a specific goal; still others contend that the goals terrorists espouse are merely smokescreens for the psychological benefits they obtain from being terrorists. In all likelihood, there is a certain amount of truth in both explanations. Perhaps a better way to think about it is not as "either/or" model but as a continuum. Certain groups may be more goal oriented than others while others may cater more toward providing members with emotional and social benefits. In reality, most groups will be an amalgam of both types of forces. Perhaps the one area that most researchers would agree upon is that most terrorists are not "crazy," at least not in the pathological or psychotic sense, although they may display behaviors at times that certainly look that way. At the very least, those who wish to study terrorist groups and individuals will have to invest a considerable amount of time and effort to understand their

motivations and behaviors.

Finally, some organizational models exist may prove helpful in understanding group

structures and behaviors. Two of these include Gilmartin's *Lethal Triad* model which explains

the circumstances under which groups may become violent and Strentz's *Terrorist*

Organizational Profile, which examines the structural roles of those within terrorist

organizations.

****

Inset One: Excerpt from "Law Enforcement and the Millennialist Vision: A Behavioral Approach." by Jensen & Hsieh (1999)
THE APOCALYPTIC MODEL
     Based either on a religious or secular model, apocalyptic belief systems contain certain universal characteristics. At the core of each, a fundamental struggle exists between good and evil. In Christianity, this struggle occurs between God and Satan. For many extremists, the evil forces of the New World Order constantly struggle with those patriotic Americans who believe that the democratic principles of this country have almost disappeared. This perspective contains little gray area: those defined as evil remain unremittingly sinister, while those defined as good stay unerringly righteous and pure.
     To this end, even those apocalyptic belief systems that are primarily secular often contain religious or supernatural rhetoric and ideas. For example, many who deplore the New World Order make liberal use of religious imagery: those parts of the U.S. Constitution with which they agree are "sacred" and "holy" while those that run counter to their beliefs (e.g., the 14th Amendment, which granted citizenship to former slaves) are cast in demonic terms.
     The battle between the forces of good and evil generally represents the final chapter in an ongoing struggle. For example, the conflict between God and Satan began in the Book of Genesis, while many who believe in the New World Order trace the roots of this grand conspiracy to the Knights Templars and the Crusades.
     Another common apocalyptic theme concerns the grand and horrific nature of the final battle between good and evil. Some predict that many individuals will perish on both sides of the conflict. In certain Christian denominations, the chosen ones will proceed to heaven and miss the battle, while those not chosen will suffer horrible plagues and consequences on earth. Other religious and secular groups believe they will participate in the struggle and play a pivotal role in allowing good to triumph. For example, these groups purport that loyal patriots who have managed to save their weapons from confiscation will defeat the forces of the New World Order.
     The final component of the apocalyptic vision includes the contention that in the end,

good triumphs over evil. In addition, those who have persevered in the fight against evil will be rewarded with either everlasting life in heaven or the defeat of tyranny and the fulfillment of heaven on earth.

****

References

American Psychological Association (1994). *Diagnostic and statistical manual of mental disorders, 4th edition.* Washington, D.C.: American Psychological Association.

Ames, R. T. (1993). *Sun-Tzu: The art of war.* New York: Ballantine.

Bandura, A. (1977). *Social learning theory.* New York: General Learning Press.

Borum, R. (2004). *Psychology of terrorism.* Tampa: University of South Florida.

Corrado, R. (1981) "A critique of the mental disorder perspective of political terrorism." *International Journal of Law and Psychiatry 4* (3,4): 293 - 309.

Crenshaw, M. (1988). "The subjective reality of the terrorist: Ideological and psychological factors in terrorism." In R. Slater and M. Stohl (eds.) *Current perspectives on international terrorism.* New York: St. Martins. Pp. 12 - 46.

Crenshaw, M. (1992) Current research on terrorism: The academic perspective." *Studies in Conflict and Terrorism 15*: 1-11.

Crenshaw, M. (2000). "The psychology of terrorism: An agenda for the 21st century." *Political Psychology 21* 405-420.

Davis S.F., M. T. Huss and A.H. Becker. (1995). "Norman Triplett and dawning of sport psychology." *Sport Psychologist 9* (4): 366-375.

Gilmartin, K. M. (1996). "The Lethal Triad: Understanding the nature of isolated extremist groups." *FBI Law Enforcement Bulletin.* Retrieved from URL http://www.fbi.gov/publications/leb/1996/sept961.txt on 04/222009.

Gurr, T. R. (1970). *Why men rebel.* Princeton, N.J.: Princeton University Press.

Hacker, F. J. (1976). *Crusaders, criminals, crazies: Terror and terrorism in our time.* New York: W. W. Norton.

Hoffman, B. (1999). "Old madness, new methods: Revival of religious terrorism begs for broader U.S. policy." *RAND Review* (Winter 1998 - 99): 12-17 at URL http://www.rand.org/publications/randreview/issues/rr.winter98.9/methods.html accessed 06/20/2005.

Hubbard, D. (1983). "The psychodynamics of terrorism." In Yonah Alexander, T. Adeniran, and R. A. Kilmarx (eds.) *International violence.* New York: Praeger. Pps. 45 - 53.

Hudson, R. A. (1999). *The Sociology and Psychology of terrorism: Who becomes a terrorist and why?* Washington, D.C.: Library of Congress.

Jenkins, B. (1975). *High technology terrorism and surrogate warfare: The impact of new technology on low-level violence.* Santa Monica: RAND.

Jensen, C and Y. Hsieh. (1999). "Law enforcement and the millennialist vision: A behavioral approach."*Law Enforcement Bulletin 68* (9): 1 – 6.

Lowe, S. (2003). "Terrorism and Just War theory." *Perspectives on Evil and Human Wickedness 1* (2) at URL http://www.wickedness.net/ejv1n2/ejv1n2_lowe.pdf accessed 06/04/2005.

Martens, W. H. (2004). "Terrorist with antisocial personality disorder." *Journal of Forensic Psychiatry Practice 4*(1): 45 – 56.

Michaels, J. W., J. M. Blommel, R. M. Brocato, R. A. Linkous, and J. S. Rowe. (1982). "Social facilitation and inhibition in a natural setting." *Replications in Social Psychology 2*:21-24.

Milgram, S. (1974). *Obedience to authority: An experimental view.* New York: Harpercollins.

Moskos, Jr., C. C. (1970). *The American enlisted man: The rank and file in today's military,* New York: Russell Sage Foundation.

Oots, K. and T. Wiegele. (1985). "Terrorist and victim: Psychiatric and physiological approaches." *Terrorism: An International Journal 8* (1): 1 – 32.

Pfohl, S. (1994). *Images of deviance and social control* (2ⁿᵈ ed.). New York: McGraw-Hill.

Post, J. M. (1984). "Notes on a psychodynamic theory of terrorist behavior." *Terrorism: An International Journal 7* (3): 242 – 256.

Post, J. M. (1990). "Terrorist psycho-logic: Terrorist behaviour as a product of psychological forces." In W. Reich (ed.) *Origins of terrorism: Psychologies, ideologies, theologies, states of mind.* New York: Cambridge University Press. Pp 25 – 40.

Post, J. M. (2003). "Killing in the name of God: Osama Bin Laden and Al Qaeda." In B. R. Schneider & J. M. Post (eds.) *Know Thy Enemy: Profiles of Adversary Leaders and Their Strategic Cultures, 2ⁿᵈ Edition* Center Sponsored Books: 17 – 39. At URL http://www.au.af.mil/au/awc/awcgate/cpc-pubs/know_thy_enemy/post.pdf accessed 06/20/2005.

Raine, Adrian (1997). " Antisocial behavior and psychophysiology: A biosocial perspective and a prefrontal dysfunction hypothesis." In D. Stoff, J. Breiling, & J. Maser (eds.) *Handbook of antisocial behavior*. New York: Wiley. Pgs. 289 - 304.

Ruby, C. L. (2002). "Are terrorists mentally deranged?" *Analyses of Social Issues and Public Policy 2*(1): 15 - 26.

Sageman, M. (2004). *Understanding terror networks*. Philadelphia: University of Pennsylvania Press.

Stouffer, S. A., et al., (1949). *The American Soldier: Combat and Its Aftermath, Volume II,* Princeton, NJ: Princeton University Press.

Strentz, T. (1981). "A terrorist organizational profile: A psychological role model." In Alexander, Y. & J. M. Gleason (eds.) *Behavioral and quantitative perspectives on terrorism*. New York: Pergamon Press: 86-104.

Sutherland, E. (1939). *Principles of Criminology*. Philadelphia: Lippincott.

Valls, A. (2000). "Can terrorism be justified?", in A. Valls (ed.) *Ethics in international affairs: Theories and cases*, Lanham, MD: Rowman & Littlefield: 65-79.

Wong, L., T. A. Kolditz, R. Millen, & T. Potter. (2003). *Why they fight: Combat motivation in the Iraq War*. Carlisle, PA: Strategic Studies Institute.

CHAPTER 4
TERRORISM AS A WEAPON FOR CHANGE

Greatest weapon of terrorists is fear playing on irrational emotions of public. Patrick Dixon,
(Terrorism Fear Is Their Greatest Weapon How to Defeat)

Introduction

By the end of the first decade of the 21st century, terrorism had become an all too familiar word in the mind of Americans and our allies. Media coverage of terrorism and terrorist attacks numbed our senses to their actions. The sight of burning cars in a Middle Eastern market place or a bus destroyed on the streets of an Israeli city became a frequent image in the media. With the explosion of technology and the internet, terrorist organizations could now reach countless individuals with their messages. The western allies were learning to accept terrorism as a reality of life, much as the Israelis had accepted it. We had painfully learned that terrorism had become a threat to be taken seriously and that terrorism could be attacked, but never be fully eliminated by force alone.

As the first decade of the 21st century concluded, terrorism and groups labeled as terrorist organizations were viewed as the greatest challenges to our national security. They replaced the Soviet Union as our national adversary and with this change we were forced to re-think our foundational approaches to national security.

The United States had witnessed domestic terrorists and international insurgent groups operating around the globe for decades. For the most part, America viewed terrorists as distractions, but not a major threat, even as groups scrambled to gain headlines. Even when Americans or American interests were targeted, calculated and measured responses were employed.

For those that choose terrorism as a way to advance their cause, they selected a strategy in which to wage conflict that does not require extensive investment in military infrastructure. The terrorist does not have to purchase tanks or artillery, maintain extensive logistical bases, or concern themselves with so many of the issues conventional militaries must face. Thus, those that resort to what we term "terrorism" have selected an approach to warfare that requires great skill, not only to inspire others to join the struggle, but to do so while avoiding a decisive engagement.

Clash of Cultures

The Cold War between the United States and the Soviet Union was a conflict that frequently used surrogate nations as military proxies. Conflicts such as those seen in Vietnam and Afghanistan flooded regions with weapons and military supplies supplied by the super powers. These weapons, and the military training provided to groups in conflict, would later prove costly to the post Cold War world.

Upon the collapse of the Soviet Union, the United States emerged as the world's only global super power. This status placed America in a position of world influence, admired by some and resented by others. The culture of the United States, to include clothing, food, entertainment and lifestyles, spread around the globe. McDonalds restaurants in Russia and China, movies and American music in theaters around the globe signaled the encroachment of U.S. culture around the world. This was viewed, especially in some parts of the Middle East, as a direct challenge to the fundamental social values and beliefs deeply rooted in religion.

The post Cold War conflicts in Iran and Afghanistan demonstrated the capability of the United States to wage war and inflict its will upon others. As a super power, even nations that might be inclined to challenge the United States militarily were reluctant to take on the challenge. Additionally, with a world economically linked, few nations could continue in isolation or ignore the benefits of international trade and investment. Once Cold War foes, China not only has evolved into a major trading partner with the United States, but also a major investor.

Many hoped the end of the Cold War would allow the world to settle into a period of peace and prosperity; however, events in the Middle East would soon eliminate that possibility With the invasion of Kuwait by Iraq in 1990, the United States and its Coalition partners shifted significant military power into the region and forced Iraq out of Kuwait. To ensure security, the United States stationed a large military presence in Saudi Arabia. Many in the Middle East saw the western influence as a danger. For those intent on challenging this western influence militarily, few options were available. Rather than engaging in direct confrontation, anti-western forces resorted to to unconventional warfare in the hope to wearing down the stronger power, convincing it that the price to continue the struggle was greater its potential benefits.

As Seen by the United States: The Concept and Definition of Terrorism

Terrorism is not new. The September 11, 2001 attack which so captured the attention of the world was not the first nor would it be the last strike by terrorists. Instead, this attack was gripping; it succeeded in shaking the United States and sparking it into action.

Interestingly, a A total of terrorist 457 incidents took place in the United States from 1980 to 1999, to include272 acts, 55 suspected acts and 130 prevented terrorist acts. In 70% of the cases, attacks involved bombings. Assassinations and arson were the other most popular methods, used in roughly 5% of the events.

The FBI didn't start tracking terrorist attacks until the mid-1970s. In the 1970s and 1980s, the vast majority of attacks were committed by left-wing and anti-war groups, such as the Weather Underground, the Black Liberation Army, the Symbionese Liberation Army, the Jewish Defense League, and the Armed Forces of Puerto Rican Liberation. Many of the incidents recorded in the early 1980s took place in Puerto Rico, conducted by groups committed to the country's independence from the United States. By the mid to late 1980s, however, most of these groups had lost their influence. Many were dismantled by law enforcement officials. Some left-wing groups that subscribed to largely socialist views were made irrelevant by the fall of Communism.

Terrorism Defined

Terrorism has been described variously as both a tactic and strategy; a crime and a holy duty; a justified reaction to oppression and an inexcusable abomination. It has often been an effective tactic for the weaker side in a conflict. As an asymmetric form of conflict, it confers coercive power with many of the advantages of military force at a fraction of the cost. Additionally, due to the secretive nature and small size of terrorist organizations, they often offer opponents no clear organization to defend against or to deter.

While the definition of terrorism within our own government varies, the understanding of the danger it poses is real. Three major elements within the Executive branch of our government define terrorism differently. The United States Department of Defense defines terrorism as "the calculated use of unlawful violence or threat of unlawful violence to inculcate fear; intended to coerce or to intimidate governments or societies in the pursuit of goals that are generally political, religious, or ideological." (cite??) Within this definition, there are three key elements—violence, fear, and intimidation—and each element produces terror in its victims.

The Federal Bureau of Investigation, a primary organization within the United States Department of Justice, defines terrorism as "the unlawful use of force and violence against persons or property to intimidate or coerce a government, the civilian population, or any segment thereof, in furtherance of political or social objectives."

Finally, the United States Department of State defines terrorism as the "premeditated politically-motivated violence perpetrated against non-combatant targets by sub-national groups or clandestine agents, usually intended to influence an audience."

No matter the definition, terrorism is an act whose intent is to influences an audience beyond the immediate victim. The strategy of terrorists is to commit acts of violence that draws the attention of the local populace, the government and the world to their cause. Terrorists typically plan their attack to obtain the greatest publicity, choosing targets that symbolize what they oppose. The effectiveness of the terrorist act lies not in the act itself, but in the public's or government's reaction to the act.

Terrorism may be viewed from several different perspectives: the terrorist's, the victim's and the public's. The terrorists, if actually understanding the purpose of their action, see themselves as warriors in a struggle, fighting for a cause they have embraced. Not all involved in the use of terrorism as a tactic within a conflict embrace the idea of sacrificing themselves nor do they see themselves as evil. Instead, they see themselves as using the tools available to them. For example, Timothy McVeigh viewed the Federal Building in Oklahoma City as a legitimate target. He did not see himself as evil, but rather as a warrior. This is one of the real dangers in the struggle against terrorism, either from domestic or international threats; the terrorists view themselves as legitimate combatants, fighting for what they believe in, by whatever means possible.

A victim of a terrorist act sees the terrorist as a criminal with no regard for human life. The intent of the modern terrorist is to inflict fear and often shake the confidence of the victim in the safety provided by their government.

The view of the public of the actions of the terrorist is typically determined by the public's orientation to the cause advocated by the terrorist. Terrorists, unless they work independently, cannot operate, much less survive, without some degree of public support. So it is important for a terrorist organization to generate public support or at least reach of level in the society while continuing its struggle.

The Use of Terrorism

Terrorism is continually evolving in intent, tactics and technologies. It is a method of waging a conflict with limited resources. Today, aircraft hijacking has given way to suicide bombings and improvised explosive devices (IEDs). Terrorist tacticians and strategists continue to view violence as a means to publicize and advance their cause and win adherents. In 1870, anarchist Mikhail Bakunin expressed it this way: "We must spread our principles, not with words but with deeds, for this is the most popular, the most potent, and the most irresistible form of propaganda" (para. 32). The challenge for the terrorist is to inflict enough damage to gain attention, but not enough to alienate those who may support your cause. As an example, in Afghanistan in 2009, a decision was made not to continue the policy of the destruction of the poppy crop being produced in the country-side. In the case of the Afghan farmers, they viewed their production of poppies as a crop whose production provided for their families. The United States and its Allies viewed the production of poppies as fueling the world supply of opium and heroin. The decision to stop the program of crop eradication was based on the realization that the destruction of the poppy crop drove many of the farmers into the arms of the Taliban and thus against Afghan and Coalition efforts within the nation.

As another example, within the Israeli Palestinian conflict, both sides have used the tactics typically associated with terrorism to advance their political agendas. Though much of the conflict has been confined to the Middle East, the 1972 attack by the Palestinian sponsored Black September Organization at the Munich Olympics shocked the world. The tragic deaths of the Israeli athletes was magnified because it played out on the world stage. Terrorism at the Olympic Games sent a message to Israel and the world that any location might well become a target for the next terrorist attack. The Black September Organization selected the Munich Olympics to capture world attention; in this they succeeded.

Response to Terrorism

The use of terrorism to advance a political objective has historically proven to be effective. Examples abound of movements which have used terrorism to topple governments. For those tasked with responding to terrorism, the challenges of response are as varied as the terrorists themselves. What appears to be common is that terrorism cannot survive long without support. If the population support base can be removed from the terrorist, it is difficult for their movement to survive.

It is difficult to successfully combat terrorism if the terrorists control the pace of operation. To successful combat terrorism, the operational tempo must be taken from the terrorist and their operations cycle must be disrupted. To disrupt the operational cycle of the terrorist, the collection, processing and use of information and intelligence is critical.

Types of Terrorism

Robert Pape, University of Chicago Professor of Political Science and author of *Dying to Win*, categorizes terrorism as demonstrative, destructive, or suicidal. Pate describes demonstrative terrorism as the least aggressive form of terrorism which has as the objective of gaining attention and inflecting fear while avoiding serious destruction or harm that could produce sympathy for the terrorist cause. The intent is often to publicize a cause, recruit more activists, demonstrate resolve toward grievances, or gain attention from soft-liners on the other side or third parties who might exert pressure on the other side. The desire is a lot of people watching, not a lot of people dead. The next category, destructive terrorism, is more aggressive; the objective becomes the coercion of opponents with the threat of injury or death. The method seeks to inflict harm on members of the target audience while balancing the risk of losing sympathy and support for the cause. The final category, suicide terrorism, is the most aggressive. This method pursues coercion even at the expense of angering not only the target audience but neutral communities as well. It is worth noting that coercion can be an aim of any of these forms of terrorism; however, coercion is the paramount objective of suicide terrorism (Pape, 2005.).

The Tactics of Terrorists

One of the first things to understand about a terrorist is that they are all different. Terrorists possess varied capabilities, different agendas and diverse motivation for their actions. To achieve success, they must typically gain or at least not lose popular support of the people in the area they operate. If they are intent on developing or maintaining a terrorist organization, they must have a message that attracts followers.

Terrorists will typically operate within a fairly restricted geographical area, using what may become predictable tactics which may vary on occasion. If their tactics fail to shock, they will seek ways to return the shock value to their actions. Terrorists typically seek targets that are vulnerable; they generally try to force those who oppose them to spend extensive resources and energies in the effort to harden targets from attack. The terrorists realize that it is impossible to protect all targets, and thus, the effort to protect creates opportunities for attack. In seeking shock value, terrorists typically rely on actions such as bombings, suicide bombers, improvised explosive devices, hijackings, assassinations, property damage and kidnapping as their more frequent tactics to advance their agendas.

Bombings

Bombs have been one of the most popular weapons in the terrorist arsenal. Typically easy to build, deploy and detonate, they have the shock value so desired by terrorists. Bombs can be constructed in all sizes and can be detonated in a wide variety of ways, from direct detonation triggered by the victim, to command detonation by the terrorist to a delayed timer.

History is filled with examples of bombs and bombers. In the early 1600s, a group of conspirators attempted to detonate a large quantity of gunpowder beneath the English Parliament in a plot to kill King James I and English lawmakers (Robinson, 2001). In the United States, during the early 20th century during a period known as the "Red Scare," anarchists used bombs as they targeted government officials and corporate interests.

Bombing is not confined to a single movement or ideology. Groups as divergent as the Ku Klux Klan and the Weather Underground have engaged in bombing campaigns within the United States. Internationally, the use of bombs has proved popular since shortly after the development of gunpowder. Bombers can work alone or in small groups.

Attacks have occurred around the globe. In 1972 on what has been called "Bloody Friday," an Irish Republican Army (IRA) bomb attack killed 11 people and injured 130 in Belfast, Northern Ireland. Ten days later, the IRA placed three car bombs in the village of Claudy. The exploding cars left six dead. In 1975, Puerto Rican nationalists bombed a Wall Street bar, killing four and injuring 60. Two days later, a bomb exploded in a bathroom at the U.S. State Department. The Weather Underground, a dissident group, claimed responsibility. In 1993, the World Trade Center was damaged and more than 1,000 people injured when a car bomb planted by Islamic terrorists exploded in a parking garage.

One of the most shocking bombing attacking in the United States was the 1995 bombing of the Alfred P. Murrah Federal Building in Oklahoma City which killed 168 and injured 800 by Timothy McVeigh. McVeigh used a rented truck to deliver his bomb which was constructed of fertilizer/diesel fuel mixture, easily obtainable.

Suicide Bombers

The steady rise in suicide terrorism over the past 25 years, the unprecedented lethality of the 9/11 attacks, and the dramatic surge in suicide operations over the last few years present a clear and present threat to national security. To gain as much shock value as possible, we have witnessed a growing trend in the terrorist use of suicide bombers, especially in the Middle East. Much can be written on the use of suicide bombers, how they are recruited, what motivates them and those that sponsor them. Suicide bombers add a greater shock value to terrorism. The idea that someone is willing and expects to die to advance his agenda is foreign to most of us. In some cases, suicide attackers attach bombs to their bodies while in others they drive vehicles loaded with explosives to their desired target.

In examining the use of suicide bombing as a tactic, nearly all suicide terrorist attacks occur as part of organized campaigns, not as isolated or random incidents. Pape traced 301 of the 315 attacks to large, coherent political or military campaigns with only five percent as random or isolated attacks. Typically, the target state of every suicide terrorist attack has been a democracy, with the intent to force the government to institute policy changes. Democracies are generally considered soft and especially vulnerable to coercive punishment. The United States, France, India, Israel, Russia, Sri Lanka, and Turkey have been the target of almost every suicide attack in the past two decades. The typical strategic objective of the suicide terrorist campaigns is to maintain political self-determination by compelling a democratic power to withdraw from the territories they prize. Therefore, the increasing trend of suicide attacks over the past 25 years suggests terrorist groups are increasingly relying on these types of attacks to achieve major political objectives, especially when dealing with democracies.

An example of the effective use of a suicide bombing was the attack on the United States Marine Compound in Beirut, Lebanon in 1983. The attack, delivered as a truck bomb, resulted in the deaths of over 200 Americans and a decision to change United States policy in the region and withdraw the military force deployed there. Thus, the Marine Compound was not the target; rather, it was a tool to force the target, the United States, to change its policy in region. The success of the attack sent a message that the United States did not have the strength to remain on task if causalities were inflicted upon it. An example of another suicide attack was the 2000 bombing of the USS Cole in Yemen. Using a small explosive laden boat, the Cole was attacked, receiving extensive damage and the loss of 17 sailors.

Through her research, Mia Bloom observed that terrorist groups appear to use suicide bombing under two conditions: 1) when other terrorist or military tactics fail, and 2) when a terrorist organization is in competition with other terrorist groups for popular or financial support. Bloom contends that suicide attacks generally occur in the second stage of conflicts, not as an initial tactic or strategy. The Chechens' struggle for independence from Russia is a good example of the evolution toward suicide operations. The wars in Chechnya began with intense battles in 1994 and 1996. The rebels waged a terrorist campaign in Moscow in 1999, which Russia responded to with decisive military action. It was not until July 2000 that Chechen rebels initiated a suicide offensive.

Since 1993, suicide bombing has become a popular tactic among Palestinian groups, such as Hamas, Islamic Jihad, and the Al-Aqsa Martyrs Brigade. In addition, U.S. soldiers, local police and government ministries in Iraq and Afghanistan have been the target of individual and vehicle borne explosive devices. In Afghanistan, coordinated attacks by multiple suicide bombers have demonstrated the devastation they can inflict.

Bombers generally seek out locations where they can do the most damage: crowded streets, enclosed locations such as buses or targets of significance. Their bombs often contain anti-personnel materials, such as nails, to maximize loss of life and their intent is to instill fear and send a message that the government is powerless to defend against such attacks.

Suicide bombing may be a growing phenomenon for the United States. According to U. S. government sources, of the 658 suicide bombings conducted around the world in 2007, 542 occurred in Afghanistan and Iraq. Between 1983 and 2008, more than 21,350 people have been killed and about 50,000 injured by suicide bombers (Wright, 2008).

Aircraft and Ship Hijackings

Hijacking of aircraft and ships has long been a tactic of terrorist groups. During the 1970s and 1980s, a disturbing pattern of hijackings occurred, especially targeting major airlines.

Terrorist groups, including the Popular Front for the Liberation of Palestine, the Japanese Red Army, Kashmiri and Croatian separatists, and Sikh and Shi'a extremists have all used hijackings to capture world attention. Aircraft make a desirable target for terrorists. In the first place, they are highly mobile, making a well-planned rescue difficult. As well, hostages are well contained and easy to control. In addition, for a time, aircraft hijackings were highly newsworthy, guaranteeing hijackers plenty of media attention.

The first recorded aircraft hijacking for political purposes occurred in 1931 in Peru when armed revolutionaries attempted to commandeer a Ford Tri-Motor on the ground; when the pilot refused to comply with their orders, the hijacking failed (AirDisaster.com, n.d.). In May 1961, the first U.S. aircraft was hijacked when Puerto Rican born Antuilo Ramierez Ortiz forced at gunpoint a National Airlines plane to fly to Havana, Cuba where he was given asylum.

On July 23, 1968, one of the first major terrorist hijackings in modern times occurred when three members of the Popular Front for the Liberation of Palestine hijacked El Al Flight 426 en route from Rome to Tel Aviv. As with many early hijackings, the terrorists attempted to have comrades in Israeli custody released. Bargaining went on for forty days; eventually, the hostages were released. Despite many attempts and the numerous security challenges faced by Israel, this has been the only successful hijacking to date of an El Al flight in the 60 year history of the company. El Al takes extraordinary precautions in all phases of its operations. The El Al hijacking mirrored many of the other terrorist hijackings of the day: the terrorists used the plane and passengers as bargaining chips to gain something of value from governments. Very often, it was the release of jailed comrades; in other cases, there were ransoms involved. Well-planned, organized aircraft hijackings by terrorist groups peaked in the 1970s and 80s. Better security precautions as well as some spectacular rescue efforts may have deterred potential hijackers.

Though terrorists appeared to have the advantage in aircraft hijacking, one major event would prove to be an example of decisive response to all nations. On June 27, 1976, Air France Flight 139 departed Athens, Greece, en route to Paris. Soon after takeoff, the flight was hijacked by two members of the Popular Front for the Liberation of Palestine and two Germans from a radical German terrorist organization. At first, the plane was diverted to Libya, where it remained on the ground with the passengers and crew for seven hours. To this point, the typical response to aircraft hijacking included negotiation, agreeing to all or limited demands of the hijackers and ultimate release of the hostages. It soon became clear this hijacking was different. The hijackers ordered the plane to Entebbe Airport in Uganda, where they were welcomed by pro-Palestinian president Idi Amin. The intent of the hijackers became obvious when they released all but the 83 Israeli and/or Jewish hostages. Twenty others, including the Air France crew who refused release, were also held. The hijackers demanded the release of various jailed Palestinians; they stated that they would begin executing hostages if their demands were not met.

The Israeli government conducted negotiations while quickly developing a military response. Israeli forces conducted a bold attack that resulted in a successful rescue of the majority of the hostages. In the short but fierce battle, all hijackers, 45 Ugandan soldiers, 5 hostages and one Israeli soldier were killed. In addition, the Israelis destroyed 11 Ugandan MIG aircraft on the ground so they could not pursue the escaping rescuers. The Raid on Entebbe has become the classic successful response to an aircraft hijacking by terrorists.

Of course, the most famous aircraft hijackings for the United States occurred on September 11, 2001, when al Qaida terrorists led by Mohammad Atta hijacked four airliners, three of which would eventually be flown into the World Trade Center and Pentagon. While commercial aircraft had never been used as weapons against targets in the United States, al Qaeda's intention to do so and to target aircraft for destruction was not unknown. In 1995, al Qaeda operative Ramzi Youssef's plot to blow up 11 airliners over the Pacific, code named "Operation Bojinka," became known to authorities. As well, Youssef had devised a plot to fly a hijacked or stolen small airplane filled with explosives into CIA Headquarters in Langley, Virginia (Jenkins, 1996). One issue that favored hijackers was that airport and aircraft security around the world had traditionally been lax. The desire on the part of the traveler for convenience and what was believed to be a limited threat, resulted in a causal approach to air travel that provided a significant opportunity for exploitation.

Because the vast majority of previous hijackings had ended peacefully, flight crews had been instructed to go along with terrorist demands. The 9-11 hijackers exploited this weakness, reasoning that they likely would not be met with resistance from either the crew or passengers. It wasn't until the passengers on the last flight airborne, United 93, received reports that other hijacked planes had been flown into buildings that passengers decided to act to regain control of the plane; their heroic efforts resulted in the hijackers intentionally crashing the plane into an isolated field in Pennsylvania, thus likely sparing a final target. The most likely target of the hijackers of United 93 was either the United States Capitol building or the White House.

The 9-11 attacks have not ended al Qaida interest in targeting airliners. In late 2001, al Qaeda operative Richard Reid unsuccessfully attempted to set off a bomb that had been built into his shoe while aboard a flight from Paris to Miami, Florida. Had he been successful, the flight would have no doubt crashed, killing all aboard. More recently, in 2006 officials in the United Kingdom arrested 25 individuals who they claimed were affiliated with al Qaida who were plotting to blow up several airliners en route from England to the United States and Canada.

As a result of the 9-11 attacks, nations around the world have acted to improve airline security. Efforts have included the reinforcement of doors to cockpits to prevent unauthorized entry, Federal Air Marshals serving aboard several flights, the creation in the United States of the Transportation Security Administration and the development of data banks on suspected individuals whose air travel is restricted.

Though we have concentrated on the hijacking of aircraft by terrorists, they are not the only people who hijack airplanes. Aircraft hijacking has occurred to seek asylum as well as to extract ransom. In the late 1960s, aircraft hijackings from the United States to Cuba became common. In a rare show of international cooperation with the United States, Cuban authorities jailed most hijackers and did not treat them as political celebrities. In the 1970s, a trend in aircraft hijacking for ransom became all too frequent. The most famous case of this type occurred in 1971 when a man who called himself D. B. Cooper hijacked a Northwest Airlines 727 which had taken off in Portland. After the plane landed in Seattle, Cooper was given a $200,000 ransom and parachutes. Upon receiving these items, Cooper released the passengers and ordered the plane airborne. Somewhere over Washington State, Cooper parachuted from the plane into the darkness. Considering the altitude and freezing weather conditions in which Cooper left the aircraft, the chances of his survival are remote. Since this hijacking, some of the money supplied to Cooper has been recovered by campers and hikers in remote portions of the northwest, but neither Cooper nor his parachutes have ever been located (Himmelsbach & Worcester, 1986).

Aircraft are not the only conveyances that terrorists have hijacked. Throughout history ships have been captured, cargo stolen and crews enslaved, impressed or held as hostages. Piracy has always been a threat to commerce. Today, pirates operating out of Somalia have turned the hijacking of ships and the capture of hostages into an international business, not unlike the Barbary pirates that kept the young United States at bay in the early 1800s.

Terrorist have traditionally viewed ships as a difficult target to seize and control, but on October 7, 1985, four militants from the Palestine Liberation Front (PLF) took control of the passenger liner *Achille Lauro* off the coast of Egypt. Holding the passengers and crew hostage, they demanded the release of fifty Palestinians who were being held in Israeli prisons. During the ordeal, the hijackers murdered a Jewish-American passenger, Leon Klinghoffer, who was confined to a wheelchair. After two days of negotiations, the hijackers agreed to be flown to Tunisia aboard a commercial Egyptian jet. En route, the plane was intercepted by United States Navy fighters and forced down in Italy and the terrorists were arrested.

Assassination

One of the oldest tactics used by terrorists and anarchists has been assassination. Leaders from Julius Caesar, Arch Duke Ferdinand of the Austrian Hungarian Empire, Czar Nicholas of Russia, Egyptian President Anwar Sadat, United States Presidents Abraham Lincoln, James Garfield, William McKinley, John F. Kennedy and American political leaders such as Robert Kennedy and Dr. Martin Luther King have all fallen victims to assassins. The murder of a public figure can have enormous consequences; it can shake governments and spark international conflict. The assassination of Austrian Archduke Franz Ferdinand and his wife in Bosnia in 1914 was one of the major causes of World War I.

In the current wave of violence in the Middle East, suicide bombings targeting government officials have become quite frequent. In Afghanistan in 2009, coordinated attacks by suicide bombers on two governmental offices left twenty dead and many more injured.

Protecting a single individual against all threats is a daunting task. For example, despite the best efforts of the United States Secret Service, a highly competent and professional organization, Lee Harvey Oswald was able to assassinate President John F. Kennedy in November 1963. The Secret Service has been credited with helping to thwart attempts on the lives of other Presidents, to include Harry Truman, Gerald Ford and Ronald Reagan.

While assassinations have the practical effect of removing a particular individual from a position of authority, their real power is largely symbolic. When someone assassinates the head of a state, it represents an assault against the entire country. When President Kennedy was assassinated, the United States endured a long period of shock and mourning. For some, the young president's death signaled the beginning of a period of national malaise and turbulence that culminated in race riots and violent protests against an unpopular war by the end of the decade.

On October 6, 1981, President Anwar al-Sadat was attending an annual military parade celebrating the "successful" campaigns during the 1973 Yom Kippur War. He was saluting the troops when an assassination team ran from one of the parade vehicles and began firing weapons and throwing grenades into the reviewing stand. Sadat was killed and 20 others, including four American diplomats, were injured. Also in the reviewing stand with Sadat were future UN Secretary-General Boutros Boutros-Ghali and Hosni Mubarek, the Air Force officer who succeeded Sadat as President. Neither Mubarek nor Boutros-Ghali were injured.

Following Sadat's assassination, the killers were identified as Muslim radicals, members of the Egyptian Islamic Jihad. They opposed Sadat's landmark peace treaty with Israel and hoped to impose Islamic rule in Egypt. Hosni Mubarak and General Fouad Allam, head of Egypt's security service, waged a campaign against radical Islam that featured unlawful arrests, detention without trial, and torture to force confessions. Thousands of suspected terrorists were rounded up and jailed, among them Sheik Omar Abdel Rahman, who was later convicted of conspiring to blow up New York City landmarks, and Ayman al-Zawahiri, one of Osama bin Laden's two top lieutenants (wrong type of cite: http://www.palestinefacts.org/pf_1967to1991_sadat_assassination.php). In 1995, Israeli Prime Minister Yitzhak Rabin was assassinated by Yigal Amir, an extremist orthodox Jew who believed there was divine justification for killing a head of state.

Property Damage

Some terrorist groups, like the Animal Liberation Front (ALF) and Earth Liberation Front (ELF), engage in acts of vandalism and damage to property to publicize their message and advance their cause. The FBI estimates that, since 1979, eco-terrorists have committed over 2,000 acts that have resulted in losses of over $110 million (Federal Bureau of Investigation, 2008a). Some of these acts include the release of animals at research facilities and farms, arson and the destruction of equipment.

Groups that engage in property damage hope that attacking their enemy's assets will be sufficient to cause them to change their ways or at least bring their "immoral activities" to the public's attention. Groups like ALF and ELF who act in this manner are quick to point out that they do not harm living beings; hence, they view themselves as morally superior to violent groups such as al Qaeda. However, law enforcement officials are concerned that, should property damage prove insufficient in bringing about the change they desire, ALF and ELF may escalate their attacks to include violence. For example, the FBI has noted an increase in violent rhetoric and tactics on the part of eco-terrorists (Federal Bureau of Investigation, 2008a, par. 5):

[O]ne recent communiqué sent to a California product testing company said: "You might be able to protect your buildings, but can you protect the homes of every employee?"

Kidnapping

Kidnapping is also a common tactic on the part of terrorists. In some cases, the kidnap victim is held for ransom while in other cases, the victim is used as a trading item to obtain the release of others; in still other cases, kidnapping is used to demonstrate the seriousness of the intent of the terrorist. Finally, terror groups have been known to kidnap the young and force them into the service of their cause. For example, Palestinian terrorists often take Israelis hostage and bargain with authorities to have their comrades released from prison. In some parts of the world, kidnapping is a lucrative business that helps fund terrorism. In Colombia in 2000, it was estimated that the rate of kidnapping was so great that on average one person was kidnapped every three hours (CNN, 2001). Many of these abductions were the responsibility of the Revolutionary Armed Forces of Colombia (FARC) which used kidnapping as one method of generating funds to support its operations. The practice was so accepted by FARC members that it became known as "taxing" the rich; the group went so far as to order all Colombians whose worth was in excess of $1M to pay this "tax" or risk abduction (Nettleton, 2001).

Perhaps the best known terrorist-related kidnapping in U.S. history occurred in 1974 when newspaper heiress Patty Hearst was kidnapped by members of the Symbionese Liberation Army (SLA), a radical left-wing group that declared war against America over racial injustice. The SLA was a particularly violent group that raised funds primarily by robbing banks.

At first, the group demanded that Hearst's father donate food to the poor; after he distributed $6 million worth of food to the needy in the San Francisco Bay area, the group refused to release Hearst because they deemed the food of "poor quality." Two months after she had been kidnapped, Hearst recorded an audiotape in which she stated that she had joined the SLA and had adopted the name "Tania." As authorities debated whether Hearst had been forced to make the tape, she soon put all doubts to rest. On April 15, 1974, she participated in the robbery of the Sunset District branch of the Hibernia Bank in San Francisco. Throughout the robbery, Hearst wielded a rifle and barked out orders to customers; her participation in the robbery appeared voluntary to all involved.

In 1975, Hearst was arrested by the FBI. She was later found guilty of bank robbery and sentenced to prison, despite the best efforts of her defense team to convince the jury that she had been "brainwashed" by the SLA. Hearst was sent to prison, but, after two years, President Jimmy Carter commuted her sentence; she was later pardoned by President William Clinton (Ramsland, 2007).

On the evening of December 17, 1981, U.S. Army Brigadier General James L. Dozier, senior American official at a NATO headquarters in Verona, Italy, was abducted by Red Brigades terrorists. The targeting of General Dozier broke the pattern of previous terrorist activities in Italy; until that time terrorist groups had concentrated their actions against senior Italian politicians, industrialists, jurists, newspaper publishers and police officials. In the days that followed General Dozier's kidnapping, numerous additional threats were received which, in combination, seemed to provide a clear indication that other Americans and U.S. facilities were potential targets for terrorist actions (cite: The Dozier Kidnapping: Confronting the Red Brigades: Col Thomas D. Phillips, USAF, Retired, http://www.airpower.maxwell.af.mil/airchronicles/cc/phillips.html).

Narco Terror

According to the Drug Enforcement Administration (DEA), in 2003 thirty nine percent of the State Department's list of designated foreign terrorist organizations had some degree of connection with drug activities (2003).

The DEA has obtained evidence that suggests that the rebel FARC organization trades cocaine for weapons and fund its activities with cash derived from cocaine sales. In addition, another Colombian terrorist organization, the United Self-Defense Groups of Colombia (AUC), conducted 804 assassinations, 203 kidnappings, and 75 massacres with 507 victims in the first 10 months of 2000; its leader claimed that 70 percent of AUC's funding came from drugs (Drug Enforcement Administration, 2003).

Of even greater concern to the United States, opium production in Afghanistan is at record levels. Many experts believe that drug money is helping to finance the Taliban's war against NATO in Afghanistan; further links between opium cultivation and sales and al Qaeda are also suspected (Drug Enforcement Administration, 2004). In a statement before Congress, the DEA Administrator provided evidence of links between narco traffickers and terrorists (Drug Enforcement Administration 2004):

> In October 2001, a joint DEA/FBI investigation targeting two heroin traffickers in Peshawar, Pakistan led to the seizure of 1.4 kilograms of heroin in Maryland and identification of two suspected money launderers, one with suspected ties to al Qaida. Similarly, Operation Marble Palace in 2001 determined that several members of a targeted heroin trafficking organization had possible ties to the Taliban and that a connected bank account had been used to launder proceeds to alleged Taliban supporters in Pakistan.

To that end, the DEA and other law enforcement agencies have multiple reasons to shut off the supply of illicit drugs: they are in and of themselves dangerous and their profits help to fund terrorist activities.

Transnational Organized Crime

International organized criminals...threaten our physical, economic and national security, indeed, in many circumstances without even setting foot inside U.S. borders."
Assistant Attorney General Alice S. Fisher (Federal Bureau of Investigation, 2008b, para. 7).

Historically, when one discussed organized crime (OC), she was usually referring to the Mafia or a small number of other criminal organizations. Today, that is no longer the case. According to the FBI (2008b):

International organized crime is defined as those self-perpetuating associations of individuals who operate internationally for the purpose of obtaining power, influence, monetary, and commercial gains, wholly or in part by illegal means, while protecting their activities through a pattern of corruption and violence. International organized criminals operate in hierarchies, clans, networks, and cells. The crimes they commit vary as widely as the organizational structures they employ.

Both globalization and technology, such as the Internet, have increased the reach of organized crime (OC). In addition to traditional activities like gambling, prostitution and drug sales, today's OC figures are also involved in the energy and financial sectors and cyberspace, perpetrating sophisticated fraud schemes, trafficking in humans for illegal purposes and laundering billions of dollars in illicit monies throughout the world. Officials fear that OC today has the power to manipulate securities exchanges in such a way as to threaten the entire global economy (Federal Bureau of Investigation, 2008b), see text box 2.

In order to address this significant and growing problem, in 2007, the Attorney General unveiled *The Law Enforcement Strategy to Combat International Organized Crime*. This strategy addresses eight specific threats that include such 21st century realities as identity theft and cyber fraud schemes. It also calls for increasing cooperation between federal, state, local and international law enforcement bodies (Federal Bureau of Investigation, 2008b).

Cyber terrorism

The cyber world is a prime area for attack; it is a world with almost unlimited targets, each with varying degrees of vulnerabilities. The nature and potential impact of a cyber attack has added a new and very dangerous element in the global struggle against terrorism. Cyber terrorism represents a convergence of cyberspace and terrorism; it refers to unlawful attacks and threats of attack against computers, networks, and the information stored therein when done to intimidate or coerce a government or its people in furtherance of political or social objectives.

Terrorists have moved into cyberspace to facilitate traditional forms of terrorism such as bombings. They use the Internet to communicate, coordinate events, and advance their agenda. While such activity does not constitute cyber terrorism in the strict sense, it does show that terrorists have some competency using the new information technologies.

To qualify as cyber terrorism, an attack should result in violence against persons or property, or at least cause enough harm to generate fear. Attacks that lead to death or bodily injury, explosions, or severe economic loss would be examples. Serious attacks against critical infrastructures could be acts of cyber terrorism, depending on their impact. Attacks that disrupt nonessential services or that are mainly a costly nuisance would not (Denning, 2000).

Conclusion

Terrorist tactics have evolved over the years. Throughout history, most groups with a political agenda restrained their use of violence, so as not to alienate the public they were trying to influence. However, as the attacks of 9-11-2001 made clear, groups like al Qaeda no longer exercise such restraint and seek to kill and injure as many of the "enemy" as possible. Coupled with advancements in technology that make the development of weapons of mass destruction more likely and the existence of failed and failing states that may possess WMD, this is a dangerous proposition.

Hijacking aircraft has been a staple of many terrorist groups, including the Popular Front for the Liberation of Palestine, the Japanese Red Army, Kashmiri and Croatian separatists, and Sikh and Shi'a extremists. In the 1970s and 80s, there were numerous hijackings by Palestinian groups, often to secure the release of jailed comrades. As well, individuals have also hijacked planes for money and, in the 1960s, many individuals commandeered planes to fly to Cuba in the hope of obtaining political asylum.

Because most aircraft hijackings had ended peacefully, aircraft crews were instructed to go along with hijacker demands and not resist. This proved to be an advantage to the 9-11 hijackers who correctly surmised that they would meet with little resistance in taking over the planes they hijacked.

Aircraft are not the only conveyances that terrorists have hijacked. On October 7, 1985, four militants from the Palestine Liberation Front (PLF) took control of the passenger liner *Achille Lauro* off the coast of Egypt. They killed an American passenger and obtained the release of 50 jailed terrorists.

Perhaps the best known and most popular terrorist weapon is the bomb. Groups as diverse as the Ku Klux Klan and the Weather Underground and loners like Eric Rudolph and Theodore Kaczynski all employed bombs as their weapon of choice. Terrorist bombings have a long history in the United States; some of the more famous ones in recent memory include the bombing of an African American church in Birmingham, Alabama during the Civil Rights era and the April 19, 1995 destruction of the Murrah Federal Building in Oklahoma City by Timothy McVeigh.

Although they are historically not a new phenomenon, Americans have become familiar with suicide bombers as a result of the Palestinian intifada and the wars in Iraq and Afghanistan. As well, the term "IED" is now a familiar one to most Americans.

Another tactic employed by terrorists throughout history is assassination. While these have the practical effect of removing a particular individual from a position of authority, their real power is largely symbolic: when someone assassinates the head of a state, it represents an assault against the entire country.

Some terrorist groups, like ALF and ELF, eschew violence and instead engage in acts of vandalism and damage to property. Law enforcement officials, however, are concerned that, should property damage prove insufficient in bringing about the change they desire, ALF and ELF may escalate their attacks to include violence.

Another terrorist tactic that has been used over the years is kidnapping. The reasons for kidnapping vary widely and include obtaining funding, abducting individuals to employ as slaves or in the sex industry and having states comply with other demands, such as releasing jailed comrades.

Two other related international phenomenon have been identified by the U.S. government as a threat to national security. The first involves narco-terror, or the sale of drugs to finance terrorist operations. Groups as diverse as the Taliban in Afghanistan and the FARC in Colombia are suspected of receiving millions of dollars through the drug trade.

Finally, buoyed by globalization and improved technology, transnational criminal organizations have sharply increased their activities. In response, the Attorney General has unveiled *The Law Enforcement Strategy to Combat International Organized Crime,* which addresses eight different threats and calls for increased cooperation between federal, state, local and international law enforcement bodies.

Similarly, in October 1983, Middle Eastern terrorists bombed the Marine Battalion Landing Team Headquarters at Beirut International Airport. Their immediate victims were the 241 U.S. military personnel who were killed and over 100 others who were wounded. Their true target was the American people and the U.S. Congress. Their one act of violence influenced the United States' decision to withdraw the Marines from Beirut and was therefore considered a terrorist success.

Clearly, Osama bin Laden and his followers do not share this philosophy. Instead, theirs is a holy war, where numerous casualties are both inevitable and acceptable. Curiously, history has shown the willingness of many different religiously-based terrorist groups to engage in events designed to produce mass casualties. Consider, for example, the case of Aum Shinrikyo, a Japanese -based sect that released sarin gas in the Tokyo subway system.

How is it that religion can be such a strong motivator to violence for some? After all, most of us think of religion as promoting peace and harmony, and, indeed, most religions do. However, many also contain a millennial component that speaks to the transformation and purification of society (Jensen and Hsieh, 1999). This oftentimes takes on the character of an apocalyptic battle between good and evil. When one sees himself as an extension of a divine force, several factors come into play.

In the first place, the normal constraints society imposes on individuals to refrain from deviant or violent behavior no longer apply; in some cases violence is commanded if one wishes to "work" himself into heaven.

In addition, political goals are less important than being a "good soldier." Since one's reward will be in Heaven and not on Earth, achieving a particular political outcome in one's lifetime no longer matters; likewise, Jenkins' admonition against mass casualty violence does not apply: since God has already ordained the battle, killing as many of the enemy as possible is one's mission.

Finally, martyrdom becomes not only understandable, it becomes desirable. Whether one straps on a suicide belt, drinks poison-laced Kool Aid, or restrains her children as the fires of a religious compound rage, giving one's life in the name of God is the ultimate form of devotion. While many of us have trouble understanding the motivations of the 9-11 hijackers, far fewer would question the dedication, devotion, and even saintliness of Joan of Arc.

It bears pointing out that nothing in the above should be read to conclude that al Qai'da or other religiously-oriented groups lack a strategic, political vision. In fact, Osama bin Laden seems convinced that large-scale, mass casualty events will sufficiently frighten his enemies into capitulation; that, indeed, America will remove its troops from the Middle East and no longer support Israel and what he sees as corrupt Arab governments.

To successfully accomplish this, terrorism is a threat. That is why preemption is being considered to be so important. In some cases, terrorism has been a means to carry on a conflict without the adversary realizing the nature of the threat, mistaking terrorism for criminal activity. Because of these characteristics, terrorism has become increasingly common among those pursuing extreme goals throughout the world. But despite its popularity, terrorism can be a nebulous concept. Even within the U.S. Government, agencies responsible for different functions in the ongoing fight against terrorism use different definitions.

Birmingham Church Bombing (1963)

On September 15, 1963, a bomb exploded at the 16th Street Baptist Church in Birmingham, Alabama, killing four young girls. Investigation revealed that the perpetrators were members of the Ku Klux Klan who wanted to send a "message" to those who wanted to end segregation and enforce court-ordered integration of public schools. It was determined that the bomb was composed of dynamite. Given the difficulty of prosecuting cases against the Klan, the final perpetrator wasn't convicted until 2002 (Lamb, 2004).

UNABOMBER (1978 - 1995)

From 1978 until 1995, 16 bombs linked to a single individual, code named "UNABOMBER" by the FBI, were sent to various individuals, including university professors and airline executives. Three people died and 23 were injured. Over the course of his bombing spree, the UNABOMBER communicated with law enforcement authorities. Eventually, he stated that he would cease his bombings if the government agreed to allow his "manifesto," a 35,000-word manuscript titled *Industrial Society and Its Future*, to be published in a major media outlet. After the manifesto was published in the *Washington Post* and *New York Times*, the FBI received many tips about its possible authorship; one came from David Kaczynski, who stated that it resembled previous writings by his brother, Ted. After extensive investigation, it was determined that Ted, a Harvard graduate and one-time promising mathematician, was indeed the UNABOMBER. Ted Kaczynski was arrested at his remote cabin in Montana in 1996. In 1998, he pled guilty to illegally transporting, mailing, and using bombs and murder (Johnston, 1998).

Eric Rudolph (1996 - 1998)

On July 27, 1996, during the 1996 Summer Olympics in Atlanta, Georgia, an explosion in a park adjacent to the Olympic venue killed a spectator. Initially, suspicion fell upon Richard Jewell, a security guard, who was subsequently cleared of involvement. In early 1997, blasts rocked the Otherside Lounge, a gay and lesbian nightclub, and a women's clinic in Atlanta, Georgia. Finally, on January 29, 1998, a bomb exploded at an abortion clinic in Birmingham, Alabama, killing a part-time security guard and critically injuring a nurse. Ultimately, it was determined that Eric Robert Rudolph, a rabid opponent of abortion and homosexuality, was behind the bombings. Rudolph was placed on the FBI's Ten Most Wanted List and a massive manhunt was launched in the mountains of western North Carolina. Rudolph escaped capture until May 31, 2003, when he was apprehended by a rookie police officer while going through a dumpster in Murphy, North Carolina.

Of note, Rudolph placed a secondary device at the women's clinic and nightclub in Atlanta. These devices were timed to explode several minutes after the initial devices; it was clear that Rudolph was targeting the first responders to these events: police, firefighters and EMS personnel.

1993 World Trade Center Bombing (1993)

On February 26, 1993, a 1310 pound bomb consisting of urea nitrate, aluminum, magnesium and ferric oxide exploded below Tower One of the World Trade Center in New York City; six people died and several were injured. A group whose members would ultimately be linked to al Qai'da were implicated.

Murrah Federal Office Bombing, Oklahoma City (1995)

By 1995, elements of the radical right wing in the United States had become convinced that their government was conspiring to erode their rights as guaranteed by the U.S. Constitution. They cited the federal actions against Randy Weaver and his family at Ruby Ridge, Idaho and the Branch Davidians at Waco, Texas as proof of governmental animus against the citizenry. Timothy McVeigh, a former Army enlisted man who was a particularly angry member of the radical right, decided that the government would have to pay for its actions at Ruby Ridge and Waco. Working with a few associates, McVeigh conspired to destroy the Alfred P. Murrah federal building in Oklahoma City, Oklahoma. On April 19, 1995, two years to the day that the Branch Davidian complex in Waco, Texas had gone up in flames, McVeigh drove a Ryder truck loaded with 5,000 pounds of ammonium nitrate and nitromethane (a motor-racing fuel) next to the Murrah Building. Shortly after 9:00 am, the truck exploded, killing 168 in the building. McVeigh was put to death for this heinous action (Michel & Herbeck, 2001).

References

AirDisaster. (n.d.) *Feature: Hijack, part 1*. Retrieved November 8, 2008, from http://www.airdisaster.com/features/hijack/hijack.shtml.

Bakunin, M. (1870). *Letters to a Frenchman on the present crisis*. Retrieved November 7, 2008, from http://www.marxists.org/reference/archive/bakunin/works/1870/letter-frenchman.htm.

Benmelech, E. and Berrebi, C. (2007). Human capital and the productivity of suicide bombers. *Journal of Economic Perspectives*, 21 (3).

Bradley, M. (2005). *The Secret societies handbook*. London: Cassell Illustrated.

Crenshaw, M. (1988). The subjective reality of the terrorist: Ideological and psychological factors in terrorism. In R. Slater and M. Stohl (eds.) *Current Perspectives on International Terrorism*. New York: St. Martins. Pp. 12 - 46.

Crenshaw, M. (1992). Current research on terrorism: The academic perspective. *Studies in Conflict and Terrorism 15*: 1 - 11.

Denning, D. (2000). Cyberterrorism. Retrieved November 25, 2009, From www.cs.georgetown.edu/~denning/infosec/cyberterror-GD.doc

Drama of the desert: The week of the hostages. (1970). *Time*. Retrieved November 8, 2008, from http://www.time.com/time/magazine/article/0,9171,942267-10,00.html.

Drug Enforcement Administration. (2003). *Drugs and terrorism a dangerous mixture, DEA official tells Senate Judiciary Committee*. Retrieved November 8, 2008, from http://www.usdoj.gov/dea/ongoing/narco-terrorism_story052003.html.

Drug Enforcement Administration. (2004). *Statement of Karen P. Tandy, Administrator Drug Enforcement Administration, before the Committee on International Relations, U.S. House of Representatives, February 12, 2004*. Retrieved November 8, 2008, from http://www.usdoj.gov/dea/pubs/cngrtest/ct021204.htm.

Eisenhower, J. S. D. (1993). *Intervention: The United States and the Mexican Revolution, 1913-1917*. New York: W. W. Norton.

Fendell, H. (2006). *Israel commemorates 30th anniversary of Entebbe rescue*. Retrieved November 8, 2008 from http://www.israelnationalnews.com/News/News.aspx/106568.

Federal Bureau of Investigation. (2008a). *Putting intel to work against ELF and ALF terrorists*. Retrieved November 8, 2008, from http://www.fbi.gov/page2/june08/ecoterror_063008.html.

Federal Bureau of Investigation. (2008b). *Department of Justice launches new law enforcement strategy to combat increasing threat of international organized crime.* Retrieved November 8, 2008, from http://www.fbi.gov/pressrel/pressrel08/ioc042308.htm.

Himmelsbach, R. P. and Worcester, T. K. (1986). *Norjak: The Investigation of D. B. Cooper.* West Linn, OR: Norjack Project

IslamOnline (n.d.). "Fatwa bank". Retrieved November 8, 2008, from http://www.islamonline.net/servlet/Satellite?pagename=IslamOnline-English-Ask_Scholar/FatwaE/FatwaE&cid=1119503545134 on 11/08/2008.

Jane's. (n.d.). "Suicide terrorism: a global threat." *Jane's Terrorism and Security Monitor.* Retrieved November 9, 2008, from http://www.janes.com/security/international_security/news/usscole/jir001020_1_n.shtml.

Jenkins, B. (1975) .*High technology terrorism and surrogate warfare: The impact of new technology on low-level violence.* Santa Monica: RAND.

Jenkins, B. (1996). *Terrorism trial begins in New York.* Retrieved from November 8, 2008, from http://www.cnn.com/US/9605/12/terror.plot/.

Jensen, C. and Hsieh, Y. (1999). "Law enforcement and the millennialist vision: A behavioral approach." *Law Enforcement Bulletin 68* (9)

Johnston, D. (1998). "17-year search, an emotional discovery and terror ends." Retrieved November 8, 2008, from http://query.nytimes.com/gst/fullpage.html?res=9E01E2DE1631F936A35756C0A96E958260&pagewanted=all.

Lamb, Y. S. (2004). "Birmingham bomber Bobby Frank Cherry dies in prison at 74." Retrieved November 8, 2008, from http://www.washingtonpost.com/wp-dyn/articles/A61428-2004Nov18.html.

Michel, L and Herbeck, D. (2001). *American Terrorist: Timothy McVeigh and the Oklahoma City Bombing.* New York: Harper.

Nettleton, S. (2001) Kidnapped: pinned by the sword and the wall" *Colombia: War Without End.* Retrieved November 8, 2008 from http://www.cnn.com/SPECIALS/2000/colombia.noframes/story/reports/kidnapped/index.html.

Ramsland, K. (2007). "The kidnapping of Patty Hearst" *Crime Library*. Retrieved November 8, 2008, from http://www.crimelibrary.com/terrorists_spies/terrorists/hearst/1.html.

Robinson, B. (2001). "The Gunpowder Plot" Retrieved November 8, 2008 from http://www.bbc.co.uk/history/british/civil_war_revolution/gunpowder_robinson_01.shtml.

Roig-Franzia, M. (2008). *From Mexico, drug violence spills into U.S.* Washington Post. Retrieved November 9, 2008, from http://www.washingtonpost.com/wp-dyn/content/article/2008/04/19/AR20080419019.

Smith, T. (1976). Hostages freed as Israelis raid Uganda airport. *New York Times*. Retrieved November 8, 2008, from http://select.nytimes.com/gst/abstract.html?res=F60816FA38591B728DDDAD0894DF405B868BF1D3.

Washington Post. (2007). "More attacks, mounting casualties. Retrieved November 8, 2008, from http://www.washingtonpost.com/wp-dyn/content/graphic/2007/09/28/GR2007092802161.html.

Wright, R. (2008). Since 2001, a dramatic increase in suicide bombings. *washingtonpost.com*. Retrieved November 8, 2008, from http://www.washingtonpost.com/wp-dyn/content/story/2008/04/18/ST2008041800913.html.

Yonghe, Y. (2004). *Small Sea Travel Diaries* (translated by Macabe Keliher) Taipei: SMC Publishing.

CHAPTER 5
TRANSNATIONAL THREATS: ORGANIZED CRIME AND TERRORISM

The expansion and sophistication of transnational crime represents one of the most dangerous threats we confront in the next millennium. Rand Beers Under Secretary for the National Protection and Programs Directorate (NPPD) at the United States Department of Homeland Security

Introduction

Until recently the two phenomena of organized crime and terrorism were considered separate problems for law enforcement and governments to address. Both are now part of a major concern in a developing trend of cooperation and networking between terrorist and transnational organized members. Both are considered strategic threats by governments, law enforcement, and the military. The development of transnational organized crime is considered by many in both law enforcement and academia as the most defining and compelling problem of the 21st century because of the economic and political impact that the alliances between crime groups and terrorist will have due to the international demand for illegal services and goods.

The gap between the poor and rich has added to the rise of both groups, in particular in countries that are developing or are a weak state. The lack of consistency in law enforcement, regulation, and laws add to this problem (Shelly 2002, Lyman and Potter, 2004). There has been some history of the nexus of the two threats, but until the events of September 11th, the two were considered separate and distinct. The new age of globalization has produced a borderless, paperless, and cashless society, with rapidly expanding technology all of which have contributed to the ability of many criminal and terrorist groups to network and become more of a threat to national and international security of many nations. The objective of examining the nexus of the links between terrorism and other forms of crime such as transnational organized crime is to develop strategies to prevent, investigate, and disrupt the criminal activity of these criminal organizations.

Drug trafficking, fraud, arms trafficking, human trafficking, cigarette smuggling, money laundering, armed robbery, and counterfeiting are among the diverse and dynamic criminal activity in which there has been a connection between terrorist and transnational organized crime. There is also the question of the extent of terrorist and organized crime illegal trafficking in nuclear, chemical, biological or other dangerous material. A particular concern is the drug trade and human trafficking networks that may be used by terrorist to enter the U.S. with dangerous material. Al Qaeda, Hezbollah, Hamas, and other groups also have found that criminal activity can support them financially and expedite their efforts to move funds to resource their operations. The question is to what extent terrorist are involved in other forms of crime given that most terrorist acts are themselves crimes.

Defining transnational organized crime can be controversial in regard to structure, functions, activities, group membership, and leadership. Defining terrorism can be problematic as well when dealing with the differences between cultures and governments.

Both have in common the ability to operate across borders or operate transnational. This has been viewed by many as impacting local, regional, and national communities.

Louise Shelley (2003), Director of the Transnational Crime and Corruption Center, listed the following illustrations of the links between the two phenomena:

- Organized crime activity is a means of financial support for terrorist
- Both terrorist and organized crime operate in areas where there are weak governments or law enforcement and open borders
- Both groups launder money using common methods and operators to transfer their money
- Both groups use corruption as a means to achieve their goals and objectives
- Terrorist and organized crime operate using networks that often intersect
- Both groups use similar means to communicate and take advantage of developing technology

This chapter will examine the history of the nexus of transnational organized crime and terrorism, the definition of the two phenomena, methods of operation, the current trend in activities and groups involved, and finally, offer suggestions for addressing the developing threat the nexus between the two present. The importance of understanding the operations and activities that are common to these two significant threats to homeland security of the U.S. and other nations is critical to developing strategies to defeating the threats and preventing the developing trend of the dangerous alliance of the two criminal organizations. There is a need to conduct additional research into the extent terrorist are involved in forms of crime, whether for financial support or to develop additional means to carry out their acts. The conclusion that state sponsorship of terrorism has decreased in recent years suggest that the terrorist have resorted to enterprise crime and alliances to achieve their goals and finance their operations (Bantekas, 2003, Cutis and Karacan, 2002).

While this chapter focuses on the transnational threat of organized crime and terrorism, a brief discussion of additional threats such as cyberwarfare/cybercrime, pandemic infectious diseases, proliferation of weapons of mass destruction, competition over scarce resources and ethno-religious and nationalistic conflict will be included.

Defining and comparing terrorism and transnational organized crime

Before examining the activities, structure, and methods of operations of the two phenomena, the characteristics that classify a group as terrorist or organized crime is helpful to understanding why these separate groups would find common ground to achieve their purpose for existence. Terrorist groups and transnational crime groups operate on a network structure often functioning as temporary networks which allows them flexibility while reducing the ability of law enforcement to penetrate these organizations. The modern versions of both terrorist and transnational organized crime operate much like legitimate business structures. While organized crime groups are often of the same nationality that form alliances of diverse ethnic origins for specific criminal activity, terrorist groups have brought together Middle East with Far East; Russian, North and South Koreans, Japanese, Chinese and etc. (Shelly, 2002). While there remains disagreement of what are the attributes and structure of a group classified as organized crime, there are a number of attributes that are universality accepted as distinguishing organized crime from other criminal groups. The definition of terrorism has a similar problem, in particular between countries such as Iran, China, Russia, and the United States; guerrilla warfare or terrorism? The thought that one country's terrorist is another country's freedom fighter is a problem in defining terrorism globally.

The Federal Bureau of Investigation defined terrorism as the unlawful use of force or violence against persons or property to intimidate or coerce a government, the civilian population, or any segment thereof in furtherance of political or social objectives (Terrorist Research and Analytical Center, 1993). The Bureau divides terrorism into two types: Domestic (involving groups or individuals whose activities are directed at elements of the government without foreign direction) and International (terrorist activities committed by groups or individuals who are foreign based).

One major difference between terrorism and organized crime is the motivation. The motivations of terrorist include religious fanaticism, postwar developments, existence of democracy, economic distress, Israeli actions, and a combination of these factors that may be classified as rational, psychological and cultural types of motivation. Democratic principles have been described as an impetus to terrorist activity. People who disagree with the majority rule often feel left out or marginalized and form groups that carry out terrorist acts to change government policy and procedure. In the United States the Oklahoma City bombing serves as an example of this view. Other groups in the U.S. that fall into this explanation include the Weather Underground, The Anarchist, the Ku Klux Klan, American Nazi groups and the modern far right or left groups such as anti-abortionists, Christian militants, animal rights or environmental extremist groups. According to this view the spread of democracy in the 19th century was associated with increasing violence associated with terrorism. William Eubank and Leonard Weinberg of the University of Nevada-Reno research led them to conclude that terrorist groups are nearly four time as likely to develop in democratic than in non-democratic states. John Stuart Mill argued that tensions in multiethnic society are generally increased when democracy is introduced.

Palestinian suicide bombers are believed to be motivated by the act of avenging the deaths of other Palestinians or achieving a martyr status on the belief that this act will guarantee entrance into Paradise. However, they do not consider themselves to be committing suicide, but acting as examples of religious war justification or a struggle to resist secularization. Rational motivation thinks through the goals and options with cost-benefit analysis or the ability to succeed against the target. Psychological motivation involves personal dissatisfaction with life or accomplishments or becoming what is called a "true believer". The cultural motivation is the identification with a family, clan, or tribe with a willingness of self-sacrifice. Fearing the values of others results in a perceived threat to an ethnic group's survival. Values the groups are protecting include language, religion, group membership, and their homeland territory. Terrorist groups also flourish in countries or environments where the youth have limited chances or opportunity for advancement of success. Some U.S. corrections administrators are concerned about the recruitment of terrorist in American prisons. Religion based motivation can be the most dangerous and produce the most violent outcomes of the cultural type motivations. These motives help explain the commitment and willingness to die among the extremist groups.

From the 1960's to the present, there has been a dramatic increase in identifiable religious terrorist groups. Religion and politics are difficult to separate in Muslim terrorist groups. Both Hezbollah and Hamas operate within a framework of religious ideology (What motivates terrorist? 2000).

On the other hand, transnational organized crime goals are money and power (Lyman and Potter, 2004, Mallory, 2007, Abadinsky, 2003). However, the other major characteristics that are used to classify a group as organized crime or transnational organized crime are often shared by terrorist groups. These include: hierarchical structure, limited or exclusive membership, willingness to use violence and corruption, monopolistic in there activities of providing goods and services, perpetuates itself, governed by rules and regulations, and demonstrates specialization or a division of labor. As many as eighteen characteristics have been used to identify a group as organized crime (Mallory, 2007). The differences of opinions of what is organized crime often center on the word "organized" rather than on what is crime. Perhaps the terms of efficiency and effectiveness are more associated with the term organization. The law of supply and demand results in an enterprise that uses corruption, violence, planning, and organization to control and expand illicit markets. Kenny and Finckenauer (1995) determined that organized crime consist of conspiracy as the how, ethnicity often the who, and illicit enterprise as the what. Criminal-community relationships exist where organized crime is accepted just as legitimate enterprises (Potter and Lyman, 2004). Public demand and corruption are necessary for the existence of any type of organized crime including transnational organized crime that operates with no geographical boundaries. Albanase (1996) list three factors that explain the existence of organized crime:

- Opportunity factors-economic, governmental, law enforcement and social and technological changes that these groups use to become more effective.
- The criminal environment-the existence of black markets in the country
- Special skills-technological expertise, smuggling expertise, management skills

Shelly (1995) described three characteristics that define transnational organized crime:

- Based in a single state
- Commit crimes in several countries as opportunities occur
- Conduct illicit activities with low risk of discovery and arrest

When reading the Al Qaeda manual, it becomes apparent that the objective was to make the terrorist more efficient and effective. When reviewing the rules of the La Cosa Nostra or an outlaw biker group, the same conclusion is apparent. Again the most observable difference between terrorist and organized crime members is the ideological motive of the terrorist versus the motive of power and greed/money of organized crime.

Another similarity of both terrorist and organized crime is that both function where there is weak law enforcement or governments, and porous borders. The examples of Moscow, the Golden Triangle, Philippines, Southern China, Laos, Myanmar, Fukian province in China, and Thailand illustrates this view where law enforcement structures are corrupted by organized crime and terrorist who operate with almost impunity (Shelly, 2002, 2005). Although most transnational crime and terrorist groups are based in transitional countries, the connections are not unique to either developed or developing countries. Arrest in Spain and the United States of terrorist for criminal offenses have occurred.

The exploitation of technology is still another area of the link between terrorist and transnational organized crime. The proliferations of information technology and international mobility have been an impetus to the expansion and growth of both transnational organized crime and terrorism (Shelly, 2004). Satellite telephones, the Internet with email and chat rooms with anonymizer features, electronic banking, and cellular telephones allow these organizations to communicate anytime, anyplace, to anyone without being detected. Both groups employ specialists that operate these communication networks, conduct intelligence operations, move money, and insure anonymity of group membership. Terrorist solicit and move funds through charities using the internet that funds their operations. Both groups employ encryption and steganography to avoid detection. Technology has made these criminal groups much more efficient and effective. Money laundering is required of both groups and with the absence of regulation in international banking system it is possible to move money anywhere, anyplace, to anyone. This leads to the conclusion that transnational organized crime, terrorism, and corruption should not be viewed as separate phenomena, but as linked by structures, networks, and activities. Terrorist groups vary in the reliance on crime to achieve their objectives, but there is an emerging trend that they are progressively moving toward a greater involvement in both conventional and organized crime (Dishman, 2001, 2002). The debate continues on the issue of the nexus of organized crime and terrorism because the data is difficult to confirm and sometimes contradictory or based on intelligence. However, there is sufficient evidence based on the above discussion that defining and comparing transnational organized crime and terrorism is useful in developing an understanding of why the two groups would develop links or associations.

Types of cooperation between terrorist groups and organized crime

In their research Dandurand and Chin (2004) sent a questionnaire to Member States of the United Nations through the UN Office on Drugs and Crime. The research examined the links between terrorism and other forms of crime including organized crime. The survey gave respondents five choices of types of cooperation or linkages between terrorist groups and organized crime groups that may occur in their respective countries:

- Operational
- Logistical
- Financial
- Political
- Ideological

Seven countries responded that there was an operational cooperation observed, nine countries observed a logistical cooperation, 12 countries observed a financial link, four countries observed a political connection, and six countries observed an ideological link between terrorist and organized crime groups. Twenty-five respondents did not report the presence of cooperation in their country.

In research by Traughber (2007) a terror-crime continuum was developed to study the link between terrorism and arms, drug and human trafficking in Georgia of the former Soviet Union. Rather than use the terms of "nexus" or "hybrid, the methodology of

Preparation of the Investigative Environment (PIE) was used. The terror-crime interaction spectrum included the following means of describing the links between terrorism and crime groups:

- Activity appropriation-terrorist and crime groups use similar methods without working together
- Nexus-the two groups rely on support and expertise of the other group
- Symbiotic relationship-the groups develop cooperative relationships of mutual benefit or dependence
- Hybrid-the groups share methods and motives
- Transformation-terrorist abandon ideological/political motives for criminal objectives or criminal groups become terrorist groups.

The researchers found that terrorist were using the same routes as arms, drug, and human traffickers thus benefitting from same environment. Terrorist were using arms and drug trafficking to finance their activities which indicated a nexus or even hybrid organization. Both nexus and symbiotic relationship between terrorist and drug and arms traffickers was revealed.

Curtis and Karacan (2002) concluded that overlapping and cooperation of activities of organized crime and terrorist has increased during 2001 and 2002. Their research described the two groups cooperating using three broad patterns. They describe the first pattern as an alliance for mutual benefit, in which the terrorist enter into agreements with transnational criminals to gain funding, without engaging directly in commercial activities or giving up their ideologically base mission. The second pattern is the direct involvement of the terrorist in organized crime, removing the middleman while maintaining the ideological mission. The third pattern occurs when the terrorist replace their ideology with the profit and greed motive. The researchers concluded that most terrorist groups follow the second pattern; they engage in the direct sale of commodities such as arms, narcotics, and people, and are involved in money laundering their profits. The researchers found that often a natural progression occurs from the first pattern toward the third. Association of terrorist with transnational criminals may cause the terrorist to think as businessmen engaged in criminal activity. The terrorist often diversify their activities to become more profitable businessmen. This transformation is described by the Mararenko,(2002) as "fighters-turned-felons". Examples given by the researchers include Revolutionary Armed Forces of Colombia (FARC), The Kurdistan Workers' Party (PKK), and the Real Irish Republican Army (RIRA). The terrorist have actually preserved the environment of instability in a country to protect the group's criminal activity.

The integration of legitimate and illegitimate funds, activities or businesses is characteristic of both organized crime and terrorist groups. Al Qaeda has used charities to move funds. This type of operations make tracking illicit funds difficult as in the case of the publicized Bank of New York Case where the integration of millions of illicit funds with legitimate accounts occurred.

Chepesiuk (2007) reported the case of al Qaeda using the Italian mafia network and expertise to forge documents and use the same transportation the Camorra uses to traffic drugs and contraband. The journalist and Fulbright Scholar quoted security experts as concerned about the growing connection between terrorist and organized crime. The report cited a arrest in 2002 of a Hezbollah cell in Charlotte, North Carolina for involvement in credit card fraud and cigarette smuggling to finance a Lebanon-based group. Dawood Ibrahim, a major crime figure in India, was reported in this article to have shared smuggling routes with terrorist that were involved in the 1993 Mumbai bombing. The cases are illustrations of the interaction of organized crime and terrorist taking advantage of globalization.

Schweitzer (2005) concluded that there is a clear overlap between terrorist and organized crime networks that rely on the same global transportation, communication, and financial infrastructures and both take advantage of the breakdowns in authority and enforcement in states under siege. He predicts that organized crime will collaborate in spawning high-tech attacks on western countries. This is due to:

- Membership of terrorist groups growing and recruiting technically skilled Members
- Terrorist are emboldened by successful operation of groups in the U.S., Europe, and Russia
- Money laundering networks that are expanding and becoming more complex
- Terrorist using the Internet in growing numbers and in more operations
- Drug trafficking expanding with clear link to terrorist organizations in the Middle East and Asia

In his testimony Schweitzer was concerned with radiological terrorism becoming a present danger and cited 85 other experts as reaching the same conclusion. Radioactive material needed to build a "dirty bomb" can be found in most countries and many countries have inadequate control and monitoring programs according to Schweitzer. Examples given were:

- Arrest of an international criminal group for possession of Osmium-187 by Russian and Ukrainian forces
- The arrest by Ukrainian security of an organized crime group in possession of six containers of Cesium-137
- The arrest by Ukrainian police of 3-4 members of a criminal gang with Strontium-90 along with a large number of arms

These and other incidents are clear indications of the interest of terrorist and organized crime in dirty bombs which is a link and type of cooperation between the two groups. Both types of organizations use force, violence and intimidation to achieve their goals whether political, religious, ideological or power and greed.

Both organized crime and terrorist engage in white-collar crime. White collar crime is commonly defined as illegal acts characterized by guile, deceit, and concealment-and not dependent upon application of force or violence. Often committed by means of conspiracy, the objective is to obtain money, property, or services. This crime my include avoiding the payment or loss of money, property, or services and to gain business or personal advantage.

Structure of Terrorist and Transnational Crime

The structure of terrorist organization varies with the size of the group. Larger organizations can create complex branches that provide methods for acquiring resources, administrative support, and operational control. Terrorist organization like transnational organized may be categories of loose networks formed for specific operations or hierarchical rigid structures that are well defined vertical chains of command, control, and responsibility. Danduran and Chin (2004) reported the structure as one that can be compared with major economic enterprises that have extensive logistical infrastructure. They describe these structures as non-tempororary, structured, powerful, anonymous, and discreet organizations that specialized in diverse unlawful activity. Both large and small terrorist groups are concerned with security as a means of survival. The primary method of achieving this is the clandestine cell. Normally, only the cell leader has knowledge of other contacts or cells and only the top leadership has knowledge of the entire organization. Groups vary in size from 20-50 members to groups as large as several hundred. The elements of the terrorist cell are command and control then in order of importance tactical and logistical support. Smaller groups typically have 40-50 members with 2-3 cell units of 2-5 persons in each cell:

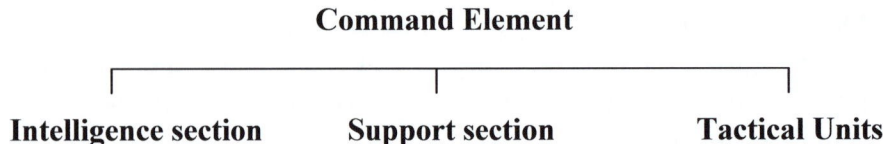

Larger or medium-sized groups add levels to leadership and sometimes resemble a corporate model much like that of many transnational organized crime groups. The leaders provide vision and policy and are often religious extremist that are intellectuals. There are exceptions to this model with leadership that is not educated or intellectual. The second level in the organizational structure is composed of individuals who perform missions or assignments. This cell structure of this second level insulates the command and support components which insure security of the organization. One cell cannot reveal the identity, location, or mission of other cells or the leadership of other cells. The following is a group structure taken from Intelligence in Terrorism, the U.S. Army Institute for Profession Development Correspondence Course (Newport News, 1989):

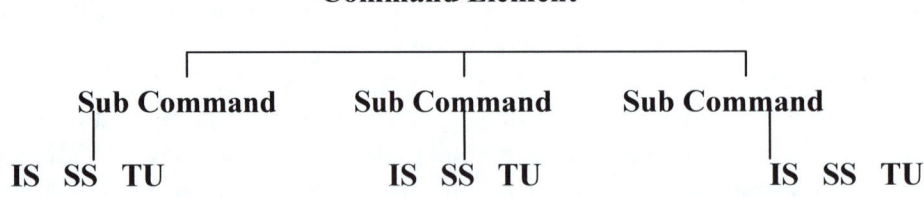

Each sub command has a intelligence section, a support section and tactical units. As the groups expand more sub commands are added and sometimes a third level of command. The sub commands are the forces that carry out attacks or missions. The structure consists of command, active cadre, active supporters and passive supporters. The active cadre performs missions depending upon skills and resources. These individuals are often the most dangerous and active members of the terrorist organization. Active supporters provide vital logistical networks; safe houses, communication technology, and provide intelligence for the organization. Passive supporters help maintain political support and credibility or legitimacy to the organization. The structure and leadership provide training that often results in military precision supported by intelligence, surveillance/reconnaissance, security and realistic training exercises. The terrorist planning cycle consist of a pre-incident phase, initiation phase, a climax phase, a post incident phase, after action briefing, and finally a new planning phase based upon lesions learned or success and failure of missions. This structure and the long term planning are consistent with that of most transnational organized crime and offer an explanation why these two groups can network and work together. Terrorism, like transnational organized crime can be a local, national, transnational or international problem (Baker, 2005). The types of structure have been described by the U.S. Military as being chain, hub, and the all channel network. This is a remarkable similarity to the concept of conspiracy. The chain network has each cell linking only to cells on each side of the cell (A--------B-------C-------D-------E). Communication is passed along the line. The hub and Star networks communicate with one central element like the spokes of a wheel with the center of the wheel comprising the command element. Some groups combine the chain and wheel to form a more complex organization. In the all channel network all nodes or cell are connected to each other with no hierarchical command. Command and control is distributed throughout the network and can be a security risk to the cells if the links can be identified and traced. Transnational terrorist or organized crime may use all three methods in large operations or groups.

Tamara Makarenko (2003) presented a view of the nexus of transnational organized crime to terrorism in what she described as convergence and the black hole syndrome. The blurring of crime and terror results in the difficulty of distinguishing between terrorist and transnational organized crime. The following is the continuum of activity that results in the crime-terror nexus:

Convergence

Black Hole
Syndrome

Organized crime	**Terrorism**
Alliances with terrorist	**Alliances with criminals**
Use of terror tactics	**Use of criminal tactics**
Political crime	**Commercial terrorism**

At the left, transnational organized groups form alliances with terrorist, use terror tactics in their operations and blur the line of political crime with commercial terrorism. The right of the above diagram illustrates terrorist transformation from the pure ideological terrorist to criminals. The structure of both groups results in being dynamic and flexible due to this trend or transformation of both types of criminal groups. Both groups lose their individual attributes and become similar entities that are both violent and enterprising or driven by profit.

The structure of transnational organized crime often mirrors that of the terrorist structures described above. Organized crime enterprises, however, are still localized, often fragmented and ephemeral entities, but have adapted effectively to changes in the global community. The structure of these groups develop cohesiveness with vertical integration, numerous sources of supply and much like the terrorist structure exploit social and political conditions while insulating leaders. In the 1980's the term nontraditional organized crime was used to describe the emerging groups that were less diverse that the traditional La Cosa Nostra (LCN). The structure of LCN (traditional organized crime) closely resembles many of the modern terrorist organizations:

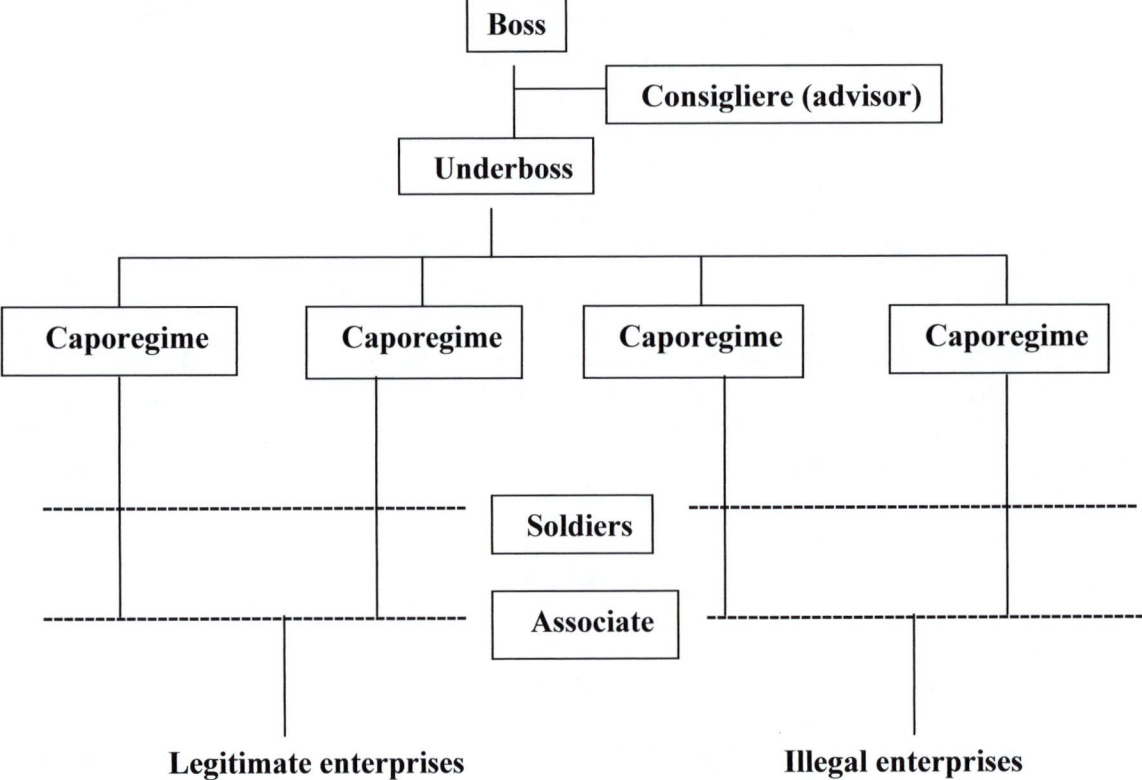

The structure of the Cali Cartel used the cell structure much like terrorist are doing today. This structure was very successful for the largest drug trafficking group in the 1980's. An example of the structure is the following:

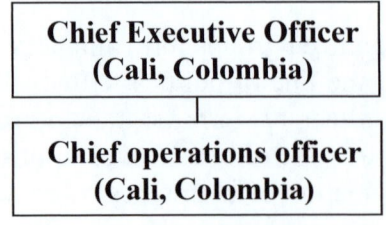

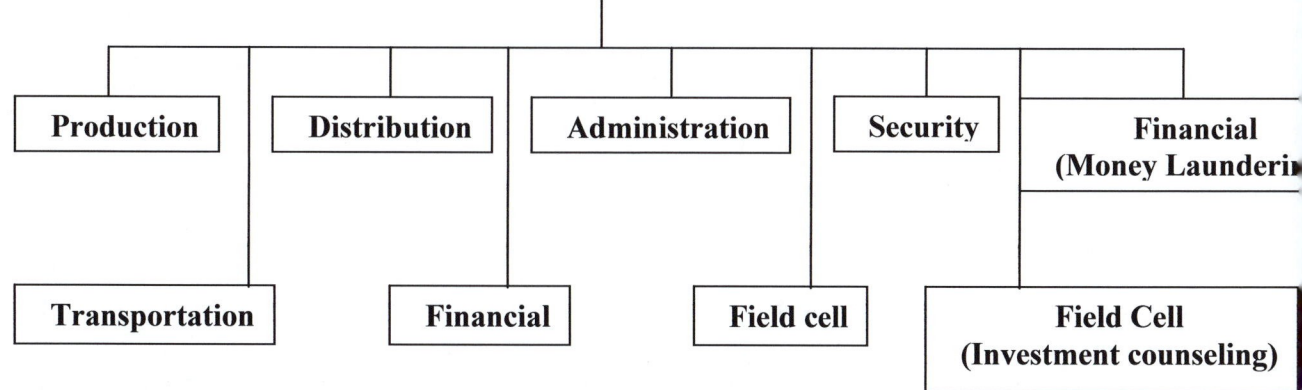

The structure of the Russian Mafia parallels the structure of both the LCN and drug cartels of Colombia and Mexico:

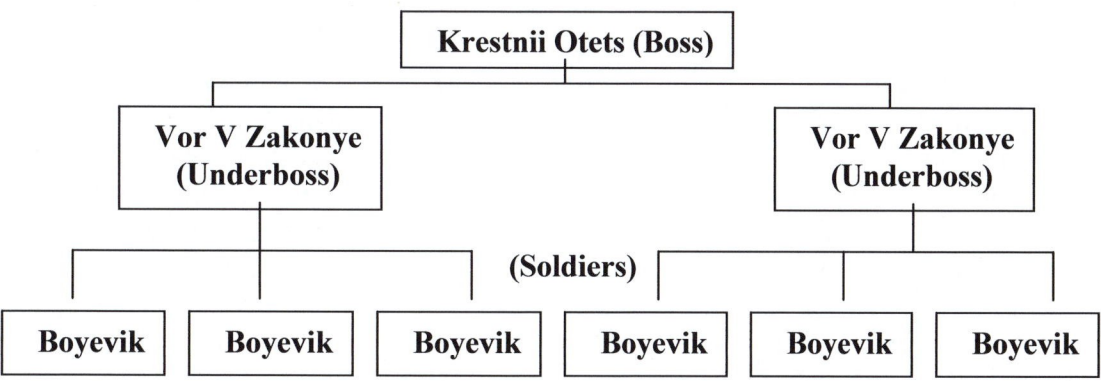

The boss of the Russian groups is also called a Pakhan who controls four specialized cells through a brigadier and two under-bosses or spies. Again the cell structure is employed much the same as with terrorist organizations. At the bottom of the structure are enforcers know as Kryshas who are extremely violent. Russians transnational crime has management and organization groups (Elite), support groups, security groups, and working groups who carry out the operations of the organizations. As with terrorist and other organized crime groups the structure is debatable and often discussed by both law enforcement and academia (Mallory, 2007).

The Yakuza, Chinese tongs and triads, the Red Mafia, outlaw bikers, and Mexican cartel all have some type of structure that lends to their effectiveness and efficiency. While each structure may differ, these structures serve transnational crime organizations just as they serve the terrorist organizations. Whether the boss is called Oyabun (Yakuza), the Shan Chu (Triad), the president (Outlaw bikers), Chairman (Gangster Disciples Gang), Krestnii Otet (Boss of a Russian Mafia group, Osama Bin Laden or his Finance Chief, Mamdouth Mahmud Salim of Al Qaeda, leadership and some type of command structure exist that is critical to understanding and investigating the activities, methods of operation, and the nexus of transnational organized crime to terrorism. These organizations are dynamic and flexible and adapt to market demand and political change forming symbiotic relationship with any entity (business, governments, or other criminal organizations) to achieve their missions, goals, and objectives. As demonstrated by the above structures, it is apparent that structure plays a role in the formation of networks that are often a nexus of transnational organized crime and terrorist.

Early History of the Nexus of Terrorist to Organized Crime

During the 1960's and 1970's, organized crime was not part of the study of terrorism even though terrorist groups had financed their operations by criminal activity. Laqueur (1999) describes a number of events that demonstrate this type of activity by terrorist:

- In the 1990's Russian terrorist robbed banks as did the anarchist terrorist, the Macedonian IMRO, and the Irgun in Palestine.
- Many groups ran a variety of protection rackets
- Groups engaged in smuggling
- Pancho Villas and his group engaged in horse theft
- The Bakunin and the Narodnaya Volya enlisted criminals in their efforts

Before the event of September 11th, 2001, the Assistant Director of Criminal Intelligence Directorate International Criminal Police Organization, Ralf Mutschke, along with Director of the Central Intelligence Agency, the Drug Enforcement Administrator, and the Director of the Federal Bureau of Investigation expressed an increasing concern of the links between terrorist and transnational organized crime.

These experts cited the decline of state sponsorship as a means of financing the terrorist's operations. Mutschke gives the examples of the Colombian drug cartels, Mexican cartels, and La Cosa Nostra associations/links with the two terrorist groups: the National Liberation Army (ELN) and Revolutionary Armed Forces of Colombia (FARC). FARC also established a relationship with Hezbollah according to Mutschke and others. In 2006 the Drug Enforcement Agency reported the convictions of two members of FARC for narcotics trafficking in the U.S. Profits from FARC's coca fields and clandestine laboratories for converting the raw product to cocaine hydrochloride were used by the organization to purchase weapons. A report by Marianela Jimenez (2006) detailed the arrest of FARC member Hector Orlando Mariinez Quinto for exchanging arms for drugs. This age that begin in the 1970's has been described as the age of "narcoterrorism".

One of most significant acts of terrorism in Latin America was the attack on the Colombian Supreme Court in 1984 where 115 civilians were killed including nine Supreme Court justices. The attack was carried out by the terrorist group M 19 and was linked to Carlos Lehder of the Medellin drug cartel. FARC has also been linked to Sendero Luminoso and other movements in the early years. These early events were the beginning of a new type of terrorist who is characterized by a different motivation and outcome. Laquer (1999) reported that in the beginning the terrorist and guerrillas were mortal enemies. Terrorist often punished their members for using drugs. It is interesting to note that many terrorist groups such as the Sunni Taliban in Afghanistan and extreme Shiite groups in Lebanon have not allowed the consumption of drugs, but have not forbidden the production and trade of drugs. It is apparent that many of the modern terrorist groups and individuals have increased their criminal activity and nexus to organized crime groups and are not likely to stop this trend when they have made enormous profits that go beyond supporting their operations or missions. The line between patriotism, terrorist ideology, and organized crime activity has blurred as demonstrated by the Chechen Mafia and terrorist in that country as well as in Caucasus and Central Asia. Organized crime has flourished in Moscow with the growth of gangs from Azerbaijani, Dagestan, Chechnya, Armenia, North Ossetia, and Ingushetia. This is due in part to organized crime becoming politicized thus moving closer to terrorism (Laquer, (1999). The nexus of drug crime and terrorism is widely recognized not only in Colombia as discussed above, but is prevalent in Asia as well. Again, the most frequent examples given are the Taliban and Al Qaeda in Afghanistan. The Sir Lanka Tamil Tigers are still another example of this trend. Louise Shelly of the Transnational Crime and Corruption Center list the following geographical areas as examples from the Pacific Region where links have developed between organized crime and terrorism:

- Russian Far East
- Southern Philippines
- Sri Lanka
- Golden Triangle
- Parts of Indonesia

Corruption has played a vital role in the early history of organized crime and terrorist groups. In the early years, for the most part, terrorism and organized crime had no common ground or interest, but did have common enemies and methods. Shelly writes that collusion of government officials was and is central to the capacity of operations such as smuggling to operate. The Colombian and Mexican Cartels have a history of corruption of government, business, and law enforcement. This was certainly the case in the early development of LCN in the U.S. with the merging of political machines and gangs such as well the documented cases of Tammany Hall machine in New York and the Pendergast machine in Kansas City.

It is often debated as to where gangs such as the Black P. Stone Nation or El Rukins are organized crime. They do meet many of the criteria that is used to classify a group as organized crime. A gang that was lead by a native Mississippian serves as an example of the link between what many classify as organized crime and terrorism. Jeff Fort, a high school dropout, formed a coalition of 21 warring gangs in Chicago, Illinois, that became the Black P Stone Nation in 1969. While serving time in prison he formed El Rukins which was alleged to be a Muslim religious organization. In addition to trafficking in drugs the gang was involved in diverse criminal activity. In 1983, Fort was convicted of selling cocaine and later tried for terrorist activities where the gang cooperated with Libya. Testimony by a gang member revealed that the Libyan Government agreed to pay $2.5 million to the gang to plant bombs on US airplanes (Lyman and Potter, 2004, Mallory, 2007). If this is an example of the extent to which gangs such as El Rukin will go, the shear number of gangs in America could result in a recruitment ground for terrorist. The American prisons are crowded with gang members who could become future terrorist. Gang members have used violence to achieve their goals that rival that of many terrorist groups.

In addition to the corruption role in the early history of organized crime and terrorism, the diverse criminal activity of both groups may well have contributed to the nexus, cooperation, or associations by these groups. The illegal trafficking in arms and narcotics is increasing worldwide with stockpiles of arms in Eastern Europe and the former Soviet Union, and tons of cocaine being produced in South American. This has resulted in the following groups increasing their criminal activity and forming alliances or increased cooperation. The Basque Fatherland and Liberty organization (ETA) and the Irish Republican Army (IRA) of Northern Ireland have been involved in arms and narcotics. Both of these groups have done business with FARC and other narco-terrorist organizations in Latin America. The Kurdistan Worker's Party (PKK) is now involved in narcotics and arms trafficking in Turkey and Western Europe. Yugoslavia arms traffickers are active suppliers of terrorist groups in Western Europe and other countries. The result is the more variable, flexible, and multinational relationship between terrorist and transnational crime groups (Cutis and Karacan, 2002).

Although the most recent events concern international terrorism, past events in the United States are indicative of a trend in domestic terrorism that should not be ignored. The Skinheads, the White Aryan Resistance, and the Ku Klux Klan among others are considered domestic terrorist groups by American law enforcement. The bombing of the Alfred P. Murrah building in Oklahoma City in 1995 where 169 men, women and children died is a grim reminder that there are "home grown" terrorist in the U.S. that are a significant threat to homeland security. The one link of domestic terrorist groups to organized crime that comes to mind is the associations of outlaw bikers and members of hate groups such as the Klan. Outlaw bikers are often known for their prejudices toward minorities (Mallory, 2007). Although there is little or no evidence other that intelligence of the Klan or other group conducting arms transactions or criminal activity with domestic terrorist, large stashes of weapons are common among the bikers and domestic terrorist groups. The outlaw bikers are often involved with other organized crime groups such as LCN in illegal activity according to the Nathansocentre on Transnational Human Rights, Crime and Security. The ability of a group such as LCN to use their extensive worldwide networks to obtain the business of terrorist groups should not be questioned. They are in the business of making money and obtaining power to maintain and protect their operations. The history of such groups indicates that they will sell and do business with anyone who has the money.

Activities Common to both Terrorist and Organized Crime

Terrorist and transnational organized crime not only share structure and modus operandi, but engage in the same type of criminal activity. Terrorist engage in various forms of organized crime including drug trafficking, falsification of documents and illicit migration, arms and munitions trafficking, drug trafficking, using communication devices for illicit activity, illegal transportation of goods and smuggling of a variety of illegal goods. Berry (2002, 2003) found that terrorist groups are involved in cultivation, manufacture, distribution and sale of controlled substances. Terrorist often tax the drug trade or operate a protection racket. A large number of what Berry described as indigenous guerrilla groups operate in drug producing areas of the world where a relationship exist that is of mutual benefit to both terrorist and drug traffickers. However, violence and confrontation can occur between the terrorist and drug traffickers for control of the drug trade as happens between organized crime groups. According to Berry (2002) terrorist linked to drug traffickers use the same corrupt contacts of government to protect their operations and operate with impunity. Shelly

(2001) reaches the same conclusions that terrorist and criminal organizations use corruption to neutralize governments and law enforcement efforts. Curtis (2002) gives the example of the fight between Chechen guerrilla forces and Georgia crime organizations. Turkey reported that the PKK is involved in production and trafficking of narcotics as well as extorting a tax from drug traffickers.

Case studies have revealed that Hezbollah cells in North Carolina used cigarette smuggling to fund terrorist operations in Lebanon. In a study by Sharon Melzer at American University, evidence was found to support the nexus between terrorism and organized crime. The research focused on cigarette smuggling as means of funding both organized crime and terrorist activities.

Thompson and Turlej (2003) described crimes committed by isolated cells of terrorist that included kidnapping, robbery and extortion. Groups listed as involved in these criminal activities included the Weather Underground, Armed Resistance, the United Freedom Front, May 19th, and Islamic Guerillas of America. The researchers reported protection rackets and contract murders by the Commandos of Armenian Genocide (JCAG). Similarly, transnational organized crime in Germany, the United Kingdom, and the United States have been reported by law enforcement as engaging in kidnapping, robberies, and extortion operations.

Dandurand and Chin (2004) reported the involvement of terrorist in the smuggling of migrants in eleven countries and a link between terrorism and falsification of travel and official documents in nineteen countries. The researchers also reported links between terrorism, money laundering, fraud or other forms of economic crimes.

One of the more serious threats posed by an alliance between terrorist and transnational is the existence of the nuclear, chemical and biological material available on the black market that may be controlled by organized crime. Lilly (2003), William and Woessner (1999), and Rosenbaum (1977) have reported that organized criminal groups have acquired nuclear material and are willing to sell to the highest bidder. Laqueur (1999) described the new face of terrorism as the use of biological and chemical weapons in their operations. Sonia Ben Quargrham-Gormley (2007) reported that Al Qaeda has been determined to obtain weapons of mass destruction (WMD). In 2004 the Abdul Qadeer Khan network was linked to organized crime in the black market of nuclear material. The report cited a number of analysts that warned that organized crime will likely channel WMD to terrorist. The article mentioned the interest of the Japanese cult Aum Shinikyo in gaining nuclear, biological and chemical weapons. Much of the attention was focused on the former Soviet Union, Central Asia and the Caucasus. However, the article based on an analysis of 183 trafficking incidents that occurred between January 2001 and December of 2006 concluded that trafficking of WMD material does not appear to have been escalated during this period. Lyudmila Zaitseva (2007) reported that of 400 nuclear trafficking incidents between 2001 and 2005, about ten percent involved elements of organized crime and that there were "marriages of convenience" between organized crime and terrorist involving nuclear trafficking.

The conclusion was the threat of terrorist obtaining nuclear material was small but real. However, there is no evidence in this report or research that terrorist have employed a WMD. Schweitzer (2005 reported that radiological terrorism is becoming a near and present danger citing a poll of 85 experts that was conducted by Senator

Richard Lugar on the threat of weapons of mass destruction. Radioactive materials needed to build a "dirty bomb" can be found in almost any country in the world. He concluded that money is required for both international networks of criminals and terrorist, and the largest source of funds is available by means of illegal drug trafficking. Schweitzer writes that drug networks should be of greatest concern in considering the future of international smuggling of material for dirty bombs. He cites linkages of terrorist groups to the opium/heroin trade in Afghanistan and drug smuggling in the Philippines. Once nuclear, biological, or chemical material enters the black market, it is no way to predict where the material will end up.

Transnational organized crime groups are deeply involved in large scale white collar crime and employ state-of- the-art encryption to safeguard their communication. Groups such as L Mala Salvatrucha (MS-13) enter the US to increase membership and may offer these networks to other groups including terrorist. Albanian transnational clans are now involved in weapons trafficking, loan sharking, alien smuggling, stock market manipulation, human trafficking, and drug trafficking (Kouri, 2009). These activities are lucrative criminal enterprises that now a major source of funding for terrorist groups. The transformation of both organized crime and terrorism has resulted in both group's potential involvement and future involvement in any criminal activity that produces enormous profits. The arrest of 22 suspects operating an immigration fraud demonstrates the growth of organized crime. This group operated in Eastern Europe, Russia, and the United States. The organization run by Viktar Krus of the country of Belarus, a former Soviet bloc country, has brought hundreds of immigrants into the US. Although there is no apparent connection to terrorist groups, this type of operation is ideal for the entry of terrorist into the US (McGlone, 2009). Today, the U.S. Department of justice reports that Mexican drug trafficking organizations is the greatest threat to the United States.

According to the report by the Justice Departments National Drug Intelligence Center, Mexican trafficking cartels operate in over 230 cities across the United States (Byrnes, 2009). Given the evidence of the nexus/link between drug trafficking and terrorism discussed previously, it is probable that terrorist will become associated, if not already, with the Mexican cartels which will allow them extensive smuggling networks to enter the U.S. From the research and media reports, it can be concluded that there is a natural partnership possible between organized crime and terrorist. Authors such and Helfand (2003), Berry (2002), and Sanderson (2004) found evidence of the cooperation between criminal organizations and terrorist groups, and found that this merger is a trend that is expanding possibly due to globalization and criminal activities shared by the groups. Terrorist and organized crime groups do share a number of characteristics, organizational attributes, and criminal activities that make cooperation between the two likely. Both organizations employ similar methods and have similar requirements for moving people, money, weapons and etc. around the world. Both groups often operate under a common set of contingencies. However, none of this leads to a defined and continuous cooperation between terrorist and transnational crime.

Impediments to cooperation between terrorist and organized crime

Researchers such as Helfand (2003) point out that terrorist organizations mimic methods and activity of organized crime, or work with transnational crime groups to exploit illicit markets. However, neither of the two wishes to risk compromising the group's secrets, thus each group maintains their own clandestine networks and opts to control their operations in order to minimize the risk of infiltration. The terrorist and organized crime groups also have different objectives and may define success differently. As discussed earlier, priority for terrorist is ideological and political goals while that of transnational organized crime is money and power. Cooperation may often be sporadic or impermanent that does not lend itself to long term cooperation or alliances. Like alliances that are encountered in transnational organized operations, these partnerships are formed for a particular goal that once achieved, the alliances dissolves. The concern of many researchers such as Berry (2002), Dishman (2001), and Makarenko (2003), in not the cooperation between terrorist and organized crime or criminals, it is the transformation of terrorist to that of a criminal group where the criminal activity has replaced the ideological or political goals. The formation of these hybrid groups (criminal/terror) is an alarming trend and may well be the future of terrorism. While there is evidence of the nexus/link between terrorist and transnational crime, these impediments should be taken into consideration when forming strategies and policy to address this perceived trend.

Current Events That Support the Link between Terrorism and Transnational Crime

Mustsche (2000) identified an area where Argentina, Brazil, and Paraguay meet as the "triple border" where terrorism is linked to organized crime in the activities of arms trafficking, vehicle theft, and counterfeit currency. Assistant Director Mutschke cited other links of terrorism and crime including:

- Algerian terrorist in Montreal and Moudjahidin groups (Groupe Islamique Arme or GIA) specializing is computer theft
- Albanian organized crime/terrorist working with Italian organized in drug trafficking
- Links between the Sacra Corona Unita and Ndrangheta and Albanians in drug trafficking

Ashcroft (2002) cited two cases that linked terrorist to organized crime. A cocaine and cash for weapons transaction for the United Self Defense of Columbia (AUC) terrorist group resulted in the arrest of organized crime members and AUC members. The other case was an attempt to sell heroin and hashish to purchase Stinger missiles for Al Qaeda.

Dandurand's and Chin's (2004) work found links between organized crime and international terrorism in 14 countries: Algeria, Colombia, Comoros, Ecuador, India, Kenya, Kyrgyzstan, Lithuania, Mauritius, Saudi Arabia, Sweden, Turkey, The United Kingdom, and the United States. Angola reported a link in the use of commodities such as diamonds by both terrorist and criminals. Sri Lanka referred to a link between human trafficking operations and terrorism. Tunisia found a firm connection in trafficking in drugs, women and arms in addition to money laundering that funded terrorist organizations. The Federal Republic of Yugoslavia and the United Kingdom linked drug trafficking and terrorism. The United Kingdom reported that paramilitaries are involved in two thirds of criminal groups identified by law enforcement. These groups are involved in extortion, tobacco fraud, drug trafficking and arm and munitions trafficking. Germany had concern about terrorist involvement in money laundering operations and drug trafficking.

In examining the funding of Al Qaeda, Abuza (2003) found eight sources that supported the transformation idea of terrorist becoming criminal enterprises. Drug trafficking, petty crime, money laundering, extortion, arms trafficking, kidnapping and racketeering were identified as sources of funding for the terrorist organization. He described this trend as "criminal terrorism".

The case of Mark Siljander, a former Republican congressman from Michigan, supports the findings of Abuza. Siljander was indicted in 2008 for money laundering, conspiracy and obstruction of justice in an operation which he is alleged to have funneled $1.5 million to terrorist fronts in Pakistan and Sudan (Bell, 2008).

Antonio Maria Costa, Executive Director of the United Nations Office on Drugs and Crime (UNODC) outlined his concerns of the nexus between drugs, crime and terrorism to an international audience in Rome, October 1, 2004. He stated that drug trafficking is the source of the financing of terrorism. He concluded that there is an increasing reliance of terrorist organizations on revenue from arms trafficking, trafficking of human being, and drug trafficking. He described the nexus of organized crime and terrorism using three case studies:

- The production of opium in Afghanistan (3600 tons in 2003) result in terrorist and warlords in Afghanistan, insurgents in Central Asia, the Russian Federation, and traffickers in the Balkans as sharing an estimated $30 billion world heroin market.
- Coca cultivation by insurgents and paramilitary groups of Ejercit de Liberacion Nacional (ELN), Fuerza Armadas Revolucionarias de Colombia (FARC), and the Autodefensas Unidas de Columbia (AUC) as benefiting from billions generated by the coca industry.
- Drug trafficking in Morocco in excess of $12.5 billion was a major source of funding for three major terrorist events: the March attack on rail passengers in Madrid, the bombing of sites in Casablanca in May 2003, and the aborted attack on the US Navy vessel in Gibraltar in 2002.

Director Costa concluded that these and other events have made it difficult to distinguish between terrorist and organized crime groups. He called for global responses to these threats he classified as global threats (Press Release SOS/CP/311, 2004).

The Drug Enforcement Administration (DEA) has reported a link of 14 designated Foreign Terrorist Organizations to ties with the drug trade. Members of FARC, AUC and others have been indicted for drug trafficking by the US. Jorge Briceno-Suarez (member of FARC Secretariat), Thomas Molina-Carcas (Commander of the FARC 16th Front), and Carlos Castano-Gil (Political leader of the AUC) were all indicted and brought to the US and later convicted as members of a foreign terrorist organizations. DEA also reported a nexus between terrorism and the criminal offenses of medical insurance fraud, visa fraud, mail and wire fraud, and cigarette smuggling. Groups that are terrorist and involved in drug trafficking include Al Qaeda, AUC, ELN, FARC, tri-border Islamic Group in Argentina, Paraguay and Brazil, the Shining Path of Peru, the PKK in Turkey, IMU in Uzbekistan, the Islamic Jihad in Palestine, the LTTE in Spain, Hizballah in Lebanon, and the RIRA in Northern Ireland (Casteel 2003).

Ambassador Francis Taylor (2004), Assistant Secretary for Diplomatic Security and Director, Office of Foreign Missions noted that terrorism is like a seven-headed viper. If you cut off the head, another group replaces it; another similarity between terrorism and organized crime. He concluded that there is a defined nexus between organized crime and terrorism. Asian organized crime groups were given as an example of the commonalities of the two groups. Asian groups are involved in cyber crimes, trafficking in explosives, identify theft, credit card fraud, money laundering, smuggling of contraband, and trafficking in prostitution. The ambassador stated that terrorist use the same criminal enterprises to fund their activities. He concluded that there has never been a terrorist organization defeated by military force alone, it is done through the rule of law that addresses these crimes. The example was given of Muhammad Atta being stopped twice on traffic violations before 9/11; he was wanted for questioning and had he been interrogated 9/11 may have been prevented. The point is that focusing on the crimes that terrorist commit can be effective.

Traughber (2007) concluded that the end of the Cold War with the Soviet Union has been an impetus to the growth of both transnational crime and terrorism. Drug trafficking, arms trafficking, and human trafficking are now lucrative criminal activities in the former Soviet Union. This research found that a reported $1 billion in illicit drugs are flowing through Georgia each year. Both terrorist and criminals cross borders and violate nation laws while operating outside the state they reside.

Brigadier Dr. Mohammed Ahmed bin Fahad, Director General of Dubai Police Academy stated that organized crime and terrorist who work together to obtain funds to support their operations employ mass media to deliver messages, and use terror to gain cooperation of recruits. He said that these organizations use legitimate companies such as building and construction businesses, take advantage of modern means of air and land transport, and transfer money through banks and money exchanges with ease. Common activities cited by Fahad include bank frauds, money laundering and corruption of financial regulators or administrators, theft of antiquity, terrorism, piracy, and IT hacking. He called for international policy makers to focus their efforts on countering organized crime in the 21st Century (Over 200 Delegates Attend, 2009).

In 2004 Italy's national prosecutor, Pierluigi Viga stated on frequent occasions that the Camorra of Sicily has been involved in providing arms for Muslim terrorist and has a long standing alliance with the Colombian FARC. He alleged that mobsters in Sicily and Calabria were involved in trafficking of illegal immigrants which has an implication of additional alliances organized crime with terrorist.

The seizure of submarines carrying as much as 3 tons of cocaine and the use of surplus soviet military aircraft to smuggle large quantities of cocaine by the Amado Carrilo-Fuentes organization (the Juarez cartel) are areas of concern because of the apparent alliances of Colombians, Sri Lankans, and Russians and enormous profits that may well attract the attention of terrorist groups in need of funding. Cash seizures of over $19 million is evidence of the reported $300 billion annual drug trade reported by the Drug Enforcement Agency, an amount that should be attractive for funding of any terrorist operation.

The arrest of Monzer al Kassar reported by the Drug Enforcement Administration in 2007 revealed a massive network of transnational organized crime that supplied terrorist organizations. This organization was selling rocket-propelled grenade launchers, surface-to-air weapon systems, automatic weapons and ammunition to factions in Somalia, the United Kingdom, Spain, Romania, Iran, Iraq, Nicaragua, Brazil, Cyprus, Bosnia, and Croatia. Kassar sold millions in weapons to FARC in Colombia.

As early as 2002 the British Tobacco Manufacture's Association was reporting that cigarette smuggling is now second to drug trafficking. This activity has been cited as a major source of income for both transnational crime and terrorist groups. This activity is growing in the U.S., Canada, and Great Britain due to differences in taxes. Profits are reported by law enforcement to be more than $30 per carton. Cigarette smuggling as cited earlier in this chapter is still another source of funding for both terrorist and organized crime.

On February 8, 2009 Fox News was reporting that drug trafficking was the source of over $100 million for terrorist in Afghanistan. The United States military was planning to put into operation strikes against drug lords or opium growers in that region. This is yet another example of the link between terrorist and crime groups and is an indication of the future of both transnational crime and terrorism.

Additional Transnational Threats and World Order

Transnational organized crime is among the major threats to world order and stability of states by non-state actors and non-governments. Other examples of transnational threats include:

- Infectious diseases such as AIDS, Pandemic viruses
- Weapons of Mass Destruction and conventional weapons proliferation (biological, nuclear, and chemical)
- Terrorism that is international/transnational
- Conflict over scarce resources such as oil or water
- Conflict among ethno-religious groups in areas of weak state control and where sovereignty is in question

Although transnational threats have been in existence for some time, they appear today as more violent, dynamic, and complex. The rapid growth of technology and a dynamic security environment has allowed these threats to become more dramatic. The ability to destabilize states and governments has experienced a rapid growth and this growth has produced major efforts on the part of all elements of governments, military and civilian, to engage in major operations such as counter-drug, counterinsurgency, and counterterrorism operations in foreign countries as well as within the borders of the U.S. Transnational threats have the potential to control critical territory or infrastructure, compromise critical resources, and result in conflict between nations. To address these threats requires all elements of national power including military, economic diplomatic and information.

The National Strategy for Combating Terrorism includes six principle objectives:

- Advance the idea of democracy as a weapon against terrorism ideology

- Ensure that terrorist do not control any nation where a base of launching terrorist operations could occur
- Ensure that the terrorist organizations have not sanctuary and support of states or governments
- Engage in prevention of terrorist attacks
- Do not allow governments that support terrorist to develop and obtain weapons of mass destruction
- Ensure interagency coordination and planning where support for these strategies will be built and maintained (Command & Staff College Distance Education Program, 2009)

The National Strategy for Combating Terrorism in consistent with six principles of transnational threats:
- The barriers between agencies, the public, and private sectors must be minimized-jointness
- In addressing these threats, entities must abide by the Constitution even with the possible failure of security-remain within the bounds of law
- We still do not have all the answers and critical thinking must be expanded to address these dynamic threats-creativity
- Technology is very dynamic and in a state of rapid change. To address the emerging threats agencies and government entities must stay on the cutting edge of technology providing the front lines with the most advance planning and tools to answer the threats-speed

- Agencies and entities in the fight against transnational threats must reduce or eliminate the bureaucracies that are slow to respond to the dynamic nature of these modern threats-adaptability

- Define and clearly understand the nature of the threat/conflict and develop clear tactics and strategies to respond-clear thinking

Cyberspace as Target for Transnational Threats

Without a discussion of cyberspace as a security risk, this chapter would be incomplete. The United States is a nation dependent on cyberspace and the Internet. To date, the US has been unable to protect the infrastructure from hackers or identify and prosecute them. Cyberrisk management includes detecting vulnerability, assessing threats, and developing and successfully applying countermeasures. There are no geographic borders in cyberspace which makes this threat attractive to groups such as terrorist, hackers, and organized crime with little risk of being identified or located. Terrorist have used the internet to communicate, recruit new members, conduct surveillance, select targets, publish their agenda, and plan terrorist attacks (Cullison, 2004). Organized crime has continuously used the internet to communicate, launder money, and plan their actions.

The National Strategy to Secure Cyberspace has addressed this problem by outlining a plan for security efforts. It provides direction for federal agencies as well as state, local, and private companies. The priorities of the strategy include:

- Creating an effective response system
- Creating a program to minimize threats and vulnerabilities
- Develop international liaisons and cooperation
- Develop effective awareness and training programs
- Increasing the security of the US Government computer networks

The Department of Homeland Security formed the National Cyber Security Division in 2003 to address the nation's critical information infrastructure. The Division is responsible for providing technical assistance and recovery planning, indentifying, analyzing, and reducing any cyberthreat or vulnerability.

There are a large number of threats including viruses, worms, phishing, attacks that destroy information system and those that disclose or reveal sensitive information. With a minimum investment in equipment, power plants, dams, railways, shipping, transportation, and financial institutions are all possible targets all with possible devastating result. There is intelligence that at least some of the terrorist groups are attempting to mount a coordinated cyber attack on the US infrastructure. It is apparent that sources such as the Pentagon and many federal agencies are very sensitive to public disclosure or discussion to what has been termed as cyber warfare. The threat remains a major concern for the US with the Nation Institute of Standards and Technology revealing that there are up to 45 new types of means to carry out a cyber attack discovered each month. The potential impact on private and government systems by cyber criminals/terrorist is one that could rival a nuclear, biological, or chemical event. However, thus far cyber warfare has been less damaging that physical attacks by terrorist, and hopefully will remain at this level due to increased security and efforts by those responsible for the security of cyberspace.

Conclusions

Whether it is called a link, nexus, alliance, association, or symbiotic relationships, there is a connection between transnational organized crime and terrorism. The war against terrorism cannot be separated from the battle against transnational crime. Both of these groups used networks to become efficient and effective. There appears to be a trend of terrorist groups abandoning their focus on ideology or political motives and replacing them with the objectives more associated with that of a criminal enterprise. There are now more groups that are now labeled hybrids who share methods and motives. It is also apparent that terrorist and organized criminal groups share organizational attributes and are often involved in the same criminal activity. The methods used by terrorist do not differ from that of transnational criminals. The message is that nations should focus on the crimes that both groups commit. Strategies that are used against organized crime (money laundering investigation, drug trafficking investigations, arms and weapons trafficking investigations, and etc) are likely equally effective against terrorist.

With the threat of WMD's (chemical, biological, and nuclear) being sold to terrorist by criminal organizations, the global community needs to form networks as effective as those used by the terrorist and transnational crime. With billions of dollars in possible funding from criminal activity, terrorist are using criminal activity to attempt to purchase these weapons. Because drug trafficking appears to be the major money maker for any group, the investigative and policy focus should be on means to combat drug manufacturing, production, and trafficking. With the extensive global criminal networks of transnational crime well in place, there is motive for the alliances between terrorist and organized crime to form. Both groups are taking advantage of the global market with extensive technology, unlimited communication ability, and the ability to transport anything or anybody to anyplace in world at anytime without detection. This alone should serve as an impetus for the global community to form networks that work and cooperate to address the apparent magnitude of connections and partnerships between terrorist and transnational crime.

The additional transnational threats such as cyber warfare, pandemic infectious diseases, and weapons proliferation have created a modern bad guy that has suggested that an asymmetrical effort that dynamic and global be mounted by the United States and its allies. The 21st century has brought with it a new violent world order that is borderless and more violent that every in history. Aided by every evolving technology, the new bad guys require strategies and tactics that are way beyond the edge of the box in this new age of information.

References

Abadinsky, H. (2003). *Organized Crime (Seventh Edition)*. Belmont : Thomson Wadsworth.

Abuza, Z. (2003, August). Funding terrosim in Southeast Asia: The financial network of Al Qaeda and Jemaah Islamiyah. *Contempoarary Southeast Asia: A Journal of International and Strategic Affairs, 25/2* . Institute of Southeast Asian Studies.

Albanese, J. (1996). *Organized Crime in America (Third Edition)*. Cincinnati: Anderson Publishing.

Ashcroft, John & Arena, Kelli. (2002, November 6). *Ashcroft Hails Joint Efforts in Wars on Drugs, Terrorism*. Retrieved February 12, 2008, from CNN: http://archives.cnn.com/2002/LAW/11/06/ashcroft.terror/index.html

Baker, T. (2005). *Introductory Criminal Analysis*. Upper saddle River: Pearson Prentice Hall.

Bell, D. (2008). *Ex-lawmaker charged with funding terrorism*. Retrieved January 12, 2009, from Free Press: http://www.freep.com/apps/pbcs.dll/article?AID=/22080117/NEWS06/801170462/1001

Berry, L. C. (2002, May). A Global Overview of Narcotics-Funded Terrorist and Other Extremist Groups. *Federal Research Division, Library of Congress* . Washington (D.C.): Library of Congress.

Berry, L. C. (2003, October). Nations Hospitable to Organized Crime and Terrorism. *Federal Research Division, Library of Congress* . Washington (D.C.): Library of Congress.

Byrnes, R. (2009, January 22). *Mexican Drug Traffickers Now 'Greatest Organized Crime Threat' to U.S.* Retrieved January 30, 2009, from CNSNews: http://www.cnsnews.com/Public/content/article.aspx?RsrcID=42329

Casteel, S. (2003, May 20). "Narco-Terrorism: International Drug Trafficking and Terrorism - A Dangerous Mix", Testimony of the Assistant Administrator for Intelligence, US Drug Enforcement Administration, before the U.S. Senate Judiciary Committee.

Chamber of Commerce of the United States. (1974). *White Collar Crime*. Washington D.C.: National District Attorneys Association.

Chepesiuk, R. (2007, September 11). *Dangerous Alliance: Terrorism and organized Crime*. Retrieved January 12, 2009, from Global Politician: http://www.globalpolitician.com/23435-crime

Congressional Statement of Ralf Mutschke Assistant Director, Criminal Intelligence Directorate International Criminal Police Organization. (2000, December 13). Retrieved January 12, 2009, from American Russian Law Institute: http://www.russianlaw.org/mutschke.htm

Cullison, Alan (November, 2004). "Inside al-Qaeda's Hard Drive" Atlantic

Curtis, G. E. & Karacan, T. (2002, December). The Nexus Among Terrorists, Narcotics, Traffickers, Weapons Proliferations, and Organized Crime Networks in Western Europe. *Federal Research Division, Library of Congress* . Washington (D.C.): Library of Congress.

Curtis, G. (2002, October). Involvement of Russian Organized Crime Syndicates, Criminal Elements in the Russian Military, and Regional Terrorist Groups in Narcotics Trafficking in Central Asia, the Caucus, and Chechnya. *Federal Research Division, Library of Congress* . Washington (D.C.): Library of Congress.

Dishman, C. (2002). *"Terrorism, Crime and Transformation", in Griset, P.L. and S, Mahan (Eds)*. Thousand Oaks: Sage Publication.

Dishman, C. (2001). "Terrorism, Crime, and Transformation". *Studies in Conflict & Terrorism , 24*, 43-58.

Fahad, B. D. (2009, January 19). *intersec trade fair and conference.* Retrieved January 30, 2009, from Messefrankfurtme: http://www.messefrankfurtme.com/intersec/downloads/INTERSEC-CONFERENCEDR-MOHAMMED-BIN-FAHAD_DRAFT-Press-release.pdf

Helfand, N. (2003, July). Asian Organized Crime and Terrorist Activity in Canada, 1999-2002. *Federal Research Division, Library of Congress* . Washington (D.C.): Library of Congress.

Jimenez, M. (2006, 8 10). *Costa Rive Arrests Suspected Guerilla*. Retrieved July 3, 2007, from Fox News: http://www.foxnews.com/wires/2006Aug10/0,4670,CostaRicaRebelSuspect,00.html

Kenny, Dennis J. & Finkenauer, James O. . (1995). *Organized Crime in America.* International thomson Publishing Inc.: Wadsworth Publishing Company.

Kouri, J. (2009, January 21). *The Transformation of Organized Crime*. Retrieved January 30, 2009, from The American Chronicle: http://www.americanchronicle.com/articles/view/88515

Laqueur, W. (1999). *The New Terrosim: Fanaticism and the Arms of Mass Destruction.* Oxford: Oxford University Press.

Lilley, P. (2003). *Dirty Dealing -- the Untold Truth about Global Money Laundering, International Cirme and Terrorism. (2nd ed.).* London: Kogan Page.

Lyman, M. D., & Potter, G. (2004). *Organized Crime (Third Edition).* Upper Saddle River: Pearson Prentice Hall.

Makarenko, T. (2003). 'the ties that bind': Uncovering the relationship between organized crime and terrorism. *Global Organized Crime. Trends and Developments* . The Hague, Kluwer Law International.

Mallory, S. L. (2007). *Understanding Organized Crime.* Sudbury: Jones and Bartlett Publishers.

McGlone, T. (2009, January 17). *Prosecutors tie illegal workers to international crime syndicate*. Retrieved January 20, 2009, from Hampton Roads: http://hamptonroads.com/2009/01/prosecutors-tie-illegal-workers-international-crime-syndicate

National Institute of Standards and Technology, Computer Security Resource Center, http://csre.nist.gov/.

Quagrham-Gormley, S. B. (2007, July/August). *An Unrealized Nexus? WMD-related Trafficking, Terrorism, and Organized Crime in the Former Soviet Union.* Retrieved January 12, 2009, from Arms Control Association: http://www.armscontrol.org/act/2007_07-08/CoverStory

Riley, K. J., & Hoffman, B. (1995). *Domestic Terrorism: a national assessment of state and local preparedness.* Santa Moncia: Rand.

Rosenbaum, D. (1977). "Nuclear Terror". *International Security , 1* (No. 3), 140-161.

Sanderson, T. (2004). "Transnational Terror and Organized Crime: Blurring the Lines". *SAIS Review , 24* (No. 1), 49-61.

Schweitzer, G. E. (2005). The Nexus of Internatinoal Organized Crime and Terrorism, The Case of Dirty Bombs. *Testimony to the Subcommittee on Prevention of Nuclear and Biological Attacks of the Committee on Homeland Security, U.S. House of Representative*

Shelley, L. (2002). "The Nexus of Organized International Criminals and Terrorism". *International Annals of Criminology*, *20* (1/2), 85-92.

Shelley, L. I. (2004, September 27). *Organized Crime, Terrorism and Cybercrime*. Retrieved January 12, 2009, from Computer Crime Research Center: http://www.crime-research.org/articles/Terrorism_Cybercrime/

Shelley, L. I. (June, 25 2003). *Statement to the House Committee on International Relations, Subcommittee on International Terrorism, Nonproliferation and Human Rights,"*. Retrieved January 12, 2009, from American.edu: http://www.american.edu/traccc/resources/publications/shelle18.pdf

Shelley, L. I. (2001). The Nexus of Organized International Criminals and Terrorist. Transnational Crime and Corruption Center.

Taylor, F. X. (2004, April 12). *A Global Perspecitve on Terrorism and Organized Crime*. Retrieved January 12, 2009, from United States Department of State: http://www.state.gov/m/ds/rls/rm/31861.htm

Terrorist Research and Analytical Center, Counter-Terrorism Section Intelligence Division. (1993). *Terrorism in the United States 1982-1992*. Washington, D.C.: United States Department of Justice, Federal Bureau of Investigation.

The National Strategy to Secure Cyberspace (February, 2003), www.whitehouse.bov/pcipb/.

Thompson, J.C. & Turlej, J. (2003). *"Other People's Wars: A Review of Overseas Terrorism in Canada"*. Toronto: A Mackenzie Institute Occasional Paper.

Traughber, C. M. (2007, Spring). *Terror-Crime Nexus?: Terrorism and Arms, Drug, and Human Trafficking in the Caucasus*. Retrieved January 12, 2009, from All Academic Research: http://www.allacademic.com//meta/p_mla_apa_research_citation/1/8/0/1/4/pages180143/p180143-1.php

United Nations Press Release SOC/CP/311. (2004, January 10). *UN Warns About Nexus Between Drugs, Crime and Terrorism*. Retrieved January 1, 2009, from United Nations: http://www.un.org/News/Press/docs/2004/soccp311.doc.htm

What Motivates Terrorists?: Chapter 2 from Terrorism. (2000). San Diego: Greenhaven Press, Inc.

Williams, P. & Woessner, P.N. (1999). "The Real Threat of Nuclear Smuggling", in Passas, N. (Ed.). *Transnational Crime*, 181-185.

Yalowitz & Cornell. (2004). The Critical but Perilous Caucasus. *Orbis , 48 (No. 1)* , 107.

Zaitseva, L. (2007, August). *Organized Crime, Terrorsim and Nuclear Trafficking*. Retrieved January 12, 2009, from Center for Contemporary Conflict: http://www.ccc.nps.navy.mil/si/2007/Aug/zaitsevaAug07.asp

CHAPTER 6

INTERNATIONAL TERRORISM: STATE SPONSORS OF TERRORISM

Iran has been the country that has been in many ways a kind of central banker for terrorism in important regions like Lebanon through Hezbollah in the Middle East, in the Palestinian Territories, and we have deep concerns about what Iran is doing in the south of Iraq. Secretary of State Condoleezza Rice, March, 2006 (Rice, 2006)

Introduction

On July 23, 1968, a new phrase suddenly and forcefully entered the world's lexicon: "airline hijacking." It was on that day that El Al flight 426, en route from Rome to Tel Aviv, was hijacked by three young members of the Popular Front for the Liberation of Palestine (PFLP) who wished to draw the world's attention to the plight of Palestinians. The flight was diverted to Algiers where 40 days of tense negotiations ensued; eventually, both the hijackers and the hostages were allowed to go free. The hijackers correctly believed that such a spectacular act would attract huge media attention and force the world to consider their cause.

However, it wasn't until four years later that the words "international terrorism" became a regular part of nearly everyone's vocabulary. On September 5, 1972, as the world was enjoying the Games of the XX Olympiad broadcast live from Munich, Germany, sports coverage was interrupted and replaced by much more serious news: Terrorists from the Palestinian group Black September had taken the Israeli Olympic team hostage. In a drama that played out live over international television, German authorities attempted to resolve the crisis. Ultimately, after a botched rescue, 11 Israelis, 5 Palestinians and 1 German police officer lay dead (Beyer, 2005).

Almost forty years have passed since the 1972 Olympics; most Americans today equate international terrorism with al Qa'ida and a handful of other groups. However, that perception does not line up with reality. In fact, the U.S. Department of State has designated 42 groups as foreign terrorist organizations and 3 countries as state supporters of terror (United States Department of State, 2008a, 2008b). In this and the following chapter, we provide an overview of international terrorism, to include how the U.S. government defines it, how it designates groups and individuals as international terrorists, and the scope of the problem in the world today. We also examine various groups involved in international terrorism, to include their histories and motivations.

International Terrorism Defined

We have previously provided various definitions for terrorism. Most intelligence and law enforcement agencies further describe terrorism as being either **domestic** or **international.** For example, the FBI defines domestic terrorism as occurring "primarily within the territorial jurisdiction of the United States" while international terrorism occurs "primarily outside the territorial jurisdiction of the United States or transcend[s] national boundaries in terms of the means by which they are accomplished, the persons they appear intended to intimidate or coerce, or the locale in which their perpetrators operate or seek asylum" (Federal Bureau of Investigation, n.d.: iv).

Therefore, even though they occurred inside the United States, the FBI considers the attacks of September 11, 2001, to be acts of international terror because al Qa'ida is a group that was formed and operates primarily outside of U.S. borders. On the other hand, even though it was founded in England, the Animal Liberation Front is considered a domestic group because its activities are primarily planned and executed in the United States by American citizens.

Designating a terrorist group as either domestic or international is not merely a matter of semantics–it has significant ramifications for those groups and individuals under investigation. For example, the FBI has two sets of guidelines, one for international groups and one for domestic ones, that outline the conditions under which investigations can be opened and carried out and the techniques permitted under each; the two sets of guidelines differ markedly. As well, the State Department has the authority to restrict U.S. financial activities for groups designated as foreign (international) terrorist entities.

History of International Terrorism in the United States
Beginnings

Until the 20th century, most activities that could remotely be considered acts of international terrorism directed against the United States are better described as acts of war. These include the burning of the White House by the British in the War of 1812 and the sinking of the USS Maine in Havana Harbor in 1898.[1]

The first acts that could reasonably be termed an act of international terror inside the United States came at the hands of the world anarchist movement and occurred with regularity in the early part of the 20th century.[2] The anarchists advocated the abolition of the state, private

---

[1]The cause of the sinking of the USS Maine remains a source of controversy to this day. Despite two official inquiries and two major private investigations, a definitive explanation for the explosion that killed 266 U.S. sailors has yet to emerge. The two leading theories suggest that either an external mine or an accidental coal fire sparked the conflagration (Allen, 1998).

[2]There was no distinction between international and domestic terrorism at this point in history.

property and capitalism in favor of common ownership of all things. Revolutionaries such as Luigi Galleani, an Italian who moved to the United States in 1901, called for the use of extreme violence against the government and private companies (Avrich, 1996).

The first major anarchist-inspired act occurred on September 6, 1901, when Leon Frank Czolgosz, a factory worker and farmer, assassinated President William McKinley in Buffalo, New York. Although Czolgosz was clearly influenced by anarchist literature and had briefly met with some prominent Socialists, there is no evidence that McKinley's assassination was anything other than Czolgosz's own idea (Briggs, 2007).

By 1914, however, anarchists began a series of bombings and violent activities that lasted through 1920. Numerous police departments, churches and government buildings were targeted, which resulted in several deaths. In addition, high ranking officials who had investigated the anarchists and called for their deportation were attacked. On September 16, 1920, a horse-drawn wagon filled with 100 pounds of dynamite exploded in New York's financial district; 38 people were killed and 400 were injured. Although no one was ever found guilty of this attack, most officials believed it was carried out by anarchists aligned with Galleani (Baily & Kennedy, 1994).

In response to these attacks, Attorney General A. Mitchell Palmer, himself a target of the anarchists, carried out a series of raids between 1919 and 1921 on suspected subversives. Dubbed the Palmer Raids, they were led by a young attorney who worked at the Department of Justice named John Edgar Hoover. Hoover, who never lost his zeal for investigating suspected

---

We have designated the acts of the anarchists as international because the movement had its intellectual genesis and conducted many of its first acts of violence overseas and because many of its actors in the U.S. came from outside the country.

subversives, would later go on to serve as the Director of the Federal Bureau of Investigation (FBI) from 1924 until 1972.

At first, the public applauded the Palmer Raids. However, the Attorney General had overstated the threat posed by anarchists and communists, going so far as to predict that an "American communist revolution" was scheduled to commence on May 1, 1920. When no such revolution occurred and when the American Civil Liberties Union released a scathing report charging that the Department of Justice had unlawfully arrested suspected radicals and had engaged in illegal entrapment during his reign, Palmer lost a great deal of credibility (Murray, 1955; Irons, 1999).

Violent anarchist activity subsided in the United States after the Palmer Raids. From the 1920s until the 1970s, external terrorist threats to the United States consisted primarily of unsuccessful Nazi sabotage during World War II. The bipolar era was a war between spies in which little violence was directed at the American homeland. Instead, authorities were more concerned with domestic threats like the Ku Klux Klan, the Weather Underground and the Black Panther Party.

1970s: International Terrorism Attracts the Attention of the U.S. Government

It would be incorrect to assert that terrorism did not exist prior to 1970s; indeed, America watched at a distance for years as its allies suffered at the hands of terrorist entities. For example, Israel was a constant target of displaced Palestinians who desired a return of their homeland and who challenged Israeli's right to exist. Longtime friend England had been violently victimized by the Irish Republican Army (IRA) throughout much of the 20th century.

Sensing that its natural borders and intelligence agencies would somehow keep it safe,

America somehow believed that international terrorism was a distant, and unlikely, concern. As the 1970s progressed, however, the United States government realized it could not remain above the terrorist fray. Early in the decade, Communist inspired terrorist groups, such as Italy's Red Brigades and Germany's Baader-Meinhof Gang, began deadly operations in Europe.

However, it was the aforementioned Black September attack on the Israelis at the 1972 Olympics that prompted heightened U.S. concern. Because it had played out live on international television, the attacks had a profoundly traumatizing effect on the American populace. Adding to this, the Olympic Games had always stood as a symbol for peace and fraternity, even during periods of war. That such an event could occur in such a venue forever shattered whatever illusions America had of escaping the long reach of international terrorism.

Shortly after the attacks, President Richard Nixon established the Office for Combating Terrorism at the Department of State to provide day-to-day counterterrorism coordination and to develop policy initiatives and responses for the United States Government (United States Department of State, n.d.). Since that time, international counterterrorism operations at the State Department, and in most other Executive Branch agencies, have increased significantly. Today, the Coordinator for Counterterrorism oversees all State Department efforts at countering international terrorism. This is a very important position, with the incumbent being appointed by the President of the United States subject to the approval of the Senate (ibid). As we shall see, the State Department plays a very significant role in coordinating U.S. efforts against international terrorism.

Staring in the 1970s, both the CIA and the FBI gradually expanded their roles in pursuing international terrorists. As the bipolar world ceased to be, each agency was able to redirect more resources to counterterrorism. Beginning in the 1970s, the world was shaken by numerous terrorist events carried out by individuals and groups promoting various causes. U.S. interests were attacked with regularity overseas and occasionally here in the United States. Finally, the 2001 terrorist attacks on the World Trade Center and Pentagon forcefully drove home the point that innocent Americans were vulnerable in their homeland; natural barriers and law enforcement and intelligence agencies seemed no longer enough to keep us safe.

The State Department's List of Foreign Terrorist Organizations

United States' law requires the Secretary of State to provide Congress with a yearly report that identifies countries and groups that the United States believes to be involved with international terrorism. This list is used to help craft sanctions, direct investigative and diplomatic efforts, and guide immigration policies. There two primary parts of the list are a) State Sponsors of Terrorism and b) U.S. Government Designated Foreign Terrorist Organizations. Taken together, this provides the most authoritative listing of international terrorist threats facing the United States today; we will examine it in great detail.

State Sponsors of Terror[3]

State sponsors of terror are those countries the State Department believes support terrorist groups and movements against U.S. interests. Countries that finance and otherwise support terror are especially worrisome to the United States because they generally have access to significant funding, weapons, materials, and safe havens from which groups can operate. Also,

---

[3]Unless otherwise noted, information contained in this section was taken from United States Department of State, 2008a.

some have the capability to manufacture weapons of mass destruction (WMD).

When a country is placed on this list, it is subject to a host of diplomatic, trade and financial sanctions. Historically, these have been shown to have some effect on designated countries. For example, Libya was on the list for a number of years for its culpability in the downing of Pan American airlines flight 103 and other atrocities. After it made a number of concessions and reforms, Libya was removed from the list (see text box 1).

The State Department's list is itself the subject of much controversy. Critics charge that political considerations count more than actual evidence of terrorist sponsorship when determining whether a country will be included on the list. For example, in response to allegations that Cuba had been sharing expertise with terrorists, former President Jimmy Carter remarked:

> I asked [high level White House and State Department intelligence personnel] specifically on more than one occasion is there any evidence that Cuba has been involved in sharing any information to any other country on earth that could be used for terrorist purposes. And the answer from our experts on intelligence was *no*. (Carter, 2002)

The State Department lists the following four countries as state sponsors of terror:

- Iran
- Cuba
- Sudan
- Syria

Iran: It may be hard for some Americans to recall, but not too many years ago, Iran was a staunch ally of the United States. In the early part of the 20th century, the British struck a deal with the Iranian royal family to form what came to be called the Anglo-Iranian Oil Company. This proved to be an extremely lucrative relationship for the British, who had to share only a meager 16% of the company's enormous profits with Iran. However, the Iranian citizenry was not enamored with the arrangement. In response, in 1951 the popularly elected prime minister, Mohammed Mossadegh, nationalized the company. The British became enraged and initiated a boycott against Iran. When this failed to produce the desired result, the British government approached the United States and suggested that the two countries engineer a coup to topple Mossadegh. The Eisenhower administration, eager to please an ally it needed during the Korean Conflict, readily agreed. In 1953, the CIA-run Operation Ajax successfully wrested Mossadegh from power Kinzer, 2003).

Excerpts from a State Department Press Release Announcing Rescission of Libya's Designation as a State Sponsor of Terrorism

Libya was first placed on the State Department's list of countries which sponsor terror in 1979. That designation was removed in 2006. The following excerpts from the State Department press release that announced Libya's removal from the list provide a good discussion of the criteria used to determine whether a particular country is a state sponsor of terrorism:

Libya was designated a state sponsor of terrorism in 1979. Relations deteriorated further during the 1980s, particularly in the aftermath of Libya's role in the destruction of Pan Am flight 103 over Lockerbie, Scotland in December 1988, killing 270 people. In 1999, Libya began seriously to address our terrorism concerns and began the process of fully meeting the requirements to distance itself from terrorism by transferring the suspects in the Pan Am 103 case for trial by a Scottish court sitting in the Netherlands. Beginning in 2001, the United States and the United Kingdom initiated three-way direct talks with Libyan representatives to secure Libya's compliance with the remaining international terrorism requirements. Based upon these discussions, on August 15, 2003, Libya sent a letter to the United Nations Security Council confirming its commitment "not to engage in, attempt, or participate in any way whatever in the organization, financing or commission of terrorist acts or to incite the commission of terrorist acts or support them directly or indirectly" and to "cooperate in the international fight against terrorism." Libya also accepted responsibility for the actions of its officials in the Pan Am 103 incident, agreeing to pay over $2 billion in compensation to the families of the victims of Pan Am 103 and pledged to cooperate in the investigation.

On December 19, 2003, after intense discussions with the United States and the United Kingdom, Libya announced its decision to abandon its programs to develop weapons of mass destruction (WMD) and MTCR Category I missile delivery systems. President Bush responded that the United States would reciprocate Libya's good faith in implementing this change of policy. At the same time, Libya moved forward in implementing its pledge to cooperate in the fight against international terrorism. Since September 11, 2001, Libya has provided excellent cooperation to the United States and other members of the international community in response to the new global threats we face. Based on this cooperation, Secretary Rice also announced on May 15, 2006, that, for the first time, Libya will not be certified this year as a country not cooperating fully with U.S. antiterrorism efforts.

Text Box 1 (United States Department of State, 2006)

Mossadegh was replaced by Mohammad Reza Pahlavi, better known as the Shah of Iran. The Shah proved to be a huge friend to the United States; for the next 25 years, the two countries enjoyed close ties. For example, as late as 1978, the United States was selling F-14 fighters and diesel submarines to Iran and training their pilots and crews.

The Shah, however, was not popular at home. While his close ties with the West enabled him to modernize the country, he brutally suppressed any form of dissent. His ruthless secret police force, the SAVAK, routinely arrested, jailed, and tortured anyone who spoke out against his regime. By the late 1970s, however, Iranians in increasing numbers began to protest against the Shah's rule. In 1979, he was persuaded to leave the country and, shortly after his departure, a popular uprising ended his rule.

The interim Iranian government invited a popular exiled religious leader, Ayatollah Ruhollah Khomeini, back into the country. Soon, Iran re-formed itself as a theocracy based on Shi'a Islam and appointed Khomeini the Supreme Leader. In sharp contrast to the Shah, the Ayatollah detested the United States. As early as 1964, Khomeini had spoken out against the coup against Mossadegh and U.S. support for the Shah. However, the final straw came when the United States allowed the Shah, then a fugitive of the new Iranian state, to enter the U.S. for cancer treatments. Immediately thereafter, students stormed the American embassy in Teheran, holding its occupants hostage for 444 days. During that period, the Iranian government did nothing to end the crisis.

Since that incident, relations between the United States and Iran have remained at a strained impasse. For example, the United States offered support to Iraq during its war with Iran in 1980 – 1988. During that period, elements of the U.S. Navy attacked various Iranian assets, to include destroyers, oil platforms and gunboats. In a tragic accident, on July 3, 1988, the *USS Vincennes*, believing it was firing at a hostile Iranian fighter, shot down an Iranian passenger jet, killing 290 (Martins, 1994).

According to a 2008 State Department publication (United States Department of State, 2008a):

> Iran remained the most active state sponsor of terrorism. Elements of its Islamic Revolutionary Guard Corps (IRGC) were directly involved in the planning and support of terrorist acts throughout the region and continued to support a variety of groups in their use of terrorism to advance their common regional goals. Iran provides aid to Palestinian terrorist groups, Lebanese Hizballah, Iraq-based militants, and Taliban fighters in Afghanistan.
>
> Iran remains a threat to regional stability and U.S. interests in the Middle East because of its continued support for violent groups, such as HAMAS and Hizballah, and its efforts to undercut the democratic process in Lebanon, where it seeks to build Iran's and Hizballah's influence to the detriment of other Lebanese communities.
>
> Iran is a principal supporter of groups that are implacably opposed to the Middle East Peace Process, and continues to maintain a high-profile role in encouraging anti-Israel terrorist activity – rhetorically, operationally, and financially. Supreme Leader Khamenei and President Ahmadinejad praised Palestinian terrorist operations, and Iran provided Lebanese Hizballah and Palestinian terrorist groups, notably HAMAS, Palestinian Islamic Jihad, the al-Aqsa Martyrs Brigades, and the Popular Front for the Liberation of Palestine-General Command, with extensive funding, training, and weapons.
>
> Despite its pledge to support the stabilization of Iraq, Iranian authorities continued to provide lethal support, including weapons, training, funding, and guidance, to some Iraqi militant groups that target Coalition and Iraqi security forces and Iraqi civilians. In this way, Iranian government forces have been responsible for attacks on Coalition forces. The Islamic Revolutionary Guard Corps (IRGC)-Qods Force, continued to provide Iraqi militants with Iranian-produced advanced rockets, sniper rifles, automatic weapons, mortars that have killed thousands of Coalition and Iraqi Forces, and explosively formed projectiles (EFPs) that have a higher lethality rate than other types of improvised explosive devices (IEDs), and are specially designed to defeat armored vehicles used by Coalition Forces. The Qods

Force, in concert with Lebanese Hizballah, provided training outside Iraq for Iraqi militants in the construction and use of sophisticated IED technology and other advanced weaponry. These individuals then passed on this training to additional militants inside Iraq, a "train-the-trainer" program. In addition, the Qods Force and Hizballah have also provided training inside Iraq. In fact, Coalition Forces captured a Lebanese Hizballah operative in Iraq in 2007.

Iran's IRGC-Qods Force continued to provide weapons and financial aid to the Taliban to support anti-U.S. and anti-Coalition activity in Afghanistan. Since 2006, Iran has arranged a number of shipments of small arms and associated ammunition, rocket propelled grenades, mortar rounds, 107mm rockets, and plastic explosives, possibly including man-portable air defense systems (MANPADs), to the Taliban.

Iran remained unwilling to bring to justice senior al-Qa'ida (AQ) members it has detained, and has refused to publicly identify those senior members in its custody. Iran has repeatedly resisted numerous calls to transfer custody of its AQ detainees to their countries of origin or third countries for interrogation or trial. Iran also continued to fail to control the activities of some AQ members who fled to Iran following the fall of the Taliban regime in Afghanistan.

Cuba: Another former ally of the United States in the 1950s, Cuba has been on the State Sponsors of Terrorism list since 1984. Ruled from 1959 until 2008 by committed Communist Fidel Castro, Cuba has proven to be a stubborn thorn in the side of every American President since Dwight Eisenhower. In the 1960s, the CIA undertook a concerted, if ultimately unsuccessful, program to remove Castro from power. Buoyed by successful covert operations in the late 1950s in Iran and Guatemala, the United States government funded, trained and otherwise supported a brazen group of Cuban expatriates who wanted to mount a coup against Castro. In 1961, their plans came to fruition. Dubbed the "Bay of Pigs" operation, what started out as an invasion under the cover of American airpower quickly devolved into a fiasco of major proportions. The invading army was quickly overcome and captured; any hopes the United States had to distance itself from this horrible blunder were quickly dashed.

Stung by an embarrassment of this magnitude early in his Presidency, John Kennedy nevertheless held firm to his commitment to limit Soviet expansion in Cuba. He did not have long to wait before his mettle would be tested. In 1962, American intelligence received word from the French that the Soviet Union was placing nuclear missiles in Cuba. Not surprisingly, the Soviets denied this allegation.

Using a combination of human intelligence (HUMINT) and imagery intelligence (IMINT) obtained from U-2 spy planes, U.S. intelligence became convinced that the French intelligence was correct. When the Soviet Union refused to back down, President Kennedy instituted a naval quarantine to halt all offensive missiles being shipped into Cuba. For two tense weeks in October, in what came to be known as "the Cuban Missile Crisis," the United States and Soviet Union came as close as they ever would during the Cold War to nuclear war. Finally, both sides made concessions—the Soviets agreed to remove missiles from Cuba and the United States agreed to remove nuclear missiles it had placed in Turkey. The nuclear standoff was over.

However, relations between Cuba and the United States have remained tense over the years. The United States has maintained restrictions on travel to Cuba and has not allowed for the importation of Cuban goods since the 1960s. Some thought that Fidel Castro's turning over power to his brother Raul in 2008 would improve things; to date, that has not been the case.

The State Department includes Cuba on its list of countries that sponsor terror for the following reasons:

- The government of Cuba provides safe haven to individuals from terrorist groups; these include the Basque Fatherland and Liberty (ETA) and the Revolutionary Armed Forces of Colombia (FARC).

- Cuba allows more than 70 U.S. fugitives to live there legally, including two who have killed U.S. police officers. In addition, Cuba has refused almost all U.S. requests for their return.

Sudan: The Republic of the Sudan, located in northeastern Africa, is geographically the largest country on that continent. A country with a rich history extending back to at least 8,000 B.C., Sudan has recently witnessed extreme levels of violence, including two civil wars and what the United States government has termed genocide.

The northern region of Sudan is predominantly Arab and Muslim while the south is a mixture of Animism and Christianity. Since its independence from Britain in 1956, the north has attempted to create a single, federated state while the south has attempted to increase its autonomy. Most recently, great attention has been focused on Darfur, a region made up of various tribes in western Sudan. Starting in the 1970s, rebels accused the government of neglecting the Darfur region economically; in addition, entrenched intertribal warfare became a frequent occurrence. In an attempt to control the violence, the Sudanese government supported a series of Arab militias who have been accused by the United States of killing thousands of tribe members and displacing hundreds of thousands more. Few would argue that a horrific humanitarian crisis persists in Sudan to this day.

The violence, large scale violations of human rights and dreadful living conditions have prompted the Fund for Peace to rank Sudan as one of the most politically unstable country in the world (Fund for Peace, 2009).

Despite its inclusion on the State Department list, officials have applauded recent efforts by Sudan to crack down on terrorist activity. However, al Qa'ida-like groups, such as the

Palestinian Islamic Jihad (PIJ), HAMAS, and the Lord's Resistance Army (LRA), continue to operate in Sudan. However, in some cases terrorist related activities have been controlled. For example, Sudanese officials have limited HAMAS to raising funds.

Syria: The Syrian Arab Republic is an ancient Arab country in Southwest Asia. Once the seat of the powerful Umayyad Empire, Syria is today a major power in the Middle East. Its location is strategically important, bordering Lebanon, Israel, Jordan, Iraq to the east, Turkey, and the Mediterranean Sea.

Modern Syria emerged from French rule in 1946. Its first years as an independent nation were marked by military coups and violence. In 1963, the Baath Party took control which it has held ever since. In reality, the country's president, Bashar al-Assad, enjoys a great deal of power. Both al-Assad and his father, who served as president from 1970 until 2000, have shown a great willingness to interfere in the affairs of neighboring countries, particularly Lebanon. While Syria's population is predominantly Sunni Muslim, there are significant Alawi, Shia, Druze and Christian minorities.

According to the State Department, Syria offers strong support to a variety of terrorist groups, to include Hezbollah, HAMAS, Palestinian Islamic Jihad (PIJ), the Popular Front for the Liberation of Palestine (PLFP), and the Popular Front for the Liberation of Palestine-General Command (PFLP-GC). Syria also stands accused of attempting to undermine Lebanon's sovereignty and security and is being investigated for involvement in the assassination of former Lebanese Prime Minister Rafiq Hariri in 2005. In addition, it is estimated that nearly 90 percent of all foreign terrorists known to be in Iraq have used Syria as an entry point.

Conclusion

International groups are judged to be the greatest terrorist threat facing the United States today. While acts of anarchists and their associates gripped the country in the early part of the 20th century, most Americans felt immune to the dangers of international terrorism, even as events such as the Munich Olympic massacre unfolded in the 1970s. As we shall see in the next chapter, however, the United States has been in the crosshairs of various groups and individuals for quite some time.

The State Department is required to identify those countries and groups it deems as sponsors or purveyors of terror. These designations carry with them great significance: countries so designated face sanctions, enhanced investigative and diplomatic efforts, and limitations on immigration to the United States. The countries currently designated by the State Department as State Sponsors of Terrorism are:

- Sudan

- Cuba

- Iran

- Syria

The list is a dynamic one. In recent years, North Korea, Libya and Iraq have been removed when it was judged that they were no longer sponsors of terror. The example of Libya (text box 1) is instructive in revealing the criteria the State Department uses to compile the list. Such things as forsaking terrorism, owning up to past acts, and paying reparations to victims and their families are weighed heavily when deciding whether to rescind or extend the status of a state sponsor of terror.

References:

Allen, Thomas B. (Ed.) (1998) "What really sank the Maine?" Naval History 11: 30-39.

Avrich, Paul (1996) Anarchist Voices: An Oral History of Anarchism in America, Princeton: Princeton University Press.

Baily, Thomas A.; & Kennedy, David M. (1994). The American Pageant (10th ed.), Washington, D.C. Heath and Company.

Beyer, L. (2005, December). The myths and reality of Munich. Time Australia, 49, 24.

Briggs, Lloyd (2007) The Manner Of Man That Kills: Spencer, Czolgosz, Richeson Whitefish, Montana: Kessinger Publishing.,

Carter, Jimmy. (2002). Statement by Carter in Cuba after his visit to the Center for Genetic
Engineering and Biotechnology in Havana, The Associated Press, May 13. Retrieved from , http://ciponline.org/cuba/cubaandterrorism/CubaontheTerroristList.pdf on 07/16/2009.

Federal Bureau of Investigation (n.d.) Terrorism 2000/2001. Retrieved from http://www.fbi.gov/publications/terror/terror2000_2001.htm on 08/06/2008.

Fund for Peace. (2009). Country profiles: Sudan. Retrieved from http://www.fundforpeace.org/web/index.php?option=com_content&task=view&id=383&Itemid=540 on 07/16/2009.

Irons, Peter (1999). A People's History of the Supreme Court. New York: Viking Penguin.

Kinzer, Stephen (2003). All the Shah's Men: An American Coup and the Roots of Middle East Terror. New York: John Wiley and Sons.

Martins, Mark S. (1994). Rules of engagement for land forces: A matter of training, not lawyering. Military Law Review 143. Retrieved from URL http://www.loc.gov/rr/frd/Military_Law/Military_Law_Review/pdf-files/27687D~1.pdf on 07/05/2009.

Murray, Robert K. (1955) The Red Scare, Westport: University of Minnesota Press

Rice, Condoleezza. (2006). "State Sponsor: Iran." Council of Foreign Relations. Retrieved from http://www.cfr.org/publication/9362/ on 07/22/2009.

United States Department of State (n.d.). "Office of the Coordinator for Counterterrorism." Retrieved from URL http://www.state.gov/s/ct/ on 09/06/2008.

United States Department of State. (2006). "Press Release: Rescission of Libya's Designation as a State Sponsor of Terrorism." Retrieved from http://2001-2009.state.gov/r/pa/prs/ps/2006/66244.htm on 07/16/2009.

United States Department of State (2008a). "State sponsors of terrorism overview" Country Reports on Terrorism, 2007. Retrieved from http://www.state.gov/s/ct/rls/crt/2007/103711.htm on 09/06/2008.

United States Department of State (2008b). "Terrorist organizations" Country Reports on Terrorism, 2007. Retrieved from http://www.state.gov/s/ct/rls/crt/2007/103714.htm on 09/06/2008.

CHAPTER 7

INTERNATIONAL TERRORISM: GROUPS AND MOVEMENTS

The threat posed by international terrorism, and in particular from al Qaida and related groups, continues to be the gravest we face.   Testimony of FBI Director Robert S. Mueller, III before the Senate Committee on Intelligence, February 16, 2005 (Mueller, 2005)

Introduction

In the previous chapter, we discussed countries that are state sponsors of terrorism. However, most terrorist groups are stateless actors. While in some cases they receive funding from and do the bidding of particular countries, they generally operate autonomously. The State Department is also required to compile a list of Designated Foreign Terrorist Organizations; as with countries, being on the list brings with it a host of sanctions, to include making it a criminal violation for an individual to offer these groups material support.

U.S. Government Designated Foreign Terrorist Organizations[1]

Organizations on the State Department list represent the most significant international terrorist threats facing the United States.   Unlike the countries described in the previous chapter who would likely not launch a direct attack against the United States for fear of retaliation, many of these groups show no such restraint.   While many of the organizations listed below have to date not attacked the United States, they have either expressed enmity toward U.S. policies or

---

[1]Unless otherwise noted, information contained in this section was taken from United States Department of State, 2008 and 9-11 Commission, 2004.   Due to space limitations, we do not discuss every group designated by the State Department as a terrorist organization.   Readers who wish to learn more about these organizations are encouraged to consult this primary source document.

those of our close allies or have shown a willingness to indiscriminately engage in violence. To that end, the State Department considers them a threat or potential threat.

Despite the many names that appear on the list, they can be subsumed under particular movements or ideologies, as laid out below.

Palestinian Groups

Palestinian Groups Designated by the State Department as Foreign Terrorist Organizations
Abu Nidal Organization (ANO)
Al-Aqsa Martyrs Brigade
HAMAS
Palestine Liberation Front (PLF)
Palestinian Islamic Jihad (PIJ)
Popular Front for the Liberation of Palestine (PFLP)
Popular Front for the Liberation of Palestine-General Command (PFLP-GC)

In 1898, Austrian journalist Theodor Herzl published *Der Judenstaat* (*The Jewish State*), a book outlining his vision for the modern state of Israel. Herzl's vision developed into a movement known as Zionism, which became quite powerful among Jews in the early 20th century. Around the same time, the land of Palestine passed from Ottoman to British control. Facing oppression and discrimination in Eastern Europe, many Jewish people immigrated to Palestine prior to and during World War II. By that time, the Zionists had concluded that Palestine, the historic location of Israel, should pass to them as the new Jewish state. At issue, however, was the fate of the many Arabs who lived there.

After World War II, the British, weary of terrorism directed at them by radical Zionist groups and convinced that they would never settle the dispute between the Jews and Palestinians, convinced the newly formed United Nations to partition Palestine into two countries. One was designated as the Jewish state of Israel while the other was to remain under Arab control; the capital of Jerusalem was designated as an "international" city.

While this division was acceptable to the Jews, it was rejected immediately by the Palestinian people and all Arab countries in the region which immediately declared war on Israel. Many Arabs left the area, believing that the land of Israel would be defeated by numerically superior Arab forces and thereafter returned to the Palestinians. In 1948, Arab armies invaded Israel, expecting to win a quick victory. Instead, Israel prevailed. Subsequent to that conflict, there were three other major wars between Israel and her Arab neighbors: the Sinai War (1956), the Six Day War (1967) and the Yom Kippur War (1973) and numerous smaller conflicts, such as the 33 day action between Israel and Hezbollah forces in southern Lebanon in 2006. While Israel has never enjoyed prolonged periods of peace, it has expanded its borders through military victories, primarily into the Gaza Strip and the West Bank.

Over the years, Israel made peace with some Arab countries, such as Egypt, while it remains technically at war with others. Many Palestinians, however, have never accepted the right of Israel to exist. They believe their lands were stolen by the Zionists and have pledged to do whatever it takes to win them back, including engaging in terrorist and insurgent activities.

Palestinian terrorism can be viewed as a progression of various groups and movements. Over time, some have embraced Communism, others have pursued strictly nationalistic goals, and still others have adhered to a radical vision of Islam. Usually, each group begins with the premise that Israel must be destroyed and Palestine re-established under Arab control. While many groups never have strayed far from this core concept, others over the years have recognized Israel's right to exist and have engaged in peace talks.

The United States is a strong ally of Israel, providing it with money, arms and other support. Often, the United States is the only other country in the world to vote with Israel in the United Nations. As such, many Palestinians and other Arabs view the United States as an enemy almost as great as Israel. Therefore, while Palestinian groups generally do not directly attack U.S. interests, officials worry that this could easily change, particularly if some sort of major catastrophe further befalls the Palestinians. It is for this reason, as well as America's closeness to Israel, that the State Department continues to include many Palestinian groups on its list of designated terrorist organizations.

In the 1970s and 80s, Palestinian terrorist groups were among the most prolific in the world. The movement as a whole had its genesis in 1964 when the influential Arab League formed the Palestine Liberation Organization (PLO). Serving as both a political party and paramilitary organization, the PLO emerged as an umbrella organization for a number of Palestinian terrorist groups. It was Black September, an offshoot of the PLO, that carried out the Munich massacre that was discussed in chapter 6. The man most associated with the PLO was its longtime leader, Yasser Arafat. Arafat became a world figure, once appearing before the United Nations General Assembly armed with a pistol. For a time in the 1970s, Arafat and terrorism were synonymous in the minds of many Israelis and Americans. Groups affiliated with the PLO were responsible for numerous acts of violence which received much publicity. However, over time, Arafat's views toward Israel appeared to moderate. In 1993, the PLO officially renounced terrorism. However, this did not sit well with many other Palestinians.

If Arafat's views softened, others stepped up to fill the terrorist void. Termed the "rejectionist front" because they rejected peace with Israel at all costs, groups such as the Popular Front for the Liberation of Palestine (PFLP), the Democratic Front for the Liberation of Palestine (DFLP), the Popular Front for the Liberation of Palestine-General Command (PFLP-GC) and the Abu Nidal Organization (ANO) carried out a series of spectacular acts beginning in the late 1960s that received worldwide attention. These included airline hijackings, cross border raids into Israel using hang gliders, attacks on airline ticket counters, grenade attacks on civilians, bombings onboard busses, and the famous 1975 takeover of the OPEC summit in Vienna. In the late 1970s, the Palestine Liberation Front (PLF) split from the PFLP-GC; the PLF became famous for its 1985 attack on the Italian cruise ship Achille Lauro in which U.S. citizen Leon Klinghoffer was murdered.

Four of these groups, the PLF, the PFLP, the PFLP-GC, and the ANO remain on the State Department's list of designated terrorist organizations. Most recently, members of the PFLP have engaged in suicide bombings and the DFLP has been accused of shooting at Israeli targets. ANO chief Sabri Khalil al-Banna (more popularly known as Abu Nidal) was found dead in Iraq in 2002. While declared a suicide by the Iraqi government, there is speculation that then-President Saddam Hussein may have had him murdered.

Over the years, many attempts have been made to try to establish peace between the Israeli's and Palestinians. To date, the most successful of these occurred in 1993. Dubbed the Oslo Accords because they were conducted in Oslo, Norway, they included the first official face-to-face negotiations between the two sides. By their conclusion, Palestinian representatives conceded Israeli's right to exist while Israel granted the Palestinians limited self rule in the Gaza Strip and West Bank in the form of the Palestinian National Authority (PNA).

The first leader of the PNA was Yasser Arafat.

However, the Oslo Accords did not bring about a lasting peace. Over time, terrorism has continued and two popular uprisings, termed "intifadas" have generated much violence, particularly in the volatile Gaza Strip.

Many of the groups that formed in the 1960s and 70s were secular; that is, religion had little to do with their politics and orientation. Some, like the PFLP and DLFP, considered themselves to be Marxist-Leninist, eschewing religion completely. However, in the 1970s, a group with a decidedly Islamic agenda, Palestine Islamic Jihad (PIJ), was formed. The goal of PIJ has never wavered from its desire to destroy the state of Israel and replace it with an Islamic state. PIJ continues to attack Israel with suicide bombings and rocket attacks. However, its influence pales in comparison to one of the largest and most significant terrorist group operating against Israel today, the Islamic Resistance Movement, better known as HAMAS.

HAMAS was formed in 1987 during the first intifada. It was largely an outgrowth of the Muslim Brotherhood, a Sunni Islamic group first established in Egypt in the 1920s. Prior to 2005, it engaged in numerous attacks against Israeli targets, which included mortar and rocket attacks and suicide bombings. However, while it continues to conduct attacks, to categorize HAMAS today as merely a terrorist group would be incorrect. In fact, it has a large political arm and engages in numerous educational, charitable, and service activities in the West Bank and Gaza. While its military operatives number in the thousands, HAMAS enjoys wide support among many Palestinians. In 2006, it won a stunning victory against Yasser Arafat's party, Fatah, in the Palestinian Parliamentary Elections.[2]

---

[2] Although Arafat died in 2004, his legacy continues to influence Palestinian politics. At one

The latest incarnation of PLO terrorism can be found in the al Aqsa Martyr Brigades. Formed in 2000 as disparate cells loyal to Arafat's Fatah movement, al Aqsa members have conducted rocket and suicide attacks against Israel. Like HAMAS and other groups, they receive funding, weapons and training from Iran.

The issues in the Israeli-Palestinian conflict are complex and multi-faceted and their resolution will not come anytime soon. To that end, while the United States is generally not a primary target of Palestinian groups, that could easily change, given its close ties to Israel. As well, Americans have died at the ends of Palestinian terrorists over the years. As a result, the State Department continues to include Palestinian groups in its list of designated foreign terrorist organizations.

Radical Islamic Organizations

---

time, Arafat's popularity among his people was without peer. However, in his latter years, Arafat and Fatah were accused of corruption and mismanagement of the PNA. Many experts believe this helped pave the way for the HAMAS victory in 2006.

Radical Islamic Organizations Designated by the State Department as Foreign Terrorist Organizations

Abu Sayyaf Group
Ansar al-Sunnah
Armed Islamic Group (GIA)
Asbat al-Ansar
Gama'a al-Islamiyya (IG)
Harakat ul-Mujahadin (HUM)
Islamic Jihad Group (IJG)
Islamic Movement of Uzbekistan (IMU)
Jaish-e-Mohammed (JEM)
Jemaah Islamiya Organization (JI)
Al-Jihad
Lashkar e-Tayyiba
Lashkar i Jhangvi (LJ)
Libyan Islamic Fighting Group (LIFG)
Moroccan Islamic Combatant Group (GICM)
Mujahadin-e Khalq Organization (MEK)
Al-Qa'ida
Al-Qa'ida in Iraq
Al-Qa'ida in the Islamic Maghreb (AQIM) [Formerly Salafist Group for Call and Combat (GSPC)]

For many Americans, international terrorism starts and ends with al Qa'ida. While it is true that the United States government sees al Qa'ida and its leaders, Osama bin Laden, as "Public Enemy #1," the State Department list above should make clear the fact that many violent, radical groups with an Islamic orientation exist in the world today. Many have little interest in attacking the United States and instead strive to replace the governments of the countries in which they exist with theocracies based on their interpretation of Islam.

A Brief History of Radical Islam

Many Americans are unsure whether Islam is a "violent" religion; that is, is there anything inherent in Islam that would logically convince its adherents to engage in acts of unspeakable violence, often against innocents? While we are more than happy to leave that discussion to scholars of religion, we offer the words of columnist Fareed Zakaria regarding this question, which he wrote just after the 9-11 attacks:

> Nothing will be solved by searching for "true Islam" or quoting the Quran. The Quran is a vast, vague book, filled with poetry and contradictions (much like the Bible)...You can find in it condemnations of war and incitements to struggle, beautiful expressions of tolerance and stern strictures against unbelievers. Quotations from it usually tell us more about the person who selected the passages than about Islam (Zakaria, 2001)

Religion is often used to justify violence. The Ku Klux Klan and other white supremacist groups have developed their own interpretation of the Bible to justify their views regarding non-Aryan peoples. Indeed, the vast majority of Muslims living in the world today would no more strap on a suicide belt than most Christians. A better question to ask is how did bin Laden and his followers arrive at their own peculiar version of Islam? A brief look at history may provide some answers.

The Origins of Islam

Like Judaism and Christianity, with whom it shares a common ancestry, Islam is a monotheistic religion. The history of Islam begins officially with Mohammed, who Muslims believe to be God's final and most significant messenger on Earth. Mohammed was born in Mecca, a vibrant trading town in Arabia, in 570 A.D. Unlike Jesus, there was nothing in Mohammed's early life that suggested he would become a prophet. When he turned 25, Mohammed wed a wealthy 40 year-old widow named Khadijah; this arrangement allowed him to live as a prosperous businessman for a number of years. At age 40, Mohammed was said to have begun receiving regular visits from the angel Gabriel. The teachings of Gabriel, as revealed to Mohammed, became the Quran, the holiest book in Islam which Muslims believe to be the literal words of God.

As Mohammed began to reveal the words of God to the people of Mecca, he made many enemies, particularly among a wealthy group who organized an annual religious festival that honored many different religions. Sensing that he and his followers were threatened, Mohammed eventually fled north to the town of Medina.

By 624 A.D., Mohammed had gained a sufficient following to return to Mecca to challenge the town militarily. At first, surprising victory was followed by defeat, which included the wounding of Mohammed in battle. In 629 A.D., however, Mohammed and his followers prevailed; they returned triumphantly to Mecca where Mohammed continued to preach until his death in 632 A.D.

At the time of his passing, Mohammed had not designated a successor. Ultimately, there was considerable disagreement over who should rule the Muslim nation upon Mohammed's death. This created a schism that continues to this day; those who thought that Mohammed's successor should be elected became the **Sunnis** while those who favored the appointment of Mohammed's closest male heir became the **Shi'a**.

Islam spread very rapidly following Mohammed's death. At its zenith, Muslim culture was unrivaled. At a time when Europe was mired in the Dark Ages, Islamic scholars were making contributions in all fields of endeavor, including mathematics, philosophy, science, medicine, and law. It is said by some that their contributions speeded up the onset of the Enlightenment.

In order to appreciate how many Muslims view Islam's relationship with the West, at least two significant historical events must be considered: the Crusades and European colonialism. The Crusades, which roughly extended from 1097 A.D. - 1291 A.D., were an attempt by Christians to wrest the Holy Lands from Muslim control. For most non-Muslims, the Crusades hold a minor place in history, belonging to a long bygone era. In the Muslim world, however, the opposite is true. Scholars and lay people alike still praise the brave deeds of heroes such as Saladin, who successfully ousted Crusading armies from the territories they had conquered. And perhaps most important, many Muslims cite the Crusades as an early and significant example of the West's enmity toward Islam. They demonstrate, the claim goes, long-standing desires to occupy the Middle East and destroy Islam. Accordingly, when President George Bush used the word "crusade" shortly after the 9-11 attacks to describe the global war on terrorism, it was interpreted by many in the Muslim world to be nothing more than a declaration of war against Islam.

If the Crusades serve in the minds of some as an ancient symbol of the West's nefarious designs on Islam, European Colonialism provides a much more recent and tangible example. By the 15th century, Europeans were traveling throughout the world, with the twin goals of obtaining resources and converting the masses to Christianity. In the mid-18th century, nearly all Middle Eastern countries were financially dependent on Europe. By the early part of the 20th century, this economic dependence had evolved into direct, political control. Colonial rule proved difficult for indigenous Muslim populations. The colonizers and those they favored occupied positions of dominance and wealth while others were forced into subservient roles, often in deplorable conditions. In order for the minority outsiders to control the population, harsh measures were occasionally employed. As well, social and tribal structures that had been in place for years were replaced with those designed to benefit the colonizers rather than the colonized.

The move toward independence in the Muslim lands began in earnest after World War I and was spurred on by World War II. As the colonizers departed the Middle East, they left behind poorly integrated societies and countries where boundaries had in many cases been artificially constructed. They also left behind an angry population that blamed economic and social problems almost exclusively on European occupation. If the Crusades planted the idea of a western war on Islam, the colonial period solidified it. Even today, modern terrorists like Osama bin Laden refer to American troops in Iraq as "Crusaders" and justify their use of terrorism as a legitimate response to infidel "attacks" on Islam.

<u>Jihad</u>

One of the most controversial aspects of Islam, even among Muslims, is the concept of **Jihad**. Although many in the West translate the word as "holy war," its literal meaning is "struggle" and its practical meaning among Muslims varies widely. Mohammed was a man of both peace and war. His justification for engaging in warfare concerned the defense of the faith: surely, God would not object to His followers engaging in a defensive war, provided they were not the aggressors and followed certain rules.

Today, many Muslims view Jihad as having two parts: the lesser Jihad is the defense of the faith if Islam or the Muslim nation is attacked. Osama bin Laden uses this logic to justify his attacks on the United States. In his "Letter to America," bin Laden explains:

> Why are we fighting and opposing you? The answer is very simple:...Because you attacked us and continue to attack us (Guardian Unlimited, 2002).

Of course, many Muslims reject bin Laden's arguments. They point out that his wanton disregard for life, to include the murder of innocents, runs directly counter to the true meaning of Islam.

For a significant number of Muslims, however, the importance of the lesser Jihad (defensive warfare) is superseded by the greater Jihad, that is, the internal struggle that each Muslim endures to make himself a better Muslim. Not unlike the Christian notion of following certain behavioral norms, Muslims are exhorted to constantly strive to follow the example set by the Prophet as they go about their daily lives. In this case, Jihad has nothing to do with fighting an external enemy: rather, it is all about resisting life's temptations and the inner demons that constantly strive to lead good Muslims off course.

The Road to Radicalism

Some trace the roots of al Qaida all the way back to a 13th century legal scholar and theologian named Taqi al-Din Ahmad ibn Taymiyya, usually known simply as Ibn Taymiyya. Taymiyya lived in Syria and adhered to a very stern version of Islam. He believed that any who did not agree with him were apostates, traitors to Islam deserving of death.

In 18th century Arabia, a religious scholar named Mohammed ibn Abd al-Wahhab used Ibn Taymiyya as his spiritual model to preach a fiery version of Islam; he constantly railed against moral and spiritual laxity among his Muslim compatriots and violently opposed any who did not buy into his very conservative version of Islam, going so far as to raid the tomb of the Prophet and attack a Shi'a sacred site at Karbala.

Al-Wahhab and his religious visions might have come and gone like so many others, but for one fact: he aligned himself with a tribal chief named Mohammed ibn Saud, who later went on to rule the oil rich state of Saudi Arabia. The relationship between the House of Saud and Wahhabism, as Al-Wahhab's version of Islam came to be known, proved to be a strong one, lasting into the twentieth century.

By the turn of the century, European colonialism and the secular rule of many Muslim countries produced anger and dissatisfaction among pious Muslims. In 1928, a teacher named Hasan al-Banna, founded the Society of the Muslim Brothers, or Muslim Brotherhood. Guided by the principles of the lesser Jihad, he called for the expulsion of both the British from Egypt as well as any Arab leader who opposed the establishment of a theocratic state.

Al-Banna became the spiritual mentor of another Egyptian teacher who would go on to become perhaps the most significant architect of modern radical Islam, Sayyid Qutb. At first, Qutb was a great admirer of the West. However, a three year assignment in the United States for the government of Egypt changed his view. Shocked by what he considered to be moral depravity, racial discrimination, and rampant materialism, he returned to the Egypt in 1951, assuming a significant role in the Muslim Brotherhood.

According to Qutb, it was the duty of every Muslim to work toward the creation of a world ruled by Islam. His writings were fiery and effective: at one point, merely owning a copy of his book **Milestones** could result in arrest in Egypt.

While Qutb died in 1966, his influence is felt even today. Those he influenced include the Ayatollah Khomeini, who established an Islamic state in Iran in 1979 following the ouster of the Shah, and both Osama bin Laden and his right-hand-man, Ayman al-Zawahiri.

<u>The Birth of al Qaeda</u>

We have previously discussed the role that the formation of a theocratic state in Iran and the defeat of the Soviet Union in Afghanistan had on the foundation of radical Islamic terrorism. One of those who responded to the call for mujahedeen to oppose the Soviets in their attack on Afghanistan in the 1980s was a young Saudi named Osama bin Laden. Bin Laden was born in 1957, the 17th child of a rich engineer who enjoyed a close relationship with the Saudi royal family. After an unremarkable childhood, bin Laden attended King Abdul Aziz University in Saudi Arabia, where he studied management and economics. It was during this time that he became interested in Islamic law and politics.

In the mid 1980s, bin Laden formed an organization, the Maktab al-Khidimat (MAK), to recruit Islamic soldiers from around the world for the Afghan resistance. Bin Laden directly credited the defeat of the Soviets to the will of God:

> In this jihad, the biggest benefit was the myth of the superpower was destroyed, not only in my mind, but in the minds of all Muslims (Cable News Network, n.d.).

In spite of American support for the mujahedeen, bin Laden was not a fan of the West. Taking his lead from Sayyid Qutb, bin Laden wanted nothing more than to rid Muslim countries of western influence; this he was willing to do by any means necessary.

After the Afghan war, bin Laden returned to Saudi Arabia, a country that in 1990 granted permission for the United States to station troops inside the kingdom in preparation for the first Gulf War. Bin Laden was outraged: he considered infidels in the land of Islam's two most sacred sites (Mecca and Medina) tantamount to the invasion by the Crusaders in the 12th century. Adding to his anger was a sense of personal frustration and disappointment. In response to the invasion of Kuwait, he had first approached the royal family with a plan to assemble an army of jihadists to oust the invading Iraqis; his plan was summarily rejected. Soon, bin Laden was writing political tracts denouncing both the Americans and the Saudi royals.

Criticizing the Saudi royal family was a dangerous maneuver. In 1991, bin Laden was forced to flee from Saudi Arabia to Sudan, just ahead of the authorities. In 1994, Saudi Arabia revoked his citizenship. In Sudan, Bin Laden was embraced by the radical Islamic government. There he began to live his dream of establishing an international Islamic army, one that would eventually crush the infidels. To accomplish this, he set up numerous companies and became heavily involved in covertly funding independent Islamic terrorist operators all over the world. In 1992, he issued his first **fatwa** (religious decree) against America., principally for the "occupation" of Arab lands (see text box 1, a statement purported to be from bin Laden, in which he outlines why he has attacked the United States). By now, he began to call his group "al Qa'ida," Arabic for "the base." There are several explanations for the origin of this name. In one version, it represents the coalescing of many disparate radical Islamic groups around a single "base." Others claim it refers to a database of mujahedeen from around the world maintained by bin Laden.

By 1993, bin Laden wasn't the only radical Muslim to have the United States in his sights. On February 26, 1993, a bomb exploded in the basement of Tower One of the World Trade Center in New York City, killing 6 and injuring 1,040. Subsequent investigation estimated the bomb to weigh 1,300 pounds; it was made from urea pellets, nitroglycerin, sulfuric acid, aluminum azide, magnesium azide, and bottled hydrogen. In addition, sodium cyanide had been added in the hope of releasing poison gas.

When one of the bombers attempted to retrieve the security deposit he had put on the rental truck used in the bombing, he was arrested. The investigation quickly led to the apartment of a Pakistani named Ramzi Yousef, the nephew of Khalid Shaikh Mohammed, who would later help bin Laden plan the 9-11 attacks.

Yousef himself was initially not captured. He fled the United States and began to plan other attacks. One of his most ambitious plans, one eerily prescient of 9-11, was code named "Operation Bojinka." Along with his uncle Khalid Shaikh Mohammed, they planned to plant bombs aboard 12 U.S. commercial jumbo jets which were designed to explode in flight over the Pacific. However, before Yousef could carry out Operation Bojinka, his bomb making facility in the Philippines was discovered. Yousef, who by this time was on the FBI's most wanted list, was later picked up by Pakistani authorities in 1995 in Islamabad.

During this period, bin Laden's reputation as a terrorist financier and sponsor of training had grown. He was most definitely considered a force to be reckoned with on the terrorist scene, despite the fact that al Qaida had yet to carry out a single large-scale attack. Nevertheless, international pressure grew to the point that, in May, 1996, bin Laden was forced to leave his refuge in Sudan, returning to Afghanistan.

By this time, the most dominant group in Afghanistan was the Taliban. Led by one-eyed Mullah Omar, bin Laden found a kindred philosophical soul, one who appreciated Sayyid Qutb as much as he did. Bin Laden flourished in Afghanistan. Supported and protected by the Taliban, he established training camps for mujahedeen from all over the world. It is estimated that between 10,000 and 20,000 individuals received training in bin Laden's camps from the mid 1990s until 2001, although far fewer actually became members of al Qaida.

As the 1990s progressed, bin Laden formulated ambitious plans to attack American interests. In 1998, al Qaida operatives blew up United States embassies in Nairobi and Dar es Salaam. In what would become an al Qaida signature, the embassies were attacked simultaneously by suicide bombers, in this case driving trucks; at least 301 individuals were killed and another 5,000 were injured.   Two years later, a small boat carrying al Qaida suicide bombers exploded next to the destroyer USS Cole in a Yemeni port, killing 17 American sailors and almost sinking the ship.

The U.S. response to these attacks was tepid; a few cruise missiles were fired at suspected terrorist camps and what was believed to be a clandestine weapons factory in Sudan.   This reaction did little to impede or dissuade al Qaida from further attacks.

By the summer of 2001, American intelligence and law enforcement agencies were picking up "chatter," or non-specific communications, that convinced many that another al Qa'ida attack was imminent.   However, most experts believed that al Qaida would strike American interests overseas, as it had in 1998 and 2000.

Little did anyone realize that, by early September, 2001, an al Qaida attack team was in place in the United States, waiting to strike.   The plans for the 9-11 attacks had first been conceived many years earlier in terrorist camps in Afghanistan; they were later refined by an al Qaida cell in Hamburg, Germany.   Osama bin Laden was personally involved in planning the attacks but their actual architect was Khalid Shaikh Mohammed.   The operational leader of the attack team was Mohammed Atta, an Egyptian engineer who spent many years in Germany. Atta led his team of 19 in a plot that was remarkable for its reliance on both simple and complex technologies and its keen understanding of American security procedures and protocols for airline hijackings (see text box 2).

The 9-11 attacks changed the way homeland security is viewed and approached in the United States.   In late 2001, America embarked on "Operation Enduring Freedom," a joint military venture with Afghan dissidents, in which the Taliban government that had supported and hosted bin Laden was overthrown. The United States also set up the Northern Command, a military unit dedicated to protecting U.S. territory.   In 2002, in direct response to the 9-11 attacks, several U.S. government agencies were brought together in the newly created Department of Homeland Security. Perhaps most significantly, the United States and a small coalition of other countries invaded Iraq in 2003. The stated reason for this invasion was the belief that Iraq President Saddam Hussein had acquired or was attempting to acquire weapons of mass destruction, to include nuclear weapons, which he intended to pass along to terrorist groups.

The al Qaida attacks did not end with 9-11. In 2004, it attacked trains in Madrid, Spain, killing 191. Up to that point, Spain had been an ally of the United States in Iraq. However, immediately after the bombings, a new Spanish government was voted in; among its first acts was the withdrawal of all Spanish troops from Iraq.

In 2005, a group with philosophical ties to al Qaida, bombed trains in London, killing 57. Other bombings linked to al Qaida include a 2007 attack in Algiers and a 2008 bombing at the Danish embassy in Pakistan. Al Qaida also set up operations in Iraq to attack U.S. troops following the invasion in 2003. For a time, al Qaida enjoyed significant success in Iraq. In 2007, however, Sunni leaders began to turn against them, fearing that the group would attempt to install its harsh version of Islam if successful.

There is considerable debate today about the true character of al Qaida. Most experts agree that, as an organization, it was significantly weakened by U.S. military and intelligence efforts. By late 2008, however, intelligence suggests that al Qaida has re-opened terrorist training camps in the largely ungoverned wilderness of northwestern Pakistan, where bin Laden is believed to be hiding. Some believe that al Qaida has regained its pre-9-11 strength.

Most experts agree that al Qaida also exists as a movement in which bin Laden serves as a spiritual and political advisor. While he doesn't directly command many of his adherents, they are expected to discern and follow his general principles, which include striking out at the United States wherever and whenever possible. Law enforcement officials are concerned about these "homegrown" terrorists who use bin Laden as a model. In recent years, al Qaida inspired cells have been discovered and broken up in such places as Lackawana, New York and Miami, Florida. In addition, many of the groups included on the State Department list cited above use al Qaida as a model to oppose secular governments in their own countries.

In the early morning hours of September 11, 2001, three 5-member and one 4-member al Qaeda team boarded four American jumbo jets at different airports in the United States. Each team had "muscle," or personnel who would overpower flight crews and passengers, as well as one pilot who could fly the plane. The attack teams had correctly predicted that they would easily be able to get box cutters, with razor sharp blades, through airport security. Once each plane was airborne, the "muscle" overpowered aircraft personnel and took over the plane. Airline hijackings in the United States were nothing new; however, in every previous case, hijackers had either made demands that, if granted, would secure the safe release of hostages or had demanded that the plane be flown to a country they believed would afford them sanctuary. Never before had a hijacked plane been used as a weapon. As a result, U.S. flight crews and controllers had been trained not to resist hijackers and to agree to their demands. At 8:46 a.m., when American Airlines Flight 11 flew into the World Trade Center's North Tower, it was clear that these were no ordinary hijackings. Shortly thereafter, United Airlines Flight 175 hit the World Trade Center's South Tower. Then, at 9:37 a.m., American Airlines Flight 77 struck the Pentagon. By this time, anxious relatives and friends were relaying the unfolding events via cellphone to passengers aboard the fourth hijacked plane, United Airlines Flight 93. Those passengers made the heroic decision to attack the hijackers and attempt to win back control of the plane. Sensing they were about to be overcome, the hijackers intentionally crashed the plane into a field near Shanksville, Pennsylvania at 10:03 a.m. It is believed the target of United flight 93 was either the White House or U.S. Capitol. In all, over 3,000 people perished in the attacks.

No other terrorist event has had the impact on the United States that the 9-11 attacks did. Shortly thereafter, President George Bush declared a "global war on terrorism." As part of this "war," U.S. military forces attacked and overthrew the radical Taliban government in Afghanistan which had given bin Laden refuge and, later, the government of Saddam Hussein in Iraq. Stateside, the U.S. military set up the Northern Command for the defense of the United States' homeland and, in 2002, Department of Homeland Security was created.

Text Box 2: The 9-11 Attacks (Source: 9-11 Commission Report)

In 2002, a letter circulated on the Internet claiming to have been authored by Osama bin Laden explaining why he had attacked America. While the authenticity of this letter cannot be confirmed, many of the statements are consistent with what is known about bin Laden's beliefs. Excerpts from this letter follow:

"Permission to fight (against disbelievers) is given to those (believers) who are fought against, because they have been wronged and surely, Allah is Able to give them (believers) victory" [Quran 22:39]

…Why are we fighting and opposing you? The answer is very simple: Because you attacked us and continue to attack us…You attacked us in Palestine…The blood pouring out of Palestine must be equally revenged. You must know that the Palestinians do not cry alone; their women are not widowed alone; their sons are not orphaned alone…You attacked us in Somalia; you supported the Russian atrocities against us in Chechnya, the Indian oppression against us in Kashmir, and the Jewish aggression against us in Lebanon…Under your supervision, consent and orders, the governments of our countries which act as your agents, attack us on a daily basis…The removal of these governments is an obligation upon us, and a necessary step to free the Ummah, to make the Shariah the supreme law and to regain Palestine. And our fight against these governments is not separate from out fight against you…You steal our wealth and oil at paltry prices because of you international influence and military threats…Your forces occupy our countries; you spread your military bases throughout them; you corrupt our lands, and you besiege our sanctities…You have starved the Muslims of Iraq, where children die every day….You have supported the Jews in their idea that Jerusalem is their eternal capital…

…These tragedies and calamities are only a few examples of your oppression and aggression against us. It is commanded by our religion and intellect that the oppressed have a right to return the aggression…You may then dispute that all the above does not justify aggression against civilians, for crimes they did not commit and offenses in which they did not partake..This argument contradicts your continuous repetition that America is the land of freedom, and its leaders in this world. Therefore, the American people are the ones who choose their government by way of their own free will

Text Box 1: Excerpts from Osama bin Laden's "Letter to America" (Guardian.co.uk, 2002)

Nationalist Organizations (Marxist/Maoist/Leftist) Designated by the State Department as Foreign Terrorist Organizations

Basque Fatherland and Liberty (ETA)
Communist Party of Philippines/New People's Army (CPP/NPA)
Kongra-Gel (formerly Kurdistan Worker's Party (PKK))
National Liberation Army (ELN)
Revolutionary Armed Forces of Colombia (FARC)
Revolutionary Nuclei (RN)
Revolutionary Organization 17 November (17N)
Revolutionary People's Liberation Party/Front (DHKP/C)
Shining Path (SL)

In the 1960s, many terrorist groups had a Marxist orientation. Inspired by the revolution in Cuba led by Fidel Castro in the 1950s and supported and often funded by the Soviet Union, the goal of these groups was to overthrow the existing government in the countries in which they operated and replace it with one based on Socialist principles.

Some of these groups have operated for years. For example, Basque Fatherland and Liberty (ETA), was founded in 1959; its goal has been to oust the Spanish government from the Basque region in Spain and replace it with one based on Communism.

Others are quite large and operate along the lines of armies. The Revolutionary Armed Forces of Colombia (FARC) is estimated to have between 9,000 and 12,000 "soldiers." It raises significant funds through kidnapping-for-profit and drug trafficking activities.

> **Nationalist Organizations (Other)**
> **Designated by the State Department as**
> **Foreign Terrorist Organizations**
> Continuity Irish Republican Army (CIRA)
> Liberation Tigers of Tamil Eelam (LTTE)
> Real IRA (RIRA)
> United Self-Defense Forces of Colombia (AUC)

Not every group interested in overturning existing governments has a Marxist orientation. The Continuity Irish Republican Army (CIRA) and the Real IRA (RIRA) are descendants of the Irish Republican Army (IRA), a group originally formed in the early part of the 20th century to overthrow English rule in Ireland. Between 1919 and 1921, the IRA fought a brutal war against English forces. In 1921, England signed a truce with the IRA which led to the establishment of an independent Irish state in all but the six northern counties of Ireland.

The source of the conflict between England and Ireland was both political and religious. A majority of the Irish population was Catholic and favored independence; the population in the northern part of the country was predominantly Protestant and desired to remain affiliated with England. In order to reach a compromise, the northern part of the country became the state of Northern Ireland and remained under British control.

This partition did not sit well with Catholic elements throughout Ireland who desired a single, independent state. Beginning in the 1960s, the IRA staged a series of violent attacks against British authorities in Northern Ireland. Eventually, both Protestants and Catholics mustered insurgent forces which battled one another. IRA violence was not constrained to Ireland. Terrorists staged spectacular bombings in London and assassinated Louis Mountbatten, a popular member of the British royal family and hero of World War II.

Over the course of its existence, the IRA received much funding from Americans sympathetic to its cause. Eventually, the IRA signed a cease fire with British authorities, which it has largely followed. However, the two groups included on the State Department list, the CIRA and the RIRA, do not recognize this cease fire. In 1997, the RIRA formed from disaffected members of the IRA. It continues to attack British authorities, using both guns and firebombs as weapons. The CIRA, which formed in 1994, is small with perhaps 50 members. It also engages in small and sporadic attacks against authorities.

While most Americans equate suicide bombers with al Qa'ida or HAMAS, in fact the Liberation Tigers of Tamil Eelam (LTTE or Tamil Tigers), a group at war with the Sri Lankan government, utilized this tactic well before either group. Founded in 1976, LTTE wants to set up a Tamil homeland in the north and east of Sri Lanka. Perhaps its most famous attack occurred in 1991, when a female operative assassinated Indian Prime Minister Rajiv Gandhi in a suicide attack. Today, the LTTE has developed into a formidable fighting force, with both an amphibious and air arm and membership estimated to number between 8,000 and 10,000.

Religious Groups (Other)

> **Religious Groups (Other) Designated by the State Department as Foreign Terrorist Organizations**
>
> Aum Shinrikyo
> Kahane Chai (Kach)

As mentioned previously, radical Islamic groups are not the only religiously motivated organizations that embrace terrorism. Two others, Aum Shinrikyo and Kahane Chai, have also been placed on the State Department list.

Established in Japan in 1987 by blind acupuncturist Shoko Asahara, Aum Shinrikyo's philosophy is a mixture of Ashara's interpretation of Buddhism, yoga, Taoism, and other religious practices. Over the years, Asahara's goals have ranged from taking over Japan and the world to preparing his group for Armageddon, which he believes will be caused by the United States. On March 20, 1995, followers of Asahara released deadly sarin gas into the Tokyo subway system, killing 12 and injuring thousands. Experts believe that the attacks would have been much more deadly had the group designed a better system for distributing the gas.

The police believed that the subway attack was motivated by Asahara's goal of world domination, although others have questioned whether this was the case. As authorities investigated the group, they attributed other chemical attacks and acts of violence to Aum. In 2004, Asahara was sentenced to death for the subway attacks. Despite his imprisonment, the group continues to exist. Experts estimate that there are some 1,500 members in Japan and another 300 in Russia.

Kach and Kahane Chai are Jewish terrorist groups that operate primarily in the West Bank and Gaza strip, while enjoying support from some individuals in the United States. Kach was founded by radical Rabbi Meir Kahane in the 1970s; it advocated discrimination against Arabs and was blamed for various acts of violence aimed primarily at Arabs. In 1990, Kahane was assassinated after a speech in New York City. His son, Binyamin, founded Kahane Chai ("Kahane Lives") even as others took over Kach.

Today, both groups exist primarily as a movement. They stand accused by the Israeli government of several low level attacks against Arabs, precipitated by the second intifada.

The Special Case of Hezbollah

"Hezbollah may be the A team of terrorists…[while] "al Qa'ida is actually the B team."
Deputy Secretary of State Richard Armitage (Bynum, 2003)

Hezbollah formed in 1982, in response to the Israeli invasion of Lebanon. Unlike most other radical Islamic groups, Hezbollah is Shi'a and takes its ideological inspiration, along with significant logistical aid, from Iran. It also takes aid from Syria and its current base of operations is Lebanon.

Americans probably know Hezbollah best as the organization that U.S. authorities believe orchestrated the bombing of the U.S. Marine barracks in Lebanon in 1983; 241 service personnel were killed in the blast, which prompted President Ronald Reagan to remove troops from Lebanon.

While the United States, Canada, and Israel have designated Hezbollah a terrorist organization, many Middle Eastern countries consider it to be a legitimate armed force. Indeed, Hezbollah has changed significantly over the years. In its early days, it behaved like many other terrorist entities, using tactics that included suicide bombings, assassinations, and kidnappings. Today, however, it possesses a significant arsenal of sophisticated weapons, to include Katyusha rockets. The U.S. Department of State has described Hezbollah as the most technically capable terrorist group in the world today.

Hezbollah has demonstrated its significant military capability. In both 2000 and 2006, its soldiers fought fierce battles against the Israeli Defense Force near Lebanon's border with Israel. On both occasions, Hezbollah did remarkably well, fighting the Israelis to a tactical standstill.

Its military prowess is but one element of Hezbollah's capabilities. Evidence of its considerable political clout can be seen in its recent victories in Lebanon: it currently holds 14 elected seats in the 128-seat Lebanese National Assembly.

Hezbollah continues to be fervently anti-Israeli and, by extension, fervently anti-American. In 2007, a high ranking Hezbollah official was apprehended in Iraq providing training to Shi'a fighters in that country.

Because of its considerable capabilities and hatred toward the United States, American officials are deeply worried by Hezbollah. Some scholars claim that the war on terror cannot be won until its terrorist inclinations are somehow curtailed.

Conclusion

Most experts believe that the greatest terrorist threat facing the United States today comes from international organizations, like al Qaida. As the primary government agency dealing with international relations and diplomacy, the State Department is responsible for designating which organizations and countries pose the greatest terrorist threat to America. Being designated a Foreign Terrorist Organizations brings with it a host of sanctions. These include making it a crime to support for an individual to offer them logistical or financial support.

While there are many groups with many different orientations on the State Department list, we have categorized them into the different ideologies or movements they represent.

Palestinian Groups in general oppose the right of the state of Israel to exist. Because the United States is a staunch ally of Israel, many of these groups also pose a potential threat to America; some have attacked U.S. interests, to include murdering its citizens.

Palestinian terrorism has changed greatly over the years, as some groups that once engaged in acts of significant violence now recognize Israel's right to exist.

Palestinian terrorism was especially extreme in the 1970s and 80s. During that time, attacks were mounted against cruise ships, airliners, busses and other public institutions. Perhaps the most infamous attack occurred during the 1972 Munich Olympics when Black September massacred the Israeli Olympic team. Palestinian groups on the State Department list include HAMAS, the al Aqsa Martyrs' Brigade, and the PFLP.

Perhaps the strongest threat facing the United States today comes from Radical Islamic Groups, such as al Qaida. Justifying violence based on views of Islam that date back several centuries, these organizations have shown a ruthless disregard for civilian or even Muslim lives. Inspiration for this movement comes from the Iranian revolution of 1979 and the victory of the mujahideen over the Soviet army in Afghanistan in the 1980s.

Other international groups have a Nationalist Orientation, seeking to overthrow the governments of the countries in which they operate. Some of these groups, like the FARC in Colombia and the Shining Path in Peru, have a Marxist/Maoist/Leftist orientation; that is, they wish to replace current governments with communism or socialism. Still others, like the Real IRA and LTTE, are primarily interested in independence and self-rule.

Two non-Islamic Religious Groups also appear on the list. These are Aum Shinrikyo, a group that released sarin gas in the Tokyo subway system in 1995, and Kahane Chai (Kach), a radical Jewish movement that has attacked Arabs throughout the world.

Finally, perhaps the most capable terrorist group in the world today is Hezbollah, a Lebanese-based Shi'a organization that receives support from both Iran and Syria. Hezbollah has attacked American interests and has demonstrated a significant military capability in its mini-wars with Israel. It also holds significant political clout, with 14 of its members serving in the Lebanese National Assembly.

REFERENCES

9-11 Commission. (2004). The 9-11 Commission Report. Retrieved from http://www.9-11commission.gov/report/911Report.pdf on 09/06/2009.

Bynum, Daniel (2003). "Should Hezbollah be next?" **Foreign Affairs 82**:6. Retrieved from URL http://www.foreignaffairs.org/20031101faessay82606/daniel-byman/should-hezbollah-be-next.html on 10/04/2008.

Cable News Network (n.d.) "The myth: The reality: The mission and method of Osama bin Laden." Retrieved from http://www.cnn.com/CNN/Programs/people/shows/binladen/profile.html on 08/26/2009.

Guardian.co.uk (2002) "Full text: bin Laden's 'letter to America'" Retrieved from http://www.guardian.co.uk/world/2002/nov/24/theobserver on 10/01/2008.

Mueller, III, Robert S. (2005) ATestimony of Robert S. Mueller, III, Director, Federal Bureau of Investigation, Before the Senate Committee on Intelligence of the United States Senate, February 16, 2005.@ at URL http://www.fbi.gov/congress/congress05/mueller021605.htm accessed 06/27/2005.

United States Department of State (2008). "Terrorist organizations" **Country Reports on Terrorism, 2007**. Retrieved from http://www.state.gov/s/ct/rls/crt/2007/103714.htm on 09/06/2008.

Zakaria, Fareed. (2001). The politics of rage: Why do they hate us? Newsweek (October 15). At URL http://www.fareedzakaria.com/articles/newsweek/101501_why.html accessed 8/18/2005.

<h1 style="text-align:center">CHAPTER 8
DOMESTIC TERRORISM</h1>

At the root of extremism are radical ideologies, radical religious beliefs and pent-up anger and frustration, all of which can lead to violent acts ranging from hate crimes to terrorism. In the United States, the 1995 Oklahoma City bombing and the 9-11 terrorist attacks six years later, have made it painfully clear that Americans cannot ignore the dangers of extremism. *Anti-Defamation League*

Introduction

Domestic terrorism involves operations within one's own country. In the United States, domestic terrorists are usually American citizens, acting on their own initiatives. International terrorists, sometimes called transnational terrorists, are foreigners attacking an institution, assassinating a notable, or threatening our political system. Most terrorism within the United States is from domestic individuals and/or groups. American terrorists are harder to detect here in the United States. They look like the rest of us. They dress and act like the rest of us. They talk like us and they dress like us. They fit and they are hard to discern because of these likenesses.

The Federal Bureau of Investigation defines domestic terrorism as "acts of violence that are a violation of the criminal laws of the United States or any state, committed by individuals or groups without any foreign direction, and appear to be intended to intimidate or coerce a civilian population, or influence the policy of a government by intimidation or coercion, and occur primarily within the territorial jurisdiction of the United States "(Lewis, 2004).

There have been many transitions in the application or the attempts to apply terrorism here within the United States. The activities normally referred to as domestic terrorism are usually related to:

- Racist and separatist violence

- Homophobic violence

- Anti-Semitic violence

Jewish responses to anti-Semitic violence (Jewish Defense League)
- Labor violence (not all labor violence is terrorism)

- Radical political violence

- Animal Rights/Environmental Activist violence

- Religious and separatist violence (or violent eschatology)

- General vigilantism

- Insurgent terrorism, which can also be racist, anti-Semitic, and political. Groups such as the Aryan Nations, The Republic of New Africa, the American Indian Movement and Puerto Rican irredentists (the focus being "we want our land back" or we want our own national identity, an independent government, and control of that government).

Left-wing terrorism

Left-wing radicals want to replace our current form of property ownership and destroy our government. They want a socialist state in which all people would be politically and economically equal. Private businesses would be commonly owned, but controlled by the government. Some socialists and communists were also anarchists, seeing all government as evil or believing that government should be restricted to public safety issues such as public safety, clean water, clean air, and a clean environment.

Other than the encroachment of the American Communist Party and the tendency of the intellectual community to choose a more socialistic way of life, the primary left-wing and nationalist group operating within the United States during the 1950's was FALN, a group using the Spanish acronym for the Armed Forces of National Liberation. FALN attempted to assassinate President Truman. They also attacked the Halls of Congress. Another group of Puerto Rican nationalists was named 'Macheteros."

These two groups and independent organizations of the same persuasion, caused problems both in Puerto Rico and within the continental United States. They supported their movement through armed robberies and emphasized their resolve through bombing attacks. In recent years, the ideology of the Macheteros and of FALN is perceived to have juxtaposed with the ideals of al-Qaida. The ideology goes something like this. "The U.S. government, in spite of having a superpower status, is morally corrupt! It's people are morally weak, and the government is controlled by Jews living both here in the United States and in Israel." Since the government is perceived to be corrupt—it therefore no longer has the moral authority to exist in its present state, and should be defeated in an expeditious manner and replaced with an Islamic Regime.

More recent examples of leftist radicalism are nationalistic. A Nation of Islam splinter group now calls itself the New Black Panther Party for Self-Defense. The BLA (Black Liberation Army) fugitive, Joanne Chesimard remains in Cuba, after escaping from a state prison where she was sentenced for assisting in the murder of a New Jersey police officer. Members of the defunct militant group, the Republic of New Africa, avoided arrest and incarceration here in the United States, are also believed to have accepted Cuban sanctuary. Some have now lived in Cuba for several decades.

Up until the 1960's, most terrorism, with the exception of common vigilantism, was left wing. Leftist memberships are usually made up of young people, primarily associated with colleges and universities. Starting in the early 1960's there were many anti-war and anti-draft protest groups. The WUO (Weather Underground Organization) was a classic example. Operating from the early 1970's and throughout the Vietnam War, the group began with demonstrations, simple political activism and anti-war protest rallies. Later they set off explosives at Harvard University and the nation's Capitol. Military recruitment centers and draftee records centers were also targeted.

Other left-wing groups are active today. The animal rights activist groups and the environmental activist groups have also become violent. The Animal Liberation Front wants to improve the treatment of all animals and wants to stop the use of animals in medical or cosmetic testing and any and all business ventures associated with the fur trade. Any exploitation of animal rights is targeted both politically and, on occasion, violently. In fact, animal rights activists have destroyed more property than any other American group. Until far-right radical Timothy McVeigh blew up the Murrah Building in Oklahoma City, the animal rights activist groups had killed more citizens in their attempts to influence medical research, the cosmetics industry, and universities than any other violent domestic subversives of other priorities..

The Eco-terrorists of the ELF (Earth Liberation Front) want to stop the destruction of wetlands and the intrusion of logging efforts in national forests and other timber stands, whether they are publicly and privately owned. ELF's response to any development in traditional forest or wetland environments is arson, and "monkey-wrenching" (equipment sabotage). As late as 2003, a California condominium complex was set on fire and a Colorado Ski Resort was also destroyed because of allegations concerning the destruction of animal habitats.

<u>Right-Wing Terrorism</u>

Domestic terrorists are also right wing. In fact, most contemporary American terrorists operating within the continental United States today are right-wing. Right wing ideologues have many unique philosophies. These are generally opposite from the left wing beliefs, but violent right wingers do not necessarily agree one with one another. The right wing ideologue does believe in government, essentially a strong centralized government, unlike his anti-government left-wing counterpart. However, the form of government, especially our government, promoted by the right winger may be considerably different from our current democratic political system.

As with many left-wing groups, right-wingers often believe that the United States government is hopelessly corrupt. Right-wingers claim "to love America—but to despise our government." Because they believe the government is corrupt, they believe that it doesn't have the right to exist! They also perceive that they have the right, indeed the obligation—to destroy our current government, restoring it to a true Constitutional standard and to the "original" (first Ten Amendments) Bill of Rigts). When the right-wing belief system is also associated with a conservative or radical religious philosophies, the group becomes even more dangerous because they believe that they are "accomplishing God's will on this earth." Most right wing terrorists in the United States are religious! These violent ideologues want to destroy our government and create a theological government; one ruled by "their interpretation" of the Holy Bible, or in the case of Muslims, of the Koran.

Even right-wing radicals who do not agree on specific issues usually have some type of core belief system. Their beliefs coincide on several points. Most oppose the present government. Most believe that some special interest group is going to take over the government or that this group has already usurped control, bypassing the democratic process. Right wingers are usually nativist and oppose increasing social integration and the immigration of foreigners into our land. Some are racial separatists and some are racists who believe that people of color should no longer be allowed to immigrate or be accepted as United States citizens.

Many, in looking for a conspiracy, have accepted the rationale that some international cabal has unduly interfered and profited from the world economy. Quite often that cabal is believed to be controlled by Jews, thus creating anti-Semitic prejudice. When this anti-Semitic conspiracy theory is believed, the radical right calls the United States government a ZOG (a Zionist Occupied Government), one primarily interested in the welfare of Israel and of Jews living within the United States.

Radical right wingers also believe in *severation*. They want disappear from the infrastructure. They want a camouflaged existence and invisibility from governmental influence. They no longer use credit cards or bank accounts. They don't use social security cards. They pay their rent and other bills with cash or money orders. They don't leave an economic tracer in any of their business transactions. They severate! "Severation "(Dees, 1996, 87),"involves dropping off the identifiable citizen grid and becoming a non-entity." Both Timothy McVeigh of Oklahoma City bombing fame and Eric Rudolph who blew up abortion centers and set off a bomb at the Atlanta Olympics, severated. They were here in the United States, but no longer accepted the benefits of sovereign citizenship. McVeigh was pulled over by an Oklahoma Highway Patrolmen because he didn't have a vehicle license tag and then arrested because he had a concealed weapon. Both McVeigh and Rudolph rejected the political values of our country. Severation was first used by the tax protesters of Posse Commitatus in a plan to "retire from America."

Until recently the federal laws dealing with terrorist activities, plans, and attacks were inadequate. If citizens were killed in a terrorist initiated bombing or arson, the homicide or manslaughter statutes would usually be applied instead of a terrorism law. If people were intimidated, threatened, or extorted, for terroristic purposes, then other standard criminal statutes would be applied. The same thing could be said for using explosives to blow up a public building, or arson to harm a family in their own home.

Often the criminal statutes suffice, and because local prosecutors are much more skilled in using these older and more traditional crime statutes, they apply the simple crime charges versus a complicated terrorism or terrorism conspiracy charge. Money laundering for terror groups is a difficult charge to demonstrate "beyond a reasonable doubt." However, proving that someone transferred money illegally is not that difficult. In many cases, prosecutors avoid the conspiracy aspects of terrorism and present the more simple elements of a specific crime to a court and jury.

Contemporary Domestic Terrorism

Today, terrorism within the United States is more likely to be committed by right-wing Americans. While the World Trade Center 9/11 event was planned and accomplished primarily by Saudi Arabians, most terror acts within the United States have been completed or attempted by Americans. The 1993 attack on the same complex was planned by a loose coalition of men somewhat affiliated with al-Qaeda, so this major

attack was also an exception. The February 26, 1993 Tower attack killed six people and

injured nearly 1,000. The intent of the group was to topple the North Tower into the

South Tower, destroying both buildings. However, the majority of terrorist attacks

within the United States were perpetuated by right-wing Americans—white (Aryan)

Americans.

Dr. Brent Smith, studied this phenomenon extensively and reported in his book,

Terrorism In America: Pipe Bombs and Pipe Dreams that from 1980 to 1989, that a total

of 170 men and women were indicted by our courts for domestic terrorism or activities

related to the planning, preparation or accomplishment of terrorist acts. Of these

defendants, Dr. Smith revealed that a significant number of those indicted were affiliated

with the religious ideology known as Christian Identity (Smith, .1994, 14)

While Smith's research covered the 1980's, a later research effort estimated that

between 1995 and 2005 "there were some additional 60 domestic terrorist acts committed

by Americans known to be members of "hate groups." (Blejwas, Griggs, & Potak, 2005).

In a February 26, 2009 Newsletter from the Southern Poverty Law Center, Morris Dees

claimed that the number of domestic "hate" groups has increased by more than 50%

since the year 2000. "Immigration fears," Dees says, "along with the recession and the

election of a black president, has caused another increase in 2008." (Dees, 2009).

On another front, Kevin Borgenson and Robin Valeri, in writing *Terrorism in*

America, reported a new clandestine alliance between traditional sworn enemies. While

traditionally the radical right has "loved America—but hated our government,"

Borgenson and Valeri reported that their confidential interviews with members of the

Aryan Nations and followers of the Christian Identity network revealed a growing relationship between the Aryan Nations and the followers of Islamic Jihad. This included membership of Islamic Fundamentalists with the Aryan Nations. This is a shocking affiliation, one that most Americans would reject, because most right-wing conservatives or radicals are usually supportive of all American efforts against foreigners within our borders.

An unusual compromise has resulted in some conciliatory efforts to combine resources between Christian militancy and Islamic Jihad. The philosophy behind these efforts goes something like this. "The enemy of my enemy, is my friend!" Since both Aryan Nations and Islamic Jihad hate the Jews and the United States government (described by hate groups as the ZOG [Zionist Occupied Government]), these two opposing groups now claim a relationship with each other.

This new conspiracy transition must be carefully scrutinized. Since Islam and Fundamentalistic Christianity are in direct opposition, as is the branch "Christian Identity Movement" from the precepts of radical Islam, it appears that at some point in time, there will be a schism or all-out war.

The justification by right-wing white American radicals for this affiliation is that the Aryan Nations is a two pronged movement, one with a religious orientation (the Phineas Priesthood), and another with a secular approach (the Aryan Nation, a separatist state within the traditional borders of the United States). The merging of Islamic Jihad with Aryan Jihad is an interesting merger and should be carefully reviewed, rather than being rejected because it seems so bizarre.

Another twist in terms of domestic terror is to review the contemporary terror acts occurring within the jurisdictions of other western powers. Recently there was a series of attacks in London, England. While each of the individuals involved in these suicide bombings were most certainly of Islamic belief, they weren't foreigners! They were British citizens, brought up in British society and educated in British schools.

Social psychologists who believed that these young men had not successfully integrated into their schools and the established secular society were shocked to learn that these young men were respected colleagues of their English friends at school and in their neighborhoods. They were not marginalized men angrily seeking revenge on a society limiting their economic or social opportunity; instead they had apparently integrated successfully into their new homeland successfully. That did not prevent radical Mullah's from targeting them for their suicide bomber recruiting efforts.

Single Issue Terrorism

Single-issue or special issue terrorism can be from the ideological left or the ideological right. The Weather Underground was an anti-war movement (specifically the war in Vietnam, Laos, and Cambodia). The Irish Republican Army was focused on Irish independence and a new national autonomy, an irredentist (we want our homeland back) movement. Similarly, on the right wing side of violent American politics, the right-to-life or anti-abortion movement is focused on this single issue.

The Ku Klux Klan is another single-issue group, at least for the majority of its 141 year lifetime. The Ku Klux Klan was primarily a racial supremacy group for most of its history. During certain of the Klan "revivals" they accepted unique beliefs. The original Klan simply wanted to control the black people of their jurisdiction and resist the

Yankee Reconstruction government. In later eras the Klan promoted nativist (American born preference policies) and anti-immigration regulations.

During the 1920's the Klan was anti-Pope and anti-Catholic, believing that the Pope had more influence over American Catholics than did our government. During the 1960's the Klan became anti-Semitic, believing that Jewish people were supporting racial integration with their jewish lawyers and jewish money. As the unique creeds of this organization and others paralleling its values began to accept additional doctrines, these multi-issue anti-government groups became more virulent and thus the danger from these groups increased at exponential levels.

The Puerto Rican Nationalist groups were initially focused on a single issue, the freedom of their homeland. The groups who espouse violence to "right the wrongs" of their issue, are all dangerous, but become incredibly so when they join forces with other single issue groups, increasing their own influence. Several of the nationalistic groups also accepted communism as an ideal social/economic/ political system, as well.

Extreme environmental and animal rights groups have also proven to use violence to advance their agendas. Animal rights activists are focused primarily on the humane treatment of animals issue. Environmental quality activists are also primarily focused on clean air, food and water topics. Since 1977, when disaffected members of the ecological preservation group Greenpeace formed the Sea Shepherd Conservation Society and attacked commercial fishing operations by cutting drift nets, acts of "eco-terrorism" have occurred around the globe.

The Earth First Organization was first accused of sabotage in 1986. The first attack of the Animal Liberation Front took place in 1983 with the theft of 12 research dogs in California. These groups have been charged with malicious destruction and theft through the 1990s. The Earth Liberation Front has conducted a series of arson campaigns in recent years. Its attack on a ski resort in Vail, Colorado in 1998 — one of its more high profile efforts — did more than $12 million in damage.

Multi-Issue American Terrorist Groups

While contemporary multi-issue terrorism group cooperation is not unique, it nevertheless has limited application. One of the earliest cooperative ventures seems to have taken place during the early 1980's. In 1984, the Committee of the States, was formed. While there had been loose-knit coalition associations in the past, "this was the first time in history that several far right groups of varying emphasis had united under one banner."(Seymour, 1991). The Committee of the States had two primary objectives that of eliminating the federal income tax system and "replacing" the Congress of the United States. The Committee of the States also intended to use its' own militia to insure the success of the organization.

The Committee of the States (COS) quickly came to the attention of the intelligence divisions of the United States Department of Justice. Federal attorneys from California, Oregon, Washington, Colorado, Idaho and Alabama began to target right wing leaders who were espousing violence and other forms of criminal activity. The Committee of the States meeting ultimately resulted in a federal law enforcement emphasis known as "Operation Clean Sweep." Ultimately some thirteen COS members were indicted, arrested and tried for the crime of sedition in Fort Smith, Arkansas. The defendants included the following men, well known in the radical right, as well as several others who did not have national reputations:

- Robert Edward Miles, former Grand Dragon of the Michigan Ku Klux Klan, he became obsessed with racial purity and the Christian Identity Movement

- Louis Ray Beam, Former Grand Dragon of the Texas Ku Klux Klan. He moved into active participation in the Christian Identity Movement. Beam also served as the Ambassador-at-large for the Aryan Nations and was considered the heir apparent of the Aryan Nations upon the death or retirement of Richard Butler.

- Richard Girnt Butler, Christian Identity Pastor and head of Aryan Nations at Hayden Lake, Idaho

- Richard Joseph Scutari, an active follower of Christian Identity and the Order. He is presently incarcerated in a federal penitentiary.

- Bruce Carroll Pierce, a Christian Identity follower and a member of "the Order". He is presently incarcerated in a federal penitentiary.

- David Edin Lane, an active member of "the Order," and driver of the get-away-vehicle in the murder of Jewish talk show host, Alan Berg, of Denver, Colorado

- Richard Wayne Snell, former CSA member, he killed a pawn shop owner he mistakenly believed was a Jew. He also murdered an Arkansas State Trooper, who was of African American descent. Before his execution he had planned to blow up the Murrah Building in Oklahoma City. Timothy McVeigh detonated the truck bomb on the day of Snell's execution.

The chief prosecution witness was for the Sedition trial was James Dennis Ellison, the former head of the Covenant, the Sword, and the Arm of the Lord (CSA), who also met with the group at Hayden Lake. James Dennis Ellison, who at an earlier time had been proclaimed the white supremacy movement's "Warlord" claimed that the men indicted were planning a guerilla war within the continental United States. The indictments charged that this group intended to support the revolution with robberies and counterfeiting. Also planned were bombing attacks, utility service center attacks, municipal water system attacks and personal attacks and murder against federal officials, leading Jewish citizens and non-white Americans.

At the time of the trial, Ellison had already been convicted for weapons violations and the crime of racketeering. His testimony was seriously questioned by jurors because many of the jurors thought he perjured himself in order to get an early release from federal custody. The jury of ten men and two women found all thirteen defendants "Not Guilty," greatly embarrassing federal agents and prosecutors.

After the Sedition Trial, Louis Beam, Jr., mocked the federal authorities with his newsletter "The Seditionist." He also began to actively promote the "leaderless cell resistance" concept, recognizing that the larger the organization, the greater the likelihood that someone would gossip inappropriately or would turn state's evidence against the group.

Beam was a Vietnam veteran who returned from that war as a disenchanted and disenfranchised citizen. He was an angry young man and believed that the United States government was becoming an "evil empire." He joined the Ku Klux Klan as an act of rebellion, ultimately becoming the Grand Dragon of the Texas Ku Klux Klan. Beam first gained notoriety when he shot at the fishing boats of immigrant Vietnamese fishermen working along the Texas Gulf Coast. Two movie documentaries were made about his efforts.

Beam quickly recognized the potential of the internet, which he called the Liberty Net. He then began mass communication through a radical right computer network bulletin board. Working with Don Black, he made powerful inroads into recruiting right wingers into their "unorganized system." Black, the former Alabama Knights Imperial Wizard, was also convicted of violating U.S. Neutrality laws in an attempted takeover of the Caribbean Island of Dominica.

The Ku Klux Klan had failed because of an bloated bureaucracy and the Committee of the States had failed because of its size and the number of people who reported its secrets. Beam recommended that the far-right militants should copy the "communist cell" concept, and promoted a "leaderless cell resistance concept" which was sometimes called a "phantom cell." Some scholars also referred to a variant of Beam's leaderless cell as "lone-wolf terrorism (Lifton, 1999, 338.). "Leaderless resistance," Beam stated vehemently," would present the government with an intelligence nightmare."(Lifton, 1999, 339)

The phantom cells of Beam's leaderless resistance suggest the idea of a *phantom guru*, an invisible and nonmaterial source of compelling wisdom for movement activists. Its form of resistance, Barkun tells us, implies lawbreaking or acts of violence at a local level, as exemplified by the Oklahoma city bombing, which was accomplished by a phantom cell or two or conceivably three people moving through a larger population of like minded individuals.

There are now a plethora of small and not-so-small groups: "militias" [which have bloodline Identity influences} like the militia of Montana, the Michigan Militia and the Citizen's Militia of Chemung County, New York: Christian Identity groups ranging from the non-violent Church of Israel to the more aggressive Christian Patriots Defense League, to the action-prophesy-oriented Covenant, Sword, and the Arm of the Lord; and the more traditional far-right groups like the Ku Klux Klan and the American Nazi Party—not to speak of the phantom cells of which we can know little. (Nobles, 1998, 132).

Beam also advocated a resistance "meritorious awards" program for "Warriors." Any armed fighter could become recognized as an Aryan "Warrior," by killing the enemies of ZOG (the Zionist Occupied Government): They would be awarded points or fractional points for each murder, although they would call it a killing, "because they were at war."

This approach awards fractions of points for assassinations [of personnel representing the United States Government, and sometimes state or local government). Members of Congress are worth one-fifth of a point each. Judges and the FBI director are worth one-sixth of a point. Journalists and local politicians are worth one twelfth of a point each. The President of the United States is worth one point. Upon achieving one full point, the rank of Warrior is given to the Aryan National (Stinson, 1987, 2).

Terrorologist Bruce Hoffman reported that almost a quarter of the world's terrorism groups and about a half of the most dangerous ones, a motivated primarily by religious concerns (Hoffman, 1993). These people believe that God authorized, even commanded, them to kill for their cause. Their cause is sacred, approved by Jehovah, Yahveh, or Allah. Whether Islamic, Christian Fundamentalist, or "Christian" Identity, these committed men and women believe that God approves their actions, their crimes (by earthly standards), and their killings which they redefine as "acts of war" versus the homicide or murder definition.

Most of these groups have studied eschatology, which is a field of study of the last days of this earth. Studying the end times by Islamic, Christian Fundamentalist, or Christian Identity standards gives those believers the push they need for vigilance and commitment to the cause of their faith. They then look forward with a hope inspired by faith. They have a pistol on their hip, a Bible or a Koran in one hand, and an assault rifle in the other. They are incredibly committed and extraordinarily dangerous. A zealot for "the" cause, especially one where the protagonists are well-trained, is a dangerous instrument in the free world.

The White American Bastion

While some of the groups listed here are now seriously weakened, or even destroyed through arrest, prosecution, incarceration, litigation or internal dissent, it is appropriate to describe the history of several of them. The Ku Klux Klan was the first major radical racist organization. It often participated in vigilante behavior during the reconstruction period, attacking politicized former slaves and the Yankee reconstructionists.

During the early 1900's the Klan emerged from a period of inactivity into a national nativist organization. Nativism is the practice of favoring native-born people over recent immigrants, especially people of difference races. During the several Klan revivals, it became more or less militant and assumed additional roles. Most of the leaders of the radical right are still, or once were heavily influenced by one or more units of the Ku Klux Klan.

Another strong influence was the John Birch Society. It's founder was Robert Welch. He was strongly influenced by the anti-communist McCarthy Hearings. When Senator McCarthy's "communism conspirator" Congressional Hearing attacks dwindled, Welch took over the anti-communist movement with the John Birch Society, named after an American Missionary killed by the Chinese Communists during the early 1940's. Welch was a firebrand. During the early 1960's Welch claimed by both President (Former General of the Army) Eisenhower and Secretary of State John Foster Dulles were communist agents, "and part of a master conspiracy to subvert the American way of life." (George and Wilcox, 1996, 7).

Welch supported the McCarthyites who fought the American Communist Movement. Publicly and privately McCarthy attacked the wealthy, intellectual elites, and politically influential public figures who had dabbled in communism or socialism or who were accused of associating themselves with the American Communist Party. McCarthy believed, and Welch accepted his claims, that communist subversives had infiltrated almost every unit of American government. He also investigated Hollywood, America's favorite movie stars and all of those associated with the screen industry. He questioned the commitment of many of the young intellectuals employed within the U.S. Department of State.

Robert Welch kicked over a lot of conspiracy rocks when he claimed that the Illuminati, a secret division of the Masonic Movement, was responsible for a monumental plot to control the world economy. Welch claimed that the Illuminati, having existed for centuries, were now an active, subversive, super-secret, covert cabal with far-reaching influence. Some of Welch's supporters went so far as to claim that the Illuminati "were responsible for the French Revolution, the War of 1812, the American Civil War, World War I, Word War II, the Korean War and the Vietnam War."(George and Wilcox, 1996, 81).

The John Birch Society (JBS) created a huge array of right-wing material, includes, books, brochures, phamplets, and flyers. Probably the book *None Dare Call it Treason* by John A. Stormer and the *Protocals of The Learned Elders of Zion* capped the list. The *Protocols* book was an early anti-Semitic fictional account describing the Jews as being in charge of the criminal financial conspiracy cabals of our world.

While Welch claimed that he was not anti-Semitic and the JBS organization was officially not anti-Semitic nor was it racist, its conspiracy theories nonetheless opened the doors to those prejudices. JBSers were never accused of being violent. However JBS membership was often the first organizational step towards right wing radicalism. The best (or worst) known far-right radical names to be associated with the JBS before moving on to more subversive activities and organization included Gerald L.K. Smith, Colonel William Potter Gayle, Colonel Gordon "Jack" Mohr, Tommy Tarrants (Quarles, 1987), Robert Matthews (Flynn and Gerhardt, 1989, 15) and Timothy McVeigh.

During the peak of its influence during the 1960's the JBS claimed four thousand chapters and an annual budget of over 5 million dollars. No American group open to the general public did more to promote the belief in a radical left-wing, one world government, communist conspiracy than any other organization.

Early Militant "Identity" Leaders:	

- William Pelley

- Gerald L.K Smith

- Wesley Smith

- Gordon Kahl

- Colonel William Potter Gayle

- Richard Girnt Butler

- William Pierce

William Pelley (died in 1965)

William Pelley's father owned a toilet paper factory and Pelley worked for him as a young man. Later he was a reporter and wrote for the Boston Globe Newspaper. At one time Pelley owned two newspapers, but these failed. Pelly was best known for writing more than 200 stories in *Redbook, Colliers, and the Saturday Evening Post* magazines.

When he began studying eschatology, predicting the imminent return of the Lord Jesus Christ, he began radicalizing. He prophesied that he had a vision for a nation he called a "Christ State" claiming that the Lord Jesus Christ would return during his (Pelley's) lifetime. He taught that the Jews were involved in a conspiracy to control the economy and that they had even "engineered the Great Depression." (Ridgeway, 1990, 62). Preparing to develop a theocratic state to await Christ's return, he formed the Silver Shirts, preparing to "bring the work of Christ *militant* into the open."(Ridgeway, 1990, 62). Pelly began to openly support Hitler during this period, resulting in his indictment, arrest, prosecution and conviction for the crime of treason and certain violations of the United States Espionage Act. He received a 15 year sentence for these crimes.

Gerald L.K. Smith (died in 1976)

Gerald L.K. Smith is well known among traditional, liberal and conservative, fundamentalist and evangelical Christians as the founder of the internationally reknown *Passion Play,* Bible Museum, and replica City of Jerusalem in Eureka Springs, Arkansas. However, Michael Barkun, in writing *Religion and The Racist Right: The Origins of The Christian Identity Movement* claimed that "Gerald L.K. Smith…more than anyone else, is responsible for promoting [Christian] Identity in the form we know it today (Barkun, 1994, 4).

Smith joined the Silver Shirts run by Pelley, in 1933 (Newton and Newton, 526, 1991). He was also involved in pastoring a church and was active politically. His church during this period was at King's Highway Church in Shreveport, Louisiana. He also was involved with the politician, "Kingfish" Huey Long. When Long was assassinated, Smith wasn't sufficiently established to take over Long's political organization, however.

Smith then relocated to Michigan where he ran for the United States Senate in 1940. He was arguably a charismatic public speaker, but some commentators of the time suggested that he was not a good politician. It is highly probable that Smith's right-wing and extremist affiliations harmed his political career. In 1946, the Georgia State Attorney General announced that Smith and his associates were "forging formal alliances with the Ku Klux Klan." (Newton and Newton, 526). By the early 1950's Smith sponsored a European anti-Semitic conspiracy theorist to help him radicalize Americans. Claiming to enter the U.S. to address church groups, he distributed his anti-Semitic book entitled *Know Your Enemy.*

Smith possessed considerable wealth and was an astute businessman. In 1953 he moved again to Los Angeles, California and began interacting with the primary movers and shakers of right wing radicalism and the Christian Identity Movement.

Smith remained in radical right-wing extremist groups throughout his life, at various times writing, speaking and promoting the Ku Klux Klan, the National States Rights Party, and the John Birch Society. Smith ran for the U.S. Presidency on the Christian Nationalist Party ticket in both 1952 and 1956. During the early 1960's Smith purchased the Eureka Springs, Arkansas property and funded, as well as developed the construction of the Passion Play Outdoor Theater and the seven story mortar statue of Jesus Christ extending his arms over Magnetic Mountain and the Eureka Springs countryside. He is now buried at the foot of the Magnetic Mountain statue of Christ.

Wesley Swift (died in 1970)

Wesley Swift, however, was probably was the best known Identity advocate. While attending a conservative Bible School in California, he claimed that he was "re-converted." to a form of white peoples Christianity. He then established an Anglo-Saxon Christian Congregation, originally known as the Church of Christ, Christian, in Hollywood, California. Later he moved the church to Lancaster, California. Swift became well established as a radio evangelist and developed a thriving ministry selling tape recordings of his sermons and secular presentations.

Some called Smith the first American "Identity" Bishop. He counseled many from the radical right, including Tommy Tarrance, a night rider for the White Knights of the Ku Klux Klan. The White Knights were headquartered in Laurel, Mississippi during the

1960's. Swift had been a Ku Klux Klan organizer during the 1920's and later founded the anti-Semitic organization commonly known as the Christian Defense League. He preached that "all Jews must be destroyed. I prophesy that before November 1993 there will not be a Jew in the United States, and by that I mean a Jew that will be able to walk or talk." (Anti-Defamation League, 1996, 21).

Swift was pre-imminent in the development of the Identity doctrine. He and several other advocates, all of the same Identity network, introduced the idea that Jesus Christ was a Caucasian and an Aryan, not a Jew. The primary founders of this network were all within Swift's church or had been at one time. Swift believed that the Jews were "of the synagogue of Satan…and are not, but do lie." (Revelation 3:9 KJV). Swift also frequently quoted Jesus in a confrontation with the Scribes and Pharisees. Jesus said, "Ye serpents, ye generation of vipers, how can you escape the damnation of hell." (Matthew 23:33 KJV).

Himself once a Klansman, Swift welcomed Klansmen into his congregation. "Over the years members of the National States Rights Party, Minutemen, and the California Rangers served with him and contributed to his organizations such as the Christian Defense League, the Southern California Defense Councils…and the Christian National Alliance." (Newton and Newton, 1991, 549).

Swift taught an anti-Semitic version of Identity. Jews were said to be planning the establishment of a one-world government, run and controlled by the United Nations. "Caucasians," he said, "would be ostracized" from the government, the economy, and the military. Those who followed Swift's teachings now had someone specific to blame, and Swift, even though he died in 1970, his legacy lives on and several of those who were influenced or trained by Swift continued active anti-Semitic and racialist diatribes, often supporting violence through to the early 2000's.

Gordon Kahl (killed in 1983)

Gordon Kahl was a decorated (Silver Star) Korean War II veteran who turned into a tax protesting farmer when he lost his farm due to falling wheat prices in the late 1960's. Angry at the loss, he blamed the United States government and our politicians for his loss. In protest, he joined an anti-income tax group called Possee Commitatus. Possee Commitatus called the U.S. personal income tax "Satan's Tithe" and Kahl refused to pay it any longer. He also became an aggressive leader in the radical underground, claiming that the federal government was seizing the assets of workers and redistributing those funds to those who don't work or will not work. Claiming we were becoming a socialistic state, if not a communist state, he became more and more active in the radical right movement.

Then Kahl was introduced to Christian Identity and became a member of the most conservative sect within Identity called "Bloodline-Identity." Some call this belief system by the name "Seedline Identity." Seedline Identity does not parallel traditional Christian inerrancy. Seedliners accept many of the tenets of Darwin's theory of evolution. Most Christians believe that the earth was created by God some six to 12,000 years ago. Seedliners believe that the world was created hundreds of thousands of years ago.

Seedliners believe that God created man on the sixth day of the creation process (Genesis 1:26). Since the name "Adam, describing a man of ruddy complexion (a Caucasian), was first referenced in the second chapter of Genesis, the seedliner believes that the white man (by their Identity standards, a more perfect man) was created later than the men of other races. Seedliners describe the men of Genesis I, as from the "mud races" and believe that mud-race men (Genesis: I) has been procreating for thousands of years before the creation of Adam, and ultimately the white race. Christian Identity followers accept the ethnocentric value that the white man and the white race is the preferred race "created in the form of Almighty God" and thus is the most perfect race on earth.

Further, they believe that Eve was sexually seduced by Satan rather than having eaten of the Fruit of the Tree in the Middle of the Garden of Eden. Insofar as the flood Noah's family survived, they believe that it was provincial rather than world-wide. This explains why race-mixing could continue after the flood, although some Seedline Identity theologians believe that a mixed-race person was allowed on the ark. They believe that Jesus Christ was a Hebrew and an Israelite, but that he was not a Jew. Some Seedliners believe that only white people can go to heaven. Others believe that it is possible for other races and mixed race people to receive salvation and a heavenly reward.

United States Deputy Marshals and local police officers attempted to arrest Kahl after a Possee Comitatus meeting. Four officers of the law were wounded and two were killed in the resulting gunfight. Later Kahl killed an Arkansas sheriff who thought he could bring Kahl in peacefully. The attempt to force Kahl out of a rural home resulted in both an explosion and a fire. At his death Gordon Kahl became the first radical right wing martyr!

Since he had received national publicity, many journalists began studying the doctrines of Possee Commitatus and the Christian Identity Sect. Many letters to the editor and those he had written to other members of the "patriot community" were later published, many of them in the Aryan Nations Newsletter. He was usually described as a "Christian Patriot" (Newton and Newton, 307) and even in death has influence over the radical right movement in America.

Colonel William Potter Gayle (died in 1988)

Colonel William Potter Gayle was an active member of the U.S. Army during World War II and served on General McArthur's staff in the Philippines. When he left the army, he was ordained as an Episcopalian minister. Later he founded his own church. In looking at his secular membership, it is recorded that he was once a member of the John Birch Society before moving ever further to the right wing activist groups. Colonel Gayle was an active recruiter for the California Rangers and the Christian Defense League. He was also known to preach for Wesley Swift in his Church of Jesus Christ, Christian in Lancaster, California.

Then Gayle networked with many other diverse radical groups. He may have been the first far-right activist to "branch out," serving in several radical groups simultaneously. He came in frequent contact with Klansmen, Rangers, the Christian Defense League, the National States Rights Party, the Minutemen and other groups of paramilitary and political persuasion. At one time he was accused of being a leader in the Unorganized Militia, years before the militia movement became a national phenomenon.

Gaye was a prime mover and shaker in what today is called the "Patriot Movement." During the later years of his life, he merged the doctrines of Christian Identity and political activism into a group he called "The Committee of the States." Gayle even claimed that he was the individual who re-named the old Anglo-Israel Movement (white people in both Great Britain and the United States are the descendants of the lost tribes of Israel) (Seymour, 86) to the term "Identity," describing what he called the birthright of Caucasian Christians.

Richard Girnt Butler (died in 2002)

Richard Girnt Butler was also in the service. He was a flight engineer and pilot instructor during World War II. Returning home, he worked in manufacturing, gradually transitioning into the aeronautics industry. In 1968 he was promoted to the senior manufacturing engineer post for Lockheed Aircraft Company at one of its California plants.

He returned from the war with a political agenda as well, that of grave concern for the future of the white race. He quickly connected with Wesley Swift and another Identity minister named Bertrand Comparet. The three of them established the Christian Defense League, with Butler as the national director. When Wesley Swift died in 1970, Butler took over the pastorate of the Lancaster, California Church of Jesus Christ, Christian. During this period Butler purchased some property in Hayden Lake, Idaho, and claimed that the location housed the office for the Aryan Nations, an all-white segregated multi-state province that he envisioned.

From watching documentary films of the Aryan Nations worship center, one can see that the Cross of Christ normally positioned in many evangelical and fundamentalist Christian churches, is the Nazi Cross symbol at the Aryan Nations rather than the traditional symbol. Butler was a big fan of Adolph Hitler, and followed Hitler's anti-Semitic positions. Butler, like Hitler, wanted to eliminate anyone of Jewish blood.

Most racist groups began interacting with the Aryan Nations organization. Continuing to reach out to diverse anti-government, racist, anti-Semitic, and those who were opposed to abortion, he began establishing dissimilar relationships. Aryan Nations and Possee Commitatus established a Charter for an all-white Christian township in 1982. The Aryan Nations boundaries were to be established by the borders of the Rocky Mountains, the Mississippi River, the Canadian Plains and the Mexican Border, but eventually the plan included only properties in the Northwest United States. The States of Washington, Oregon, Idaho, Montana and Wyoming were to form the separatist Aryan Nations state. Butler died in 2002, never realizing his lifelong obsession.

William Pierce (died in 2002)

William Pierce was once a physics professor at the University of Oregon. While he was an atheist and was not associated with Christian Identity, nevertheless, he helped train and he certainly influenced many of those who were. A large number of bloodline identity believers came first under the influence of the John Birch Society, moving on to embrace the secular tenets of National Socialism. While he was an atheist, he still had strong racist and anti-Semitic leanings.

The Anti-Defamation league claimed that Pierce was one of the principal contemporary leaders of the American Nazi Party, subsequently renamed the National Socialist White People's Party and even later, the National Alliance (Anti-Defamation League, 1996, 107). Pierce edited and published a magazine called the *National Vanguard* and ran a right-wing mail order book sale operation.

Pierce's rhetoric and writings influenced both Robert Mathews of the Order, and Timothy McVeigh of a small, but militant, leaderless cell resistance group. Pierce was generally credited with writing a novel entitled *The Turner Diaries*, which he also marketed. The book 's pseudonymous author was listed as Andrew McDonald. However, one of the editors of *American Pulp* claimed that Robert J. Randisi wrote *The Turner Diaries* for Pierce (Gorman, et al, 1997, 213).. Under any circumstance *The Turner Diaries* is the best welling right wing novel of the last two decades. From psychological autopsies of the life and work of both McVeigh and Mathews, it is clear that they both used the book's theme as a model for their revolutionary activities.

The book's back cover material describes *The Turner Diaries* in the following manner:

What will you do when they come to take your guns?

Ed Turner and his fellow patriots face this question and are forced underground when the U.S. government bans the private possession of firearms and stages the mass Gun Raids to round up suspected gun owners. The hated Equality Police begin hunting them down, but the patriots fight back with a campaign of sabotage and assassination. An all-out race war occurs as the struggle escalates. Turner and his comrades suffer terribly, but their ingenuity and boldness in devising and executing new methods of guerilla warfare led of a victory of cataclysmic intensivity and world wide scope.

The FBI has labeled *The Turner Diaries* "the Bible of the racist right. If the government had the power to ban books, this one would be at the top of the list. *The Turner Diaries* is the most controversial book in America today—and it's a book unlike any you've ever read (McDonald, back cover).

Pierce was well-known on the right-wing lecture circuit. He was deliberative and profound, but was not a charismatic presenter. His style was more like that of a boring college professor, closely adhering to his notes. However, his contact with Robert Matthews of the Order who had frequented Pierce's National Alliance properties, as well as the Aryan Nations properties was a strong indication of his influence. Mathews had also spoken at the public meetings held at the National Alliance properties.

Conclusion

While many historians would lead you to believe that our nations' founders were revolutionaries who used terroristic methods, the methods used against the British Army was organized along a guerilla approach. While members of the Boston Tea Party and the members of individual militias may seem to possess the characteristics of the contemporary terrorist, there is still a considerable difference.

While the Minutemen and the participants of the Boston Tea Party were revolutionaries and criminals by the express law of the land during these years of revolution, they were quite different from those mentioned in this chapter who want to subvert democracy, espouse hatred towards members of minority races and Jews, and overwhelm the government of the United States. Innocent women and children may have been inadvertently killed by friendly fire during the American Revolution, but they were not targeted by Americans, nor by the British, with some few exceptions towards the British involvement.

The next chapter will cover many of the contemporary leaders of radical right and revolutionary groups. With the exception of kidnappings and suicide bomb attacks, these groups usually behave just as international terrorists do, using the same tactics, strategies, and goals to achieve their purposes.

References

Lewis, John E., Statement of the Depurty Assistant Director of the Counterterrorism Division, FBI before the senate Judiciary Committee (May 18, 2004), www.fbi.gov/congess/congress 04/lewis051804.htm

Blejwas, A., Griggs, A., and Potak, M (2005) "Terror From the Right," *Intelligence Report* 118 (Summer): 33-46.

Borgeson, Kevin and Valeri, Robin, *Terrorism in America*, (Sudbury, Massachusetts: Jones and Bartlett Publishers, 2009).

Smith, Brent, *Terrorism in America: Pipe Bombs and Pipe Dreams*, (Albany, New York: State University of New York, 1994).

Lifton, Robert Jay. *Destroying the World to Save it: Aum Shinriko, Apocalyptic Violence and the New Global Terrorism*, (New York: Harper and Row, 1999).

Noble, Kerry. *Tabernacle of Hate: Why They Bombed Oklahoma City.* (Louisville, Quebec, Canada: Voyageur, 1998).
Stinson, James, "Domestic Terrorism in the United States," *Police Chief,* September 1987.

Hoffman, Bruce, *Holy Terror*. (Santa Monica, CA: RAND, 1993).

George, John and Wilcox, Laird, *American Extremists: Militias, Supremacists, Klansmen, Communists, and Others*, (Amherst, New York: Prometheus Books, 1996)

Flynne Kevin and Gerhardt, Gary, *The Silent Brotherhood: Inside America's Racist Underground*, (New York: The Free Press, 1989).

Ridgeway, James, *Blood in the Face The Ku Klux Klan, Aryan Nations, Skinheads, and the Rise of a New White Culture.* (New York: Thunder Mouth Press, 1990).

Seymour, Cheri, *Committee of the States: Inside the Radical Right* (Mariposa, California: Camden Place Communications, 1991).

Barkun, Michael, *Religion and the Racist Right: The Origins of The Christian Identity Movement*, (Chapel Hill, NC: University of North Carolina Press, 1994.

Newton, Michael and Newton, Judy Ann. *The Ku Klux Klan: An Encyclopedia.* (New York: Garland, 1991).

Anti-Defamation League, *Danger: Extremism: The Major Vehicles and Voices on America's Far-Right Fringe.* (New York: Anti-Defamation League, 1996).

Gorman, Ed; Prozini, Bill; and Breenburg, Martin H. *American Pulp.* (New York: Carroll and Graff, 1997).

CHAPTER 9
COMBATING TERRORISM: THE UNITED STATES

The world will face continued growth in terrorist attacks in the next decade, and large – scale incidents involving hundreds of deaths will become more common.
Brian Michael Jenkins, 1987

Introduction

The networks of terrorist organizations now resemble the infrastructure that supports transnational organized crime. The emergence of resilient networks of connections, alliances, safe houses, arms suppliers, providers of counterfeit documents, and funding from criminal enterprises such as drug trafficking have changed the face of efforts to combat terrorism. In the 1970's terrorist activity concentrated their attacks on property. In the 1980's more than half of attacks were directed against people. Terrorist killed people, blew up targets, and seized hostages.

The most significant advantage that terrorist have and will continue to have is the unlimited range of targets; they can strike anything, anywhere, anytime, and can target soft or hard targets (Jenkins, 1987). The era of modern terrorism began in the 1960's and for the first time in history it became possible for a small group of individuals to cause massive damage to people and property. Four areas have made modern terrorism what is it today: communications, technology, weapons, and transportation. Prior to the Internet, communication consisted of personal verbal exchanges: written, books, periodicals, newspapers and etc. The telephone and telegraph and then creation of the Internet have benefited the terrorist in their ability to communicate anytime, to anyplace or group. Modern communication allows the terrorist to receive maximum exposure of their message. Computers have allowed terrorist to communicate and benefit from the knowledge that can be found on the Internet. Computers control much of the infrastructure such as water systems, communication systems, and electrical and nuclear power which are all now targets of modern terrorist groups.

Weapons have become much more effective, less difficult to obtain, and offer an arsenal for the terrorist that can be traditional (advanced sniper rifles) or can be used for mass destruction (biological, chemical, and nuclear). Transportation has allowed any terrorist group to become global and strike anywhere in the world including the United States (Dyson, 2001). The United States is a target from not only Middle Eastern extremist, but of extremist that are "home grown", including right-wing extremist, single-issue terrorist or specific issue terrorist and eco-terrorist. However, the tools needed to combat terrorism have developed and now offer law enforcement the same advantages as they do the terrorist. Modern weapons, extraordinary means of transportation and communication systems that can connect units globally, offer law enforcement much needed means to address the modern global threat that terrorism presents.

Modern Terrorism and the United States

The United States began experiencing modern terrorism in the 1960's due primarily from opposition to the Vietnam War. Over time other social issues began to evolved and produced violence which was classified as terrorist acts. Local agencies began to respond to violent attacks where crime scenes were very difficult to work. Bombings, assassinations, armed assaults, kidnappings, hijackings, and barricade and hostage incidents were the six basic tactics that accounted for 95% of all terrorist incidents (Jenkins, 1987). Groups such as FALN (Puerto Rican Armed Forces for National Liberation) carried out over 100 attacks during the 1980's.

The 1970's produced groups such as the New World Liberation Front and the Weather Underground Organization. Armored truck robberies and bombings by these groups resulted in the formation of task forces such as the New York Terrorism Task Force. Chicago Police Department, Illinois State Police and the FBI formed the Chicago Terrorism Task Force and the result was cooperation between agencies to combat terrorism. By the 1990's there were more than 20 operations tasks forces dedicated to combating terrorism in the United States (Dyson, 2001). The FBI has been in the process of restructuring itself since the events of 9/11 and has sought to strengthen the functions of intelligence, partnerships, and investigations in response to the threats of modern terrorism.

The United States has over 2000 miles of border with Mexico, 6000 miles of border with Canada, and 13000 miles of coastlines which present a major challenge to the protection of the country from terrorism. The 1993 bombing attack on the World Trade Center in New York was a clear indication that the United States was not only subject to real and lethal attacks by domestic terrorist groups, but was subject to attack from international terrorist groups. The bomb used in this attack was the largest homemade bomb seen in the United States at that time and consisted of approximately 1200 pounds of explosives. Six people were killed and over 100 injured by the attack. Both international and domestic terrorism are now major threats to the security of the United States. The events of 9/11 and the Alfred P. Murrah Federal Building bombing suggest that America is not as safe as many have assumed. Groups such as the Branch Davidians, Montana Militia, and the discovery of sleeper cells of international terrorist such as Hamas, Hezbollah, and Al Qaeda are major concerns for law enforcement in the United States. The front line of defense against terrorism has and will always be local law enforcement.

The United States is a primary target of modern terrorist, whether domestic or international, right-wing or left-wing, and must develop tactics and strategies that will effectively address this threat. This chapter will present investigative techniques that apply to terrorism and discuss the law, statues, and legislation that have evolved due to the modern terrorist threat. Local, state, and federal units and task forces are now in place along with the creation of the Department of Homeland Security and over 15 agencies that collect and disseminate intelligence information and products that support terrorist investigations. Although modern technology has greatly improved the ability of law enforcement to address terrorism, the competent investigator will always play the major role along in addition to the intelligence function to effectively and successfully combating terrorism. Local law enforcement and first responders are ultimately responsible for the threat of terrorism and will be the first line of defense of any plan to combat terrorism. The chapter concludes with a discussion of future trends of terrorist activity and strategies of response to modern terrorism.

Antiterrorism and Counterterrorism Strategies

Terrorism may be described as low cost warfare with the objective to demonstrate the inability of governments, military, and law enforcement to protect the homeland. Terrorist have operated covertly while engaging in countersurveillance, elaborate security, and extensive long term planning to carry out their operations. The two major strategies to address terrorism are antiterrorism and counterterrorism. Counterterrorism includes the practices, tactics, techniques, and strategies that governments, militaries, and a number of other groups use to address terrorism. The concept includes groups form a number of levels of society such as businesses that have security plans and units, local police, firefighters, and emergency first responders. These entities engage terrorist and prevent attacks. The majority of counterterrorism operations that are tactical are conducted by state, federal and national law enforcement agencies. The intelligence function may involve covert surveillance by signal intelligence, satellite intelligence (GEOINT or SATINT), human intelligence (HUMINT), and electronic intelligence (ELINT).

Antiterrorism examines the concept of terrorism and attempts to understand and articulate what constitutes terrorism. This results in antiterrorism legislation and suggests diplomatic and less confrontational methods than counterterrorism (encyclopedia. the freedictionary.com, 2009). Antiterrorism techniques include focusing on crime-prevention and target hardening security measures. Antiterrorism is defensive and is aimed at reducing the chance of an attack by terrorist groups or individuals. Intelligence analysis and planning by law enforcement are critical to antiterrorism strategies: collecting and analyzing information to produce intelligence products or actionable intelligence, analyzing target vulnerabilities, and developing strategies and techniques for preventing destruction by terrorist acts. Antiterrorism planning includes the three dimensions of operations security, physical security, and personnel security. Proactive measures and threat analysis are two components of the planning cycle. Target hardening produces security measures that make it more difficult for a terrorist group to obtain information on the target and attack or penetrate the target. Targets (hard and soft) may include airports, dams, bridges, locations of gathering of large numbers of people, and nuclear plants. Billions of dollars are now being spent on security measures and target hardening.

Counterterrorism techniques involved responding to specific terrorist attacks. Counterterrorism techniques are designed to deny an opponent the use of terrorist tactics and may prevent, deter, preempt, and respond to terrorism. Counterterrorism units are created, trained, and equipped to respond anytime and anywhere to any type of attack by a terrorist group. Critical targets that must be considered when planning counterterrorism and antiterrorism strategies include the nation's water supply, telecommunications, the financial infrastructure, power plants, oil and gas distribution and storage centers and transportation. Units may have to respond to hijackings, hostage incident, bombings, chemical, biological, or nuclear attacks, armed assaults or active shooters, assassinations, and kidnappings. Biological agents may be bacteria, toxins, viruses or rickettsia, nuclear attacks may include bombs or devices that disperse radiological agents, and chemical agents may be nerve gases, irritating agents, blister agents, and etc. (Baker, 2005). The counterterrorism units face a variety of threats and must be trained and equipped for any of these types of attacks. The magnitude of threats and number of targets mandates that local, state, the private sector, and federal resources be coordinated to form efficient and effective antiterrorism and counterterrorism strategies. A proactive response by the United States in underway to identify and interdict the activities of terrorist. Cases such as the 1993 arrest of the New York City World Trade Center bomb conspirators demonstrate that terrorist acts can be prevented with proactive intelligence and interdiction. However, there will be another attack and units must continue to be prepared to respond.

Intelligence, the First Line of Defense

The 1993 bombing attack on the World Trade Center was the impetus that demonstrated the real and lethal threat of terrorism in the United States by international terrorist groups. The FBI's response was to augment its Counterterrorism Program by committing additional resources, including reallocation of personnel, conducting counterterrorism training, refining collection and analysis techniques, and enhancing cooperation within national and international law enforcement and intelligence communities. After the events of 9/11 that resulted in the lost of almost 3000 lives and an enormous economic and psychological impact on the United States, for the second time is less than a decade, the failure of the intelligence community resulted in calls for strengthening the intelligence function. Members of law enforcement and intelligence experts concluded that the sharing of intelligence must be coordinated and developed the National Criminal Intelligence Sharing Plan. The vision was to develop a model intelligence sharing plan to promote intelligence-led policing. Recognizing that the key to combating terrorism is with local and state law enforcement and the intelligence they can provide has led to a more united effort between state, local and federal agencies. This plan was to be a blueprint for administrators to follow to build an intelligence system than would result in sharing of vital information among federal, state, and local entities. This plan called for increased availability of information, establishing minimum criminal intelligence training standards, and ensuring that all law enforcement is involved at some level of the intelligence function.

To prevent events such as 9/11 or the Murrah Federal Building bombing, the intelligence community cannot fail again and must produce sound, professional analytic products that are shared by law enforcement entities that are proactive in preventing or intervening in terrorist plots to attack the United States. The vision was to promote a policy of openness in communication with the public and all interested parties regarding the criminal intelligence process, when it does not affect the security and integrity of the process. The plan called for the partnership with public and private sectors to be able to detect and prevent attacks against the nation's critical infrastructures. The International Association of Law Enforcement Intelligence Analyst (IALEIA) has developed minimum standards for intelligence analysis to ensure that intelligence products are accurate, timely, factual, and relevant and include recommendation for implementing policy and actions. The twenty seven recommendations of the plan are not all accomplished, but progress has been made (The National Criminal Intelligence Sharing Plan, 2005). The vital importance of human intelligence has been rediscovered and the intelligence community no longer relies on technical intelligence (signal and image intelligence) to conduct anti- and counter-intelligence operations. The transformation of the FBI into an organization that focuses on collecting domestic intelligence has been a challenge. The priority of the FBI is now protecting the United States by preventing additional attacks. It has strengthened its intelligence function and created partnerships with local, state, federal, and international entities and law enforcement that enhance its ability to collect intelligence and produce intelligence products that have application.

Civil aviation security that was in place at the time of 9/11 was composed of seven layers of defense that included the following:

- Intelligence
- Passenger prescreening
- Airport access control
- Passenger checkpoint screening
- Passenger checked baggage screening
- Cargo screening
- On-board security

Intelligence was the first layer of defense but FAA was not a member of the intelligence community. The agency had a civil aviation intelligence division that was a collection point for information from a number of intelligence agencies including the FBI, CIA, State Department and had officers assigned as liaison to these agencies, but none to the National Security Agency or the Defense Intelligence Agency. The International Criminal Police Organization (Interpol) is a clearinghouse for information worldwide and produces intelligence from information collected by member nations. The U.S. has a representative assigned to Interpol which allows sharing intelligence to U.S entities such as FAA. Al Qaeda conducted surveillance and studied the tactics and techniques needed to succeed in the 9/11 events.

The conclusion of the 9/11 commission was that the intelligence function failed to stop the terrorist actions or produce actionable intelligence; there were missed clues, failure to connect the "dots", and a lack of coordination between law enforcement due mainly to "turf" wars. The National Criminal Intelligence Sharing Plan identified a lack of sharing intelligence among state, local, and federal agencies and the Homeland Security Act of 2002 mandated new procedures for sharing classified information. At present over 6000 state and local have access to classified material involving terrorist threats and federal agencies now are sharing more information that prior to 9/11. Two major obstacles to intelligence sharing have been deconfliction (eliminating rules and jurisdictional problems that inhibit sharing of information) and interoperability (compatibility of information systems to communicate). Communication among state, local, and federal agencies is now the priority of the intelligence community and the importance of actionable intelligence in now recognized by law enforcement throughout the United States.

All source analysis centers have now been resourced and restructured to address the modern threats of terrorism. The Counter Terrorism Center of the CIA, the FBI, State

Department's Bureau of Intelligence Research, the Defense Intelligence Agency's Joint Intelligence Task Force Combating Terrorism now focus not only on tactical overseas operations, but are more focused on strategic analysis that addresses threats to the United States. The following are among the recommendations of a number of committees including the 9/11 Commission that is being implemented:

- Review and coordination of relationships among the members of the intelligence community including foreign intelligence and law enforcement
- Consistent priorities for the collection, analysis, and dissemination of intelligence throughout the intelligence community
- Moving personnel between elements of the intelligence community
- Develop human intelligence and sources that penetrate terrorist organizations and networks both overseas and within the United States
- Strengthen counterterrorism within the FBI including field offices and develop career tracks that provide incentives for skills demonstrated by counterterrorism agents and analyst (The 9/11 Investigations, 2004)

These and a significant number of recommendations were made by 9/11 investigative committees that mandated change throughout the intelligence community. Improvement in the cooperation, training, and skills of state, local and federal agencies has improved, but there is still room for improvement. There have been a number of counterterrorism successes even before the event of 9/11 based on intelligence and criminal investigations. The FBI created the Counterterrorism Center in the 1990's and an exchange program between the FBI and the CIA in 1996. A number of plots were indentified and prevented and arrest and conviction occurred in other events: the world trade center bombing in 1993, the landmarks plot in 1993 labeled the "Day of Terror" that was a plot to blow up the Lincoln and Holland Tunnels in New York, the George Washington Bridge, the United Nations and the New York FBI office, the 1999 Millennium plot against the Los Angeles International Airport, Manila Airlines 1995 plot to blow 12 airplanes bound for the United States, the Khobar Towers bombings investigations, and the U.S.S. Cole Bombing in 2000.

However, the FBI determined that solving cases was not enough and shifted its priorities to a preventive posture by the late 1990's that focused on intelligence collection and analysis, counterterrorism training, information technology, and requiring counterterrorism capacity in all 56 field offices. The agency has now allocated more agents to terrorism and less to other types of criminal activity including drug enforcement. The FBI's Joint Terrorism Task Forces are the primary means for sharing counterterrorism information with state and local law enforcement. Members are from local and state law enforcement and other federal agencies that work as a team to address terrorism and share intelligence information. However, many state and local entities in the 1990's reported that they have not gained much from have a officer/agent assigned to this task force. The agency also struggled with improvement of its networks, systems and software. An additional impairment to the intelligence function has been the Foreign Intelligence Surveillance Act (FISA) that imposed a stringent barrier between the FBI and criminal prosecutors. The approval for electronic surveillance under FISA is slow and long, but efforts are being made to improve the process. The Church Commission was aimed at limiting the spying on American citizen by the National Security Agency, the FBI, and the Central Intelligence Agency.

In 1978 the Foreign Intelligence Surveillance Act was passed by Congress. The Act established a secret Foreign Intelligence Surveillance Court that approves or denies domestic surveillance in regards to national security. The Act protected civil liberties during the gathering of foreign intelligence within the U.S. borders. The Act required that Intelligence agencies establish cause before the court before conducting domestic surveillance that involved nation security. Agencies must follow specific guidelines to qualify for FISA warrants which were reviewed by the FISA court. FISA limited spying to foreign powers and their agents and was not intended to address domestic law enforcement investigations (Bamford, 2006). In 1980 the U.S. Congress passed the Intelligence Authorization Act that was designed to make the intelligence community fiscally accountable for their actions.

The USA Patriot Act has provided additional tools for the FBI and has removed a number of obstacles that hindered the intelligence investigations. In 2003 the FBI established the position of the Executive Assistant Director for Intelligence and made the intelligence function a priority of the agency. FBI analyst now are offered benefits and opportunities comparable to positions in other intelligence agencies and as a result of these changes the agency has now developed the strategic analytic capability recommended by the 9/11 Commission. The agency integrated with the CIA's counterterrorism center and the Terrorist Threat Integration Center. The FBI appears to have taken a more active role in the intelligence community (The 9/11 Investigations, 2004). Information sharing remains a goal of all law enforcement in the United States and with the implementation of strategies such as intelligence-led policing and participation of state and local law enforcement in task forces the future of developing actionable intelligence appears bright. For a more detailed discussion of the role of intelligence in the war on terror, see chapter 13.

The Department of Homeland Security

President Bush signed Executive Order 13228 in October of 2001 that established the Department of Homeland Security (DHS). It was established to consolidate domestic security agencies to coordinate anti-terrorism and respond to major disasters, natural and manmade. The agency consists of 22 agencies and is under the authority of the Secretary of Homeland Security who answers to the President of the United States. These agencies include FEMA, the U.S. Coast Guard, Immigration and Customs Enforcement, The U.S. Secret Service, the Transportation Security Administration and a number of other entities. It is now the largest U.S. Government entity ever created. The question of its efficiency and effectiveness is one that will be answered in the near future.

The challenge of overseeing the activities of such a large bureaucracy is one that will require exceptional leadership and resources. DHS operates an awards free equipment program (Commercial Equipment Direct Assistance Program) for local police departments. The goals of the program include communications interoperability, intelligence sharing among law enforcement, and equipment needed to respond to a major disaster. The government recognizes the fact that local and regional response in required in any major disaster. This Executive order was the most significant restructuring of federal law enforcement since the establishment of federal agencies. The structure of DHS includes a number of agencies:

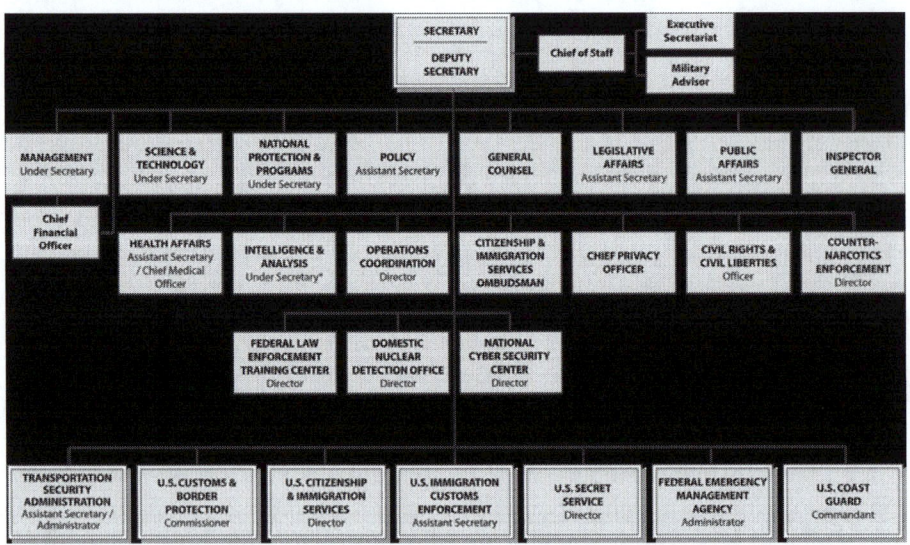

Source: Department of Homeland Security, www.dhs.gov

The government of the United States in now implementing the leadership model of managing for performance or results management. This model shifts the focus from inputs, processes and outputs to results measured by the twin elements of production of efficiency and effectiveness and the concept of accountability. The national vision is to make the United States more secure by effective leadership with accountability. The National Strategy for Homeland Security defined the mission and goals of the government. The strategy listed six critical mission areas to address prevention, vulnerability, response and recovery:

- Intelligence and warning designed to prevent and prepared for an attack
- Protection of the infrastructure
- Develop a defense against catastrophic threats including biological, radiological, and nuclear events
- Identify and prevent domestic terrorism and their sources of support
- Develop an efficient and effective border and transportation security
- Develop a national system for emergency preparedness and response

The National Strategy includes the security of cyberspace, a plan to address money laundering, and a plan to strengthen security and go on the offense at home and abroad to combat terrorism. The strategy suggests four foundations that support the six goals: science and technology, information sharing, international cooperation, and law (Office of Homeland Security, 2002). To address the issues of homeland security that include prevention, reducing vulnerability and response and recovery, the Homeland Security Act of 2002 created the Department of Homeland Security (DHS). The department is charged with combating terrorism and the threats they posed to domestic targets. The concept includes preparing the nation for any major disaster or emergency.

The mission of the DHS is to develop and coordinate the implementation of a comprehensive national strategy to secure the United States from terrorist threats or attacks. The agency has developed a plan to detect and prevent terrorist attacks and has established goals to accomplish this mission. Among the goals is security of the U.S. borders, information sharing among all law enforcement and partners, protection of the U.S. infrastructure, improvement of port security, and to become more prepared for catastrophic events. The Federal Emergency Management Agency (FEMA) is among the agencies now under the DHS. Signed into law in November, 1988, FEMA has authority for most Federal disaster response activities including terrorist attacks. It became part of the DHS in March, 2003 with the primary mission to reduce the loss of life and property and protect the Nation from all hazards, including natural disaster and acts of terrorism by leading and supporting the Nation in a risk-based, comprehensive emergency management system of preparedness, protection, response, recovery, and mitigation. FEMA has over 2600 full time employees and partners with local emergency management agencies, 27 federal agencies and the American Red Cross. The agency also has approximately 400 standby disaster assistance employees who are available for deployment after disasters (www.fema.gov). The FBI is the lead Federal agency that responses to acts of domestic terrorism.

The National Law Enforcement Telecommunications System (NLETS) has been the central means of domestic law enforcement communication. However the system is not without its problems and as a result the National Plan has created the fusion center as a means to collect all available data that concerns terrorism and make this information available to all agencies.

The development of fusions centers in all states is a goal of DHS. These centers are as a mechanism for exchanging information and intelligence, analysis of information, and providing resources to prevent acts of terrorism and other threats to public safety. These centers process information from all possible sources in the states into actionable intelligence and serve as a location for the exchange of intelligence among law enforcement at the state and federal level. The Mississippi Analysis and Information Center is an example of the establishment of these centers in all states in the U.S. It serves as an integrated multi-discipline sharing network to maximize public safety agencies ability to detect, prevent,, apprehend and respond to criminal and terrorist activity. It serves to reduce duplication of effort by agencies or departments and supports intelligence led policing and national security strategies/initiatives designed to protect critical infrastructure and the public (msaic@mdps.state.ms.us).

Each state has now established an Office of Homeland Security. The purpose of these departments is the protection of citizens and property from both foreign and domestic attacks by terrorist. They are also tasked with recovery from any man made or natural disaster/attack. A coordinated effort between law enforcement and first responders is the responsibility of the offices. Part of the job of these departments is to inform and educate the public to become vigilant and prepared for any disaster. The department encourages the public to provide any information that may be related terrorist activity (www.homelandsecurity.ms.gov). In addition to creating DHS and the Federal response, a number of statues, legislation, and laws are critical to the investigation and combating terrorism.

Major Statutes, Legislation, and Laws that apply to Terrorist Investigations

There are no investigative techniques that are used to investigate groups or individuals such as those of transnational organized crime that cannot be used against terrorist. Modern terrorist may now be motivated by greed and financial gain rather than ideology and political agendas. Terrorist often study the enemy (law enforcement) and develop techniques to avoid detection and apprehension. The terrorist organizations may be very security focused as are many in organized crime and offer a challenge for law enforcement investigators. Terrorist organizations have layers of leadership that are well insulated and are involved in planning but not in carrying out operations. Businesses and individuals who support terrorist organizations by financial or other means are insulated as are the leaders and not subjected to arrest and prosecution under laws that address traditional crimes such as murder, assault, kidnapping, and hijacking. The following discussion involves statutes, legislation, and laws that were designed to address organized crime, but have been found to be successful in the arrest and prosecution of terrorist. The U.S. is now challenged by how to prosecute terrorist and enemy combatants. The following is a list and explanation of how this may be accomplished using the legislation that was successful against organized crime leaders and those who supported organized crime or were corrupted by these organizations. All terrorist activity involves criminal acts or conspiracy to commit these acts. Terrorist are criminals and are subject to the innovative statues, laws, and legislation that can address modern terrorism.

Presidential Commissions and the U.S. Congress concluded in the late 1960s that laws that existed were not adequate for addressing the complex organizations that were operating similar to business entities insulating their leaders and assets from traditional law enforcement methods. Major legislative actions increased the ability of law enforcement to address the complex and dynamic nature transnational organized crime. The Crime Control Act of 1968 allowed authorities to conduct electronic surveillance at the state and federal levels. In 1970, the Organized Crime Control Act enhanced grand jury powers and allowed more authority to protect and secure witnesses. The Racketeer Influenced and Corrupt Organization Statute of 1970 addressed the racketeering activity and funds gained through such activity.

The 1986 Money Laundering Act (18 USC 1956 and 18 USC 1957) made it a Federal crime to launder money. The Money Laundering Prosecution Improvement Act of 1988 allowed financial institutions to readily identify persons purchasing checks and money orders and added special reporting requirements to these institutions. Both state and federal governments created conspiracy statutes that enhanced the ability to prosecute leader of organized crime. The Continuing Criminal Enterprise (CCE) Statute was directed at major drug traffickers as was the Foreign Narcotics Kingpin Act of 1999 that applied to major foreign drug trafficking and provided extraordinary sanctions to them and their organizations worldwide. Acts were addressed at drug trafficking, which remains the major profit producer for terrorist groups worldwide. These acts followed controlled substances statutes passed in the 1970s by federal and state governments. Many other laws may be employed by law enforcement to establish major cases against leaders of terrorist groups, their organizations, and assets. This following will list and examine these laws and the elements needed to establish a prosecutable case or seize assets of major criminal organizations. It is critical to not only identify the "labeled" criminal element/enterprise and its activities, but also to establish the role of the upper world (corrupt business, government, and law enforcement) and seize their assets as well as prosecute them for their role in terrorist operations.

The Hobbs Act and Extortion

Perhaps one of the earliest statutes to deal with activity associated with complex crime was the Hobbs Act (18 USC 1951-1955). This act made it a federal crime to obstruct or interfere with interstate commerce. This is often accomplished by extortion, (payment of money or other reward for avoiding harm or subjection to harassment) usually requiring paying a "street tax" to continue to operate a business (legal or illegal), or by robbery. The act also makes it a crime to travel or use interstate facilities (telephones, computers, mail, etc.) to aid illegal activity. The Hobbs Act has been used to prosecute union officials who obtain kickbacks (a reward for using or buying a particular service or product), fees, loans, or any money or reward for using their influence on the unions or people they represent. Violation of the act can result in fines and up to twenty years incarceration. Property is "extorted" under law by the Hobbs Act, when a public official agrees that his official conduct will be controlled as promised or paid to do so. Extortion is also referred to as blackmail, as is common practice of organized crime to infiltrate legitimate businesses. Extortion is a means to obtain property by way of threats or intimidation. Extortion may also be defined as obtaining property from another, with his consent by use of force, fear, or under color of official right. Under color of official right, violation of the Hobbs Act is a fine of $10,000 and up to three years in prison. The Hobbs Act was a useful tool against organized crime but is often not used due to more effective statutes such as RICO or Conspiracy. Violation of the Hobbs Act can be a tool for the investigation of terrorism as it was for organized crime. Modern terrorism is dynamic and often linked to the type of violations covered by the Hobbs Act.

RICO

There are no other statues used to address organized crime, complex criminal activity such as terrorism, and white collar crime that have caused as much controversy and discussion as the Racketeer and Corrupt Organization Statute (RICO), 18 USC 1961-1965. G. Robert Blakey, known as the "father of RICO", in 1986 expressed concerns that there was no applicable definition of organized crime (OC), racket or racketeering. He wrote that the legal attempts to define organized crime were constitutionally vague and may violate the constitutional right to associate or assemble, and the rights of due process or equal protection. His concerns remain an issue for some in today's society and are still debated; RICO is attacked for being too vague, double jeopardy, Eight Amendment violations, and due process rights, including speedy trial and right to counsel of choice. Many applaud its use while others call for restriction or elimination of the statute of 1970. The Patriot Act of 2001 is perhaps the only Act to become more controversial. Before RICO, prosecution of major crime bosses was difficult at best due to their employment of underlings to carry out the criminal acts. This insulated them from identification and prosecution. This level on insulation occurs within terrorist groups as it does with organized crime groups. Rather than proving criminal agreement (conspiracy) or committing a specific crime, RICO allows for prosecution of a pattern of crimes that are committed through an organization referred to in the statute as an enterprise. RICO makes it a crime to acquire, receive income from, or operate an enterprise through a pattern of racketeering. Patterns of criminal acts committed by direct and indirect participants in criminal enterprises can be prosecuted. Some believe this statute leads to prosecution of criminals who are not organized crime and that the statute is vague or too broad. RICO can certainly be applied to terrorist operations who receive funds by means of criminal activity and used these funds to resource their operations. As part of the 1970 Organized Crime Control Act, RICO or Title IX, defines thirty-two "predicate offenses" that can be classified as racketeering activities for profit by organized crime. Not only does the statute have punishment of twenty years in prison and a fine of $20,000, it also has a civil section. Under both the civil and criminal section, assets derived from racketeering activities can be seized and forfeited. The civil section allows anyone who has been injured in his property or business by racketeering activity to sue responsible parties for triple damages and attorney fees.

Predicate offenses include fraud, Hobbs Act violations, white slavery, drug trafficking, arson, extortion, obstruction of justice, kidnapping, loan sharking, and a number of other offenses. The offenses vary somewhat from state to state in state statutes, but most are very similar in the offenses and elements of the crime. In 1910, the "White Slave Act or the Mann Act was passed to prohibit interstate transportation of women for the purpose of prostitution or any immoral purpose. Today, trafficking of humans, male and female, young and old, is common with both the Chinese Snake heads or Asian organized crime and many Russian groups. Cases, such as U.S. versus Teri in 1980, against traditional organized crime have led to the expansion of Federal RICO to include publication of obscene materials, drug trafficking by street gangs, and police corruption, and even violent anti abortion protest groups. This expansion has caused concern among some in the legal community. Most states now have RICO statutes which have also contributed to the expansion of the RICO prosecutions.

The Act specifically prohibits the following:
1. Using income received from a pattern of racketeering activity or through collection of an unlawful debt to acquire an interest in an enterprise affecting interstate commerce.
2. Acquiring or maintaining, through a pattern of racketeering activity or through collection of an unlawful debt, an interest in an enterprise affecting interstate commerce.
3. Conducting or participating, through a pattern of racketeering, racketeering activity or collection of an unlawful debt, the affairs of an enterprise affecting interstate commerce.
4. Conspiring to participate in any of these activities.

Racketeering activity may include any of the listed predicate acts in the statute. A pattern of racketeering activity includes any two acts of racketeering by a person within ten years of each other (this varies among state statutes; some only require a five year period). The acts do not have to be the same type of violation, but must be related by some criteria, such as motive or purpose, design, etc. The enterprise may be a corporation, association, or group of people or individuals, who have interaction and involved in the activities of the enterprise. This fits the description of any terrorist organization and specifically those that have a link to criminal organizations (see Chapter 5, Transnational Organized Crime and Terrorism).

Under RICO, courts can enter restraining orders before conviction to prevent transfer of potentially forfeitable property or assets. A wide range of civil actions are possible under RICO, including divestiture, dissolution, and reorganization. These actions add to the complaints and controversy of RICO. Prosecutors report that RICO statutes have dismantled large operations, such as prostitution rings, that under local or traditional statutes the offenders would be back in business after short sentences while keeping their assets. However, RICO cases do require excessive resources and time to develop and prosecute. RICO does allow the prosecutor to present a complete picture of the organization's activity and allows trials with multiple defendants, where the activity of all is presented to the jury. For the investigator developing a RICO case, it is essential to prove a pattern of racketeering or long term criminal activity and to have the group classified as a criminal enterprise. Many prosecutors and law enforcement have discovered that RICO is not that complex and has been very successful in combating organized crime, terrorism, and white collar crime; the Columbian Cartels, LCN families, and many others were successfully prosecuted under RICO. Another advantage of RICO is that prosecution is allowed in any jurisdiction where overt acts were committed. Presently over 1200 major crime figures have been successfully prosecuted under RICO by State and Federal guidelines. While critics view RICO as a threat to individual rights, it remains the law and has been a frequent tool of many in law enforcements to combat organized crime. The forfeiture provisions allow the government to take away incentive of profit and under civil forfeiture the property can be tried without charging the owner with a crime. Taking assets from terrorist organizations will result in many their operations not being carried out due to lack of resources/money. The war on terrorism has blurred the line between crime and war with a trend of terrorist committing more criminal acts that can be addressed by statues such as the innovative RICO   statue.

Forfeiture

Two type of forfeiture are used to take the assets of criminal organization such as a terrorist group:
- Civil- a legal proceeding against property that was either purchased with profits from illegal activity or used to facilitate a crime; vehicle or aircraft may be seized when used to transport illegal contraband, such as cocaine or marijuana.
- Criminal forfeiture- this requires that the defendant be found guilty of a crime and is ordered to forfeit property or funds related to the crime.

The Federal Comprehensive Forfeiture Act of 1984 enhanced the government's ability to seize assets of drug trafficking organizations such as the Mexican and Columbian DTO's and now terrorist groups that engage in this type of activity for funds to support their operations. Drug trafficking is becoming a major source of funding for terrorist organizations and the nexus of many terrorist groups to transnational organized crime makes them a target for RICO and forfeiture statues. The major advantage of civil forfeiture is that it has allowed a lesser burden of proof (preponderance of the evidence) than criminal forfeiture (beyond a reasonable doubt). Probable cause is needed to seize assets or property, and the rules are the same as with any seized evidence; exceptions for warrants required, etc. Once the property is seized, the burden shifts to the owner to prove the money or property was obtained legally or did not facilitate a crime. One advantage for law enforcement is that hearsay evidence can be used to establish probable cause. However, the U.S. Supreme Court in U.S. versus Real Property, 510 U.S. 43, ruled that real property cannot be seized without notification of the owner and opportunity for the owner to contest the seizure. Another advantage of civil forfeiture, which is in rem rather than in personam; allows the forfeiture of assets even with the acquittal of the owner of criminal activity.

Not only can money or vehicles be seized, but any assets that are proceeds of criminal activity or that have facilitated criminal activity; aircraft, ships, houses, weapons, real property, etc. Terrorism is now a crime under the PATRIOT ACT. Assets that are seized and forfeited are given to law enforcement to supplement their operations; overtime, equipment, training, and property purchases. Defense attorney fees are also subject to forfeiture and have been a hotly debated issue. Criticism of forfeiture surrounds the issues of innocent owners (who are protected by law), excessive punishment such as seizing a yacht for only marijuana traces, and taking vehicles which are necessary for a person to travel to work. The identification of hidden assets and tracing assets to criminal activity can be a long term and complex task. However, under civil forfeiture, it is only necessary to link the owner to drug trafficking in some aspect, then to make the owner prove how the assets were obtained. Taking the profit out of crime and following the money is an excellent strategy for combating organized crime and terrorism.

Violations of the Internal Revenue Code

During the 1960s, tax investigations by the Internal Revenue Service (IRS) produced most of the convictions regarding organized crime. Tax evasion or failing to pay taxes is a common crime of these criminal enterprises. The experience of the author revealed that financial analysis was a major tool for developing cases against major violators. Many organizations and terrorist such as the KKK members do not keep required records and do not file a tax return while spending large sums of money. By examining the target's spending habits and assets acquired, the investigator can establish a tax case. The methods employed by the criminal investigation division of the IRS include network and expenditure schedule, source and application of funds, and the bank deposit methods. These methods result in unexplained or unreported income. The bank deposit method examines bank deposits, cash expenditures and purchases, and any cash on hand. Once the unexplained income is discovered by investigators, the burden shifts to the suspect to prove it was obtained legally.

Money Laundering Laws

Money laundering is always present in major crime activity. It is defined as all activities designed to conceal the existence, nature, and final disposition of funds gained through illicit activities. Money laundering has been a common theme in organized crime since prohibition. Terrorist need to "clean" the illegal funds before they can use these funds to support their operations. The massive amounts of money made by criminal activity presents a challenge for them. They not only need to "clean" the money but protect it from seizure by law enforcement. The process can be as simple as mailing or body transporting cash out of the country or as complex as a bank takeover. The methods are often the same as legal business transactions except the money is obtained illegally.

The President's Commission on organized crime in 1984 made the observation that new phases were occurring in regard to organized crime funds; wire transfers, CTR (Currency Transaction Report), CMIR (Currency and Monetary Instrument Report), "fronts" and shell corporations, bank transfers, etc. The Bank Secrecy Act of 1970 was the first attempt to combat money laundering by organized crime (31 USC 5311-5326). The Act requires financial institutions to file CTR's on all cash transactions of more than $10,000. The CTR's must be filed with the IRS within 15 days of the transaction and the bank or institution must keep copies for 5 years. CMIR's exceeding $10,000 in value that leave or enter the U.S. must be filed. These records assist in tracking cash through the system. In response to these laws, organized crime would make multiple smaller transactions (under $10,000) to avoid the reporting requirement. This practice is referred to as "smurfing" is a violation of 31 USC 5324, known as the Anti-Drug Abuse Act of 1986. The penalty for "smurfing" or structuring for each transaction is 5 years unless the amount exceeds $100,000 in a 12 month period which increases the penalty to a 10 year sentence.

The Right to Privacy Act of 1978 was amended to allow the financial institution to give authorities the name of the suspect or organization, the account number, and the nature of the suspected illegal. Section 1956 of the Money Laundering Act of 1986 deals with violations in a domestic content, and violations that occur when monetary instruments or funds are transported between the U.S. and foreign country. The violator must "knowingly" conduct or attempt to conduct a transaction knowing (or with willful blindness) that the assets involved are proceeds of unlawful activity even if the launder does not know the precise activity. This action must promote "specified unlawful activity" or conceal or disguise the source, origin, location, or ownership of the proceeds or be designed to avoid Federal or State reporting requirements. It should be noted that before the 1986 money laundering act it was not a federal crime to launder money. 18 U.S. 195 7 makes it a violation to engage in monetary transactions in excess of $10,000 with property derived from proceeds of "specified unlawful activity". Both CTR and CMIR violations are predicate acts under RICO. Violations of 1956 are up to 20 years prison term and a fine of up to $500,000 or twice the value of the property involved. Violations of 1957 are up to a 10 year prison term and fine. Title 18 USC 981 and 982 provide for civil and criminal forfeiture, respectively. Other acts that address money laundering include:

1. The Drug Abuse Act 1988 which require off shore banks to record any U.S. cash transfers in excess of $10,000 and to allow government access to the records.

2. The Annunzio-Wylie Money Laundering Act of 1992 and the Money Launder Suppression Act of 1994 are assets to combating money laundering. The Annunzio-Wylie Act makes it a crime to operate a money laundering business, but also protects financial institutions from civil liability when reporting suspicious activity of their customers. The Act requires all financial institutions and gambling enterprises to report suspicious activity.

3. The Money Laundering Prosecution Improvement Act of 1988 required financial institutions to verify the identity of persons who purchase bank checks, traveling checks, or money orders in amounts of $3000 or more. Using these types of instruments was common for drug traffickers. The Act also allowed the government to target certain institutions or geographic area for special reporting requirements (USC Sections 5325-5326).

4. Recently, the USA Patriot Act created in response to terrorism is considered by ABA National Institution on white collar crime to be the broadest money laundering statute on the books. Unlike Sections 1956 and 1957, the statutes do not require listing specific offenses or "specified unlawful activity" (SUA's). Foreign crimes list has expanded to include "bribery of public official", embezzlement and misappropriation, and theft. Although transactions may not have any connection to terrorism, they are included in the Act. The Act is a complement to the Palermo Convention of 2000, which requires extradition of violators who are involved in transnational organized crime or "serious" crime that may include corporate tax violations and fraud occurring in a foreign country such as SUA's money laundering charges (This includes computer fraud). The Act expands the definition of the term "illegal money transmitting business" to include unlicensed businesses and those who transport or transmit illegal proceeds or money intended to promote or support unlawfully activity. The Act allows IRS information or CTRs and CMIRs (Forms 4789, 4790, and Form 8300 Report of Cash Payment over $10,000 received in a trade or business) to be available to law enforcement. Anyone who transports or transmits money by any method is considered subject to this Act.

    All types of major criminal activity for profit require the need for money laundering. The goal is primarily to legitimize income to allow the violator to spend the money without suspicion of criminal involvement. There is the need to get large volumes of cash into the U.S. banking system and to exchange small bulky transactions to make transporting cash less demanding. The money from international or transnational organizations much be delivered to source countries in their currency. The money can then be used to support terrorist operations.

The Money Laundering Cycle

In 1990, the Financial Crimes Enforcement Network (FinCEN) was formed under the Department of Treasury. It functions as an intelligence center for all financial crimes, including those that are linked to terrorism. FinCEN divides money laundering into three stages:

1. Placement: the illegal proceeds placed into the financial system unnoticed or transported outside the United States.
2. Layering: the funds go through a series of financial transactions in such frequency, volume, and complexity that they are difficult to trace and appear to be legitimate financial transactions.
3. Integration: the funds integrated into the economy and appear to be derived from legitimate income. At this stage, the investigation is faced with a major problem of distinguishing illicit from licit funds.

The cash transactions between the suppliers, transportation cells, and users can be considered money laundering violations. Transportation of cash out of the U.S. leaves no paper trail to follow.

Financial institutions are common players in the business of organized crime and terrorist activity:

Western Union, U.S. Banking System, Wire transfer, etc. These are also Black Market exchanges that launder money; casa de Cambio or money exchange houses which convert U.S. dollars to pesos or buy U.S. dollars at a black market rate. Remittance corporations operating as fronts under the guise of an investment company, broker, financial service provider, or check cashing operation receive and transmit illegal funds. The CTR or CMIR will often only reflect the name of the company, not the terrorist group or organization. The money is transmitted through a number of "fronts" before being placed in the violator's account or company and again appears to be legal income. It is not uncommon for funds to go through 15-20 financial institutions, charities, businesses or banks.

Investigators need to be trained in banking and financial procedures to better understand how money is laundered. A key strategy is attacking assets of terrorist organizations. The El Paso Intelligence Center (EPIC) and FinCEN are staffed by personnel from a variety of federal agencies who have access to the Treasury's computer system (TECS II) which has a database of all CTRs, CMIRs, and 8300s. The Multi-Agency Financial Investigative Center (MAFIC) was formed to identify, target, seize, and forfeit any significant assets of major organized crime figures. The FBI uses software that can trace financial transactions that can identify front organizations, safe houses, weapons storage locations, travel routes, stash houses, and financial entities that support terrorist operations (Baker, 2005). By following the money the identity and location of individuals and cells can be determined. These agencies have been and continue to be an essential asset in combating money laundering by terrorist organizations.

Controlled Substances Acts

Because drug trafficking has become a major profit producer of terrorism worldwide, acts that address illegal drug distribution may be used to bring terrorist to justice. The Controlled Substance Act is a statute that exists in all U.S. states. The Comprehensive Drug Abuse Prevention and Control Act of 1970, which has been amended to add new substances almost each year, gives Federal Jurisdiction for investigating drug trafficking and provides substantial penalties for violation of the Act. The Act divides substances into five schedules according to their potential for addiction and harm. The procedures for controlling a substance are provided in the Act and requirements for legal distribution of pharmaceuticals are part of most statutes regarding controlled substances, security, records, reporting loss, etc. by pharmacists and the medical profession. Other Acts that supplement this Act include:

1. The 1988 Chemical and Division and Trafficking Act- controls substances known as precursor chemicals needed to produce certain drugs. Records of purchases and transactions of these precursors are required by the Act to allow investigators to trace these products to clandestine laboratories that produce or manufacture illegal drugs.

2. The Comprehensive Crime Control Act of 1984 and the Anti-Drug Abuse Act of 1986- enhanced prison sentences for specific drug offenses.

Other drug abuse Acts and amendments have been directed at the demand side of the equation; penalties for using drugs and loss of license to drive, etc. Drug enforcement can be major strategy against terrorism.

Conspiracy Statutes

The term conspiracy is essentially the essence of organized criminal activity including terrorism. Conspiracy is an unlawful agreement by two or more persons to violate the law or to conduct a legal act by illegal means. The success of the conspiracy is not necessary for conviction of the charge, and the conspiracy charge is distinct and separate from the substantive crime that was the goal of the conspiracy. Most states and the Federal government have conspiracy laws with substantial penalties. Most prosecutors desire or require overt acts (any act that further the objective of the conspiracy which may be a lawful or unlawful act). Overt acts need not be known by all participants. The conspiracy or agreement may be established by any contrivance, either impliedly or tacitly, for two or more persons to come to a common understanding to violate a law. Conspiracy laws have many advantages for case development and include the following:

1. Conspirators do not have to know each other.
2. Each is responsible for the actions of the others (Pinkerton Theory).
3. All are agents for each other.
4. Conspirators do not have to be aware of the actions of others.
5. Anything done to carry out the objective of the conspiracy is an overt act.
6. Overt Acts need not be criminal in nature.
7. Over acts need not be known by all participants.

8. Any act or statement by one conspirator can be used in court against all other conspirators.
9. All conspirators may be responsible for the substantive crimes of their co-conspirators provided
   a. they were in the conspiracy at the time the offense was committed,
   b. the offense was committed in furtherance of the conspiracy, and
   c. the offense was a foreseeable consequence of the conspiracy.
10. Venue lies in any jurisdiction in which an overt act occurred or where the agreement was made.
11. The conspirator must do something affirmative to withdraw from the conspiracy such as inform the police about the conspiracy and inform known co-conspirators of their intention to withdraw.
12. The statute of limitations normally runs five years from the last overt act or when the conspiracy ends (varies between states).
13. The case can eliminate the entire criminal organization.
14. Evidence against one defendant is evidence against all.
15. Exception to the hearsay rule where a defendant can testify concerning statements, deeds, or actions of the co-conspirators.
16. Asset forfeiture laws apply to drug conspiracy cases.

The disadvantage of a conspiracy includes long term involvement to gather evidence, which is likely to be manpower intensive. In major investigations, extensive surveillance is conducted and testimony of witnesses needs to be verified and corroborated, which again requires time and manpower. Multiple venues encountered in terrorism investigations often pose political and logistical problems.

Although conspiracy investigations are complex, they are much simpler to develop and understand that such offenses as RICO and money laundering cases. This type of case allows prosecution of leaders of terrorist groups even with a level of insulation of subordinates and the fact that leaders remain in a foreign country, never entering the U.S. where the objective of the conspiracy is reached. Statutes, such as RICO, have an offense of conspiracy to violate RICO. It should be noted that mere association or knowledge of the existence of the conspiracy does not constitute joining.

The types of conspiracies developed by organized crime activity and terrorist activity include:
1. Historical- the object of the conspiracy has already been met. Investigators must locate witnesses, conduct warrants for physical evidence, including documents, and use informants to produce a case of this nature. Again, the goal is to prove the agreement to violate the law existed.
2. Ongoing- conspiracy still exists while it is being investigated.
3. Chain- all members are connected, yet only by some members interact with the others:

A------------B----------C----------D----------E

Chain conspiracy

In the chain conspiracy, not all members know each other and no single member knows all members. In the above diagram, A and B make the agreement to violate the laws and

C, D, and E carry out overt acts where E and D do not interact with A and B and C only interacts with B and D and etc.

4. Wheel- like the spokes of a wagon wheel, the area between the spokes interacts with certain members. Although all are connected, only some of the links or members interact with others: Wheel Conspiracies are also called cell structures or compartmentalization and are common in terrorist and organized crime groups. The group may be referred to as a sleeper cell in a terrorist group when they are dormant waiting for instructions to carry out their mission or objective.

5. Combination Wheel and Chain Conspiracies- occur when members of the wheel and chain frequently interact for operational purposes and are part of the same objective in the overall conspiracy:

Conspiracy Case Development

The development of a conspiracy case results in a wide variety of investigative techniques and methods. The investigator must be well trained in these methods and be allowed time and resources to conduct such complex and long term cases. The following are some of the methods frequently used to develop conspiracy cases:

1. Management and Development of Informants
2. Title III Investigations and Electronic Surveillance
3. Mail Covers
4. Photo Spreads and Line Ups or Show Ups
5. Use of Grand Jury Testimony and Immunity of Witnesses
6. Physical Surveillance
7. Asset or Financial Investigations
8. Undercover Operations
9. Trash Runs
10. Search Warrants for Documents
11. Grand Jury Subpoenas or Investigative Grand Juries
12. Analytical and Intelligence Support
13. Testimony of Co-Conspirators

Conspiracy cases have been praised by Federal and State prosecutors and investigators as a valuable tool against organized crime and terrorist activity. The penalty for violations is normally the same as if the object of the conspiracy had been completed.

Continuing Criminal Enterprise (CCE)

The CCE statute (21 USC 848) was enacted as part of the Comprehensive Drug Abuse Prevention and Control Act of 1970. The author's experience suggest that nothing puts fear in a violator or defense council as that of the possibility of a CCE conviction; most often the violator ask to cooperate and provide information in exchange for a lesser charge. The statute is directed as any person who occupies a position of organizer, supervisor, or in a position of management in a narcotic producing and distribution enterprise. The minimum sentence under CCE is twenty years with no possibility of parole. The court may impose a life sentence and fines up to $100,000. Additionally, all profits and assets of the operation are subject to forfeiture as prescribed in 21 USC 853.

The elements of the statute are the following:
1. Violate a Federal felony drug offense of the Control Substance Act.
2. The violation is part of a continuing series of violations (three or more related transactions).
3. Be in concert with five or more persons and occupy a position of organizer, supervisor, or position of management.
4. Obtain substantial income from the violations.

The proof of CCE usually involves both direct and circumstantial evidence. This may include evidence of defendant's position in the organization, quantity of drugs involved, and the amount of money that changed hands or lavish personal expenditures without any legitimate source of income. The investigator must demonstrate specific illegal acts that were committed by a defendant to prove CCE.

The Kingpin Act

The Foreign Narcotics Kingpin Designation Act was signed into law in December 1999. It was an Amendment to public law 106-120, Intelligence Authorization Act of FY2000. Modeled after the Specially Designated Narcotics Trafficker (SDNT) program it seeks to expose, isolate, and incapacitate the financial infrastructure of Major Drug Trafficking Organization (DTOs). Sanctions such as denying major traffickers and their businesses access to the U.S. financial system and prohibiting U.S. citizens and companies from conducting business with them are major parts of the Act. The U.S. government now prohibits companies for dealing with countries that sponsor or support terrorist.

Electronic Surveillance

The Federal government and states have authorized enforcement to intercept telephone conversations and electronic communications and record them for presentation as evidence at trials. Title III of the Omnibus Crime Control Act (18 USC 2510-2520) authorized Federal law enforcement to eavesdrop on suspects when authorized by a warrant. Most states have similar statutes. The Electronic Communications Privacy Act of 1987 expanded electronic surveillance to include cellular telephones and electronic mail. Normally, before a "wiretap" is started, computerized pen registers (records of numbers of outgoing calls) and the trap and trace (records of number of incoming calls) are placed on communication devices to help establish probably cause that the communication device is being used by suspects to conduct criminal business. The pen register and trap and trace capability is now one computerized device that prints out the results and can print out a link analysis of the calls, e-mails, or communication exchanges (location, time and length of call, and identification of callers). The government is allowed under FISA guidelines to conduct domestic electronic surveillance when there a threat against national security. Advanced software programs are now in place that can decode conversation and electronically transmitted messages such as email. Echelon is a program used by the NSA to capture and analyze telephone calls, faxes, and any type of telecommunication messages. The program has the ability to search descriptors, code words, and phrases in addition to the capability of voice recognition. The FBI with court authorization uses the Carnivore program to intercept e-mail and electronic communication.

The USA PATRIOT ACT

The act was signed into law by President Bush in October, 2001. The act is view by law enforcement as a significant improvement in the ability to combat terrorism. The act allows tools that have been used to investigate organized crime and drug trafficking. The act updated the law in regard to new technology and the threat of modern terrorism. It has allowed for the improved sharing of information and intelligence between state, local and federal agencies. The act was renewed in 2006 and has strengthened border security.

The Patriot Act of 2001 has enhanced the ability of Federal agencies to share criminal information obtained by electronic surveillance. This includes contents of foreign intelligence and counter intelligence obtained by National Security Agency (NSA) or Central Intelligence Agency (CIA) and any Federal agency. Prior to the Patriot Act, Federal law enforcement had very limited authority to delay notification of "sneak and peak" searches. The Act expands this to "reasonable cause" showing of adverse impact on the investigation. Title III authorizes covert entry to install interception devices such as "bugs" (a transmitter that picks up conversations in a room or area). Without court approval or an extension, the target of the intercept must be notified of the wire tape within 90 days after the termination of the court ordered intercept. Most orders for electronic surveillance are for 30 days unless extended.

The Patriot Act clarified that law enforcement can use Title III trap and trace and pen registers on computer networks. The Act also made possible a warrant that, once issued, was legal on any communication device a target used and in any jurisdiction he traveled (Roaming Wiretap). This type of warrant has been used prior to the Patriot Act in major drug investigations.

The requirements to obtain an electronic intercept include:
1. Probable cause that a crime is being committed or about to be committed by the target and that the crime is an offense under Title III.
2. All other investigative methods have failed or will not provide the evidence to succeed in the goals or objective of the investigation.
3. Probable cause exists that the intercept will provide the communication evidence sought.
4. Probable cause that the area or device is being used or will be used by the target or targets to violate a particular law.

These types of investigations are extremely manpower and time intensive and can be complex, requiring special equipment. Most departments cannot support an intercept operation. Training is also required of investigators to use equipment and gain knowledge of the rules and limitations. The equipment must be monitored for 24 hours a day, and monitoring is discontinued when communication is privileged, not covered by the court order or not related to an offense. There is also the possibility that no valuable communication evidence will be recorded despite the effort and expense. As communication becomes more "high tech", new equipment and training become necessary to intercept (Digital and cellular phones, e-mail, etc.). For these reasons, electronic surveillance can be problematic, even though it can produce evidence needed to charge RICO, money laundering, and conspiracy during terrorist investigations.

Investigative Grand Juries

Federal and State prosecutors have had success with the investigative grand jury concept. These juries have the authority to subpoena testimony and documents, grant immunity, and remain in session long term to allow a complete investigation while maintaining secrecy. Refusal to honor a subpoena results in punishment. The testimony of reluctant persons can be compelled upon a grant of immunity from prosecution. Two types of immunity are possible:
1. Derivative Use Immunity- prohibits the information provided by the witness from being used against them. However, if evidence of a crime is developed independent of the testimony, the witness can be prosecuted.
2. Transactional Immunity- this is broad and prohibits prosecution from the crime or criminal act they are testifying about.

The Witness Security Program (WITSEC) implemented in 1971 has benefited major crime investigation and encouraged testimony without fear of retaliation. The program gives a new identity to witnesses and places them in a secure location with lifetime protection. The program has been successful in protecting essential organized crime witnesses and may prove to be an effective tool to encourage terrorist who are normally not cooperative to become sources of information and give testimony.

Other Statutes Frequently Used During Major Criminal Investigations

1. 18 USC 4- misprision of felony
2. 18 USC 111- assaulting, resisting, or impeding federal officers
3. 18 USC 924 (c)- use or possession of a firearm during and in relation to drug trafficking offenses
4. 18 USC 1071- concealing person from arrest
5. 18 USC 1073- flight to avoid prosecution or giving testimony
6. 18 USC 1341- mail fraud
7. 18 USC 1503- influencing or injuring an officer or jury
8. 18 USC 1503- influencing a juror by writing
9. 18 USC 1510- obstruction of a criminal investigation
10. 18 USC 1511- obstruction of state or local law enforcement
11. 18 USC 1512- tampering with a witness, victim, or informant
12. 18 USC 1513- retaliating against a witness, victim, or informant
13. 18 USC 1542- false statement in application of a passport
14. 18 USC 1543- forgery or false use of a passport
15. 18 USC 1952- interstate and foreign travel or transportation in aid of racketeering enterprise (ITAR)

16. 18 USC 1621- perjury
17. 21 USC 843 (b)- use of a communication facility to facilitate a drug crime (known as phone counts)

Most indictments include a number of these statutes and are fairly easy to develop. It is obvious that terrorist activity includes violations of all of these statutes.

Application of Traditional Investigative Techniques to Terrorism Investigations

The acts of terrorist are criminal acts that include murder, bank robbery, human trafficking, arms trafficking, drug trafficking, kidnapping, assault, arson, bombings, assassinations, hijackings, and hostage incidents. The law enforcement community in the United States has never had better methods and techniques to address these and other crimes committed by terrorist. In addition to the laws and statues discussed previously, law enforcement has technology and techniques that have produced numerous arrest and conviction of leadership of major criminal enterprises including terrorist organizations. The FBI has shifted their efforts from methodically building airtight cases against perpetrators of crime to preventing future terrorist plots. The agency made the decision to sacrifice prosecutions and uncovering coconspirators to making prevention the priority. Law enforcement must use every tool available to accomplish this priority (Cloud, 2004). Techniques used to solve traditional criminal cases can be used in terrorism investigations.

One of the most successfully concepts has been the establishment of the task forces. Today there is over 30 terrorism task forces in operation across the United States. The burden of homeland security is with local governments and law enforcement who are the first responders. Terrorist investigations must be well organized and require coordination with a large number of entities. These first responders are now often members of task forces that are trained and equipped to response to crime scenes such as bombings that challenge the most experienced and trained officers. These task forces have been very effective in addressing domestic terrorist groups and are now tasked with the challenge of international terrorist activity.

Terrorist appear to be more concerned with security and have greater knowledge of law enforcement techniques than most criminals that law enforcement traditionally encounters. The Al Qaeda Manual discovered by the Manchester Metropolitan Police during the search of a member of the terrorist organization reveals the extent of knowledge and training given to Al Qaeda members. The manual covers organization requirements, describes missions of the organization and crimes such as destroying bridges, kidnapping, gathering intelligence on targets and law enforcement, espionage, and assassinations. The manual addresses forged documents and describes how cells and individuals avoid detection and apprehension. It goes into detail about security precautions and how to detect surveillance by law enforcement. Means of communication and transportation are covered in the manual along with methods to avoid interception of communication. The subject of obtaining weapons and explosives is covered with emphasis on how to transport and store weapons. The value to law enforcement of the discovery of the manual is apparent. The manual gives insight of the operations of individuals and cells that operate in the United States. Advances in technology have aided criminal investigations tremendously, but the skills, knowledge, and experience of competent investigators remains critical to any criminal investigation.

One skill that is critical to good investigation is the ability to conduct covert surveillance of individuals, groups, and locations. There is no better witness than that of a well trained and experienced investigator. In addition to technical surveillance discussed previously, physical surveillance is often needed to produce a prosecutable case or prevent a terrorist act. However, this type of surveillance like electronic surveillance in manpower intensive and requires considerable skills, equipment, and time and must be done without the surveillance being compromised or detected by the target. Surveillance teams from task forces and state, local, and federal agencies become skilled and are a considerable asset for both antiterrorism and counterterrorism operations. Teams have to deal with counter-surveillance conducted by terrorist groups. The three types of basic physical surveillance are moving, fixed (stationary or picket), and combination surveillance. These methods may be employed 24-7, at specific times and places as indicated by intelligence, or during times that the target is more likely to be engaged in criminal activity. Other methods of conducting surveillance include:

- Capsule-coverage provided to a target (location or individual) for a period of time to develop a pattern of behavior
- Event coverage-designed to observe a person or location in conjunction with a specific event; terrorist have often developed a pattern of attacking or conducting criminal activity on a particular symbolic date
- Spot check coverage-observing a specific location periodically to determine if activity is occurring (Dyson,2001)

An additional requirement of effective surveillance is the equipment necessary to communicate. Without the ability to communicate, surveillance is impossible.

Surveillance is a planned activity and there must have adequate resources to ensure success: manpower, equipment, time, and money. Innovation is critical to successful surveillance; ability to get on an airplane if necessary to follow a subject, the use of disguises, the ability to change the appearance of vehicles. The team must blend in with the environment and be aware of counter-surveillance methods. Teams often employ aircraft and documents events with photographs, diagrams, and notes. Agents may use tape recorders to documents the events during a long term surveillance operation. In additions to telephone wiretaps, cameras can be used in fixed positions to documents events. Tracking devices or beepers installed on the targets vehicle or any form of transportation allows team members follow at distances to avoid being detected (made) and never lose the target. Most models of new vehicles now have tracking devices that can be monitored. Surveillance is a valuable tool in the investigation of terrorism and can identify members of a terrorist cell, recover evidence, establish probable cause for warrants, and determine patterns, method of operations, and trends of the terrorist organization.

Skills in interviewing, interrogation, and statement analysis are essential to produce successful and effective terrorist investigations. Training in these skills is available to investigators throughout the United States. The Reid Technique, the Kinesic Interview Technique, and the L.S.I Course on Scientific Content Analysis as developed by Avinoam Sapir offer the investigator excellent opportunities to become effective at obtaining information and detecting deception. Statement analysis or SCAN is about obtaining information from a person's words or dealing with verbal information and not dealing with people. The process examines a statement using three test; the test of structure, language, and pronouns. There is nothing to compare with using the words of a suspect to convict them. Obtaining admissions or confession is an art that must be developed by training, education, and experience. During the detection phase of the interview, three behavior types are observed and studied to determine if there is deception: verbal behaviors or speech patterns, structured questions and responses, and non-verbal behaviors or body language. Reid has developed a two part process that consists of a nine step process of interrogation and a behavioral analysis interview. A confession obtained from a suspected Al Qaeda member foiled a plot to bomb the American embassy in Paris. Large numbers of suspects have been questioned since the events of 9/11. The interview and interrogation skills of the agents have produce actionable intelligence that has prevented numerous terrorist acts. In the United States the roads have over 30,000 vehicles that transport poisonous gas, toxic liquids and explosives (Cloud, 2004). Agents have interviewed people in dozens of truck driving schools. With over 250 million people and unlimited vulnerabilities, agents must conduct hundreds of interviews and interrogations to gain information that may well prevent a disaster. There are large numbers of investigators now trained and experienced in these methods and they have applied these techniques with tremendous success. Any investigator who has not acquired these skill is at a disadvantage in developing information and detecting deception from terrorist suspects who are known for their resistance to questioning.

One of the most effective tools of law enforcement in combating terrorism is the confidential informant or CI. An informant is a person, directed by law enforcement, and usually compensated, who furnishes information regarding unlawful activity or performs tasks as specified by investigators. The majority of criminal cases are brought to a successful conclusion through the use and development of informants or sources of information. Informants can provide insider information that cannot be obtained by other means. The CI can help determine what sequence to follow during an investigation, explain what evidence is available, who possesses the evidence, and where it can be located. The identity of members, leaders and structure of the organization, methods of operation, scheduled criminal activity, targets, information needed for interview and interrogation, indentify assets of the organization, introduction of the undercover agent, and information regarding the reconstruction of criminal activity can be provided by informants. Informants can provide the identity of other potential sources of information or weak links in the terrorist organization. Information from informants must be corroborated by investigators before any action is carried out based on the CI's information. Terrorist fugitives are extremely difficult to locate and apprehend. They often have assumed identities and have blended into the environment. Terrorist may have support groups that hide them and assist them in avoiding apprehension. Informants are essential in locating the terrorist fugitive. Fugitive task forces frequently have informants that are recruited to locate fugitives. The development and control of informants is a skill that like interview and interrogation comes form training, education, and experience. Informants can be double-edged swords and are sources of many problems such as corruption of law enforcement. Agencies have written policy and procedure on the development and management of informants that mandate the oversight by experienced supervisors or agents; today's informant may be tomorrow's defendant. However, informants are necessary for effective and efficient law enforcement; they save money, manpower, and time. Developing informants into a terrorist organization is a significant challenge for an agency. The sociology, brainwashing, and culture of the terrorist do not lend itself to a member of a terrorist group becoming an informant, but it does occur. Informants are like children, you must know where they are at all times and what they are doing; control is the key to successful management of informants. Motivation, the psychological incentive which moves a person to action that comes from within, must be examined by the investigator. Informants are motivated and will produce for the investigator who properly identifies the motives for cooperation and stimulates these motives into action; understanding human behavior is critical to development and management of informants. Common motives included greed/money, ideology, competition, and ego. Vanity, altruism, fear, revenge, repentance, and greed are often found as key motivators of informants. Informants used in the World Trade Center bombing case were paid in excess of $1 million and relocated with new identities. There are over 6000 individuals in the federal witness protection program. Informant control is a learned skill and determines the level of productivity of an informant. Having an informant that prevents a major terrorist attack or provides information that leads to the arrest and conviction of terrorist is the result of competent and effective investigation; it does not occur by accident. The protection and confidentiality of informants are areas that require a significant commitment from the agency and investigator (Mallory, 2000).

Developing an informant that occupies apposition within a terrorist organization that knows about the operation and identity of members or leaders is the ultimate goal of informant development. This informant can provide information to develop an historical conspiracy and provide information on future criminal activity by the organization. Determining motivation is critical to developing this level of informant. Interviewing or interpersonal skills are needed to be successful in "turning" the informant. Periphery informants are people that may have a minor position in the organization or be an associate on the fringes of the group. This level is not as valuable as the true insider, but will be of value to the investigation and is less difficult to develop. Informants that are considered outsiders provide the least amount of information, but may be able to penetrate the organization under the guidance of the investigator (Dyson, 2001).

Undercover operations can be successful, but are extremely dangerous and time consuming. The law enforcement officer is more often than not a more desirable and effective witness. However, the investigation of a terrorist group is likely to take a long period of time to complete. Long term/deep cover undercover work is problematic is that the agent undergoes extreme physical and psychological stress. It is also probable that an introduction form an insider (CI) will be necessary for the agent to be accepted by the terrorist group. If the informant goes bad, the agent is placed in extreme danger. There must be considerable preparation including developing a background and cover story that can withstand any level of scrutiny. Rather than deep cover, agencies my consider using limited undercover contact where the agent is not placed in as much danger or contact with the target of the investigation.

Undercover operations require tremendous surveillance efforts and assigning a handling officer to the deep cover operation. The selection of the undercover officer is an additional challenge to the agency. With the cell method of operation being employed by terrorist groups, the penetration of the group by an undercover agent is not likely. For these and other reasons, the use of the informant is most often the choice made by agencies investigating terrorism. It is often said that informants are the bread and butter of law enforcement. Informants present a major challenge for the investigator; you can's live with them and you can't live without them. Informants are a type of human intelligence that provides significant information that often leads to effective prevention of terrorist acts and prosecution of terrorist.

Whatever the agency's choice of investigative methods, a prosecutor should be brought into the investigation at the earliest date. Legal advice on warrants and obtaining court orders is extremely beneficial to the investigation. As discussed previously, the investigative grand jury is one of the most powerful tools used in criminal investigation. Most investigators will agree that involving the prosecutor in the investigation leads to more attention to the case during the process and a higher probability for success including a conviction.

The terms of source of information and informants is often used interchangeable. However, a source of information is a person or organization furnishing information without compensation, often on an occasional basis, and without specific direction from law enforcement (compare to previous definition of Informant). Sources of information include open sources such as information included in civil suits and public records, banks, professional associations, motel and hotel employees, airline ticket agents, licensing bureaus, and etc. Considered as outsiders with no involvement in criminal activity, these sources often supply information that is critical to the investigation of terrorism (Mallory, 2000).

Most U.S. intelligence agencies and law enforcement entities have internally managed reward programs for informants. Those classified for national security purposes include the following:

- The Department of State rewards program established in the Omnibus and Diplomatic Security Act of 1986-The PATRIOT Act amended the amount of reward to $5 million and allows the Secretary to offer a reward without monetary limit
- Responsible Cooperators Program awards alien groups regarding any knowledge their members may have about criminal acts, particularly terrorism
- The Violent Crime Control and Law Enforcement Act of 1994 created a "S" visa that may be issued to aliens who posses critical reliable information regarding criminal activity and willing to share that information with a U.S. agency
- The 1984 Act to Combat International Terrorism establish rewards up to $500,000 with respect to acts of terrorism within the territorial jurisdiction of the United States that leads to the arrest and conviction in any country of individuals who commit acts of terrorism-a reward of more than $100,000 requires the approval of the Attorney General or President of the United States
- Rewards for Information Concerning Terrorist Acts and Espionage

- The PATRIOT Act amended the reward program's authority by increasing the amount of money of the preceding program of up to $250,000 with the approval of the President or the Attorney General
- The Air Transport Association of America and the Air Line Pilots Association supplement rewards paid by the U.S. Government to a maximum of $2 million (Kash, 2002)

The Intelligence community and law enforcement have developed programs that offer significant rewards for information regarding terrorism. The failure of the intelligence community was due as least in part to the decline in human intelligence. Informants and sources of information provide the human intelligence that along with other sources can make the United States a more secure country.

The area that is the result of terrorist activity is treated as a crime scene. Rescue operations to save lives takes priority, but eventually the crime scene must be addresses to successfully complete the investigation. Witness statements must be taken immediately after the disaster to determine what happened and identity of those responsible established. The responsibility to protect the crime scene, identify, collect, and preserve physical evidence is still another major challenge of the investigation of terrorism. The most common forms of terrorist attacks in the United States are bombings and arson, both which present major challenges during the examination of the crime scene. Local and state law enforcement are most often responsible for conducting the crime scene, but the FBI has a team that responds to major disasters and has proven very capable in past investigations. Crime scenes may cover an area of miles such as in the case of the bombing of an aircraft as in the case of the 1988 destruction of Pan American flight 103 by Libyan. Agents at the crime scene discovered a small part of the explosive device which leads to the identity of the terrorist. The crime scene in examined for the signature of the bomber which is often unique and can lead to the identification of the bomber.

Legislation was passed by the United States after this incident to require manufacturers to incorporate a detection chemical in explosives such as Semtex. Finding this critical piece of evidence was the result of patience and training by competent crime scene personnel and the later analysis of the evidence. Everything that was there before an explosion will be there after the explosion. The trick is locating and identifying it as evidence. Physical evidence is not subject to poor memory and is difficult for a suspect to dispute in court. Evidence is often in an environment that presents unique problems for crime scene personnel. Rapid response is critical to the preservation of evidence due to weather and other contaminates. Locard's principle of the transfer of evidence between victims, suspects, and the scene mandates that all evidence be preserved, collected, and analyzed to be used in the reconstruction of the crime. A criminal investigation proceeds from determining "what" happened, "why" it happened, which leads to "who" made it happen. The scene is documented by narrative description or notes, depicting the scene photographically, and preparing a sketch or sketches of the scene.

Science alone does not solve cases. However, the development in technology has improved the probability of identifying, collecting, and connecting evidence to those responsible for the crime. From ballistics to DNA, science has proven to have revolutionized police work. The ability to separate background noise from audio-surveillance tapes and now the use technology to clean up video tapes to produce crisp digital images have produced a significant improvement in solving cases. The proliferation of data bases such as CODIS, the Integrated Automated Fingerprint Identification System, and the National Integrated Ballistic Information Network has allowed law enforcement to match evidence to suspects on a scale never before achieved in criminal investigations. The ability to collect and analyze trace evidence and the discovery of the ability to trace human ancestors using mitochondrial DNA has been applied to connecting evidence such as fingernails, teeth, and hair shafts to suspects. The new gas chromatography and mass spectrometry machines have allowed the crime lab to test traces of evidence and determine chemical composition. Conducting competent and complete crime scenes is a tremendous asset to terrorist investigations.

First Responders

The burden of combating terrorism and responding to terrorist events and major disasters is with states and local governments. First responders include police, firefighters and emergency medical professionals who save lives and limit destruction. There are a number of organizations that respond to major disaster including the Red Cross, the Salvation Army, Citizen Corps, and thousands of volunteers. Events after 9/11 demonstrated that the national and local response was still lacking in many areas. The inability of communications systems to talk to each other was a major obstacle in the response to Katrina. The response by FEMA was highly criticized by local and state governments. However, the response to hurricanes after Katrina was viewed as an improvement. Scenarios based training by federal, state, and local governments have improved the national response. Local governments are reaching out to private entities to establish contact information, exchange information and intelligence, conduct joint drills, and obtain support from the private sector.

First responders have obtained WMD equipment that contains antidotes for toxic agents, materials for testing for the presence of WMD's, and protective suites to prevent exposure. Considering the possibility that the next major disaster or terrorist attack could happen tomorrow, governments are aggressively training and planning for the next incident. Important changes for federal and national responses have been implemented that affect state and local agencies and nongovernment organizations. The Homeland Security Act of 2002 and Homeland Security Presidential Directive 5 (HSPD 5) addresses incident management. HSPD 5 creates a single comprehensive national approach and ensures that all levels of government and the private sector work together. Crisis and consequence management are now integrated with the secretary of DHS given the principal responsibility for managing domestic incidents. The learning curve produced the current relationship between the National Incident Management System (NIMS) and National Response Plan (NRP). Organizational structure, terminology, communications protocols, resource allocation have achieved an improved level of synchronization. The NRP provides the national framework for managing domestic incidents and establishes protocols for monitoring and reporting any potential incident. Under the NRP, DHS takes the lead during terrorist attacks or major disasters in coordinating operations and resources. Border security, critical infrastructure, and cyber security are areas now being address by federal, state, local governments and the private sector (The National Response Plan, White House, 2003). The FBI has the Disaster Squad and the Evidence Response Team that have demonstrated outstanding performance in both terrorist events and natural disasters:

- http://www.fbi.gov/hq/lab/disaster/disaster.htm
  The *FBI Disaster Squad* is a forty person team of agents trained in fingerprint identification methods, forensic dentistry, forensic anthropology, and the proper operational procedures to follow after a disaster. These agents are ready to travel to the scene of a disaster at a moment's notice to assist local authorities in identifying victims.

- http://www.fbi.gov/hq/lab/ert/ertmain.htm
  The *FBI Evidence Response Team* (ERT) is a group of highly-trained and well-equipped FBI personnel specializing in organizing and conducting major evidence recovery operations. They manage the identification, collection, and preservation of evidence at crime scenes.

The National Transportation Safety Board (NTSB) and the FBI Response Team (ERT) are conducting joint training and have formed a partnership to work and improve communications between the two entities (TrainingCenter@ntsb.gov).

Counterterrorism Units

States, major municipalities, federal agencies and the military have formed counterterrorism units that respond to terrorist acts. Many cities and all states employ "SWAT" units to address violent crime and have added training, equipment and techniques that may be used against any type of terrorist attack.

The New York City Police (NYPD) has one of the largest units in existence. A special 1000 member unit is dedicated to counterterrorism. The unit has officers stationed overseas who provide intelligence to the unit in New York. They report the successful techniques by foreign police against terrorist to the unit for adjustments and improvement of operations. The unit monitors radical and terrorist web sites and developments informants that supply information on terrorist and their supporter's activity. The NYPD created Operation Nexus that is a nationwide network of businesses and enterprises joined in an effort to prevent another terrorist attack. Detective have made over 25,000 visits to businesses that support NYPD counterterrorism efforts and report suspicious business encounters that may be linked to terrorist. Operation NYPD Shield is the department's umbrella program that pertains to private sector security and counterterrorism. The National Nuclear Administration's Remote Sensing Laboratory (RSL) is supporting NYPD counterterrorism efforts by retrofitting high-tech speedboats, vans and portable backpacks with radiation detection equipment. RSL has performed wide-area radiological surveys to enhance security of the city. The TRACS system employed is designed to detect neutron and gamma radiation and puts the NYPD on the cutting edge of applying technology to counterterrorism efforts.

The Los Angeles Police Department has created the Counter Terrorism and Criminal Intelligence Bureau that is comprised of the Major Crimes Division and Emergency Services Division. Major Crimes consist of Criminal Conspiracy, Criminal Investigations, Intelligence Investigations, and Surveillance and Liaison Sections. The

Emergency Services Division includes Field and Community Support, Emergency Planning, Operations, and Hazardous Devices Sections and the Bomb Squad Unit. The Unit is responsible for planning, response, and intelligence. The reputation of LAPD to respond to violent crime is unprecedented.

The FBI has the elite Hostage Rescue Team (HRT) that responds to major events including terrorist attacks. Each state has FBI agents that are trained and can employ "SWAT" tactics. The HRT team is headquartered at Quantico, Va. at the FBI Academy. The unit is part of the Tactical Support Branch of The Critical Incident Response Group of the FBI. The unit can deploy to any location within four hours of notification by the Director of the FBI or his designated representative. In the 17 year history of the unit has been deployed on over 200 occasions in support of FBI terrorism, violent criminal, foreign counter-intelligence and other investigations. Training includes weapons of mass destruction, maritime operations, mobile assaults, hostage rescue and barricaded subjects, high risk arrest/searches, helicopter operations, manhunt and rural operations, and cold weather operations. The unit was activated in 1983 and in addition to performing traditional law enforcement it has been involved in hurricane relief operations, dignitary protection missions, tactical surveys, and has supported special events such as the Olympic Games and presidential inaugurations. It has conducted successful rescue of United States person and others who have been held illegally by a hostile force including terrorist. Assignment to the HRT is voluntary is open to all Special Agents of the FBI. The unit is prepared to meet any crisis that may develop (www.fbi.gov).

The events of 9/11 were the impetus to a directive by Attorney General John Ashcroft for the all U.S. Attorneys to make the war on terrorism the first and overriding priority. Offices such as the Western District of Texas created Anti-terrorism and National Security Units that had a mission to investigate and prosecute all terrorist related offenses. Intelligence analysts have been assigned to the unit which works closely with the Joint Terrorism Task Forces in the state. The addition of these units can enhanced the ability of investigators to obtain legal evidence necessary for the prosecution and conviction of terrorist and their supporters.

The Posse Comitatus Act of 1878 was created to make a division between the military and domestic police forces. The act outlaws any direct involvement by the U.S. military in any enforcement of domestic law. However, the President of the United States by Presidential order can deploy members of the Department of Defense in cases of emergency or national security. This occurred during the Los Angeles riots of 1992, Hurricane Katrina, and the Beltway Sniper incidents. Additionally, Governors can activate the National Guard of their respective states in times of emergency and have done so on numerous occasions. The military is the only entity of American government with the equipment and assets capable of responding to events such as Katrina or 9/11. During and immediately after the 9/11 attack, the Air force had aircraft protecting the city of New York. Two of the nations most elite counterterrorism units, Delta Force (1st Special Forces Operational Detachment-Delta (1st SFOD-D) a component of the Joint Special Operations Command (JSOC) and the United States Naval Special Warfare Development Group composed of approximately 200 men (known as DEVGRU or SEAL Team Six-ST6) can be employed upon a presidential waiver of the Posse Comitatus Act. These units are composed of the best of the best of the armed services. Delta's prime mission is counterterrorism, counterinsurgency and national intervention operations.

The Delta unit was created by Colonel Charles Beckwith in 1977 and was modeled after the British Special Air Service (SAS). SEAL team Six was formally created in 1980 by Richard Marcinko and its missions and personnel remain top-secret. In 1987 the new counterterrorism unit became DEVGRU after SEAL Team Six was dissolved. The structure, operations, size, weapons, equipment, missions, organization, recruitment, and training of these units are kept secret for the most part and the units operate with an enormous amount of flexibility and autonomy. These units often train with other counterterrorism units around the world and are rumored to have trained with the FBI's HRT team. The books, Black Hawk Down by Mark Bowden and Inside Delta Force by Command Sergeant Major Eric L. Haney have brought Delta an unwanted amount of media attention. There is no fact sheet on either of the units produced by the military. Rumors of the involvement of Delta in events such as Waco and other domestic incidents have been denied by the U.S. Government. These units are a considerable asset that can be employed during a terrorist attack such as active shooters or hostages situations upon presidential order to combat terrorism within the U.S. borders (Wikipedia, 2009, Simonsen and Spindlove, 2000).

Conclusions and the Future

Combating terrorism has become a priority for the United States after the events of 9/11. The unthinkable has now happened and the U.S. Government and law enforcement have made considerable efforts to prevent and respond to terrorism. Police are not the only emergency responders and considerable resources from the private sector, the military, firefighters, and emergency professional are now forming partnerships to become more efficient and effective in addressing terrorism. The key to combating terrorism lies at the community level with support from partnerships from every aspect of the nation.

Massive changes in state, local, and federal levels have occurred during the past decade. The Department of Homeland Security was formed at federal level and States have now formed their own departments of homeland security. The development of fusion centers at the state level, the creation of the National Response Plan, the National Incident Management System, Homeland Security Presidential Directive 5, the National Criminal Intelligence Sharing plan and the passage of the Patriot Act are among the massive effort by the nation to respond and prevent act terrorism. The movement by the governments of the U.S. has moved toward managing for results to improve the effectiveness, efficiency, and accountability of all levels of government.

At no time in history has law enforcement had the technology, laws, and techniques to identify, arrest, and prosecute terrorist and their supporters. Along with prosecution and case initiation using traditional criminal acts such as murder and assault, the statues of RICO, conspiracy, money laundering, and violations of the Patriot Act can be applied to case initiation against terrorist. The current effort to share intelligence and form partnerships is having a positive impact on the ability of law enforcement to identify, arrest, and prosecute terrorist and seized assets of their organizations.

The future growth of terrorist, both domestic and international, will continue to be a challenge for law enforcement and the U.S. government. The eco-terrorist movement and other environmental groups such as the Animal Liberation Front and the Earth Liberation Front along with events such as the Murrah Federal building bombing will continue to occur. Future attacks by international terrorist such as Al Qaeda, Hamas, and Hezbollah and destruction of life and property by domestic single-issue terrorist (abortion and environmental issues) will remain a challenge for the United States. The "home grown" terrorist may become the more serious threat whether left wing, right wing, or single issue motivated. These and other terrorist organizations have taken advantage of the advances in technology, communication, transportation, and the borderless global society.

Perhaps the most serious threat is that of weapons of mass destruction and cyber-terrorism. Many experts are predicting a major attack on U.S. soil in the near future. Although the intelligence community has improved its ability to collect, analyze, and disseminate intelligence products and tremendous changes have been implemented in federal, state, and local law enforcement in the areas of technology , investigative techniques, and management, there remains a high probability that other terrorist attacks will happen. The eradication of international terrorist abroad and domestic terrorist and their organizations in the United States must remain a priority of the U.S. government. The strategy of identifying and seizing assets that fund these organizations and the arrest and prosecution of individual and business organizations that support terrorist must continue to be a priority of the justice system. In a country of over 250 million people, thousands of miles of shore and borders, and unlimited targets of opportunity for terrorist, the vulnerability of the United States has been revealed and now the challenge is to continue to respond in a manner that insures national security.

References

Baker, T. (2005). *Introductory Criminal Analysis.* Upper saddle River: Pearson Prentice Hall.

Bamford, J. (2006, April). *"Big Brother is Listening".* Retrieved March 12, 2009, from The Atlantic Online: http://www.theatlantic.com/doc/print/200604/nsa-surveilance

Clark, J. (2009). *The Posse comitatus Act of 1878.* Retrieved March 3, 2009, from How Stuff Works: http://science.howstuffworks.com/delta-force4.htm

Cloud, J. (2004). Search and Disrupt. *Time* , 19-21.

Dyson, W. (2001). *Terrorism: An Investigator's Handbook.* Cincinnati: Anderson Publishing Company.

encyclopedia.com. (n.d.). *Counter-terrorism units.* Retrieved March 9, 2009, from Encyclopedia: http://encyclopedia.thefreedictionary.com/Counter-terrorism+units

Federal Bureau of Investigation. (n.d.). *Critical Incident Response Group.* Retrieved March 16, 2009, from Federal Bureau of Investigation- Investigative Programs: http://www.fbi.gov/hq/isd/cirg/tact.htm

FEMA. (n.d.). *About FEMA.* Retrieved March 11, 2009, from FEMA: http://www.fema.gov/about/index.shtm

Jenkins, B. (1990). The Future Course of International Terrorism. *The 1990s & Beyond* , 90-95.

Kamien, D. (2006). *The McGraw-Hill Homeland Security Handbook.* New York: McGraw-Hill Companies.

Kash, D. (2002). Hunting Terrorists Using Confidential Informant Reward Programs. *FBI Law Enforcement Bulletin* , 26-30.

Los Angeles Police Department. (n.d.). *Counter Terrorism and Criminal Intelligence Bureau.* Retrieved March 9, 2009, from The Los Angeles Police Department: http://www.lapdonline.org/inside_the_lapd/content_basic_view/6502

Mallory, S. (2000). *Informants: Development and Management.* Incline Village: Copperhosue Publishing Company.

National Nuclear Security Administration. (n.d.). *RSL Enhances New York's Counter Terrorism Operations.* Retrieved March 9, 2009, from Nevada Site Office: U.S. Department of Energy: http://www.nv.doe.gov/library/Featured%20Items/TRACS_revise.pdf

New York (CBS News). (2006, March 20). *Inside the NYPD Counter-Terrorism Unit.* Retrieved March 9, 2009, from WCBSTV: http://wcbstv.com/topstories/60.Minutes.NYPD.2.234050.html

New York City Police Department. (n.d.). *Counterterrorism.* Retrieved March 9, 2009, from New York City- Police Department- Crime Prevention: http://www.nyc.gov/html/nypd/html/crime_prevention/counterterrorism.shtml

Nilson, Chad & Burke, Tod. (2002). Enviromental Extremists and the Eco-Terrorism Movement. *Academy of Criminal Justice Sciences* , 1-6.

Simonsen, C. & Spindlove, J. (2000). *Terrorism Today: The Past, The Players, The Future.* Upper Saddle River: Prentice Hall.

Texas Law Enforcement Management and Administrative Statistics Program. (2001, October). Responding to Terrorism. *TELEMASP Bulletin* . Texas: Sam Houston State University.

The 9/11 Investigations: Staff reports of the 9/11 Commission. (2004). *The 9/11 Investigations: Staff reports of the 9/11 Commission.* New York: Public Affairs.

The Office of the Mississippi Homeland Security. (2009). *The Office of the Mississippi Homeland Security.* Retrieved March 9, 2009, from Mississippi Homeland Security: http://www.homelandsecurity.ms.gov

United States Attorney's Office. (n.d.). *Anti Terrorism Unit- Western District of Texas.* Retrieved March 3, 2009, from United States Department of Justice: http://www.usdoj.gov/usao/txw/criminal_division/anti_terrorism_unit.html

United States Department of Justice. (2005). *The National criminal Intelligence Sharing Plan.* USDOJ.

CHAPTER 10
COUNTERING INTERNATIONAL TERRORISM

We will direct every resource at our command to win the war against terrorists; every means of diplomacy, every tool of intelligence, every instrument of law enforcement, every financial influence. We will starve the terrorist of funding, turn them against each other, rout them out of their safe hiding places, and bring them to justice.
President George W. Bush   September 24, 2001

Introduction

On September 11, 2001, al-Qaeda, an International terrorist organization was responsible for the death of over approximately 3,000 Americans when the terrorists slammed two hijacked commercial airliners into the New York City World Trade Center. A third hijacked aircraft crashed into the Pentagon causing numerous deaths and millions of dollars worth of damage to the huge U.S. Department of Defense complex.

However, September 11, 2001 was not the only occasion where the United States was victimized by international terrorist organizations. In 1983, two hundred and fifty four Marines were killed when a suicide bomber driving an explosive laden vehicle drove into the Marine Barracks located in Beirut, Lebanon. Hezbollah a radical Shi'ite Islamic terrorist organization claimed responsibility for the attack. In 1993, members of al-Qaeda were responsible for the bombing of the United States embassies located in Kenya and Tanzania. The combined embassy bombings resulted in 212 deaths and 4000 persons injured. One of the most notable attacks perpetrated by international terrorists occurred in October 2000, when the U.S.S. Cole, a U.S. Navy destroyer, was attacked while moored in the Port of Aden in Yemen. The attack resulted in the death of 17 sailors and wounding 39 and the naval warship sustained millions of dollars worth of damage.

As we well know there are approximately 109 definitions of terrorism. Fortunately for us counterterrorism is not as complicated to define. Counterterrorism refers to the practice, tactics, techniques, and strategies that governments, militaries, police departments, and corporations adopt in response to terrorist threats and or acts. Martin (2003, p.345) defines counterterrorism as "proactive policies that specifically seek to eliminate terrorist environments and groups and the ultimate goal of counterterrorism is to save lives by proactively preventing or decreasing the number of terrorist attacks." Counterterrorism involves many different options (strategies) that are available to countries in order to defend themselves from a terrorist attack.

Myo (2009, p.5) claims "counterterrorism experts agree that counterterrorism options can be grouped under several policies such as *Use of Force* (coercive, covert operations, suppressive campaigns, punitive strikes, preventive strikes), Repressive options (covert operations, intelligence, enhanced security, economic sanctions). conciliatory options (diplomacy, social reform and concessionary options) and Legalistic responses (law enforcement, counterterrorism laws and international law)."

The United States is the sole remaining super power and is a leader in the "free world," as a result of this power and influence in the international arena, the United States will remain a viable target for terrorist groups throughout the world. According to Pillar (2001, p. 57), "One third of international terrorism incidents recorded during the past two decades involved attacks on U.S. interests."

The 9-11 Commission advised America that the major terrorist threat directed at the United States emanates from radical Islamic organizations. Benjamin (2008) supports the findings of the 9-11 Commission by claiming that the Sunni jihadist organization known as ***al-Qaeda*** is the only international terrorist organization that has the ambition and the capacity to inflict catastrophic damage to the United States. Moreover, al-Qaeda is the only terrorist organization who has successfully engaged in terrorist acts on land, sea and in the air. However, we must not ignore other radical Islamic terrorist organizations such as Hezbollah and Hamas.

When a government considers counterterrorism measures, it must first develop a strategy or a plan to combat terrorism. In 2003 the United States government developed a *National Policy for Combating Terrorism.* The intent of the strategy is to stop terrorist attacks against the United States, its citizens, its interests, and U.S. friends and allies around the world (CRS, 2005). Ganor (2005, p.41) states "when combating terrorism, one must carry out various types of activities aimed at reducing or eliminating the terrorist organization's ability to perpetrate attacks, and activities aimed at reducing or eliminating the terrorists' motivation to carry out the attacks." Pillar (2001) contends that terrorism is a problem to be managed not solved because of the complexity of the issue. It is foolish to believe that all counterterrorism strategies are fail-safe. We should be mindful of the fact that terrorism poses a threat that cannot be eliminated. Moreover, the government cannot truthfully claim that it will prevent all terrorist attacks (Guiora, 2008).

The 2007 National Strategy for Combating Terrorism claims that the United States should adopt a counterterrorism strategy that includes:

- the destruction of al-Qaeda

- enlisting support from allies

- training experts in foreign languages

- and cultures with an emphasis of gaining a

   better understanding of Islam (CRS, 2007 p. 1).

Moreover, the 2007 National Strategy for Combating Terrorism reiterates the importance of using all the available elements of U.S. power to combat international terrorism such as; diplomatic, economic, law enforcement, financial, intelligence, military and criminal prosecution. When developing a counterterrorism strategy it is important to be aware that from time to time the faces of terrorism are changing and the demands of the counter actions must change. According to Bruce Hoffman (1999, p. 166-67), " a good deal of theory and practice of counterterrorism becomes out of date month by month."

This chapter is concerned with countering international terrorism and the methods that are available to the United States government to counter it. One of the most effective methods of countering terrorism is to eliminate a terrorist organization's source of funds.

Funding Terrorism

It has been widely accepted that military organizations cannot wage war without the proper funding. The same holds true for terrorist organizations. Terrorist organizations require funding to purchase weapons, explosives, and travel expenses to carry out their acts of terror. The Irish Republican Army and the Tupamaros of Uruguay often turned to bank robbery as a means to obtain funds. The Taliban and al-Qaeda continue to use drug proceeds to finance their campaign of terror. Colombian and Mexican narco-terrorist organizations have adopted kidnapping for ransom as a means to obtain funding. African based terror groups have used the proceeds obtained from the sale of hijacked humanitarian supplies such as food, and medical supplies to fund their terror operations. As of late, Somalian pirates operating off the Somalian coastline have been hijacking ships traveling through the Gulf of Aden for ransom. It has been reported that from March 2009 through October 2008, Somalian pirates have earned anywhere from $80 to $150 million in ransom payments from international maritime transportation companies. However, the most important source of funding for terrorist organizations comes from donations.

Many terrorist experts claim that it is quite costly to finance the day-to-day operations of a terrorist organization. It can even be costlier for terrorist groups to carry out their crimes. For an example, al-Qaeda spent approximately $500,000 to carry out their attack on September 11, 2001. Following a "paper or money trail" is the most essential part of any financial investigation such as money laundering. Tracing the funding of terrorist groups is essential to the dismantling of such organization. Following the "paper trail" can assist investigators in identifying the sources of funding along with identifying members and associates of the terrorist group. Mark Navias (2002) contends that the major strategy of counterterrorism should be wagging "financial warfare" with financial weapons in an attempt to stop the flow of funding for terrorist organizations.

Money Laundering and Asset Forfeiture

The United States has several financial weapons at its disposal to assist in the elimination of terrorist financing. These financial weapons are but not limited too; Bank

Secrecy Act (BSA), the Patriot Act, freezing terrorist bank accounts, seizing assets and economic sanctions. The BSA also known as The Currency and Foreign Transactions Reporting Act is a tool the United States government uses to fight drug trafficking, money laundering, and other crimes. The U.S. Congress enacted the BSA to prevent banks and other financial providers from being used as intermediaries for, or to hide the transfer or deposit of money derived from criminal activity (Office of the Comptroller, 2001). There are approximately one hundred and seventy five crimes listed in the BSA and they range from drug trafficking, gunrunning, murder for hire, fraud, acts of terrorism and the illegal use of wastelands.

According to the provisions set forth in the BSA, financial institutions are required to report all suspicious financial transactions in the amount of $10,000 or more are required to them to the U.S. Department of Treasury by completing a Currency Transaction Report (CTR), and must be completed within 15 days of the transaction date. The reporting and record keeping requirements of the BSA regulations create a paper trail for law enforcement to investigate money laundering schemes and other illegal activities (Office of the Comptroller, 2001). The U.S. government is hopeful that the paper trail operates as deterrence to illegal activity and provides a means to trace movements of money through the financial system.

The USA Patriot Act was overwhelmingly passed by the United States Congress in October 2001 as a response to the tragic events that occurred on September 11, 2001. Title III of the USA Patriot Act is known as the Money Laundering Abatement and Financial Anti-Terrorism Act of 2001. This Act contains various measures directed at strengthening the Federal government's ability to combat terrorism. With the passage of the Patriot Act, federal law now imposes significant fines and terms of imprisonment for any entity that provides material support or resources or resources knowing or intending that they are to be used in terrorists or by Foreign Terrorist Organizations (Day, Berry & Howard Foundation, 2004). In June 2002, this Federal criminal law was amended to criminalize the "financing of terrorism." This new provision punishes an individual or organization who "willfully provides or collects funds with the intention that such funds be used" to carry out acts of terrorism or who knowingly conceals the source of funds used to carry out terrorism or to support Foreign Terrorist Organizations (Day, Berry & Howard Foundation, 2004).

Freezing Terrorist Assets

Another financial tool in the "war on terrorism" is the ability of the United States to freeze the bank accounts of terrorist organizations and the accounts of countries that sponsor terrorism. On January 23, 1995, President William Clinton signed Executive Order 12947 which prohibited financial transactions with terrorists who threaten to disrupt the Middle East Peace Process. Furthermore, the Executive Order further stated "As part of the comprehensive and sustained campaign against terrorist financing all U.S. persons including U.S. based charities are prohibited from dealing with persons (individuals and entities) identified a being associated with terrorism (U.S. Treasury, 2006). Section 302 of the Anti-Terrorism and Effective Death Penalty Act of 1996, authorizes the Secretary of State to designate organizations as *"Foreign Terrorist Organizations."* The Secretary of State usually makes this decision in consultation with the U.S. Attorney General and the U.S. Secretary of Treasury. However, these designations must meet the following criteria: (1). it must be a foreign organization, (2). the organization must engage in terrorism activity, (3). the organization must threaten the national security of the United States. The reader must be mindful of the fact that it is a criminal offense for an American citizen to provide material support or assistance to a Foreign Terrorist Organization (FTO).

The lead federal agency for the seizing of assets of terrorism-supporting countries and international terrorist organizations is the Office of Foreign Assets Control (OFAC). OFAC is a division within the U.S. Department of Treasury and is supervised by the Under Secretary for Enforcement. OFAC implements these sanctions as part of its general mission to administer and enforce economic trade sanctions based upon U.S. foreign policy and national security goals. Since 1995 OFAC has implemented three sanctions programs targeting international terrorists and terrorist organizations. In addition, OFAC administers eight sanctions programs targeting terrorism-supporting governments and regimes (OFAC, 2001). In 1999, the U.S. government seized $2.8 billion in state sponsors' assets frozen in the United States. The largest amount belonged to Iraq at approximately $1.5 billion followed by Libya which totaled approximately $1 billion (Pillar, 2001, p. 96). According to the OFAC Terrorist Assets Report 2007, $20,736,920 funds were seized from various terrorist organizations. In 2006, OFAC seized or blocked $16,413,817 from designated terrorist organizations. Another financial tool that is available to the U.S. Government to counter terrorism is the usage of economic sanctions.

United States Economic Sanctions

In another attempt by the United States government to eliminate the funding of terrorism, President George W. Bush signed Executive Order 13224 (Blocking Property and Prohibiting Transactions With Persons Who Commit, Threaten to Commit or Support Terrorism). This executive order was issued in response to the grave acts of terrorism and threats of terrorism committed by foreign terrorists, including the terrorist acts committed on September 11, 2001 in New York and Pennsylvania and against the Pentagon, and the immediate threat of future attacks on U.S. nationals and the United States.

Executive Order 13224 imposes economic sanctions on persons who commit, threaten to commit, or support certain acts of terrorism. It prohibits transfers, including donations of funds, goods, or services to any organizations or individuals designated, under its authority, and it blocks all property in the United States or within the possession or control of a U.S. person in which there is an interest of any designated person. It should be noted that an Executive Order is not a law per se but it carries the force of law in that it represents the President's exercise of statutory authority granted by Congress.

OFAC considers the usage of economic sanctions as a powerful tool against international terrorism. The U.S. government and in particular the Department of Treasury strongly believes that economic sanctions is much more far reaching than just seizing or block terrorists' assets. Policy makers contend that the effects of the seizure of terrorists' assets reach far beyond just the seizure of those funds and property. It is believed that that by designating individuals or organizations Foreign Terrorist

Organizations (FTOs) notifies the United States public and the world that these parties are either actively engaged in or supporting terrorism or that they are being used by terrorists and their organization (OFAC, 2007). OFAC officials believe that economic sanctions can assist or supplement the law enforcement actions of other U.S. agencies and/or other governments.

Charitable Donations

Charitable donations have been described as being the most profitable means of financing terrorism. However, often times many donations that is intended for humanitarian reasons are diverted to terrorist organizations. Rachel Ehrenfeld (2003) states the Arabic term *"zakat"* translated means charity and is an integral part of Islam. The Islamic people believe that the *zakat* is the amount of money that every adult Muslim should contribute to those who are poor and needy and the idea of contributing to the poor is deeply entrenched in the Qur'an. According to www.Islamicity.com, Muslims are required to pay their charitable contributions by the conclusion of the lunar year and they are instructed to pay 2.5% of one's capital. The world Muslim population has been estimated at 1.6 billion people. The amount of funding that could be generated from this Muslim mandate would be mind boggling if only half the Muslim population participated. Theoretically, the potential for diverting these "charitable funds" to terrorist organizations is extremely high due to the fact that the possibility exists that a radical Islamic cleric could control the donations. Therefore, without any controls in place, donations could be funneled to terrorist organizations and the bloodshed and carnage perpetrated by radical Islamic terrorist groups would continue.

Ehrenfeld (2003) explains that in many Arab counties such as Saudi Arabia, Kuwait and the United Arab Emirates, the government controls the charities and often makes large contributions to them and occasionally these contributions are diverted "directly or indirectly" to terrorist organizations (p. 37). The International Islamic Relief Organization (IIRO) is a perfect example of a charitable organization that donates to various worthy humanitarian causes but yet also contributes to terrorist groups. The IIRO has been identified by the United Nations and the United States Department of Treasury as a charitable organization who has been a major financial supporter to al-Qaeda. Al-Mujil the leader of the IIRO has been nicknamed the "million dollar man" for supporting many Islamic militant groups. During the1990s, Al-Mujil traveled extensively in Arab countries to meet with leaders of al-Qaeda. Ehrenfeld (2003) contends that more than 70% of the IIRO's funds were allocated to purchase weapons and the remainder of the funds was used for legitimate public works. Moreover, the IIRO has been allegedly accused of funding the Egyptian branch of al-Qaeda (Ehrenfeld, 2003). According to the U.S. Department of Treasury (2206), Al-Mujil has been a major financial contributor to terrorist organizations in the Middle East along with the Philippines and Indonesia.

Financial Investigations

In an effort to eliminate the financing of terrorism, the U.S. Department of Treasury created Operation *Green Quest."* Operation Green Quest was established by the U.S. Customs Service Office of Investigations and is a multi-jurisdictional program that is comprised of the following agencies: the Internal Revenue Service, the Secret Service, the FBI, the Financial Crimes Enforcement Network (FINCEN), the Bureau of Alcohol, Tobacco and Firearms (ATF), and U.S. Postal Inspection Service. The purpose of this financial enforcement initiative is to augment the ongoing counterterrorism initiatives by bringing together the financial resources of the U.S. Department of Treasury to freeze accounts, seize assets and where appropriate bring criminal charges against individuals and organizations that finance terrorist groups (Customs Border Protection, 2002). Operation Green Quest has been described as one of the most successful financial crimes task forces having seized approximately $425 million and arrested 1,500 individuals since its inception in 1992 (Customs Border Protection, 2002).

In addition to Operation Green Quest, the government created the Federal Bureau of Investigation's (FBI) Interagency Terrorism Financial Review Group which is under the supervision of the U.S. Department of Justice (DOJ). The mission of the Financial Review Group is to identify, investigate, prosecute, disrupt, and dismantle all terrorist-related financial activities (FBI, 2002). The group consists of the Central Intelligence Agency (CIA), the National Security Agency (NSA), the Defense Intelligence Agency (DIA), the Drug Enforcement Administration (DEA), and most of the agencies assigned to Operation Green Quest.

Lehmkuhler (2003) contends that the above mentioned law enforcement initiatives that have taken place since September 11, 2001, have given the U.S. Government more tools to combat terrorism financing. However, the United States government cannot realistically combat terrorism financing unilaterally. We must have the assistance of the international community. One option is to request assistance from our allies to employ economic sanctions on those countries that help facilitate the funding of terrorist organizations.

Control of United States Borders

Another significant instrument for countering international terrorism is the "securitization" of the U.S. borders. Most Americans believe that the United States is most vulnerable along the U.S. Mexican border because of the unprecedented number of illegal immigrants who attempt to illegally enter the United States. Tom Payan (2006) claims that approximately 300,000 to 400,000 Mexican illegal aliens successfully enter the United States annually. Moreover, the overwhelming quantity of cocaine and methamphetamine is smuggled into the U.S. through Mexico. In addition to the drug trafficking, the Mexican drug cartels have brought an increase in violent crime and corruption to the border area. As a result of the large volume of political corruption transpiring along the U.S.-Mexican border, it is feared that Mexico will soon become a failed state. However, even though the Mexican border is extremely porous there is little information to indicate that terrorists have entered the U.S. via the Mexican border. The Canadian border is a completely different story.

On December 14, 1999, Ahmed Ressam, an Islamic terrorist was apprehended at the U.S./Canadian border while attempting to smuggle approximately one hundred pounds of explosives into the United States while he was traveling on a ferry from Victoria British Columbia to Port Angeles, Washington.

A follow-up investigation conducted by U.S. federal agents revealed that Ressam was intending on blowing up Los Angeles airport on January 1, 2000 (millennium). Hence, Ahmed Ressam has been dubbed the "millennium bomber." It was later learned that Ressam was a member of an Algerian terrorist group called *"Armed Islamic Group or GIA"* operating as a "cell" in Montreal, Canada. According to Anderson and Sloan (2003), the GIA is a non-state Islamic Fundamentalist organization that has sought to establish an Islamic government in Algeria.

The Canadian Intelligence Security Service (CISS) reported that Canada is home to approximately fifty terrorist organizations. It is widely believed that the reason for this large number of terrorist organizations being based in Canada is a direct result of Canada's liberal immigration policy. These loose immigration and asylum policies have become a major concern for U.S. Homeland Security Officials which will probably result in tighter security controls along the United States-Canadian Border.

The 9-11 Commission recommended that the U.S. Department of Homeland Security (DHS) develop a program that would monitor(restrict) the movement (travel) of non-U.S. citizens within the borders of the United States. Subsequent to the 9-11 Commission's recommendations the DHS developed the US-Visit program which is designed to electronically track the arrival and departure of all non-U.S. citizens. The U.S.-Visit program utilizes biometric technology that enables the U.S. government to establish and verify a traveler's identity when they visit the United States. The Program requires all aliens to be photographed and fingerprinted upon arriving in the United States. Another security feature of the Program's biometric technology is that it identifies those persons who have "overstayed" their visas. The DHS estimated that at least thirty per cent of the approximately ten million illegal immigrants residing in the United States are probably "overstayers" (Vaughn, 2004). The figure on estimated illegal population in the U.S. is realistically understated. Many immigration officials would estimate a larger illegal alien population at approximately twelve million. Moreover, and even more concerning is that we do not exactly know the number of overstayers living in the U.S., and where they came from or how long they have lived here (Vaughn, 2004). The US-Visit is not considered to be a panacea for our nation's immigration problems. The US-Visit program in conjunction with tighter visa background checks and U.S. Consulate screening will hopefully assist the DHS in improving its ability to monitor the travel of non-citizens within the U.S.

Since the tragic events of September 11, 2001, the DHS has implemented many other security initiatives along the U.S.-Mexican border. The United States has deployed additional border agents and technology to the borderlands area in an attempt to deter further illegal immigration into the U.S. Tony Payan (2006) describes the increase in security along the U.S.-Mexican border as the *"militarization"* of the border. In an attempt to counter the threat of narco-terrorism along the U.S.-Mexican border, the U.S. Congress enacted the ***Merida Initiative*** which is a $1.4 billion assistance package for Mexico along with other Central American countries to assist their law enforcement efforts against the rising threat presented by the drug trafficking cartels. Selee (2008) notes that the Merida Initiative contains a series of coordinated efforts such as; joint law enforcement operations to track, identify, and arrest cartel leaders and those involved in organized crime; to strengthen Mexico's judicial system ands significantly revamp its national and local police forces and to develop strategies in both countries to reduce the demand for controlled substances. Congress has insisted that funds will not go directly to the Mexican government. Instead, technology, equipment and will be provided.

Diplomacy

The U.S. State Department has been charged with the responsibility of conducting diplomacy on behalf of our nation. Webster's New World College Dictionary defines diplomacy as the conducting of relations between nations as in building up trade, making treaties etc. O'Connor (2008) contends that the primary purpose of diplomacy is communications, and the ultimate goal of diplomacy is peace.

Diplomacy has been an important tool in countering terrorism, and the United States Department of State has played a crucial role in the war on terrorism. According to U.S. Ambassador at Large-State Department Coordinator for Counterterrorism J. Cofer Black (2003), "Diplomacy plays a crucial role in the global war on terrorism by taking the war to the terrorists, helping to cut them off from critical resources, and strengthening political will and international cooperation." Many U.S. diplomats strongly believe that U.S. embassies and consulates are on the front line of diplomacy and helping battle terrorism. As part on the war on terrorism the State Department has developed many programs to counter terrorism.

In 1983 the U.S Department of State established the Antiterrorism Assistance Program (ATA) to help train foreign governments' law enforcement and civilian security agencies in their fight against terrorism. The Department of State has conducted training in 56 countries through 180 courses during fiscal year 2003 (Dept. of State, 2009). The ATA Program trains foreign law enforcement personnel to:

- protect national borders
- protect critical infrastructure
- protect national leadership
- respond to and resolve terrorist incidents
- investigate and prosecute those responsible for terrorist acts.
- respond to weapons of mass destruction attacks
- manage kidnapping for ransom crimes
- respond to terrorist incidents resulting in mass casualties or fatalities

In 1984 the United States Department of State created the *Rewards for Justice Program* and it is administered by the Department of State's Bureau of Diplomatic Security. Under this program, the Secretary of State is currently offering rewards of up to $25 million for information that prevents or favorably resolves acts of international terrorism against U.S. persons or property worldwide (U.S. Dept. of State, 2009). Rewards also may be paid for information leading to the arrest or conviction of terrorists attempting, committing, conspiracy to commit, or aiding and abetting in the commission of such acts.

According to the Department of State (2009), the USA Patriot Act of 2001, authorizes the Secretary of State to offer or pay rewards of greater than $5 million if the

Secretary determines that a greater amount is necessary to combat terrorism or to defend the United States against the United States.

The Program has been successful in the arrest and conviction of the 1993 World Trade Center bomber, Ramzi Yousef. There should be no surprise to hear that the Program's highest priority is the arrest of Osama bin Laden and the State Department is offering a reward of $25 million for his arrest or capture. In 2003, an Iraqi informant was awarded $30 million for information that led authorities to Saddam's sons, Uday and Qusay Hussein (Isikoff & Hosenball, 2008). Even though the Rewards Program is aimed at individuals or organizations who perpetrate acts of terrorism against Americans, the U.S. will share information received with foreign countries whose citizens are at risk. In this scenario, the identity of the reporting individual would remain anonymous.

Another option available to the U.S. State Department in their efforts to counter international terrorism is the usage of *"punitive diplomatic measures."* Punitive options could range from condemnation in international form such as the severance of diplomatic relations or by closing embassies.

According to O'Connor (2009, p.3), "The most common uses of diplomacy in counterterrorism include; developing bilateral or multilateral anti-terrorist policies; arranging for the sharing of intelligence; arranging permission for law enforcement authorities from one country; and to come in and arrest or interrogate a suspected terrorist in another country; and the establishment of appropriate sanctions on sponsors of terrorism."

Intelligence Sharing/ Improve Intelligence

One of the primary missions of the United States Intelligence Community (IC) is to prevent a surprise attack and to minimize the damage sustained in the event of a terrorist attack. There is little doubt that the tragic events surrounding September 11, 2201, can be classified as an "intelligence failure." In the waning days following 9-11, the American IC was severely criticized for failing to share information (intelligence) within the other intelligence agencies. This was partially due to the fact that the agencies within the IC were more concerned about "turf bureaucracy" or "turf protection" than the dissemination of intelligence to their counterparts. The breakdown in information sharing was a major contributing factor to the terrorist attacks on September 11, 2001.

Another contributing factor to the intelligence failure on 9-11 was that prior to the terrorist attacks, the IC was focused primarily on the "Cold War" and the defeat of the Soviet Union. During the Cold War there was a clear cut enemy and our nation's intelligence relied primarily upon our technical surveillance to fulfill our intelligence requirements. In the "War on Terrorism" the actors are non-state members and are not affiliated with any formal military organization. Al-Qaeda does not have massive troop movements to monitor, or ships or aircraft to track. Consequently, our technical surveillance is of little use with regards to these collection methods. Our intelligence collection in the war on terrorism must include "feet on the ground." We need *"human intelligence"* (HUMINT) to help identify terrorist organizations and its members. Jenkins (2003, p.5) states "Knowing what terrorists might do depends largely on human sources, under-cover agents and informants. Penetrating small terrorist groups may take months." Once our intelligence agencies identify terrorists, our signals intelligence (SIGNET) is quite capable of intercepting terrorist's electronic communications. U.S. SIGNET has been responsible for preventing several terrorist attacks in the United States as well as Europe since September 11, 2001. In the war on terrorism, our intelligence collection methods need to strike a balance between technical and human intelligence.

It was quite obvious following the tragic 9-11 terrorist attacks that our nation's IC relied too heavily upon technical surveillance and as a result we were unable to detect al-Qaeda's plan to attack the United States. The United States IC was unable to make the transition from the Cold War to the War on Terrorism prior to September 11, 2001.

Subsequent to the terrorist attacks on September 11, 2001, the 9-11 Commission along with the Subcommittee on Terrorism and Homeland Security of the House Permanent Select Committee on Intelligence made numerous recommendations for major intelligence reform. As part the intelligence reformation process the U.S. Congress enacted the Intelligence Reform and Terrorism Prevention Act of 2004 (Public Law 108-458-December 17, 2004). In the words of President George W. Bush at the signing of the Act, "Under this new law, our vast intelligence enterprise will become more unified, coordinated and effective. It will enable us to better do our duty, which is to protect the American people" (Office of the DNI, 2009, p. 4).

One of the most important provisions of the Intelligence Reform Act was the creation of the position of Director of Intelligence (DNI). The main function of the DNI is to ensure timely and effective collection, processing, analysis, and dissemination of intelligence. Furthermore, the Act mandates that the DNI replace the Director of the Central Intelligence Agency (DCI) as the primary intelligence advisor to the president, thereby ending the fifty-seven year reign of the DCI as the nation's chief intelligence officer. Another major responsibility of the DNI is to ensure better coordination and dissemination of information within the U.S. Intelligence Community and those government agencies that have"a need to know." The Act also establishes the DNI as the head of the U.S. Intelligence Community. This could become problematic for the DNI because the majority of the intelligence agencies that comprise the IC are Department of Defense agencies and therefore report to the Secretary of Defense.

According to Presidential Executive Order 13470 (July 30, 2008) The Director of the Federal Bureau of Investigation (FBI) shall coordinate the clandestine collection of foreign intelligence collected through human resources or through human-enabled means and counterintelligence activities inside the United States. In layman's terms the FBI is charged with the responsibility of gathering *domestic intelligence.* Historically, the FBI has been regarded primarily as a federal law enforcement agency and not an intelligence organization. Following the tragic events of 9-11 the FBI and the U.S. Department of Justice realized that their policy of counterterrorism had to change to a policy that is preventive in nature. Jacobson (2006, p.27) contends that "The FBI can no longer be satisfied with merely reacting to attacks with excellence and bringing perpetrators to justice; it now had to focus on preventing them." During the 1990's the FBI's Counterterrorism efforts against international terrorism organizations focused on intelligence and criminal investigations. The 9-11 Commission contends that during this time frame, the FBI devoted their efforts to after-the-fact investigations of major terrorist attacks such as the Oklahoma City bombing in order to develop criminal cases.

As part of the intelligence reform President George Bush in June 2005 ordered a restructuring of both the Justice Department and the FBI (Lowenthal, 2006). As part of the restructuring proposal, the position of assistant attorney general for national security was created. This new position is charged with the responsibility of overseeing counterterrorism, counterespionage, and intelligence responsibility (Lowenthal, 2006). In an attempt to improve the FBI's counterterrorism efforts, the FBI established a *National Security Service* which combines the missions, capabilities, and resources of the counterterrorism, counterintelligence, and intelligence elements of the FBI under the leadership of a senior FBI official (FBI, 2009).

Subsequent to 9-11, the FBI has made significant changes to improve their collection of domestic intelligence. The FBI has increased the number of agents assigned to Counterterrorism. In addition, the FBI has upgraded their computer system which will enable field offices to better communicate with each other. The use of human intelligence or confidential informants is crucial to any counterterrorism strategy. Through the utilization of informants the FBI has been able to infiltrate and dismantle several domestic and international terrorist plots to destroy

American targets. One cannot argue with the fact that these methods have been successful because the United States has not been attacked since 9-11.

There is no "silver bullet" to prevent terrorist attacks. A determined terrorist can find a "soft target'" somewhere. However, advanced intelligence is perhaps the most important element in preparedness. Perl (1998) suggests that the United States should develop good working relationships with foreign intelligence agencies

Use of Military Force

Another instrument that is available to counter international terrorism to the United States and other countries is the "use of military force." Military force is an instrument that is not used very frequently. Wilcox (2002, p. 43) claims that force is regarded as an effective message that the United States will not be intimidated by terrorism and a warning to others that such attacks will be avenged."

Historically, this instrument has been used primarily for three reasons; to rescue hostages, retaliation for terrorist attacks, and strike terrorist capabilities preemptively. The United States is a new comer with regards in developing a dedicated military capability to rescue hostages. Europeans were faced with these problems years before the U.S. In 1972, the Summer Olympics were held in Munich Germany and the games were marred when members of the *Black September* a Palestinian terrorist organization killed several members of the Israeli Olympic Team and held the remaining Israeli athletes hostage.

The goal of the Black September terrorist organization was to exchange the Israeli athletes for Palestinian political prisoners that were jailed in Israel. The rescue attempt by the Germans was inept to say the least which led to the deaths of the remaining Israeli athletes along with several terrorists were killed at the Munich airport. As a result of this failed rescue attempt, the German government established the GSG-9 Counterterrorism unit. In a short period of time, GSG-9 has become one of the most elite counterterrorism units in the world. Shortly after this tragedy, many European governments recognized the need to develop and maintain highly skilled counterterrorism units.

In 1980, the United States attempted to rescue hostages at the seized American Embassy in Tehran, Iran. The rescue attempt was marred by a lack of military coordination in executing the rescue plan which resulted in several U.S. military aircraft colliding in the Iranian desert. Wilcox (2002) contends that this failed rescue operation revealed a need for better interservice coordination and training which led to the creation of the *U.S. Special Operations Command (SOCOM)*. SOCOM is responsible for the U.S. counterterrorism responsibility and oversees each individual special operations unit of every branch of the U.S. armed forces.

Another reason for using the military in countering terrorism is *"retaliation."* Pillar (2001, p.99) states "Retaliation has been the most important counterterrorist use of U.S. military force." The United States has only used "military retaliation" against terrorists three times. In 1986, President Reagan authorized a retaliatory strike against Tripoli the capital of Libya, for the Libyan government's involvement in the terrorist bombing of a discotheque in Berlin, Germany which was frequented by off-duty U.S. military personnel. American casualties included two killed and seventy-nine wounded. Shortly following the retaliatory strike on Libya, Secretary George Schultz stated during a speech he gave in New York City asserted that the United States must be ready to use military force to fight terrorism and retaliate even before all of the facts are known (Magogoto, 2006). This strategy became known as the *Schultz Doctrine."* Furthermore, Secretary Schultz claimed that the "United States (Magogoto, 2006, p.431) had the right to use force against terrorist threats abroad, including a policy of pre-emptive strikes in foreign countries." The Reagan administration claimed that retaliatory strikes against terrorist organizations were a legitimate response and that it was an issue of self-defense.

In an attempt to justify their strategy, the Reagan administration referred to Article 51 of the United Nations Charter which states that "nothing in the present Charter shall impair the inherent right of individual or collective self-defense if an armed attack occurs against a member of the United Nations until the UN Security Council has taken measures necessary to maintain international peace and security." Many pundits claim that a by product of retaliatory strikes is that they create a sense of fear and deterrence so that terrorist organizations will think twice before engaging in acts of terror.

The third form use of military force is preemptive strikes. By The People (2004) defines *Preemptive Strikes* as "military actions against countries and groups we view as having the capacity to harm us and the intention to do so" (p.1). Many supporters of preemptive strikes believe that we cannot afford to sit back quietly and allow terrorists and terrorist organizations to strike us first; especially if they possess weapons of mass destruction (WMD) or nuclear weapons. On June 1, 2002, President George Bush outlined his National Security Strategy of the United States of America at the U.S. Military Academy (West Point) commencement. President Bush stated "Given the goals of rogue states and terrorists, the United States can no longer solely rely on a reactive posture as we have in the past…We cannot let our enemies strike first" (USA Today, 2005). Bush added "As a matter of common sense and self-defense, America will act against such emerging threats before they are fully formed" (USA Today, 2005). This strategy of utilizing unilateral "preemptive strikes" became known as the ***Bush Doctrine.***

The Bush Doctrine has many critics and has been characterized as being polarizing both domestically and internationally. Eland (1998) claims that a strong correlation exists between U.S. involvement in international situations and an increase in terrorist attacks against the United States. He further claims that the U.S. would reduce the amount of devastating terrorist attacks if our nation would adopt a policy of military restraint.

Article I, Section 8, of the U.S. Constitution authorizes the U.S. Congress the power to declare war. "That power comprehends not only the enactment of formal declaration of war but also the authorization of uses of military force which are not intended to rise to the level of a war" (Ackerman, 2001, p. 1). On September 14, 2001, the U.S. Congress authorized the President to "use all necessary and appropriate force against those nations, organizations, or persons he determines planned , authorized, committed or aided the terrorist attacks that occurred on September 11, 2001, or harbored such organizations or persons" (Grimmett, 2007, p.1). This legislation is referred to as the *Authorization for Use of Military Force* (AUMF). The AUMF was used as a pretext for the invasion of Afghanistan and for the controversial use of electronic surveillance against possible terrorists.

Criminal Prosecution/ Criminal Justice

There has been a serious debate in our country over the most appropriate strategy to counterterrorism. The Bush administration adopted a "preemptive" strategy that relied heavily upon the use of the United States military to locate and eliminate terrorists and their sanctuaries. However, there are many Americans who believe the fight against terrorism is a law enforcement/criminal justice matter. As a counterterrorism instrument, law enforcement operations are generally used when the purpose is to bring terrorists to justice (O'Connor, 2008). Many critics of using law enforcement as a means of countering terrorism claim that law enforcement has been historically reactive as opposed to being proactive in the war on terrorism. For example, the FBI responded to the 1993 World Trade Center (WTC) bombing where six people were killed and 1,042 were wounded. Following an intensive investigation the perpetrators were tried and convicted in Federal District Court. The success of the prosecution of the 1993 WTC bombers has served as a bench mark for those supporters of the criminal justice system as a counterterrorism instrument.

Another argument can be made for supporting trying alleged terrorists in U.S. courts is that since 9-11, approximately twenty-four suspects of terrorist crimes committed against United States' targets have been indicted by U.S. Courts and are publicly listed as the "FBI's Most Wanted." The FBI (2009) states that "these individuals will remain wanted in connection with their alleged crimes until such time as the charges are dropped or when credible physical evidence is obtained, which proves with 100% accuracy, that they are deceased."

Those terrorists who were responsible for the tragic attacks on 9-11 violated a host of U.S. criminal laws, including laws that criminalize acts of international terrorism and specifically when such crimes include homicide (Scheffer, 2001). Osama bin Laden has been a U.S. fugitive since before September 11, 2001 for his alleged crimes against the United States. As a result of these federal indictments, the fugitive terrorists are required to be tried in U.S. federal court.

One of the major concerns with regards to prosecuting alleged terrorists in the U.S. judicial system is the security of evidence considered to be "classified" and has national security implications. The fear is that "classified' information obtained from sensitive intelligence sources could be compromised in open court. Proponents of the use of this counterterrorism instrument claim the Sixth Amendment of the U.S. Constitution guarantees a defendant the right to confront the evidence against him, to obtain evidence in his favor, and to be tried in an opening proceeding. In 1980, Congress recognized the utilization of classified information in open court could be problematic and enacted the ***Classified Information Procedures Act (CIPA).*** The purpose of CIPA is to provide procedures for protecting classified information in criminal prosecutions. Secondly, it served as a safeguard against the practice of ***"graymail"*** which is a defense tactic that some defendants have used in national security cases in an attempt to cause the government to forgo the prosecution or risk the disclosure of national security intelligence information (DOJ-Counterterrorism Section, 2006).

Schulhofer (2001) adds that CIPA allows federal courts to filter out any classified information that is not strictly necessary to the resolution of the disputed issues in the case. According to CIPA, the presiding judge is empowered to discern what information should be withheld from open court and what information should be accessible to the defense. The main problem with utilizing classified information in the prosecution of terrorists is the issue of discovery. However, the U.S. Department of Justice (DOJ) insists that CIPA has not changed the government's discovery obligations nor has it changed the rules of evidence. Moreover, DOJ maintains that CIPA has provided the proper protections and mechanisms to protect classified information, including classified sources and methods of collection, and at the same time protecting a defendant's due process rights. One criticism of this process is that it would prolong the duration of a trial because it would take a considerable amount of time for all of the court officers to obtain a security clearance that would grant them access to classified documents and information. Many defense attorneys claim that CIPA has worked well in terrorism prosecutions. Schulhofer (2001) claims that during the 1990s when most of the terrorist's cases were brought to trial, CIPA was not need because few security issues arose. Schulhofer (2001) noted that these terrorist cases included those individuals responsible fore the 1993 WTC bombing, the prosecution of Rami Yousef for the foiled 1994 attempt to blow up twelve airliners over the Pacific Ocean, and the prosecution of Ahmed Rassam the millennium bomber. In all of these criminal investigations the government was able to collect sufficient forensic evidence against the offenders that the use of classified information was not necessary.

A potential problem associated with trying illegal combatants in the American judicial system is that it would congest the federal courts. In the beginning of the Coalition invasion of Afghanistan approximately 1,000 illegal combatants were captured. The logistics involved in transporting these individuals to the United States for trial would become problematic to say the least. In addition, the federal court docket would be overwhelmed with the addition of trying illegal combatants.

As an alternative to trying illegal combatants in the United States judicial system, the Bush administration proposed tying those individuals by a Military Commission at the Guantanamo detention facility.

On November 13, 2001, President George W. Bush announced that certain non-citizens would be subject to detention and trial by military authorities. "The order provides that non-citizens whom the President deems to be, or to have been, members of the al-Qaeda organization or to have engaged in, aided or abetted, or conspired to commit acts of international terrorism that have caused, threaten to cause, or have as their aim to cause, injury to or adverse effects on the United States or its citizens or to have knowingly harbored such individuals, are subject to detention by military authorities and trial before military commission" (American Bar Association, 2002).

According to the United States Department of Defense (DOD), Military Commissions derive their authority from Articles I and II of the U.S. Constitution and they have been historically used to prosecute enemy combatants who violate the laws of war and it was last used during World War II.

"The military commissions are designed to try terrorism suspects under rules of procedures and evidence crafted specifically with terrorism prosecutions in mind" (Schulhofer, 2001, p.63). In addition, Schulhofer, 2001) contends the military commission is intended to streamline the trial process and avoid the complexities of federal criminal procedure. However, the utilization of military commission by the Bush administration became problematic when the U.S. Supreme Court ruled against the use of military commissions. In the U.S. Supreme Court case *Hamdan v.Rumsfeld (2006),* the Court ruled that military commissions as they were established by Presidential executive order, conflicted with existing statue and treaty law and that the entire system as it then stood was therefore void. In response to the ruling by the Supreme Court, the U.S. Congress passed the Military Commissions Act of 2006.

The Military Commission Act of 2006 establishes procedures governing the use of Military Commissions to try unlawful enemy combatants engaged in hostilities against the United States for violation of the law of war and other offenses triable by Military

Commissions. Furthermore, the Military Commissions Act was written to appease the U.S. Supreme Court and to elicit Congressional approval.

In the months following the tragic events of 9-11, the United States along with Coalition forces invaded Afghanistan because the Taliban refused to turnover those al-Qaeda members who were responsible for the 9-11 terrorist attacks. While conducting combat operations there, the U.S. decided to detain *"illegal combatants"* who were captured on the battlefields of the war on terrorism in a detention center located at Guantanamo Bay, Cuba. The Third Geneva Convention defines an illegal combatant as a "person (civilian) who engages in combat without meeting the requirements for a lawful belligerent according to the laws of war as outlined in this Convention." Kanstroom (2002, p. 2) explains the situation best by stating "lawful combatants are subject to capture and detention as prisoners of war by opposing military forces. "Unlawful combatants are likewise subject to capture and detention, but in addition they are subject to trial and punishment by military tribunals for acts which render their belligerency unlawful." The Bush administration has always claimed that members of al-Qaeda were non-deserving of POW status because they were non-state actors.

Scheffer (2001) agrees that al-Qaeda members should not receive Prisoner of War (POW) status because the organization does not meet the guidelines outlined by the Geneva Convention. However, he argues that the Taliban was the ruling party of Afghanistan at the time of the Coalition invasion and thereby captured Talban combatants should be treated as bona fide POWs.

The Chief Prosecutor of a Military Commission is responsible for drafting charges and when appropriate, he/she determines if whether or not the case should go to trial. The Military Commission is comprised of a military judge, and at least five members. In a criminal case where the accused may be sentenced to death twelve members are required to preside over the trial. Any guilty verdict and the imposition of a sentence must be with the concurrence of two-thirds of the Military Commission members. However, in the event of a capital offense, a sentence of the death penalty requires a unanimous vote of at least twelve members of the Military Commission. According to Military Commission guidelines, any commissioned officer of the U.S. military is eligible to serve on a military commission. In the event an illegal combatant is found guilty of any/all charges there is an appeals process.

Proponents of the use of Military Commissions contend that this system has more safeguards for protecting classified information as opposed to criminal prosecution in civilian court. They further claim we can ill afford to have sensitive intelligence revealed or discussed in open court. Wedgewood (2001) suggests that there is a misconception that in closed portions of a military commission defendants are prohibited from viewing the evidence against them. This is not the case. Defendants in a military commission are given access to any/ all evidence that is brought against them. This is to include evidence that might be classified. The sentiment is that the military commission exerts tighter control over the court room proceedings as opposed to their civilian counterparts.

Berringer (2007, p. 4) an advocate for the use of military commissions states "our criminal courts simply do not have extraterritorial jurisdiction over the vast majority of those individuals or the vast majority of their activities. These people have never set foot in the United States or planned specific criminal acts in violation of our federal criminal statues. If you were an Egyptian, Yemeni, or Saudi, it was not a violation of our federal criminal laws to travel to Afghanistan, train in an al-Qaeda camp, or become a member of the Taliban. These were not a violation of our federal criminal laws." We should be mindful of the fact that the terrorists who were tried in U.S. civilian courts were tied to specific acts such as the 1993 bombing of the WTC and the bombings of the U.S. Embassies in Kenya and Tanzania. Berringer (2007) further argues that the majority of Taliban and al-Qaeda detainees who were captured on the battlefield cannot be tied to a specific act. Therefore, according to jurisdictional rules, they cannot be tried in our civilian criminal courts.

Military commissions are controversial because they were traditionally used to try war crimes. The Obama administration has indicated that they will continue to utilize military commissions to try illegal combatants. In a major U.S. policy change, President Obama has stated that the detainees will be regarded as POWs and will be afforded all of the protections guaranteed by the Geneva Convention.

The prosecution and indefinite detention of illegal combatants continues to arouse passionate debates regarding the constitutionality of both subjects. One thing is for sure, as long as there is a war on terrorism the debate will continue.

Conclusion

Disrupting the financing of terrorist organizations is a major instrument in countering terrorism. A terrorist group like many of types of organizations cannot exist without proper funding. This chapter has mentioned that the passing of the U.S. Patriot Act along with other financial legislation has assisted U.S. law enforcement officials in identifying organizational members and associates who assist in the financing of terrorism. Moreover, the Patriot Act has assisted federal prosecutors in the successful prosecution of those individuals who provide material support for terrorists.

The debate continues whether or not terrorists should be prosecuted in the U.S. federal judicial system or by a Military Commission. Eric Holder, the United States Attorney General, has decided to prosecute four detainees in the federal judicial system. The detainees are scheduled to be incarcerated in a correctional facility located in Illinois while they await trial.

This chapter has illustrated the importance of a nation to defend its self against any/all attacks from another nation or terrorist organization. The debate continues among the international community whether a country should act unilaterally while fighting the war on terrorism. This was a major criticism of the European Union against the George W. Bush administration.

References

Ackerman, D. (2001). Response to Terrorism: Legal Aspects of the Use of Military Force. Congressional Research Service RS21009, September 13, 2001.

Alexander, Y. (2002). Combating Terrorism Strategies of Ten Countries. Anarbor, MI: The University of Michigan Press.

American Barr Association. (2002, January 4). American Bar Association Task Force On Terrorism And The Law Report And Recommendations On Military Commissions

Anderson, S. & Sloan, S. (2003). Terrorism Assassins to Zealots. Landham, MD: The Scarecrow Press, Inc.

Buckley, P. & Meese, M. (2002). The Financial Front in the Global War on Terrorism. U.S. Military Academy, West Point, New York.

Day, Berry & Howard Foundation. (2004). Handbook on Counter-Terrorism Measures: What U.S. Nonprofits and Grantmakers Need to Know. Accessed 6/23/2009, Retrieved from www.cof.org/files/Documents/Publications/2004counterterrorismhandbook.

Ehrenfeld, R. (2003). Funding Evil How Terrorism Is Financed-and How to Stop It. Chicago, IL: Bonus Books.

Eland, I. (1998). Does U.S. Intervention Overseas Breed Terrorism? The Historical Record. Foreign Policy Briefing No. 50. Accessed 05/15/09, Retrieved from http://www.catoinstitute.com.

Ganor, B. (2005). The Counter-Terrorism Puzzle A Guide for Decision Makers. New Brunswick, NJ: Transaction Publishers.

Guiora, A. (May 15, 2008). The Resilient Homeland: How DHS Intelligence Should Empower America to Prepare for, Prevent, and Withstand Terrorist Attacks. Testimony before U.S. House of Representatives, Committee on Homeland Security Subcommittee on Intelligence, Information Sharing, and terrorism Risk Assessment.

Hoffman, B. (1998). Inside Terrorism. New York, NY: Columbia University Press.

Jenkins, B. (2003).Testimony Before The National Commission on Terrorist Attacks Upon the United States. March 31, 2003. Accessed 6/29/2009, Retrieved from www.9-11commission.gov/hearings1/witness_jenkins.htm.

www.Islamcity.com.   Zakat.   Accessed   6/23/2009,   retrieved   from www.islamcity.commosques/zakat

Jacobson, M. (2006). The West At War U.S. and European Counterterrorism Efforts, Post-September 11. Washington, D.C: The Washington Institute For Near East Policy.

Kanstroom, D. (2003, Winter). "Unlawful Combatants" in the United States: Drawing the Fine Line Between Law and War. Human Rights Magazine. Accessed 6/30/09, Retrieved from www.abanet.org/irr/hr/winter03/unlawful.html

Lowenthal, M. (2006). Intelligence From Secrets To Policy (3rd. Ed.). Washington, D.C: Congressional Quarterly Press.

Martin, G. (2003). Understanding Terrorism, Challenges, Perspectives and Issues. London,UK: Sage Publications.

Myo, K. (2009). Europe and Counterterrorism: Evaluation of the Effectiveness of European counterterrorism policies. Retrieved from www.scrib.com/doc1365103Europe-and-counterterroism.

O'Connor, T. (2008). Counterterrorism: Diplomatic and Intelligence Operations. Accessed 05/28/2009, Retrieved from www.apsu.edu/oconnor/3400/3400lect08.htm

Payan, T. (2006). The Three U.S.-Mexico Border Wars. Westport, CT. Practical Security International.

Pillar, P. (2001). Terrorism and U.S. Foreign Policy. Washington D.C: Brookings Institution Press.

Scheffer, D. (2001, Nov. 14). Options for Prosecuting International Terrorists. United States Institute Of Peace Special Report. Accessed 6/30/09, Retrieved from www.usip.org.

Schulhofer, S. (2001). Prosecuting Suspected Terrorists: The Role of the Civilian Courts.

The Federal Bureau of Investigation. (2009). National Security Branch. Accessed 06/07/2009, Retrieved from http://www.fbi.gov/hq/nsb/nsb.htm

The Federal Bureau of Investigation. (2009). Most Wanted Terrorists. Accessed 7/01/09, Retrieved from www.fbi.gov/wanted/terrorists/fugitives.htm

United States Department of State (2009). Rewards for Justice Program. Accessed 05/19/2009, Accessed from http://www.rewardsforjustice.net/index.cfm?page=Rewards_ Program&language=English

USA Today. (2005).Bush Outlines Strategy of Pre-Emptive Strikes, Cooperation. Accessed 06/28/2009 from http://usatoday.printthis.clickability.com/pt/cpt?=cpt&title=USATODAY.com+-+Bu..

Wilcox, P. (2002).

CHAPTER 11

DISASTER AND TERRORISM EVENT RECOVERY

Introduction

The key to responding to a crisis remains with the plan. Contingency plans provide structure and a systematized response. Planning is necessary and appropriate. It is vital! It is not, however, a substitute for common sense. Sometimes the best-made policies, procedures and plans are defective and their defects are demonstrated as they are used. For this reason policies are generally considered to be guidelines for senior administrators, not an absolute demand or requirement.

A major problem confronting crisis management is the choice of the appropriate response and recovery strategies. Working under significant time constraints and information restraints (often limited and uncertain), is confining at best, but especially during a terrorism crisis response. Without a trained response reaction, management is likely to quickly lose control of the terrorism event recovery.

Crisis events, especially a man-made attack, whether criminal or terroristic in nature, brings out either the very best or the worst in the personnel who must respond to it and manage it. Crises cause strain, disruption, and malfunctioning in both managers and in organizations (Lerbinger, 1997, 341). Fortunately most terrorist attacks are of a short duration. Terrorists attack and run. Terrorists scheme and hide. Most terrorist tactical cells don't have enough manpower or the physical assets to overwhelm a substantial police or military security team. It should always be remembered that an initial terrorist act may simply be a diversion.

The terrorists often want to draw law enforcement or military personnel away from their primary target. The crisis event you respond to initially may be the beginning of your response-not the end. Crisis mangers are learning to cope with a multiplicity of issues, relationships and challenges.

"The precipitous rise in the number, variety, and intensity of terrorism related crises in the last two decades indicates that the pressures and demands on public and private organizations are outstripping their ability to cope with them. Therefore, no only has the subject of crisis management risen in importance, but its relevance to general management has become more pronounced and urgent." (Lerbinger, 1997, 341).

<u>When There Has Been No Planning for Crisis Management</u>

If an organization has planned for and formulated crisis event policies, it is quite easy to expedite the assignments of individuals by position, rank, experience, maturity, or site location. If there hasn't been a formal crisis management policy development approach, then we may well encounter what some theorists call *the headless chicken syndrome.* The headless chicken syndrome (HCS) is encountered whenever there are no formal policies and there has been a dearth of planning about crisis management.

The HCS syndrome involves a strong lack of cognitive skills. During times of great stress many respondents do the right thing., but at the wrong time—and in the wrong order. An administrator is calling his lawyer instead of dialing 911 for an ambulance. He just isn't thinking cognitively. His priorities are all wrong. If the administrator had a plan, or a policy approach for this type of emergency, he or she would be doing the right thing, just by following the crisis policy response template.

The problem of great stress during an emergency is that everyone wants to do something, anything, to help, to aid, to respond, but if they do the wrong things at the wrong time or the right things in the wrong order, they are creating tertiary crises that may overwhelm the original crisis response.

Professional quality crisis management can be implemented in any terroristic event for which a pre-crisis plan has been formulated. Quality crisis management can be accomplished expeditiously when the primary crisis manager and his or her assistants have been trained to do the right thing at the right time, and have a written set of guidelines to follow. Conversely, he or she has been trained to avoid accomplishing the wrong things or the right things in the wrong order. Timing is of critical importance in any man-made crisis situation, and in most natural disasters, as well.

Time is the most critical element in crisis management. Crisis situations are actually just difficult problems if there is sufficient time available for analysis and response. As a consequence, managers and executives need to seek more time between a crisis warning signal and the impact(s) of that crisis situation. Many of these gains can be achieved in pre-crisis planning and preparedness and response deployment. Time can be gained by becoming familiar with roles, actions and tasks outlined in plans and rehearsed in readiness exercises. Rehearsing deployment and initial action tasks helps reduce time wastage and thus increases time for examining the situation and making decisions (Heath, 1998, 302).

There must be a plan—and it should be a good one—but any plan is only the first of many steps. Any forethought gives a more appropriate response than a seat-of-the-pants reaction. It is very difficult to plan for unusual or crisis events that are outside the range of normal logic or understanding, but organizations that do not plan to *confront* crises will *react* to them. Reactions are not normally of the same quality as a planned response. When there is no plan and no prior preparation, a crisis reaction is likely to be totally inappropriate. The organization that reacts inappropriately responds in this manner because there is no plan, no policy and no real forethought.

When you have well-established reaction and recovery policies and well-formulated response plans in place, the recovery efforts run more smoothly. "Response measures are the time-sensitive actions incorporated to save lives and property at the onset of an incident"(Sauter and Carafano, 2005, 316). "Recovery is the effort to restore infrastructure and the social and economic life of a community" (Sauter and Carafano, 2005, 316). Because of the pre-crisis planning process, policy articulation and training, each of your crisis team members knows what to do and the order in which each step must be accomplished. Preparedness is the answer, both in terms of policy, plans, and pre-incident training.

Steven Fink, the author of *Crisis Management: Planning for the Inevitable*, wrote that every crisis, whether if be natural, as in an earthquake, storm or flood; an accident, as in an 18 wheeler or a cargo train carrying dangerous chemicals crash; or a violent attack by terrorists has as many as four different and distinct stages. Fink listed these stages as follows (Fink, 1986, 20):

- Prodromal crisis Stage
- Acute Crisis Stage
- Chronic Crisis Stage

- Crisis Resolution Stage

<u>PINS and Prodromes</u>

If a terrorist attack has already occurred, it is obvious that your Threat Management Committee's (TMC's) analysis of the PINs (<u>P</u>re-Incident <u>In</u>dicators) has failed, or has not lived up to reasonable expectations. In writing for the American Management Association Press, management scholar Steven Fink,wrote about an ancient Greek concept which he called a *prodrome*. The prodrome was a warning sign, an indicator of a developing threat, a pre-crisis indicator. Prodromes encourage us to be more vigilant to plan better and to prepare more. Contingencies which were never considered previously are now more probable, after an untimely attack against an American institution or individuals representing our nation.

Knowing how to recognize and manage the prodromes….before they erupt into the far more serious acute crisis stage is often what spells the difference between a company (or an individual) that profits during a crisis (its or someone else's) and companies (or people) that suffer and sometimes fail.

Knowing how to spot prodromes in a crisis also has the capacity to create "overnight" heroes within a company. These are the people, the managers, who make quantum leaps in achievement within a company and promotional leaps over their colleagues.

You and your managers should understand that anytime you're not in a crisis, you are instead in a precrisis or prodromal, mode.

Anytime, all the time. Be vigilant. Be prepared.

And if you operate in a prodromal, or vigilant state, you may catch sight of
something that needs to be addressed quickly, before it gets out of control. Before
it becomes an acute crisis (Fink, 1986, 7).

The acute crisis stage, Fink says "is the point of no return." (Fink 1987, 23). The
warnings were ignored or were not responded to appropriately so the crisis situation has
progressed from the prodromal to the acute stage. Some damage has already occurred
during the acute stage. The crisis manager's responsibility is to control as much of the
crisis as they can.

Normally the acute stage of the crisis is the shortest of the four phases, though it
may be the most intense. During the 9/11 event, the New York City's Office of
Emergency Management Headquarters was located on the 23rd floor of the World Trade
Center. The Office was evacuated before the collapse, but the office, nor its staff was
able to respond immediately in recovery efforts.

Additionally, there were secondary crises. The communication system for
firefighters and other first responders in the Towers Complex was not activated properly.
Fire and police officials ordered their personnel out of the building, but since their
communication system wasn't working properly, everyone did not hear the directive.
One hundred and twenty-one firefighters, one NYPD officer and five Port Authority
police officers lost their lives when the second tower collapsed (www.9-
11commission.gov/hearings/hearings11/staff_statement_14.pdf). Several fire station
chiefs were lost in the event, as was their experience in crisis management.

Also, since this was such an encompassing event, far more chaotic than any in
recent experience, there were many additional problems, essentially influenced by the

lack of communication and information sharing between law enforcement, firefighters, emergency managers and other first responders on the local level, not to mention the plethora of federal assistance converging to the scene. "Convergence is a phenomenon that occurs when people, goods, and services are spontaneously mobilized and sent into a disaster-stricken area (Demuth, 2002, 7).

The chronic stage of the crisis is often called "the clean-up stage." In the 9/11 attack, this involved first the rescue of the survivors and then the crime scene work as the federal, state, and local public safety personnel from many different agencies recovered bodies and evidence. The chronic stage was not over until the Twin Towers was actually broken into pieces, taken apart, trucked away and used in land-fill exercises.

The crisis resolution stage is the final stage. This is when the recovery process is ongoing. The primary response organizations are feeling good again, and the public is more comfortable. However, this is the time when another prodrome appears because most crises "come in pairs, bunches, or thundering herds" (Fink, 1986, 28). Another crisis is on the horizon and you should be carefully evaluating your PIN's and your prodromes.

Are You in Recovery?

If your organization is in the process of a terrorism attack recovery, you already know that your prevention and avoidance programs were not totally successful, most certainly were flawed and may have been an abject failure. The recovery process mandates several priorities, usually focusing on the priority of saving lives and property. During the closure of the response phase, the organization needs to carefully study what went right and what went wrong. Now is the time to professionally debrief *everyone* involved.

The debrief should not be an attempt to scapegoat an individual or an operational division, but should be used to make sure that the next time an attack occurs, it is handled more efficiently and effectively. You should immediately begin improving your antiterrorism physical security plan, shoring up the weaknesses discovered by the evaluation of the recent attack. This process is generally known as "target hardening."

You want to make it more difficult for any other terrorist intelligence unit (or the same unit initially targeting you) to gain access to areas where they can collect information. You want to insure that your facility, your agency, and your personnel are more difficult to penetrate for future targeting. The most important step though is prevention. Prevent your adversary from obtaining sufficient quality information which could be used to re-target your facility or agency.

Even as you are recovering from an attack or a hostage situation, you should be devising new policies or revising old policies and plans based on your most recent experience with terror groups. You won't know what policies are appropriate or necessary until you have appropriately accessed your risk factors. This will involve a tremendous amount of research. You will want to be able to completely justify the plans and policies ultimately adopted for your future use. You can't use a Ouija Board, or roll dice to get satisfactory numeric variables to justify your response plans.

Pre-terror Attack Planning

Planning results in better decision making. Reactions during a crisis can be pre-planned and institutionalized in a Standard Operational Procedure (SOP) notebook.

Invariably, decisions made in advance of threats, critical events, terrorist attacks, or extortion demands will be better than those made spontaneously during a crisis. Any careful thinking, particularly group plans, will be advantageous during the pre-planning phases. In reviewing those things that went wrong after the 9/11 attack, one of the major obstacles to effective recovery efforts was the lack of communication between first responders.

The individual police officers could communicate with other members of their same department, but not with all responding jurisdictions. In this case, police officers needed to be able to communicate directly with firefighters, as well. The individual fire department could communicate within their own rank structure, but not with other responding fire departments. The ambulance services could communicate within their own organizations, and the hospitals communicating with the ambulances could communicate within themselves. However, there was no comprehensive interagency communication system to assist in such a catastrophe.

The Department of Homeland Security is now funding Project SAFECOM to remove the barriers of interoperability, to meet the technical challenges of radio communications and other wireless network communication systems. The SAFECOM system allows "seamless: communications between all first response agencies during an emergency of catastrophic dimensions." When the system is fully functional across America, we will all receive more prompt and effective interagency responses.

The individual business organization, governmental units, and all public safety and private security organizations have a legal, moral and ethical responsibility to respond appropriately before, during and after a crisis. Concise research, advance planning, checking with other governments and businesses on how they acted, including what they did right and what they did wrong, will serve as a guide to improve your own plans and the policies developed as a result of your studies.

Advance research, careful preparation, group thinking and concise planning will assist both public and private organizations develop an appropriate response. In the private sector, these plans will go a long way towards foregoing legal action. An organization with long-standing, well-established policies relating to counter-terrorism and crime prevention is less likely to be successfully attacked in a deep-pockets law suit.

<u>The Planning Process</u>

Each organization should decide how it will handle the planning process insofar as terrorist attacks, natural disasters, tragic accidents, or dysfunctional chaos from any source. The well-thought-out "contingency plan" should be the focal point of institutional and individual preparations. "The planning process creates awareness of potential disasters, defines actions and activities that will minimize disruptions of critical functions, and develop the capability to reestablish normal operations" (Sauter and Carafano, 2005, 336).

The first step in this process is an institutional commitment. Half-hearted administrative/bureaucratic support is transmitted throughout the organizational hierarchy and the policies, plans, and implementation procedures will only be as strong as the institutional commitment. Normally, policies should be formulated and then plans should be developed around the Steps for a Successful Disaster Recovery policy design.

- Obtain management commitment

- Establish a planning committee

- Perform a professional quality risk assessment

- Establish operational priorities

- Determine continuity and recovery options

- Develop a contingency plan

- **Implement the plan**

(Sauter and Carafano, 2005, 337).

Some organizations do not make policy in the area of terrorism, but when they neglect this duty, they must accept the financial and legal risks of failing to create the policy or policies. Plans should also be well developed and be in the hands of all appropriate managers. Terrorism, counterterrorism, and terrorism response should be a well documented, well-articulated component of any organizations policy and procedure manual.

Crisis Management Definition: "Any measure that plans in advance for a crisis…any measure that removes the risk and uncertainty from a given situation…is indeed a form of crisis management" (Cole, 1980, 75).

In planning for crisis response, the Director or Chief of an organization's first step is to call in top policy-makers. It is always the responsibility of senior management to coordinate emergency planning. Normally this would include several top-level managers including those in security, intelligence, risk assessment, legal affairs, public information, and the financial division. Perhaps other skills should be included as well, depending upon the nature of the organization. Notes should be taken and recorded of all the planning deliberations. Once the policies are in place, the planning group should begin work on specifying the basic strategies and tactics to be implemented in the event of a terrorist attack.

These documented strategies should include intelligence gathering, prevention and avoidance approaches, pre-attack issues, security issues, an operations plan for terrorist attacks as they are occurring, and post-incident strategies and tactics as well. Training strategies for incident avoidance, deterrence, prevention, and response should also be articulated in the policies. Simulations, games, and probability assessments should all be a component in the management, staff, and line training programs which will be designed around the organizational plans and policies

The Four Primary Preparedness Measures
• Deterrent measures reduce the likelihood of a deliberate attack.   • Preventive measures protect vulnerabilities and make an attack unsuccessful or reduce its impact.   • Corrective measures reduce the effect of an attack.   • Detective measures discover attacks and trigger preventative or corrective controls. (Sauter and Carafano, 2005, 341).

The federal government, even before 9/11, was working on a document designated as the *National Response Plan (the NRP)*. It was released within weeks of the Manhattan crisis. Based on the mistakes made at 9/11, another document was created shortly after that event. This document was called the *National Incident Management*

System (or NIMS). These two plans led to considerably significant procedural changes in the way and manner the federal government responds. The plans also impact state and local plans as well.

When the NRP and NIMS, the Homeland Security Act of 2002 and the Homeland Security Presidential Directive 5 (HSPD-5) relating to the Management of Domestic Incidents (including terrorism) are all included we can reliably state that a national policy revolution was formed. Charles Hess, an official with the Department of Homeland Security said that the objectives of HSPD-5 were to:

(1) create a single, comprehensive national approach

(2) assure that all levels of government and the private sector work together

(3) integrate crisis and consequence management

(4) assign the Secretary of the Department of Homeland Security as the principal federal official for managing domestic incidents (Kamien, 2006,678).

Risk Assessments

The term *risk assessment* seems a vague and elusive term if you haven't used it before, but you can complete a terrorist risk assessment with strong determination and a review of how the assessment process should be accomplished. Risk assessments should be completed at all dangerous locations, usually by a previously established and well-trained Threat Manager and Threat Management Committee.

Indeed, unless you want to be victimized again in the very near future, you must complete an assessment! Risk assessments can be relatively easily understood and can be accomplished by anyone professionally trained in the process. Gather all the information you can. Evaluate the information for credibility and quantify it to a level of statistical significance, or to demonstrate that the data is not creditable. Your data may come from governments, businesses, specialized private security and intelligence agencies, the media, and public authorities such as the police or if overseas, the State Department's Bureau of Diplomatic Security.

The NIMS approach, adopted by the Department of Homeland Security insures that a new and better way of incident management occurs. It goes far beyond just the emergency response and recovery management process. It also refocuses those involved on continuing prevention and preparedness approaches, essential in a terrorism milieu.

Local governments can use the U.S. Department of States template for risk assessment. The State Department offers security threat analysis on every continent and every country. Just go to the United States Department of State internet-based bulletin board. If you are a part of a recognized international business entity, you can obtain membership in OSAC (the Overseas Security Advisory Council). OSAC records every crime and terrorist event against every western citizen on a daily basis in every country, so you can read these unclassified raw news summary accounts every day You can also call the 24/7 State Department Security Hotline or deal with private security research databases like The Stanford Group, Business Risks International, Control Risks Group. The security departments of almost any of the Fortune 500 companies can also render service on occasion.

If an organization is surprised at the onset of a crisis, it seems apparent that something was missing in the organization's contingency planning. If whatever is occurring is significantly serious to constitute a crisis, it must be presumed that had the organization known of, or anticipated the event, it would have been prepared for it. From this, it logically follows that the organization, for whatever reason, was not aware of the potential for the crisis to occur, at least at a level of awareness that triggered action. (Klamser, 1988, 16).

You need to know *and understand* your enemy. Knowledge of how they operate, what they do, how they attack, when they attack, and the result of their attack is a weapon which can be used as your first line of defense. Number crunchers (statisticians), and other mathematically influenced risk assessment personnel are often criticized in the homeland security field, with the field agents taking all of the glory, but the men and women who track incidents, collate events, and maintain records from newscasts, newspapers, magazines, and journals render an important service. When you have a valid terror (and crime) record system, you, your city, and your organizationcan become safer and your organization will be demonstrably more protected as well.

The worst place to obtain information is the rumor mill. Patrick Collins, was a veteran CIA Agent who had been assigned to protective details throughout the world. After retiring from government service he wrote *Living in Troubled Lands*, probably the first book of its type during the early era 1970 attacks against American citizens all over the world. Collins said that "the rumor mill will *always* provide unsolicited information Rumors and rumor mills make for good gossip….but they have no place whatever in your security planning or information gathering (Collins, 1981, 31). All data must be carefully scrutinized to insure credibility. Even creditable information from reliable sources may often be skewed or in error.

<u>Planning Reduces Many of the Unknowns</u>

The Threat Management Committee (TMC) that designs or implements a policy relating to a specific response or reaction has already carefully considered many of the problems associated with a crisis. They have considered the crisis stages and realize that a serious reactive blunder may overwhelm the initial attack response. The erroneous response becomes more public and more volatile than the original crisis. These inappropriate crisis responses create what are generally called *secondary* or *tertiary crises*. If you make a mistake during response and recovery, more than likely it will take on a "life of its own."

Any planning is better than none. The planning process should be prioritized, however. When the planning is initiated each planning committee participant should be removed from the normal office setting. A strong organizational commitment should be insisted upon. While a good planning committee will ordinarily be composed of key personnel, those with many responsibilities, it should be understood that their staffs should leave them alone during the planning process.

Cell phones should be turned off. Interruptions of any sort should be discouraged. Only extreme emergencies should be allowed to interfere with the very important business of pre-planning a response effort for a future attack. Superficiality is never appropriate in terms of crisis planning or reaction. The crisis planning response committee should be totally focused on this issue, and non-other.

Planning also provides an "organizational open forum" for dealing with terrorism-based crisis issues. You will see many different attitudes demonstrated in this process. There will always be a "Rambo" or "John Wayne" ready to insist on dynamic responses, however many of these responses will be over-reactive and counterphobic (excessive or irrational) in nature. Especially when lives are threatened, both immediately or in terms of the long term, careful attention should be paid to any and all response options. "Beware and be advised: crises historically evolve in a cyclical fashion, and a crisis sufferer almost never has the luxury of dealing exclusively with one crisis at a time" (Fink, 1986, 25).

Planning also provides an opportunity for the members of every organization to have an assigned role and responsibility. Additionally, planning results in better decisions, actions and reactions during any critical incident. Those decisions made months ahead of time will invariably be better than those made under duress during the middle of a crisis. Since every organization has a primary responsibility or function, the plans should help most of those employed get on with their normal duties and responsibilities. This in itself will limit organizational disruptions and help keep everyone focused.

One proven course is the prompt establishment of a Crisis Management Team (CMT). Many organizations have these teams in place, but make adjustments if a regular team member has taken another job, retired, been killed, injured during the current crisis, or has been kidnapped. Many international organizations have CMT's established regionally. Some even have a CMT established for every country or even region of every country to which they are assigned. The Threat Management Committee is vital in predicting and deterring terror attacks. The Crisis Management team improves the response effort. For the most part, organizations continue to function during an ongoing terror event or at the conclusion of an attack in spite of the chaos of the event.

The Crisis Management team needs the approval of top management and the formal and technical authority to manage the crisis. The CMT should name all of the team players. The team should be selected by finding those eligible by location, profession, interpersonal skill, temperament, and the ability to work well with others. Some teams may need one skill. Other teams may need specially selected skills.

During a hostage event, for instance, a crisis consultant or manager with considerable experience with kidnappings should participate. In another event, such as an extortion demand coupled with the threat of the use of demolitions, an explosives or ordinance professional may be needed. If skyjacking is the threat, a professional with unique experiences in flight security should be consulted.

Recognizing the need for specialization, a list should be created by the crisis management team of the personnel resources needed for particular types of terrorism and extortion-based crises. Sometimes, specialists may need to be brought in from other agencies, or firms. No one nation has had more experience in fighting terrorism than Israel, so often the Israeli Embassy can be asked to suggest specialty consultants from their police, military, or intelligence specialties.

The Provisional Irish Republican Army radicals gave the Irish government and the British military several decades of unique experience. Using recommendations from the British or Irish Intelligence, Investigative, and Crisis Response personnel, or using these experienced professionals as CMT consultants may be advisable.

One incredibly vital member of a Crisis Management Team is a public relations or media specialist. Especially in a politically dynamic hostage negotiation, the words our politicians say can be incredibly important. In fact, words can cause death and chaos in a terror environment. An example of this behavior was displayed by former President Richard Nixon, who made an off-the-cuff remark at a press conference during an on-going crisis event.

In 1973, Palestinian terrorist, members of Black September (the same group who kidnapped and murdered the Israeli athletes at the Munich, Germany Olympics), took over the Saudi Arabian Embassy in Khartoum. In return for the release of other hostages, who included one Belgium and two American diplomats, the Ambassador the the Deputy Chief of Mission—the terrorists demanded, among other things, the release of the imprisoned assassin of Senator Robert Kennedy (Sirhan Sirhan). For the first two days, the terrorists took no action. Sudanese officials informed them that a high-ranking American official, the Under Secretary of State, was on his way to Khartoum. Meanwhile, in the course of a press conference at the White House, reporters asked President Nixon if the United States was going to release Kennedy's killer. The President replied that the U.S. would never give in to terrorist blackmail. This comment was rebroadcast to Khartoum. The terrorists reportedly heard it on their radio. Shortly after that, they murdered the one Belgian and the two American hostages (Jenkins, 1985, 307).

In another on-going event involving the negotiations for the remaining 39 hostages of TWA Flight 847 in Beirut, Lebanon, President Ronald Reagan exacerbated the dynamics of the situation with an offhand remark at an impromptu political rally in Chicago. Reagan said that the plane hijackers were:

"murderers, thugs, and thieves." He said that there was no linkage to the Israeli release of Atlit prisoners (735 Shiites not then charged with any crimes), and the release of the Flight 847 hostages. He seemed to warn of reprisals against the hijackers and their sponsors. "I don't think anything that attempts to get people back who have been kidnapped by thugs, murderers, and barbarians is wrong to to."

The U.S. press was screaming that the rhetoric had scuttled the release and that the Hizbollah, widely believed to have planned and carried out the hijacking, were scared of air strikes and other retaliation (Carlson, 1986, 161).

If the team plan has been written with professional specializations and regions in mind, and has been updated to correlate with retirement, transfer, or death, then the plan is always ready. Decisions have already been made and they don't have to be made again, or made at all during the tremendous pressures of a crisis. The decisions were made when there was no crisis and when the organization was operating smoothly. This insures that no decision is rushed because of the stress of the moment.

Steve Fink in *Crisis Management: Planning for the Inevitable,* said that: "What you are striving for in the crisis management plan is to make as many mundane, routine decisions as possible when everyone has a cool head. You want to remove as much guess work as possible from the crisis. You want to, forinstance, know where the flashlights are before you need them" (Fink, 1986, 58).

It should also be recognized that very few government agencies, or combination of public safety and service agencies within a metropolitan area can single handedly handle a terrorism event. Terrorism involves all kinds of statutory violations. In the

United States, there are jurisdictional issues. Some cities are formed at the juncture of two states, or one, two or even three counties, possibly involving multiple police and fire departments, sheriffs, prosecutors and judges. The federal bureaucracy is also to be carefully considered, with some 58 primary law enforcement or investigative agencies and some 300 non-military federal agencies having some form of police, investigative, audit, security, or arrest authority.

The terrorism event could be a bombing which would be primarily under the federal jurisdiction of the Bureau of Alcohol, Tobacco, Firearms, and Explosives (BATFE), though frequently in terrorism bombings the Federal Bureau of Investigation is assigned the lead agency position by the U.S. Attorney General. If key members of the government or the President himself is threatened, the Secret Service my have primary jurisdiction.

In a kidnapping, the FBI would have primary case-making and control authority. In an event like the Twin Towers demolition on 9/11 all of these agencies would be involved, both in response to the crisis and in some forms of investigative authority. Obviously the Federal Aviation Administration (FAA) was heavily involved in the investigation of 9/11 and in preventing additional skyjackings and explosions by "grounding"every plane in U.S. airspace. Planes already in route, were diverted to the nearest available airport. No commercial aircraft was flying by late morning, only military planes patrolling our skys.

The time to meet government officials, intelligence officers, police administrators, sheriffs, hostage unit negotiators,or hostage rescue unit coordinators is before the crisis occurs. These pre-formed relationships can save lives and countless hours of chaotic preparation. The lines of communication need to be kept open during day-to-day operations, but they are absolutely essential during perilous times. These contacts should be ongoing but any pre-formed contact is better than none at all.

Planning and programmed development of extraordinary pre-formed interagency relationships can prevent the very disruptions that terrorists intend. This disruption is one of the terrorists primary motivations. Terrorists and their financial supporters laugh at us when we founder. When we respond quickly, efficiently and effectively, they lose this benefit. When we step in with spontaneous countermeasures, they will lose their initiative and their ongoing plans will be derailed.

<u>Bombing Threats</u>

Historically, terrorism statistical data clearly indicates that bombings are by far the most common type of terrorist attack. Clearly, police agencies should be prepared for this event or for the threat of this event. Bombings involve over 50 percent of all terrorist attacks in any specific time period. In areas where bombings are occurring with any frequency, there is also the threat of bombings.

Often threats are made over the phone, received through a messenger service, or even in the mail. Fortunately, only about two percent of all bomb threats are real (Fuqua and Wilson, 1978, 57), but since bombs are so deadly the threat needs to be carefully analyzed. Many agencies have a formal procedure which is spontaneously accomplished whenever a bomb threat is received.

When a bomb threat is made by mail, organizations need to have a policy to insure that the envelope, threat letter, or anything related to the bomb threat is kept for evidenciary purposes. Do not touch the letter or envelope again! Obviously, if a strange package or bulky mailer is received, leave it alone—do not open it. Especially if the package or envelope feels sticky or greasy, don't open it. If you are not expecting a package from a vendor, then do not accept it –or open it—unless you first telephone to determine the appropriateness of the delivery. Simple policies pertaining to reasonable safety measures can save someone-s life and maybe that life will be yours.

Some agencies have bomb-sniffing dogs who can detect explosives by the smell. Some agencies have explosive detecting machinery which is used on all packages received through the mail or the alternate delivery services. Most federal and state courthouses have metal detectors to check against smuggled firearms or suspicious packages clandestinely brought into the building. If you work in an area where bombs may be brought in or if bomb threats are a probability, there needs to be a formal emergency evacuation plan. If you already have an evacuation plan for fire, earthquake, or tornado, it may be appropriate to use the same plan for a bomb threat.

By rehearsing the evacuation plan, you may prevent panic in the event of a real threat. There was real terror in Twin Towers after the first plane struck. By exiting the building promptly, countless numbers of potential victims survived.

One of the primary responses during an emergency is an evacuation plan. Many more citizens would have perished in the Twin Towers, but for a spontaneous exodus which had been pre-planned for many years. The evacuation route should always be carefully considered. Some terrorists may attempt an "Eric Rudolph" type attack. In one of Rudolph's abortion center bombing attacks, he set off a small bomb on the side of a building. Several minutes later, after many police, firefighter, emergency service and media responders arrived; he set off a bigger charge right in the midst of them. A similar event happened in Kenya when the Embassy was bombed.

A truck bomb was driven to the Embassy delivery gate, but was turned away by an alert national policeman who denied access because of inappropriate paperwork. The truck drove around the block, dropping off a passenger with a hand grenade. He pulled the pin and threw it over the Embassy wall. When it detonated, many Embassy employees rushed to the windows to see what was happening. By then, the truck pulled back in the delivery gate because the guard was checking the grounds. After exiting the truck, he detonated the explosives, blowing up the building, killing many employees and blinding others who were looking out of the windows as the larger detonation occurred.

We need to have a pre-planned and well established route of departure. Emergency exits should be marked with the primary plan, or a secondary route if this should prove appropriate.

Information and People Management

The two elements critical to managing crisis situations are information management and people management. People react differently under stress. Fight, flight, or surrender are alternatives. Fight or flight inclinations are adrenalin responses. The surrender alternatives involves the acytlcholine effect which Robert Heath called a *negative panic reaction* (Heath, 1998, 347).. The acytlcholine effect or the negative panic reaction relates to skyjacking victims or terrorism hostages who slept through most of the event. Their bodies just shut down, like a hibernating bear or possum does during the colder season of the year.

Different chemicals are released into the body which allow the body to increase sensory perception and to respond to those perceptions. "The prime essential in any crisis is to remain calm, neither reacting aggressively or defensively to the crisis, but seeking how best to escape or deal with it by liming damage and resolving the situation (Heath, 1998, 346). Acytlcholine does the opposite and shuts the body down where it does not react inappropriately, but can't act appropriately when the opportunity arises.

If your organization has planned well, however, all of the principle workers have a plan, a function, and something to do. Nobody has to run around like the chicken with its head cut off. You follow procedures. You follow the plan. You do what your are supposed to do. You avoid doing the things you shouldn't. You do the prioritized activities first and those further down the list, last.

Since you should have co-planned with other agencies and perhaps even other jurisdictions, you can contain the crisis efficiently, effectively, and economically, limiting your resources to those vitally needed, retaining personnel and equipment resources for other attacks, other emergencies and other functions. Contingency planning for terrorism, major crime, storm, fire, tornado, hurricane, flood or earthquake will allow you to meet the challenge successfully. Planning is the key to all effective terrorism response.

Conclusion

Planning for the chaotic conditions of a terrorist attack is the key to incident recovery. Once an agency or jurisdictional committee has been established, priorities established, a planning committee appointed, a risk assessment (or a series of risk assessments relating to different targets and functions), and recovery priorities are mandated, your community or your agency is well on its way to an appropriate response.

You can have an effective plan, especially if you utilized consultants who have been involved in jurisdictional disasters where plans failed, and where plans succeeded. By accomplishing the planning and the policies encompassing the plan, you can make all of your employees aware of specific terrorist attack probabilities, or those involving natural disasters. You can mandate an appropriate response through your policy manual. You can get your agency back into its normal operational ability more quickly with these plans and policies, than you could without them.

After 9/11, the loosely coordinated coalition of federal, state, local and military authorities took another look at the probability of future attacks. President George W. Bush took a giant step forward and merged twenty-two separate federal agencies into a Department of Homeland Security (DHS). While each of these agencies still has its statutory responsibilities, the Secretary of Homeland Security has the mandate to insure that all of the investigative information, intelligence findings, and prevention efforts towards the safety of all Americans from acts of terror, is processed within his or her agency.

The mergers took place quickly and perhaps without as much forethought as necessary, but now the DHS has the budget and the manpower to more effectively protect Americans and/or to respond appropriately when there is a man-inspired crisis or a natural disaster. Additionally the DHS Act has channeled billions into federal, state, and local preparation, equipment and training. Working together our frontline agencies are in a better position to protect us than at any previous time.

References:

Mark A. Sauter and James Jay Carafano, *Homeland Security: A Complete Guide to Understanding, Preventing, and Surviving Terrorism,* New York: McGraw-Hill, 2005.

Steven Fink, *Crisis Management: Planning for the Inevitable*, New York: American Management Association, 1986.

David G. Kamien, *The McGraw Hill Homeland Security Handbook*, New York, McGraw Hill Publishers, 2006.

Julie L. Demuth, *Countering Terrorism: Lessons Learned from Natural and Technological Disasters,* Washington, D.C., National Academy of Sciences, 2002.

Robert C. Klamser, "Crisis Management: A Crossroads for Law Enforcement" (an unpublished paper presented to the P.O.S.T. Command College, May 1988), 16.

Patrick Collins, *Living in Troubled Lands*, Boulder, CO: Paladin Press, 1981.

Robert Heath, *Crisis Management for Managers and Executives*, London: Pitman Publishing, 1998.

Richard Cole, *Executive Security: A Corporate Response to Abduction and Terrorism.* New York: Wiley Interscience, 1980.

Brian M. Jenkins, *Terrorism and Personal Protection*, Boston: Butterworth Publishers, 1985.

Kurt Carlson, *One American Must Die,* New York: Congdon and Weed, 1986.

CHAPTER 12
THE ROLE OF INTELLIGENCE IN THE WAR ON TERROR

Let us never forget that good intelligence saves American lives and protects our freedom
President Ronald Regan, 1981

Introduction

The intelligence process is considered by law enforcement to be the heart of both anti- and counterterrorism operations. The objective has always been to anticipate and intervene in terrorist operations. The ability to predict the activities include indentifying the mission, goals and objectives of a terrorist group. This process is critical to intervention by governments. The best defense to the phenomena of terrorism is a good offense that includes critical thinking and problem solving. Governments must continually engage in strategic and tactical planning, awareness, and educational programs. To analyze the extent of a terrorist threat, the intelligence analyst must define terrorist's goals, identify their associations, determine their capabilities, develop profiles of both individual terrorist and their organizations, and suggest strategies for effective prevention and response.

It became evident after the events of 9/11 that the intelligence function that was developed and employed during the Cold War by the military and government agencies was ineffective in addressing modern terrorism. Described as an emerging transnational asymmetrical threat, modern terrorism requires a new approach to the art and science of intelligence analysis. These asymmetrical threats are dynamic and are not easily identified, infiltrated, or observed by any means of surveillance. These organizations such as Al Qaida are transnational organizations that are not subject to laws of governments and are not limited by the means they use to conduct warfare. The 9/11 Commission found that the U.S. intelligence community had failed to protect the country, specifically in sharing intelligence information.

Many experts concluded that the intelligence community relied too much on technical sources of information ignoring or minimizing the human intelligence (HUMIT) function. Because information if fragmented and different agencies have only parts of the puzzle, the analysis of the "dots" does not result in an accurate and timely product. As with criminal investigations, small fragments of the equation that are missing or not reported can result in failure.

Antiterrorism and Counterterrorism

Governments and law enforcement engage in two spheres when addressing terrorism. Antiterrorism involves defensive measures and threat assessment which includes prevention and physical security. Counterterrorism involves taking the offensive. This phase determines the response and carries out operations against terrorist cells or organizations. The intelligence analyst in critical to both phases and produces products for critical thinking/problem solving sessions, determines the ideology and motivation of the terrorist group, and provides strategies for addressing the terrorist threat. The analyst converts information into actionable intelligence by making sense of the information for use by policy makers and those who carry out the policy.

The intelligence process requires credible raw information in addition to quality analysis by competent analyst. Contrary to common belief, there is no lack of information. The problem is that there is too much information and too little analysis to produce intelligence or products that are useful. The ability to separate valuable information from unreliable or invalid information is a skill that must be developed by the analyst. Since 9/11 there has been an effort to increase the number of analyst and provide training to produce analyst that are skilled and competent. Intelligence, unlike evidence in a criminal investigation, does not have to meet the traditional standard of being admissible in a court of jurisdiction. Intelligence information is stored and becomes part of the puzzle that may not have value for years. The critical element of the intelligence function is that information is shared in a timely manner with those that have a need or application of the information. The National Criminal Intelligence Sharing Plan (2005) concluded that there were five top impediments to the sharing of information by law enforcement:

- Lack of communication and information sharing-there was found no centralized analysis and dissemination function at the state or federal level.
- Technology issues-there is a lack of equipment to facilitate a national data system and lack of interconnectibility between computer systems.
- Lack of intelligence standards and policies-there is a lack of common standards for collection, retention, and dissemination of intelligence data.
- Lack of intelligence analysis-there is a lack of compatible analytical software and a lack of analytical support, personnel, equipment, and training.
- Poor working relationships-there is system that does not foster sharing of information or trust between agencies.

Terrorism requires both proactive and reactive responses. The intelligence analyst provides information by means of products that is critical to both strategies. The world faces a serious threat from a number of terrorist organizations. The threat of mass destruction by chemical, biological or nuclear terrorism requires that the intelligence role be at the forefront of developing strategies that are designed to prevent, predict, and react to the threat of modern terrorism.

Terrorism has been a part of globalization of crime that presents problems of jurisdiction and responsibility. Terrorist operate outside the sovereign domain of countries and cross international borders at will. Effective communication and information sharing with separate governments becomes a critical requirement for effective intervention. Terrorist organizations are forming links to transnational organized crime and other criminal groups thus creating more dynamic, flexible, and powerful threats. This chapter will address the role of intelligence as the heart of anti- and counterterrorism measures to addressing the modern asymmetrical threat of terrorism. By producing a product that is customer focused, accurate, and timely, the intelligence function becomes an essential part of proactive prevention and response.

Defining Intelligence and the Intelligence Process

Collecting information is not the same as creating intelligence. Intelligence is not just information; without analysis, there is no intelligence. Information plus analysis equals intelligence. Analysis is often defined as the separation of a substantial whole into its constituent parts to allow an examination and interpretation of the thing. It also requires synthesis of data bases into a restructured whole which provides new information or additional meaning. The need for the collection and analysis of criminal information was recognized by Sir Robert Peel, considered to be the father of modern policing whose principles are still valid in today's criminal justice profession. Both O.W. Wilson and August Vollmer suggested that a unit be created to analyze information. The intelligence function falls under the broad term of criminal analysis along with crime analysis, strategic analysis, tactical analysis, administrative analysis, criminal investigative analysis and operations analysis (Baker, 2005). The focus of intelligence analysis has traditionally been on enterprise crime. However, with the growing trend of the nexus/cooperation and alliances of terrorist groups with transnational crime and other crime groups and terrorism becoming a national security threat, the intelligence analyst is now required to apply their skills to the anti-and counterterrorism efforts. This form of analysis examines structures, associations, management and leadership roles/positions, activities, and methods of operation. The transformation of information to intelligence requires the use of complex computer programs. However, for the information to have application it must be analyzed by experienced and trained intelligence professionals. Once analyzed the information is used in decision making, planning, prevention, and for tactical and strategic purposes. While strategic intelligence involves long term planning and solutions, tactical intelligence addresses specific operations that require immediate action. Other applications of intelligence include evidential intelligence and operational intelligence. Evidential intelligence is used to identify the location of additional evidence and provide leads for agents to follow. Operational intelligence offers support for long term operations that identify targets and intervene in criminal activity.

Planning is essential to the intelligence function. Decision makers must understand the long term view of a target or operation, identify trends and patterns, know what is occurring in the sense of temporal and spatial terms, and indentify and prioritize threats. Operations and long term solutions must be based on critical thinking and accurate and timely intelligence.

The intelligence process described in the Bureau of Justice Assistance report *Intelligence-Led Policing: The New Intelligence Architecture* (2005) consists of six steps: planning and direction, collection, processing/collation, analysis, dissemination and evaluation that are illustrated below.

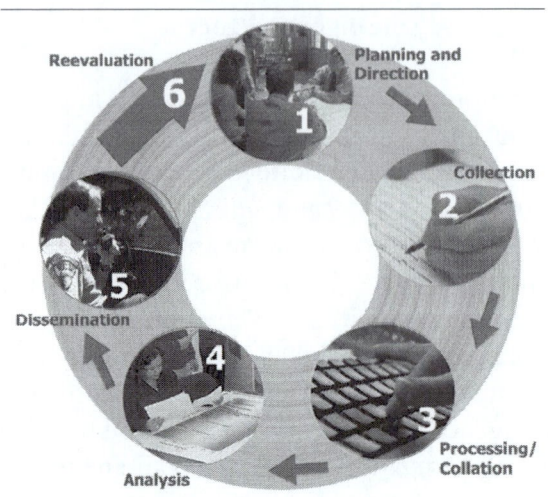

(National Criminal Intelligence Sharing Plan, 2005)

This is a continuous cycle that results in never ending improvement of the process of intelligence. This process is the same used in the Goldstein SARA model that includes assessment, response, analysis, and scanning which is very similar to the Edward Deming cycle of plan, do, study, and act. The success of the total quality movement resulted in law enforcement and federal agencies adopting the Deming philosophy of never ending improvement of processes.

The planning phase of the process ensures that the collection of intelligence is focused and coordinated and results in accurate information that is applicable to the mission. During this phase inputs and outcomes are determined and additional information is identified that is needed for established missions or operations.

Data collection is the next phase of the intelligence process and is the phase that requires considerable manpower, equipment, money, and time. The most common means of collecting information include:

- Confidential informants/operatives/human intelligence
- Electronic surveillance-wiretaps, image, signal and etc.
- Undercover operations
- Physical surveillance
- Open sources such as newspapers, public records or databases

The Collation/processing phase requires the analyst to eliminate data that is irrelevant or inaccurate and to put the data in a logical or chronological order. This process can be accomplished by means of programs such and data mining or text mining. This allows for relationships to be identified which results in applications for operations by agencies. The data is then evaluated for validity and reliability. The source is also evaluated for validity and reliability. A source that is generated by a law enforcement agent is considered much more valid and reliable that that of an informant/source/operative. Levels of source reliability may include the following:

- Reliable-this is the highest of reliability and leaves no doubt of source's authenticity based on past information always been proven true.
- Usually reliable-there is doubt of the source's authenticity-the source has been wrong on occasions.
- Not reliable-the source's information has been false on most occasions.
- Unconfirmed-there is no history or method to establish source's authenticity.

The levels of information validity may include the following:

- Confirmed by independent sources-corroborated by other methods or sources.
- Probably true-information that appears to be accurate but is not confirmed.
- Doubtfully true-information that does not appear to be true but is not confirmed to be false.
- Not true or Improbable-information that is contradicted by other sources and does not agree with other intelligence.

These levels of source reliability and information validity vary among the intelligence and law enforcement community. However, all agencies that produce and disseminate intelligence develop methods of rating the reliability and validity of the product.

The analysis phase is when the data is transformed into intelligence. This step is the process of deriving meaning from the data. The phase of analysis involves synthesizing data, identifying trends and patterns, predicting future acts by the criminal element, developing inferences or conclusions, and making recommendations for action based on the data. How a crime or act is committed, who likely committed the act, and what information is needed to continue analysis are part of the process at this phase. After an event such as 9/11 the first question most often asked is who is responsible. It is noted that the analyst does not make decisions about action to be taken, but only give recommendations. In the classic work by Peterson (1994) twenty six methods and thirty-seven products were identified as techniques in criminal analysis. The range of products produced is broad and includes but not limited to the following:

- Crime pattern analysis
- Time series analysis
- Frequency distribution analysis
- Statistical analysis
- Behavioral or profile analysis
- Telephone analysis
- Bank or financial analysis
- Threat assessments
- Vulnerability assessments
- Risk assessments
- Target profiles
- Strategic targeting
- Case analysis
- Timeline analysis

- Net worth analysis
- Commodity flow analysis
- Event flow analysis
- Activity flow analysis
- Association analysis

A more detailed discussion of selected products and their application to terrorism of the intelligence function will be included in a later section of this chapter.

The Dissemination phase involves the application of the products to strategic or tactical operations. It requires that the products get to the decisions makers in a timely manner. This phase is very sensitive and mandates a protocol or guidelines on who can receive the information. Information or products are often time sensitive and require considerable effort to produce. There is often conflict between the need to protect sources of information and the information itself and the need to make it available so it can be used. Classifications such as top secret, secret, and confidential are used by the intelligence community to protect sensitive information and sources of this information. There are other means to protect or regulate the dissemination and access to sensitive information. The following are examples:

- Sensitive but unclassified/for official use only/law enforcement sensitive (LES)-this type of information is not national security sensitive but may be dangerous in the wrong hands.
- Sensitive homeland security information-this type of information would impair federal, state, or local operations to be successful against terrorism
- Sensitive compartmented information (SCI)-this classification is an additional protection level that restricts access to people with a valid need to know the sensitive information
- Not for release to anyone classified as a foreign national (NOFORN)-this classification does not allow the sharing of the sensitive information to any foreign government or official
- Dissemination and extraction of information controlled by originator (OC)-Dissemination must be approved by the originator of the documents or sensitive information. In the drug enforcement community there is often created a pointer system that requires that the inquiry be relayed to the originator and they make the decision to release or not release the information to the agency or individual inquiring about sensitive information

Information may be termed unclassified-this means that the information is not or no longer sensitive and can be released to the public. Management specialist review all products produced by the intelligence unit and determine the level of classification and the security clearance needed to view the intelligence product or report. Federal telecommunications networks, secure digital intranets, digital networks, and Internets may be used to disseminate sensitive information. The Department of Homeland Security disseminates encrypted information over the Internet thru the Homeland Security Information Network (HSIN). The DHA Homeland Security Information Network connects all 50 states and 50 major municipalities. The DHS is extending its ability to network to all jurisdictions and is establishing communications with the private sector as well. There are other networks that are used to carry secret or top secret information.

All source agencies produce comprehensive intelligence products and reports, databases, charts, briefings, images and maps that are based on skill and sound judgment. There is a degree of collaboration among the intelligence community. Intelligence units and agencies in the United States are structured as hierarchies and around specialization. The strength of the intelligence agencies in the United States is the degree of accountability, but the system is slow to respond when information must be disseminated in a timely manner. The CIA and DIA are all source agencies. Many of the CIA's analysts are assigned to the Counterterrorist Center (CTC) and the National Counterterrorism Center. The National Security Agency (NSA) and the National Geospatial-Intelligence Agency (NGA) support all source agencies with technical collection that is validated and interpreted. Analyst can produce national products that often estimate and warn the nation of a upcoming or serious threats.

Finally the reevaluation phase examines intelligence products to determine their effectiveness. The process involves feedback from internal and external customers or users of the products/reports. Ratcliffe (2003) presented a model that depicts the concept of intelligence-led policing which is related to what the intelligence community does on a national and international level;

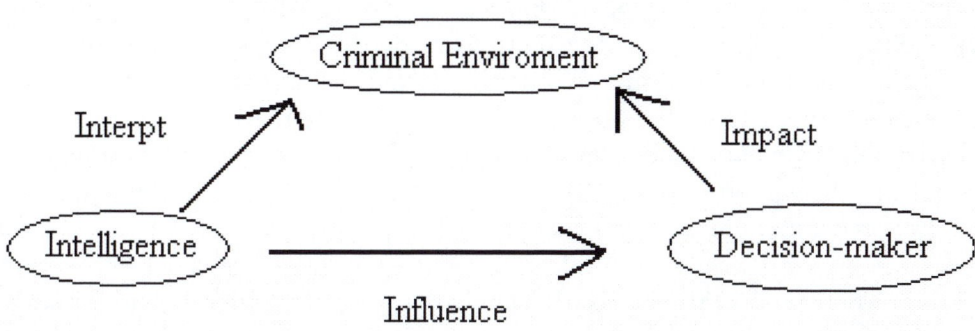

Figure 1

He explained the model (figure 1) as having a positive impact on the criminal environment that is dynamic and fluid, but one that will continue to exist. The three steps or stages include: interpreting (stage 1) the criminal environment by the intelligence unit; influencing (stage 2) decision-makers who have the ability to impact the criminal environment; the final stage (stage 3), results in an impact (desired outcome) by decision makers on the criminal environment. The point is that effective and skilled intelligence analysts are critical to influencing decision makers who can impact the success of the war against terrorism.

The United Kingdom's National Intelligence Model listed the desired outcomes of the intelligence community as crime reduction, community safety, criminal control, and disorder control. Most models of the intelligence process, whether international of national, prioritize a particular group or activity and develop products that help create an effective response or strategy to the threat. The United Kingdom's model outlines the following objectives:

- Establish a process that creates specific task and a coordination process
- Develop intelligence products that ensure the success of the operation
- Establish rules for the best training practices at all levels of law enforcement
- Establish protocols and systems that ensure the development of intelligence products (Intelligence-Led Policing: The New Intelligence Architecture, 2005).

The intelligence cycle make sense of an incredibly amount of information and is a never ending process. Without the skills and products of analyst, decision makers and planners would not have effective and efficient products to guide their decisions. Prior to 9/11 there were many serious bureaucratic barriers and rules that inhibited the effectiveness of gathering, analyzing, and disseminating information. Hopefully, the bureaucracy has diminished and a system that supports the timely and accurate production of intelligence consisting of the processes described above has been established.

Historical Background and Composition of the Intelligence Community

To develop an understanding of the intelligence role in the war of terrorism and the contribution of intelligence analyst, a brief review of the historical evolvement of the intelligence function is helpful. The roots of the intelligence process dates back to biblical time and the ancient Chinese strategies. A review of history reveals that links were made between gathering information, analyzing the information, and application of information to war. The military and tribes/clans/ governments were the first to apply intelligence to operations. Intelligence has played a critical role internationally as evidenced by the development of agencies such as the Central Intelligence Agency, the Soviet KGB, the British Secret Service, and infamous Israeli Mossad. The application of intelligence in law enforcement began in the 1920's and 1930's due to the Kefauver Committee findings of the existence of organized crime. The federal government and large police departments begin to collect information to identify and address the threat of organized crime. The 1967 the President's Commission on Organized Crime suggested the development of Intelligence units to support organized crime investigations.

Two of the first police agencies to use analytical techniques were the California Department of Justice and the New Jersey State Police. Among the first products developed were telephone toll analysis, event flow charting association analysis and visual investigative analysis. The early years did not have the benefit of today's advanced computer technology/programs or individuals that had the skill to use complex charting methods to produce effective products. By 1976, the Federal Bureau of Investigation (FBI), the Drug Enforcement Agency, the Bureau of Alcohol, Tobacco, and Firearms were applying at least some analytical methods to criminal investigations. Software packages begin appearing around 1980 and federal funded projects such as the Regional Information Sharing Systems (RISS) were developed. By the 1990's a number of professional organization were in existence including the International Association of Crime Analysts (IACA), the International Association of Law Enforcement Intelligence Analyst (IALEIA), the International Association for the Study of Organized Crime, and the Society of Certified Criminal Analyst (SCCA). Today there are a number of professional organizations and federal agencies that have developed training and offer certification and accreditation for agencies and individuals. In 1993 the FBI instituted the Crime Analyst Training program at the FBI Academy in Quantico, Virginia.

The Federal Law Enforcement Training Center (FLETC) in Glynco, Georgia has developed a program in Criminal Intelligence Analysis that is available to state, local and federal agencies. Analysts often have degrees or have taken courses in statistics, computer science, accounting, foreign languages, and economics/business. A number of universities have developed minors or courses in the intelligence function. The University of Mississippi recently added a minor in Intelligence to meet the needs of the modern intelligence agency or unit. ANACAPA Sciences of Santa Barbara, California, offers a number of courses in producing intelligence products or training programs that lead to certification or accreditation. Standards and training requirement are now in place for certification and accreditation and have contributed to the professionalization of the analyst's role in the intelligence function. To be certified requires the analyst to pass a written test and demonstrate skills during practicum's (Peterson, 1994, 1998). Powerful visual investigative analysis software such as i2 Analyst's Notebook is now available to the intelligence community and brings clarity to complex investigation and the intelligence function.

The U.S. intelligence function was practiced primarily by the military until the end of World War II. The National Security Act of 1947 established the Central Intelligence Agency (CIA) and the position of the director of Central Intelligence (DCI). The military and the Department of Defense (DOD) maintained their Intelligence function which was separate from the civilian organizations. Currently there are as many as 15 federal agencies that collect, analyze, and disseminate intelligence in addition to state and local entities. Due to the events of 9/11 and the aftermath of discovering that the "dots" were not connected and a general consensus that the intelligence community had failed the country, the U.S.A. Patriot Act was passed and the National Criminal Intelligence Sharing Plan was developed.

THE NATIONAL CRIMINAL INTELLIGENCE SHARING PLAN

In March 2002, the International Association of Chiefs of Policing (IACP) and the U.S. Government organized a summit of experts in criminal intelligence who developed the National Criminal Intelligence Sharing Plan. The objective of this plan which was revised in June 2005 is to develop solutions and approaches for a cohesive plan to develop and share intelligence. As a result of the National Criminal Intelligence Sharing Plan, the Global Intelligence Working Group (GIWG) was formed to further develop and oversee the national plan. The GIWG recognized the importance of the smaller local agencies to develop, gather, access, receive, and share intelligence information that is critical to public safety and national security. The plan outlines the responsibility of agencies, how they can be involved, and how to improve the intelligence process. The vision of the GIWG included a mechanism to promote and develop intelligence- led policing. The primary purpose of the recommendations of the National Criminal Intelligence Sharing Plan is to provide public safety decision makers with the information needed to protect the lives of citizens. The plan contained twenty-eight specific recommendations to achieve this purpose. Additionally, the plan called for a national model for intelligence training and a model for intelligence process principles and policing. Training standards are now being established in almost every state. Other major concerns and recommendations of the National Criminal Intelligence Sharing Plan involved interoperability of existing systems and the protection of individual privacy and constitutional rights. The plan calls for the development of sound, professional intelligence analytical products which support intelligence- led policing. The Criminal Intelligence Coordinating Council (CICC) was established as suggested by the IACP to advise the U.S. Congress, the U.S. Attorney General and the Secretary of Homeland Security on intelligence use, and works under the Global Advisory Committee until it is operational. The CICC has representatives from state, local, tribal, and federal agencies. These entities partner with other public and private sectors to provide intelligence.

Under the National Criminal Intelligence Sharing Plan agencies involved in the intelligence process are to adopt the standards of the Criminal Intelligence Systems Operating Policies Federal Regulation (28 CFR Part 23) and use the International Association of Chiefs of Police criminal intelligence model policy when implementing the intelligence function. Other recommendations include minimum standards for intelligence analyst including training standards. Background investigations on sworn and non sworn personnel are to be conducted initially and every three years.

Inadequacies of the law enforcement intelligence process were contributing factors in not preventing the 9-11 events. The events of September 11 demolished the sense of invulnerability to a foreign hostile action and paralyzed New York financial markets which impacted the United States economy. The National Criminal Intelligence Sharing Plan is designed to support the concept of Intelligence led policing and is now a priority of law enforcement by the United States Government (The National Criminal Intelligence Sharing Plan, 2005).

The U.S.A. Patriot Act

The act made fundamental changes at the Federal Bureau of Investigation, the Central Intelligence Agency, and other members of intelligence community including the Treasury Department. The act empowered the FBI to shift the primary mission from solving crime to gathering domestic intelligence. The Treasury Department is now responsible for building and maintaining a financial intelligence-gathering system whose data can be accessed by the CIA. The CIA will now be authorized to influence the surveillance operations of the FBI and to obtain and use evidence gathered by the FBI, federal grand juries and criminal electronic intercepts including telephone, cell phones, and computer transmissions. The CIA now has access to the powerful investigative federal grand jury. These juries have the ability to gather evidence without public notification (meet in secret) including testimony, electronic intercept transcripts, telephone records, financial records, and medical records. They also have the ability to grant immunity and compel testimony. The FBI and CIA can now share information without court approval. The FBI conduct roving wiretaps with a court order on individuals which allows them to monitor and record any communication device, without obtaining a new warrant, the individual/target uses. The act erased many of the limitations that resulted from the Watergate ear when domestic intelligence gathering was abused. The Foreign Intelligence Surveillance Act (FISA) of 1978 now has a lower standard for approving wiretaps (often referred to as Title IIIs) or electronic intercepts. Individuals suspected of working with terrorist can now be wiretapped. In the bill Congress allowed for the sharing of terrorism-related information collected by the federal agencies with local and state police. The bill expanded the ability of agencies to conduct financial investigations and is now considered to be the broadest and most effective law addressing money laundering. Congressman concluded that modern terrorist organizations are both domestic and international criminals, and are what they classified as hybrid criminals that can only be stopped by modern hybrid tools (McGee, 2001).

The Intelligence Departments/Agencies of the U.S. Government

These components of the intelligence community are charged with the collection, analysis, and dissemination of intelligence, and are part of the Executive branch of government. These elements are managed by either military or civilian organizations. The Department of Homeland Security was designed to coordinate intelligence between all elements of the intelligence community. The following is a list of the members of the agencies, departments, and offices:

Independent Component

- The Central Intelligence Agency (CIA)-the agency converts basic information collected overseas into a finished intelligence product by integrating, evaluating, and analyzing all available data (all source analysis) that concerns national security. The CIA produces products used by national policymakers, defense planners, law enforcement, and the military. They also are involved in counterintelligence abroad and serve under the direction of the President of the United States.

Defense Department Components

- The National Security Agency (NSA)-this agency collects and analyzes foreign signal intelligence or information. It is also responsible for the security of the U.S. information systems.

- Defense Intelligence Agency (DIA)-this agency provides all source intelligence analysis to both policymakers and military branches. It specialized in the collection, analysis, and dissemination of foreign military intelligence.

- The National Geospatial-Intelligence Agency (NGA)-supports national security and the Department of Defense with geospatial intelligence.

- The National Reconnaissance Office (NRO)-constructs and designs, operates, and maintains the reconnaissance satellites of the United States.

- The military has intelligence components that support their missions and national security. Military intelligence is the product of gathering information about foreign military disposition, equipment and strategic plans, analyzing the contents of that information, and disseminating the findings to decision makers. The three forms of information are tactical, operational, and strategic. Military intelligence has a rich history in the U.S. dating back to the colonial period in America. From the Revolutionary War, thru the Cold War, the Y2K threat, to the present national security threats such as terrorism and transnational organized crime, the military intelligence function has been critical to the survival of America.

Other Components

- The Department of Justice/FBI-Collects and analysis intelligence within the U.S. and conducts domestic counterespionage and counterintelligence.

- Department of Homeland Security/Directorate of Information- Analysis and Infrastructure Protection-monitors and assess national security threats, coordinates warnings, and is concerned with the vulnerabilities of U.S. critical infrastructures.

- Department of Homeland Security/U.S. Coast Guard Intelligence-responsible for security interest in maritime regions and international waters including the coast of the U.S., it ports, and inland waterways.

- Department of Treasury/Office of Terrorism and Financial Intelligence (INF)-collects and processes any financial information that may become a threat to the interest of U.S. financial institutions (Kamien, 2006).

The federal intelligence community in coordination with other members that collect and analyze information such as state and major cities provide intelligence to the government and law enforcement up and to including the President of the United States. Briefs are written and distributed to the management of intelligences agencies and policymakers/decisions makers. Once tactical or strategic plans are determined they are sent to operations to be implemented or carried out. There are entities that only collect information and pass it on to all source agencies; small municipalities, rural county law enforcement, and the private business community. All elements of law enforcement are expected to contribute to the intelligence process. The U.S. government has developed a National Security Strategy, the Homeland Security Strategy, and the National Strategy for Countering Terrorism in addition to the National Criminal Intelligence Sharing Plan, all of which address the collection and analysis of information that is directed toward protecting the U.S. population and the U.S. infrastructure. The aftermath of 9/11 resulted in major changes to the intelligence community and the governments begin to address the concern that the community had not shared intelligence information adequately or were not connecting the "dots". Intelligence analysts produce products that examines local, national, and global issues and information that may influence foreign or domestic threats to homeland security.

Categories of Intelligence

Intelligence falls within two broad categories; technical and human collection. The capabilities of technical intelligence which are for the most part managed by DOD, DCI, and the Director of National Intelligence include the following:

- signal intelligence (SIGINT)
- Imagery intelligence (IMINT)
- Measurement and signatures intelligence (MASINT)

SIGINT is the responsibility of the NSA who collects processes and reports this type of data. The electronic signals are analyzed and put into a form that can be understood by the end user. The products produced by the NSA support all source agencies such as the CIA.

IMINT involves the analysis of aerial imagery or gleaming information from photos of detailed high-altitude pictures of infrastructure, military or terrorist bases, and movement of members of these entities. The National Geospatial Intelligence Agency (NGA) gathers this type of intelligence through a network of satellites, aircraft, and a variety of sensor systems. Products produced by the NGA support all source agencies.

MASINT is method of passively collecting data on targets of interest and measuring or identifying characteristics of the individual, object, or activity. Again, the product supports the function of all source agencies.

Human intelligence (HUMINT) is the most common method of collection and is likely the oldest form of intelligence. Most investigative agencies including state, federal, and local law enforcement contribute to or create HUMINT. Collected by overt or covert methods, this type of collection involves serious risk to those collecting the information. The FBI, ICE, DEA, state law enforcement, and major cities are all heavily involved in collecting human intelligence. The CIA and DIA are limited to collecting human intelligence outside the borders of the United States. Considered to be the most valuable, human intelligence can provide insight into the targets intentions, structure, leadership, methods of operations, identity of members of the target organization, methods of communications, and capabilities of the organization to carry out its objectives. HUMINT requires that agencies place either agents or develop operatives (informants/sources) within target organizations. Management and development of these sources requires extensive interpersonal skills, time, money, and equipment. The development of sources of information can take years as with the training of an agent to carry out short or long deep undercover or covert operations. Agents receive extensive training in this area of intelligence collection which makes this method both expensive and time consuming.

Open-source Intelligence (OSINT) if a source of intelligence that escapes the attention of the public. This information is derived from publicly available media sources such as news papers, journals, magazines, television broadcast, and etc. The value of this type of intelligence can be found in its contributions to understanding who or what nations are supporting terrorism, the intentions, ideology, and strategies or terrorist or their organizations, and potential targets for terrorist activity. This data is often the least exploited by intelligence units and even may be considered too time consuming to collect. However, OSINT is a major contributor to the overall product that is produced by all source agencies.

The job of the intelligence community is to produce a product using all the above sources and types of intelligence that can be shared with those that need the information. The integration of all types or categories of intelligence can be slow due to the complexity and time consuming technical process, establishing who has access, the process of compartmentation, and the culture of exclusivity or ownership of intelligence. All of these problems slow the production of accurate and timely intelligence products. The decision of what is valuable and what is not, what to keep and what to eliminate from the voluminous amount of information is a formable task for the intelligence analyst.

Although the PATROIT Act eliminated many problems of sharing information, the chronic problem of lack of cooperation and sharing information between law enforcement and intelligence agencies remains. Who controls the information and how the product should be classified both limits access to the intelligence product and is an impairment to sharing critical data. Add to the mix establishing the reliability and validity of the source and the information, the job of the intelligence community is inundated with problems. The goals of providing timely warnings of terrorist attacks, improving awareness of the threats, and disrupting terrorist activities or destroying the organization depend largely upon the success of the intelligence community. There has been a reform effort with some success by the U.S. government to improve the intelligence function. This effort is a work in progress and requires that the problems above be addressed.

The Intelligence Products

To become effective in both proactive and reactive tactics and strategies, products of the intelligence analyst are essential to the effectiveness of operations. With the magnitude of information from state, local, federal, international sources, and open sources, the collection, analysis, interpretation and timely dissemination of accurate and competent products is the role of the intelligence analysis. The planning phase determines what data is needed to be effective against a specific terrorist threat. The work of the analyst will answer questions such as what group is the threat from, when and where will the attack occur, and how will the threat be carried out. The agents in the field need to know the preferred tactics and strategies of the terrorist to become proactive and prevent or meet the threat with an adequate response. The analyst becomes a problem solver using critical and analytical thinking (Baker, 2005). The terrorist threat like that of transnational organized crime is a dynamic and asymmetrical threat that requires the analyst to continuously redefine the tactics and strategies that are required to meet the threat. Effective responses requires the wisdom expressed by Sun Tzu, the 5th century Chinese general and General George Patton; if you know the enemy and know yourself then you need not fear the result of a hundred battles. The analyst allows our government to take the offense and avoid continuously being on the defense and only responding to the terrorist threats.

To defeat the goals of terrorism (causing governments to overreact and form negative public opinion that diminishes support for the government, obtaining recognition for their cause, and demonstrating the vulnerability and inability of governments to protect the country) the product of the intelligence analyst must include both antiterrorism and counterterrorism tactics and strategies. The antiterrorism products are proactive security methods that include collecting intelligence, analyzing vulnerabilities, and preventative measures. Counterterrorism products include those that develop a plan for the management of crisis, propose adequate responses to a terrorist event, and actual management of a crisis. The products provide the user with a deeper understanding of the culture and nature of terrorism that assist in determining the nature of the threat, the target, and the time table for the likelihood of an attack.

The intelligence analyst identifies the dimensions of terrorist groups including the organizational structure of the group and membership of the group. Baker (2005) listed five dimensions of antiterrorism that allow government to become proactive:

- First Dimension-Law enforcement patrol and reactive responses
- Second Dimension-Crime prevention proactive responses and problem-oriented policing
- Third Dimension-Personal Security operations (internal and external)
- Fourth Dimension-Personal security
- Fifth Dimension-Operations security

Baker writes that countering terrorism requires that the analyst and government operate in the third, fourth, and fifth dimensions. Analysts often identify symbolic targets of opportunity such as the World Trade Center or the Lincoln Tunnel in New York. He concludes that the problem lies with the police thinking in the second dimension only; the result is a lack of operation security, physical security, and personnel security. The vulnerability of computer systems and information systems are problematic for governments. The analyst provides products that protect from the threat of both passive an active information security challenges, produce suggestions for physical security and target hardening strategies, and identify what individuals or personnel are at risk.

Peterson in her book, Applications in Criminal Analysis-A Sourcebook (1998), listed twenty-six methods and thirty-seven products that are the role of the analyst. Many of these are used today in the war on terrorism. She concluded that the analytical products that can be used in the investigation of terrorism depend on the proactive or reactive nature of the investigation. Because of the dynamic nature of modern terrorism and the unpredictable nature of terrorism, government must gather and analyze information on all groups that are identified. The traditional hierarchal pyramid structure of terrorist groups has been replaced by loose networks structure with group members organized into cells that have little or no contact with other cells or a central leadership location. The terrorist groups of the past resemble the traditional Weberian bureaucratic structure that is more vulnerable to the intelligence community employing technical surveillance or human intelligence sources. Al Qaeda has cells in many countries and is fluid and dynamic having non-linear, semi-hierarchical organizational structure. Al Qaeda is a hybrid that has both a traditional Weberian structure and non- hierarchical networks/cells. The organization has a shur (council), media committee, travel committee, finance committee, and a military committee.

The cells of Al Qaeda function autonomously, with limited communication or support from the leader, and the ability to make decisions is at lowest possible level. Each cell cannot identify or communicate with other cells. This type of structure is problematic for the intelligence function (Diebert and Stein, 2002). The modern terrorist structure and activity result in an asymmetrical threat that requires asymmetrical responses and products from the intelligence community. Contemporary terrorist networks are now amorphous, indistinct organizations that operate on a linear nonhierarchical structure. The broad categories of products listed by Peterson include group information, financial information, personnel data, and locational data. Financial analysts look at sources of funds that may include traditional crimes such as robberies or drug trafficking operations that can support terrorist missions. Sudden influx of funds can be an indicator of preparation for a terrorist attack.

Personnel data involves group membership, leadership changes, and the capabilities of members. Associations or connections between groups or other organizations such as organized crime are part of the products that are developed under this type of data. Locational data may include the location of the groups training camp, their headquarters and safe houses. The location of weapon stash houses and supplies storage locations may be discovered using locational data. Together, these three types of information can determine the potential threat of the terrorist groups to life or property. The seizure of large amounts of supplies or weapons or the destruction of training camps or headquarters can prevent these groups from carrying out their mission; preemptive or proactive measures. The following is a partial list and explanation of the products produce by the intelligence analyst. For more information on the products see Introductory Criminal Analysis by Thomas Baker (2005) and Application in Criminal Analysis, A Sourcebook by Marilyn Peterson (1998).

- Threat Analysis-involves the analysis of intelligence information and security measures that results in the identification and vulnerable of terrorist targets such as nuclear power plants, information systems, airports, dams and symbolic targets such as the Statue of Liberty. Threat analysis results in the evaluation of security posture. The process examines the group's propensity for violence and the time and place of an attack or event. It is often termed "warning intelligence". The product includes recommendations for countermeasures. The intelligence community must now address the asymmetric threat that modern terrorist organizations present. The term "asymmetric threat" describes attempts by the terrorist to circumvent or undermine an opponent's strengths while exploiting his weaknesses, using methods that differ significantly from the opponent's usual mode of operation. The terrorist employs weapons and tactics that defeat the technological superiority of the target. Termed by the military as the "new battlespace", the terrorist may use chemical, biological, or nuclear weapons, or use computer tactics that destroy information systems that control much of the infrastructure of a country; information warfare may focus on individual, industrial or economic levels. There are over 122 countries that operate online industrial and economic espionage against the United States. Terrorist organizations are sure to note and employ this type of attack (La Carte, 2002).

- Profiles-This tool develops indicators of behavior or a model of probable activity using psychological and sociological data on terrorist. These profiles cannot predict behavior, but can link suspects and methods of operations to events or activity. Ideological positions, type of terrorist activity, method of operations patterns, and personality factors can be developed from the social, psychological, and personality needs of the terrorist. Terrorist typologies such as the lone-wolf versus the organized terrorist are discussed and compared which can link terrorist to criminal events or terrorist action (Baker, 2005).

- Biographical Sketches-The product compiles all known data on individuals or entities. It may include the query of other data bases such as FinCEN, RISS, National Crime Information Center, and other agencies' intelligence files. The information includes aliases, addresses, identifying numbers, vehicle identification, associates, place of business, any criminal activity, and group affiliations.

- Collection Plan-This is a preliminary step toward the completion of tactical or strategic assessment and focuses on what needs to be collected, how to collect the information, and when the information must be collected. Survey instruments, time tables for collection, and hypotheses may be part of this step. A major part of this process is identifying potential sources of information or types of intelligence that is needed. The collection plan includes group or activity specific questions. With terrorist investigations the plan will examine the political affiliations of the group.

- Activity Flow Chart-This product charts the general steps needed to complete a particular operation. It provides an overview of occurrences without dates. The activity flow chart explains and charts complex processes such money laundering operations by terrorist organizations to fund their activity. Domestic terrorist organizations have been involved in the criminal activity of bank robbery. An activity flow chart produces information on the method of operation that may link robberies or identify potential suspects. The following is an example of an activity flow chart of the crime of bank robbery:

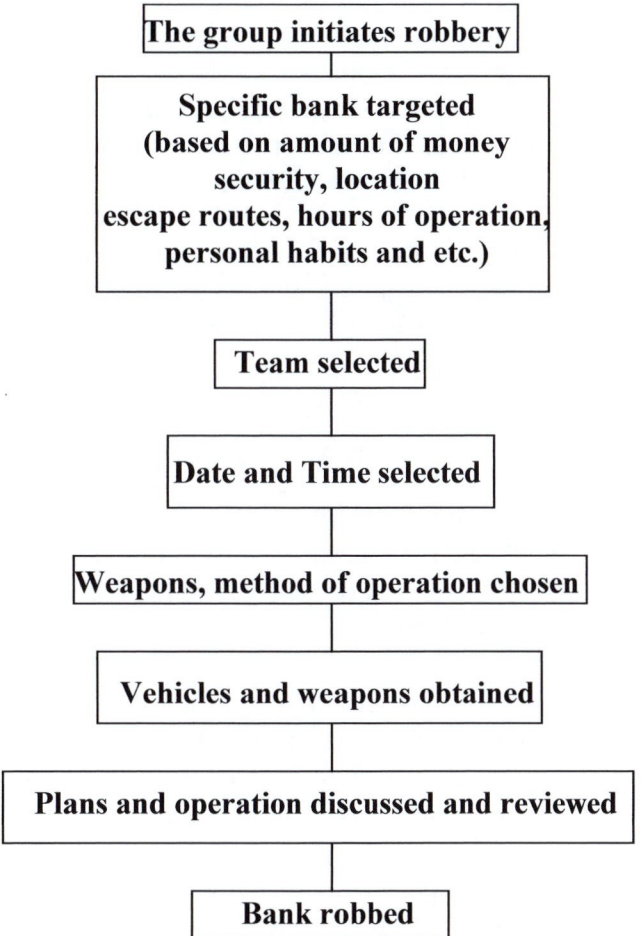

The application of the activity chart to terrorism may involve examining and depicting all activity prior to an attack. It can outline steps that are common to a specific group and may provide tactics or strategies to respond to or prevent the attack.

- Network Analysis-a conceptual tool used to study the structure and regular pattern of complex social social systems. This product discovers nodes that are interconnected by links. It can be used to describe the target of a terrorist group and organizational structure of the group. The product addresses the group as an emerging form of social organization. Conclusions about many of the terrorist groups are: they are decentralized hierarchies with multiple hubs have links or pathways between nodes, and that the level of redundancy of nodes and links is directly correlated to the level of security of the system. Nodes can include corporations, urban centers, or charities while links include highways, fiber-optic cables, railroads, and flight routes and etc. Efficiency of a network can be calculated by measuring distance between nodes. This distance can be physical such as a highway, relational distance such as the strength of relations among member of a terrorist cell, or communicational distance as in the case of ability to pass on information to members of a cell without disruption or detection. The importance of the node is correlated to the change in efficiency of the cell or organization when the node is not present (Latora, Vito and Marchiori, 2004). Valdis Krebs used network analysis to map links between the 9/11 hijackers. He calculated prior contacts and trust between the subjects which was used to determine the strength and existence of the members of the group. He created a visual network that revealed that removal of hijacker Mohamed Atta would have the most impact of the ability of the group to carry out the events of 9/11. This product is valuable to post event analysis. From this analysis, Al Qaeda is a structure that is almost completely decentralized, non-hierarchical, flexible and highly redundant which results in the likely survival of the network (Hoffman, 2004).

- Content Analysis-This is the classification of different types of data with the idea of deriving meaning from the information. Content analysis may be done on written or recorded documents. This product can determine psychological state of individuals or reflect cultural patterns. The intentions of the communications may be reveled by content analysis.

- Conversation analysis is process of examining spoken communication for meaning and intent. The role of each participant is determined along with the meaning of the exchange. This is an essential part of conspiracy investigations.

- Descriptive Analysis-A process where a summary of events and activity by a group or individual leads to recommendations, inferences, and conclusions. This product may note changes in leadership, geographic area of activity, type of activity, membership and associations.

- Association Chart-This product depicts the relationships among members of a terrorist cell or organization graphically. People are shown as circles and businesses depicted as boxes. The associations are connected by lines with dotted lines denoted weak or suspected relationships. The hierarchy of a network or operation mode of a terrorist conspiracy may become apparent from the association chart. While those who communicate or meet frequently are in the center of the chart, leaders appear in the peripheral positions indicating insulation from the activity of the organization. The product gives information about the conspiracy and the roles played by people and businesses of terrorist operations. Association charts are used within an association analysis which depicts the relationships among people, groups, business, and other entities. The following is and example of how a chart may be used to depict relationships:

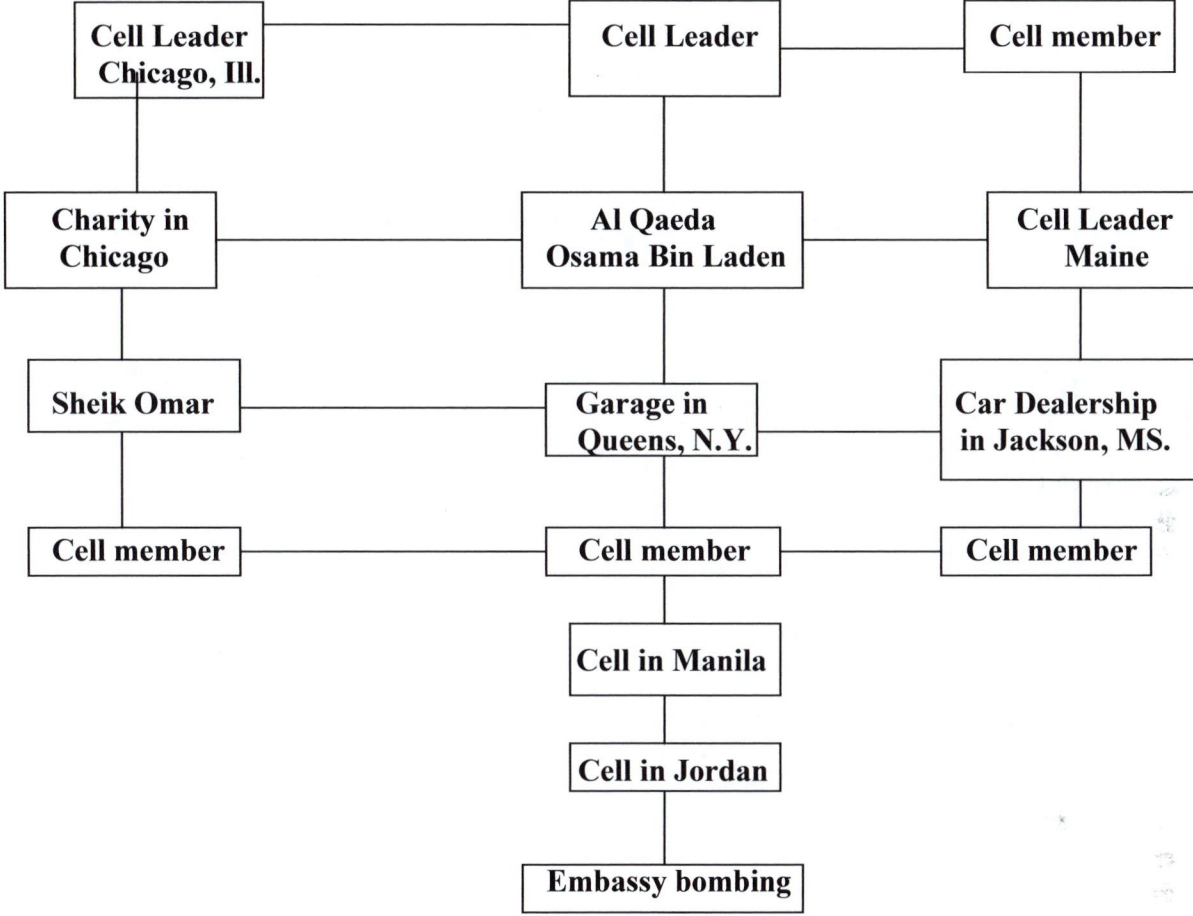

- Trend Analysis-This product uses numeric or descriptive data to make conclusions. It is used to support a prediction or forecast. A trend may be described as a terrorist group changing tactics or targets to produce a more effective event for their cause.
- Warning-this is the product of threat or vulnerability analysis that provides facts concerning future occurrences that may address threats against an individual, group, or symbolic target.
- Telephone record analysis-The analyst reviews data generated by electronic surveillance or telephone bills and develops pattern of activity that may be related to criminal activity thus establishing roles or identity of conspirators. This product often includes a telephone chart that depicts activity between multiple suspects/targets.
- Net worth analysis/financial analysis-To create this product the analysis collects and analyzes the financial records of the target/group/individual to determine source of the funding and if the target is living within the means of legally reported income; assets minus liabilities equals net worth. Another technique to determine if illegal funds are used by the target is the source and

application of funds method. This method examines the legally earned or received income and compares that with what the target has spent. This yields potential illegal income that may be used to fund terrorist activity. Bank record analysis is another tool for examining deposits, withdrawals and etc. that may be part of discovering funding for the terrorist operation. Wire transfers, checks, money orders, and any type of transfer of funds may be used to profile the method of funding of activity of the terrorist group.

Sample of Source and Application of Funds: 2008 and 2009

Known Sources of Funds:	2008	2009
Salary	40,000.00	50,000.00
Inheritance	20,000.00	
Total Known sources of funds	60,000.00	50,000.00
Expenditures		
Purchase of Building	500,000.00	
Payment on BMW	40,000.00	12,000.00
Payments of Ford truck	6,000.00	6,000.00
Mortgage payment on Condo	9,600.00	39,600.00
Purchase of Sav. Bonds	30,000.00	
Purchase of Rolex	7,500.00	
Increase in Savings Account		65,000.00
Living Expenses	40,000.00	50,000.00
Total Expenditures	633,100.00	172,600.00
Expenditures in excess of Know sources of funds	573,100.00	122,600.00

The above sample revealed that the target has $695,700.00 in unexplained income which may have been used to fund a terrorist operation or derived from illicit drug trafficking. Following the money can lead to successfully identification and arrest of terrorist.

- Commodity Flow Analysis-This product is the analysis of the flow of goods or currency among individuals or groups to determine the meaning of the activity. It often gives insight into the nature of a conspiracy, the identification of the hierarchy, or the method of operation of a distribution network. The data includes individuals or businesses and locations where a commodity has traveled, the direction of flow, type of commodity, and the dates and times of the flow. This information produces a flow chart that is a graphic depiction of the flow of goods and services among all entities. Boxes or symbols are connected by lines that connect the entities and often include dollar amounts or drug amounts with dates and temporal and spatial information. It can identify people who are benefiting from the flow of the community or service. Biographical sketches on each person or group along with conclusions and recommendation for investigative, tactical, and strategic responses are the result of this product.

- Conversation analysis-The analyst reviews and compiles data form conservations during electronic surveillance or covert operations. The meaning of the exchange is determined along with role of participants and the activity that is occurring or about to occur. Translations are often required in the investigation of the global terrorist threat.

- Strategic analysis-This process includes a variety of types of analysis including threat assessments, vulnerability assessments, warnings, market analyses, and premonitories. This product is often predictive, long range in nature, and includes recommendations of how a government should precede to addresses a threat such as terrorism.

The evolving software used by the intelligence analyst has resulted in remarkable products that providing governments with the tools to address modern terrorism. Lockheed Martin is implementing the Global Visualization Services and Analyst Roundtable products that visualize situations by integrating layers upon layers of discrete data in what is described as intuitive and dynamic interface. This allows users to access images, targets or reports using point and click on geographically represented maps, aerial photos or designs. Analyst's Notebook 7 allows the uses to perform sophisticated analyses such as commodity flow, telephone analysis, and financial analysis. This software allows the analyst to create a number of products including:
- Sequence of events
- Combine link and timeline analysis using a variety of layouts
- Relationship between people and organizations
- Reveal methods of operation of a terrorist group
- Reveal paths and clusters
- Produce products that combine photos of suspects, telephone analysis, photos of evidence, time lines, video evidence, and association charts
- Incorporate maps and imagery
- Incorporate existing intelligence into a new product

Software such as this can manage vast amounts of raw, multi-format data that is developed from any type of source, and produce a product that is actionable intelligence.

Current Assessments of the Threats and Responses of the Intelligence Community

The response of the intelligences entities of various countries has evolved to cope with events and trends of the modern terrorist organizations. However, despite the efforts and evolvement of security and intelligences services, terrorist continue to carry out successful attacks without being identified. The United States has been successful in bringing to justice many individuals or groups such as Ramiz Youussef who was responsible for organizing the first World Trade Center bombing. There is evidence that many terrorist attacks have been prevented as well. The FBI has tripled its counter-terrorism force and the CIA has created the Counter-Terrorism Center to deal with the emerging threat of terrorism. In 2003, FBI Director Mueller ordered the creation of Field Intelligence Groups (FIGs) in all 56 field offices in the United States. These groups consist of special agents, intelligence analyst, linguist, and other members of law enforcement intelligence communities. The goal is to share and collect timely threat information/intelligence for both tactical and strategic purposes. FIGs identify intelligence gaps, collect and analyze raw information and generate and share intelligence products to help guide investigative, program, and policy decisions. The FBI's intelligence cycle includes planning and direction, collection, processing and exploitation, analysis and production, and dissemination (Spiller, 2006). There has been an improvement in international cooperation, surprisingly even with some Arab League countries, Russia and China contributing somewhat to this effort. Cyber-terrorism is another emerging field that has caught the attention of the intelligence community. With the possibility of the destruction of an entire city producing over a million deaths or contaminating large areas, the threat of terrorism has expanded with the United States the primary target. Questions include: to what extent does a group have the potential to carry out such an attack, are they limited by moral and political constraints, and are they in fear of massive retaliation. These questions demand an improvement of HUMINT, counter-terrorism expertise, cultural knowledge, and language aptitudes of officers engaged in the fight against terrorism. Other areas of current efforts and concern include:

- Monitoring contacts between know terrorist strongholds and countries serving as a base for their activities
- Preventing formation of blind spots in the overall intelligence picture such as Afghanistan and Somalia
- Improve monitoring open sources such as the internet and open media
- Improve research by academia into terrorist ideologies, doctrines and strategies
- More investment into technological efforts
- Develop and improve cooperation with the private sector
- Penetrate and monitor groups that attempt to obtain weapons
- Improve sharing information between law enforcement agencies
- Coordinate intelligence agencies with that of the military and security entities including the private sector
- Improve international cooperation

The 9/11 attack was not the first time fours airplanes had been used in a coordinated attack. In September of 1970, the Popular Front for the Liberation of Palestine diverted a Pan Am, TWA, Swissair, and BOAC to Dawson Airport in Jordon where all where blown up on the ground. The intelligence community cannot allow another failure and maintain its professional image as protecting America and the world. The continuation of the war against the US will result in terrorist cells form Somalia, Yemen, Sudan, Syria, Iran, Lebanon, Philippines, Indonesia, Chechnya, Kashmir and others increasing their efforts to attack the US abroad and within its borders. This threat will require efforts on multiple levels including diplomatic, economic, financial, political, and in the form of military strikes, all of which the intelligence community's role is critical (Karmon, 2002).

There are mixed opinions and numerous predictions about how well the United States is accomplishing its task of protecting property and lives. Juval Aviv, Golda Meir's bodyguard who tracked down and brought to justice the Palestinian terrorists who killed Israeli athletes during the Munich Olympic Games, has made some predictions is a speech given in New York City during the month of January, 2009. It should be noted he predicted the London subway bombing, gave intelligence regarding the 9/11 attack, and now predicts the next terrorist attack on the U.S. will occur with the next few months. He has said that U.S. airport security is a joke and is reactionary rather that proactive. It focuses on security when people enter the gates. In Israel, security checks are done before people enter the airport. His information indicates that targets will be busy times on the front end where people are checking in. He predicts that the next attack in America will involve suicide bombers and non-suicide bombers in places where large groups of people congregate; Disneyland, Las Vegas casinos, big cities where shopping malls or subways exist. The attack will involve simultaneous detonations around the country. He also predicts that the next level of terrorist will be "homegrown", possible students who travel back and forth to the Middle East. According to Aviv, the attack will not involved sophisticated weapons, but will likely use suicide as a cheap and effective method. In regard to intelligence perspective, Aviv warns the U.S. to stop relying so much on satellites and technology for intelligence. The emphasis must be on human intelligence, both from an infiltration perspective as well as to trust aware citizens to help. A trained and aware public is necessary to the prevention on terrorist attacks (Aviv, 2009).

Another interesting perspective from the intelligence community is the conclusion by National Intelligence Director Dennis Blair that the economic crisis has replaced terrorist attacks as the most serious threat to homeland security. Director concluded that if the current economic crises last more that two years, some nations' governments will collapse. The briefing given to the Senate Intelligence Committee presents a different type of threat than is normally given by a director of an intelligence agency. The economic crises could seriously damage the U.S. strategic interest according to Director Blair. Blair cited the situation in Pakistan as one that the economic crises impacted the ability of a nation to secure its borders. He also warned of the growing availability of biological weapons (Recession tops list, 2009).

The targets of terrorist groups now include symbols of American power within its borders, not just abroad as was the case initially. This mandates the expanded role of law enforcement in the U.S. The National Criminal Intelligence Sharing Plan called for all law enforcement entities to engage at some level of contribution to the products that the intelligence community produces. With the evolving links between terrorism and enterprise crime, the intelligence analyst's role becomes even more critical to effective enforcement and identification of sources of funding of the modern terrorist organizations. Al Qaeda now receives support from organized crime in locations such as Pakistan, India and even charity organizations in United States. The role of the intelligence analyst has changed since the days of the Cold War and before the event and expansion of transnational crime. The products that were once produced for organized crime investigations are now relevant to the investigation of terrorism.

The intelligence community and law enforcement are making a case for why organized crime in Mexico is an emerging threat to homeland security. An insecure southwest border (over a million border crossings a day) allows the travel of both weapons and terrorist to and from the United States. Ellis (2009) reported that twenty-three of the thirty-one states in Mexico are being controlled by Mexican Drug Cartels. Many now believe that Mexico is in a state of "narco-terrorism" with corruption at an all time high. General Barry McCaffrey is now serving as an advisor to Mexican federal law enforcement to stem the growth of the cartels. Retiring CIA Director Michael Hayden concluded that Mexico is a threat that would rival that of Iran in regard to national security (Ellis, 2009). Mexico and the United States are interdependent on a number of commodities such as oil and labor. The loss of Mexican oil would be a major blow to the economy of the United States.

The events of 9/11 set a high standard for future terrorist attacks. To reach or go beyond the destruction of this level, terrorist may target nuclear facilities or communication systems that could result in even greater destruction. When this level of threat is added to the conventional or traditional means of attack, the role of the analyst becomes even more diverse and dynamic. The implementation of intelligence-led policing strategy and establishing fusion centers in all states in the U.S., has placed the role of intelligence on a path that will increase the amount of timely and accurate information that will prevent a number of attacks. The products produced by the "All crimes" fusion centers not only connect the dots but develop responses that save lives. Good policing results in good terrorism prevention and effective counterterrorism techniques. Addressing modern terrorism requires competent intelligence analysis and vision.

Conclusion

Both antiterrorism and counterterrorism begin with analysis. The products produced by the intelligence community have become extraordinary tools that result in desirable efficient and effective outcomes. The Intelligence Reform and Terrorism Prevention Act of 2004 was designed to align the 15 agencies of the Federal intelligence community to increase the sharing of information and become less bureaucratic. However, it appears that this goal is not yet achieved, not 100 percent. Modern terrorism now requires an expanded role by state and local law enforcement, and the military. Terrorism is an asymmetrical threat that requires an asymmetrical response. Too much reliance on technical sources of intelligence rather than on human sources is yet another problem that must be addressed.

There is no doubt that the United States has made a tremendous effort to increase the role of the intelligence analyst addressing not only terrorism, but transnational organized crime, and traditional crimes that fund terrorist operations. There is a general agreement among many experts that it is a matter of time until the next terrorist attack within the U.S. borders. The role of intelligence is to separate the useful and accurate information from information that has no value or is inaccurate. There is a demand for cooperative, fluid structures in the intelligence community that can collect and move intelligence to end users in a timely manner. With the large number of diverse targets subject to a terrorist attack including transportation, energy, telecommunications, public health, food, agriculture, and banking, the intelligence community must collaborate with a wide variety of entities at all levels to produce products that are timely and essential to preventing or responding to an attack. Using modern technology and software to accurately predict and identify trends, threats, models, and patterns of terrorist groups and individuals, the intelligence analyst of today has become a major obstacle to the success of terrorism.

References

Aviv, J. (2009, December). *Being Prepared.* Retrieved February 12, 2009, from Law Enforcement Articles: http://www.lawenforcementarticles.com/being-prepared-israeli-agents-advice-warning-december-2008

Baker, B. (1999). The Origins of the Posse Comitatus. *Aerospace Power Chronicles.*

Baker, T. (2005). *Introductory Criminal Analysis.* Upper saddle River: Pearson Prentice Hall.

Binkerhoff, J. R. (2002, February). The Posse Comitatus Act and Homeland Security, *Journal of Homeland Security.* Retrieved February 12, 2009, from
        http://www.homelandsecurity.org/journal/Articles/brinkerhoffpossecomitatus.htm

Diebert, R. & Stein, J. (2002, Spring). Hacking Networks of Terror. *Dialog IO* .

Ellis, L. (2009, February). *The Second Greatest Threat to America.* Retrieved March 9, 2009,   from   Family   Secuirty   Matters: http://www.familysecuritymatters.org/publications/id.2415/pub_detail.asp

Hoffman, T. (2004). A New Look at Terrorism: Definitions, Tactics, Organizational Structure and their Implications. Montreal, Canada.

Homer-Dixon, T. (2002, January-February). The Rise of Complex Terrorism. *Foreign Policy* , 52-62.

Karmon, E. (2002). The Role of Intelligence in Counter-Terrorism. *The Korean Journal of Defense Analysis* , 119-139.

La Carte, Lieutenant-Colonel Donald A. (2001-2002). Asymmetric Warfare and the Use of Special Operations Forces in North American Law Enforcement. *Canadian Military Journal* , 23-32.

Latora, V. and Marchiori, M. (2002, April). How the Science of Complex Networks can help developing strategies against terrorism. *20 (No. 4)* . Chaos Solutions and Fractals.

Mallory, S. (2007, September). The Concept of Asymmetrical Policing. *International Police Executive Symposium: Working paper No.12* .

McCaffrey, General Barry R. (2008, November). *Narco-Violence in Mexico: A Growing Threat to U.S. Security.* Retrieved March 9, 2009, from American Diplomacy: http://www.unc.edu/depts/diplomat/item/2009/0103/comm/mccaffery_mexico.html

McGee, J. (2001, November 4). *An Intelligence Giant in the Making.* Retrieved December 10, 2001, from Washington Post: http://www.washingtonpost.com/wp-dyn/content/article/2005/11/04/AR2005110401362.html

Peterson, M. (1998). *Applications in Criminal Analysis.* Westport: Praeger.

Peterson, M. (2005). *Intelligence-Led Policing: The New Intelligence Architecture.* U.S. Department of Justice.

Ratcliffe, J. (2003, April). Intelligence Led Policing. *Australian Institue of Criminology* . Canberra, Australia.

Spiller, S. (2006). The FBI's Field Intelligence Gropus and Police: Joining Forces. *FBI Law Enforcement Bulletin* , 1-6.

United States Department of Justice. (2005). *The National criminal Intelligence Sharing Plan.* USDOJ.

U.S. Department of Justice. (n.d.). The Posse Comitatus Act of 1878. Retrieved March 23, 2009, from http://www.dojgov.net/posse_comitatus_act.htm.

CHAPTER 13

KEY INTERNATIONAL PARTNERS IN THE WAR ON TERRORISM

We should cooperate with others in the fight against terrorism around the world, in whatever ways are appropriate and possible. Because it's a global threat, is invulnerabilityisglobal.

President William J. Clinton

Introduction

The attacks of September 11, 2001 redefined the world for the United States and most nations. Traditionally, nations looked at other nations as potential foes and had not faced the possibility of attacks of the type staged by Al Qaida. Clearly, what became known as the Global War on Terror was as much a clash of cultures imbedded in a thousand years of history as it was a product evolving world technology that threatened eventually to reach every part of the world.

The September 11th attacks were not the first terrorist attacks on the United States or its traditional allies, nor would they be the last, but those attacks were the most spectacular and of such a level of boldness that they could not be ignored. Images of the Twin Towers falling or the damage to the Pentagon spread across the globe. A response was inevitable; it was now up the policy makers as to what and where the response would occur.

For the United States, efforts were immediate to bring together allies, build coalitions, seek those responsible and determine appropriate action, military, economic and political.

For those responsible, their desire to spark the United States to action had been accomplished. Now would be the question as to how the sides in the struggle would assemble. For the United States, treaties and alliances immediately brought nations to the aid of the United States. Other nations, recognizing the dangers, quickly joined, recognizing international terrorism as a major threat to domestic security that extended much farther than the borders of the United States.

Nations are not alone in their efforts to maintain national and regional security. Included in this effort are a wide range of organizations that are dedicated to supporting security and the protection of human rights. Other organizations involved in supporting security efforts are international business organizations whose role in regional and global security support is driven by economic profit.

Within this setting are some key partners of the United States in the struggle against international terrorism. These partners include multi-national alliances, such as the United Nations and NATO, some of these organizations are non-governmental humanitarian organizations, such as the International Red Cross and Doctors without Borders, some are extremely diverse international corporations that are highly engaged with providing support such as Kellogg, Brown and Root or the former Blackwater.

The Global Community

As a global community, events that directly impact one part of the world may well have a far reaching impact upon other parts of the globe. By 2010, the world is clearly multi-polar. The fall of communism and the dynamic movement of many nations toward market democracy, in which nations recognize the international aspect of business, has altered global dynamics from the bi-polar world of the Cold War. Nations no longer fall exclusively into the camps of the United States or the Soviet Union, but range dramatically economically, socially and politically in the multi-polar world of the post Cold War era.

Using market democracy as a standard by which nations are categorized, nations can be divided into three groups: (1) those successful at implementing market democracy, (2) those in transition from authoritarianism governments which dominated the economies of their nations to market democracy and (3) troubled and failed states that have fallen behind the rest of the world while frequently struggling against ethnic or religious extremism.

Failed states can no longer perform basic functions such as education, security, or governance, usually due to fractious violence or extreme poverty. Within this power vacuum, people fall victim to competing factions and crime, and sometimes the United Nations or neighboring states intervene to prevent a humanitarian disaster. However, states fail not only because of internal factors. Foreign governments can also knowingly destabilize a state by fueling ethnic warfare or supporting rebel forces, causing it to collapse. In considering global stability, the troubled or failed states are the nations that are most likely to be the site of conflict or the source of regional instability.

Conflicts occur around the globe. Some of these conflicts are limited in scope, while others threaten regional stability. Most conflicts occur because of issues related to troubled, failed or transitional states. Some of these conflicts occur as failed nations attempt to divert attention from their domestic ills by external aggression aimed at imposing regional hegemony. Others find that the conditions within the nation are such that internal insurgencies occur.

Most conflicts have limited impact beyond their region, but a few present greater danger, especially in light of the proliferation of weapons of mass destruction (WMD). In the arsenal of a rogue nation, failed state or radical group, weapons of mass destruction can threaten even the strongest of nations and disrupting regional stability.

A multi-national effort is typically required to respond to a failed state or rouge nation. As has been seen in Somalia, a multi-national military and humanitarian effort to provide relief and stability has yet to be successful. In spite of multinational efforts to stabilize the country, Somalia is controlled by gangs and war-lords and the waters around the nation are some of the world's most dangerous as pirates continually attack shipping passing in international waters (Binnendijk, Winter 1995 - 1996).

As another example of the global impact of regional events we can look to the conflict in the Middle East. Instability and conflict in the Middle East impacts the cost of the global supply of oil. As another example of global interdependency, the 2008 economic speculation in the global commodity futures market drove the cost of oil to levels far in excess of the cost expected based upon the supply of oil. The world is clearly linked.

Global and Regional Stability

Economies are linked, businesses are multinational, labor forces and production flow to parts of the world in which cost can be minimized. The revolution in communications has stimulated a blending of cultures. Fashion and entertainment are just two areas in which we have witnessed western influence around the globe. English has become the language of business. Computers, computer operating systems and the internet have further connected the world and dramatically changed our lives and lifestyles.

Within this global community are elements that threaten regional and in rare cases, global stability. No longer do the United States and the Soviet Union face each other expecting to unleash their mighty militaries against each other on the plains of Europe. By 2010, most of the threats impacting nations and regions were not from nation-states, but rather from groups operating within nations or within a limited regional setting. The FARC in Colombia, the Tamil Tigers in Sri Lanka, Somali pirates, the conflicts in the Former Yugoslavia, the Israeli/Palestinian conflicts, warfare and genocide following ancient tribal boundaries in Africa all threaten national or regional stability. A major departure from the regional threat has been Al Qaida, the group responsible for the 2001 attacks upon the United States. Al Qaida's reach has extended outside the Middle East and has sparked the Global War on Terror.

The Middle East is the globe's current flashpoint. Tensions in the Middle East and the West have been longstanding. For thousands of years these cultures have clashed. The Middle East has been the center of conflict since the Crusades. European domination of the region, the Jewish settlement and ultimate formation of Israel in 1948 led to further conflict. As a result of the United States' need to ensure access to the oil of the Middle East, the role of the United States has increased in the Middle East since World War II, as the United States and the Soviet competed in the region for influence.

In the last decades of the 20th Century, as the Cold War came to closure, the Middle East gained increasing importance in the National Strategy of the United States. The security of the natural resources of the region, to include oil, is viewed by the United States as a Vital Nation Interest.

The 1979 fall of the United States backed Shah of Iran was an example of the volatility of the region. The 1990 invasion of Kuwait by Iraqi sent a message to the world community that action would be required to ensure security and a dependable supply of oil from the region. The Gulf War that followed the Iraqi invasion of Kuwait further increased the role of the United States in the Middle East. After that conflict, the presence of the United States in the region was significant. To some, such as Osama Bin Laden, the increased western influence in the region was unacceptable and a dynamic clash of cultures would soon occur.

A World Community

The early 21st century appears to be a time of reasonable stability between major nation states, unlike the last century that witnessed two major world wars, a cold war and countless smaller, regional conflicts. To ensure global security, efforts to enhance international coordination and cooperation continue. Nation states cannot successfully exist in a vacuum.

Nations have always varied in power and influence. Some nations are very strong and dominate their regions of the world, while other nations recognize their security is dependent upon their abilities to enter into economic and security alliances with more powerful nations.

Nation's today enter into treaties and alliances. These treaties and alliances are limited groups of nations, major regional and global organizations exist. International organizations, such as the now extinct League of Nations, the current United Nations, the World Court, the International Monetary Fund and NATO are just a few of the many diverse international organizations that link nations together in a cooperative manner. Some of these organizations have been created to provide nations alternatives to conflict to settle international disputes, others to assist economic, social and political development.

National Power

By the dawn of the 21st Century, the United States claimed the title of the only remaining global superpower and, in theory, has the greatest ability to project its power and influence on the international stage. Other nations and international coalitions, such as China, Russia, India and the European Union have taken their positions on the world stage and are positioned to challenge the United States as a global superpower.

International power and national status has proven to be ever-changing as nations gain or lose their positions on the world stage. The last thousand years witnessed Rome, Spain, France, England, Germany, the Soviet Union and the United States take positions as the world's most powerful nation or empire. Each, with the exception of the United States, has lost its position of prominence.

The 20th century witnessed the impact of the industrial revolution upon diplomacy, warfare, international aggression, informational technology and global economics. The nations that entered the 20th century as major international powers would see their power and influence on the world stage decline. The global powers of 1900 participated in both World War I and World War II. Those conflicts devastated nations, resulted in the deaths of millions and changed the international balance of power. With the end of World War

II, old world colonialism entered its last stages and the United States and the Soviet Union emerged as global superpowers in a bi-polar world with nations quickly aligned with the eastern or the western power.

In the shadow of World War II, democracy and communism faced off in a Cold War that would shape the rest of the century. The United States supported the global spread of democracy, while the Soviet Union brought nations under the control of communism. The bi-polar world of the 2nd half of the 20th century redefined the levels national power could reach and when it ended, a multi-polar world emerged.

National Survival and National Sovereignty

National survival and national sovereignty remain the top priority of all nations. To a great extent, national survival and national sovereignty has led to the development of the modern nation state, into which our global community is divided. These nation states vary in power, influence and national wealth. Each has its own system of government, culture, history and heritage. In many cases these are similar in nature, but still unique to the specific nation and constantly evolving.

National governments evolve or in some cases fall, as a result of domestic or international challenges or aggression. In the last century, colonialization, economic depressions and world conflict redefined the balance of international power. In 1900, the monarchies of Europe dominated the globe. World War I destroyed many of those monarchies and limited the power and influence of those remaining. World War II witnessed the emergence of two international superpowers, the United States and the Soviet Union, both nations thrust into their roles as a result of World War II, they fought aggressor nations who threaten their own national survival.

Threats to national survival are taken serious. History is filled with stories of nations whose aggression has sparked conflict. Even today, the world is not at peace. On any day, conflict is on-going and the threat of additional conflicts erupting remains real.

The Cold War

For almost five decades, the United States and the Soviet Union faced each other in an uneasy peace that became known as the Cold War. In retrospect, the Cold War ensured a great degree of world security. The Soviet Union and the United States realized early in the Cold War that another global conflict, employing weapons of mass destruction, to include nuclear weapons would not be advantageous to either nation. The Cold War saw the United States and the Soviet Union continually testing each other, to include both nations supporting small wars around the globe in such places as Korea, Vietnam and Afghanistan, while remaining careful not to directly engage.

During the Cold War, millions of weapons, equipment, ammunition and military supplies were distributed by the Superpowers across the globe. These weapons, combined with weapons from World War II that had been earlier distributed or discarded, made the world a dangerous place in which even the smallest, poorest or most isolated of nations could obtain arms and supplies thus endangering its neighbors.

A New International Dynamic and Threat

In the late 1980s, the fall of Communism sparked a revolution in national change for many of the nations that had operated under communist governments. Germany again united, former Warsaw Pact nations entered NATO and it appeared a new level of global peace may have been reached. Unfortunately, as the bi-polar world ended a multi-polar world emerged as many old and long standing hatreds emerged. Areas such as Yugoslavia, Africa and the Middle East erupted in violence and small wars, many of which outside the control of the international superpowers.

As the Superpowers reduced the supply flowing from their stockpiles, international arms dealers moved in to meet the demand and profited from a massive unregulated sell off of low price surplus armaments into the most fragile, conflict-ridden states and failed states. The weapons, mostly from state-owned Eastern European factories, have found their way to Angola, Sudan, Ethiopia, Colombia, Congo-Brazzaville, Sri Lanka, Burundi and Afghanistan where conflicts have led to the deaths of up to 10 million people during the past decade (http://www.sourcewatch.org/index.php?title=Private_Military_Corporations). Thus, there is a large supply of all types of weapons available to supply the demands of those who would use them in even the most poverty ridden parts of the world.

This availability of weapons, combined with violent movements in unstable regions or radical ideology, has increased to opportunity for violence.

The attacks of September 11, 2001 did not commence the Global War on Terror, rather, the struggle against international terrorism has been ongoing for decades and the 2001 attacks just redefined and expanded the struggle. Murder, kidnapping, aircraft hijacking and bombings were just a few of the tactics of terror that had been used to shock the world.

Though the world continued to witness the work of terrorist, it would be the attacks on New York and Washington DC that marshaled a major international response to the danger. Nations around the globe recognized the threat of terrorism is not isolated, but rather attacks can target almost any part of the world. Terrorists follow their own ideology to determine acceptable behavior and legitimacy of targets (Drake, 1998). They select targets to advance their agenda, instill fear and capture world attention. Dramatic attacks such as those in Spain, London and Russia demonstrate the terrorists' desire to shake public confidence in the governments they have targeted.

The March 2004 train bombings in Madrid, Spain, the July 2005 London transport system attack and the 2008 attacks in Mumbai, India, demonstrated that no country can feel safe from terrorist attack and that civilian targets are considered fair game for many of these extremist, terrorists or radical groups. Responding, nations rallied in the struggle to make the international setting more secure.

International cooperation is essential in the struggle to leverage foreign experience, intelligence, expertise and resources in the fight against terrorists to ultimately remove their safe havens and disrupt or destroy their organizational infrastructure. Since the 2001 attacks, the United States has played a major role with allied nations developing regional strategies to disaggregate terrorist networks, eliminate terror safe havens and disrupt terrorist links, including financial, travel, communications and intelligence. The international struggle against terrorism requires international cooperation and must be conducted using the all of the elements of national power available.

International Cooperation

While the United States has taken the lead in the Global War on Terrorism, the struggle is truly of international proportion. Global partners, to include governmental and non-governmental, military and non-military are engaged in struggle. Unlike traditional war, the Global War on Terror has placed a greater reliance on winning not just the war, but also the peace that must follow.

Nations are linked and international cooperation is essential to ensure security. Many of the acts of violence that have captured global attention have been planned, staged, supported and launched from national locations different from the actual target itself.

The network of international terrorism that appeared in the 1960s has evolved into various bodies of decentralized, independent groups, basing its actions on radical ideologies with significant capabilities. Many of the groups target western nations and their allies.

Though terrorism is not new nor the efforts to impact or even bring down governments, the modern era of terrorism has generated an international response. The 1963 United Nations Treaties Against International Terrorism was one of the earliest efforts to provide the legal tools to the international community with which to battle terrorism.

The continually changing tactics employed by terrorist drive international legislation and cooperation. International agreements responding to aircraft high jacking included the 1970 Convention for the Suppression of Unlawful Seizure of Aircraft which required parties to the convention to make hijackings punishable by severe penalties. The 1971 Convention for the Suppression of Unlawful Acts Against the Safety of Civil Aviation, addressed acts of aviation sabotage such as bombings aboard aircraft in flight.

Other international efforts continued to include the 1973 Convention on the Prevention and Punishment of Crimes Against Internationally Protected Persons, Including Diplomatic Agents; 1979 Convention Against the Taking of Hostages; 1979 Convention on the Physical Protection of Nuclear Material; the 1988 Protocol for the Suppression of Unlawful Acts of Violence at Airports Serving International Civil Aviation, (supplements the 1971 Montreal Convention); the 1988 Rome Convention for the Suppression of Unlawful Acts Against the Safety of Maritime Navigation; 1988 Protocol for the Suppression of Unlawful Acts Against the

Safety of Fixed Platforms Located on the Continental Shelf; the 1991 Convention on the Marking of Plastic Explosives for   the Purpose of Detection; 1997 Convention for the Suppression of Terrorist Bombings, signed by the United States on January 12, 1998, submitted to the Senate for advice and consent to ratification on September 8, 1999; 1999 Convention for the Suppression of the Financing of Terrorism, signed by the United States on January 10, 2000 and submitted to the Senate for advice and consent to ratification on October 12, 2000.

In 1994, the United Nations adopted the *Declaration on Measures to Eliminate International Terrorism*, and in 1996, the *Declaration to supplement the 1994 Declaration*. These Declarations condemned all acts and practices of terrorism and declared them both criminal and unjustifiable. The Declarations further urged all nation-states to take measures at the national and international level to eliminate international terrorism.

The 2001 attacks on the United States increased the efforts to combat international threats. Since the attacks, Article 51 of the United Nations Charter stressing a nation's right to defend itself against armed attacks has been applied to a non-state actor such as al-Qaeda.

Further actions by the United Nations Security Council emphasized the obligations of countries to prevent acts of terror in resolutions 1368 and 1373 which state that each act of international terrorism is a threat to world peace and international security and should be combated by all available legal means. Means identified by the United Nation's Security Council includes: prevention and suppression of terrorist financing by criminalizing financing, planning, preparing or perpetrating terrorist acts; prohibit nationals from making funds or economic resources available to terrorists; freezing funds and financial assets of terrorists and related entities; refraining from supporting terrorist entities, to include taking steps to prevent commission of terrorist acts and prevent use of territory for terrorist acts; denying safe haven and prevent movement of terrorists across borders; exchanging operational information and enter into agreements to prevent and suppress terrorism, including ratifying the 12 Counter Terrorism conventions and protocols; ensuring refugee/asylum laws prevent abuse by terrorists; and prohibit active and passive assistance to terrorists.

These resolutions reaffirm the principles of individual and collective self-defense, as well as the duty of every government neither to tolerate nor to support any terrorist activities. In September 2006, the United Nations Global Counter-Terrorism Strategy was adopted by Member States further strengthening international efforts against terrorism.

The European Union has been a solid partner in sustaining the global coalition against terrorism. Following the 2001 United States attacks, the European Council adopted an Action Plan to identify areas, such as police and judicial cooperation, humanitarian assistance, transportation security, and economic and finance policy, to help fight terrorism. The European Union and the United States signed Extradition and Mutual

Legal Assistance Agreements at our June 2003 Summit expanding law enforcement and judicial cooperation (European Cooperation With the United States in the Global War on Terrorism, 2004).

The European Union has become involved in a range of practical counter-terrorism initiatives which provide for an increased level of co-operation between investigatory and security services, as well as in judicial matters. The EU Declaration on Combating Terrorism (adopted 25 March 2004) and the EU Plan of Action on Combating Terrorism (passed by the European Council on 17-18 June 2004), has promoted practical co-operation among EU member states in combating terrorism. 27 members of the EU all have financial intelligence units

Responding further to the continuing changes to threats facing the international community, nations increased their efforts to counter piracy. According to the International Maritime Organization - which has been advocating greater regional cooperation - the Malacca Strait, South China Sea, the eastern Indian Ocean, the western and central-western African coast and Latin American coastal areas are especially vulnerable to pirate attacks. In 2000, there were 471 acts of piracy, representing a 150-percent increase over 1999 levels (Special Warfare, 2001). By 2008, Somali pirates had made the waters off their coast the most dangerous in the world for shipping.

In addition to international efforts to provide a legal framework to fight terrorism, many nations have enacted or upgraded counterterrorism legislation to include anti-money laundering and counterterrorism finance legislation with the intent of making it even more difficult for terrorists to operate.

Non-Governmental Organizations (NGOs)

With each conflict comes a price frequently imposed upon non-combatants, to include homes destroyed, injury and death as they are trapped in the combat zone. International efforts are on-going to provide humanitarian assistance to those nations and regions that need such assistance, with nations providing international support in the form of aid to other nations.

Literally thousands of non-governmental organizations exist world-wide. According to the 2002 UNDP Human Development Report, nearly one-fifth of the world's 37,000 NGOs were formed in the 1990's (www.globalpolicy.org/ngos/credib/index.htm). Many of these are committed to providing outstanding service, some, actually support those that threaten us. NGOs are often believed to provide well-targeted aid. They are said to be particularly close to the poor, as many of them directly cooperate with local target groups, circumventing recipient governments with a reputation of corruption (Nunnenkamp, 2008).

There are three categories of NGOs according to the type of functions they perform. The first category of NGOs are those that provide immediate relief to the victims of war, natural calamities, accidents, etc. These were the most prominent form of NGOs until the time of European reconstruction in the aftermath of the Second World War (Nunnenkamp, 2008).

The second category of NGOs focus their concentration on long-term social and economic development. These came into prominence in Europe from the 1960s. In the Third World countries these NGOs are engaged in imparting technical training, in the construction of schools, hospitals, toilets, etc. They claim to promote self-reliance, development of local productive resources, development of rural markets, people's participation in development activities, etc. They encourage self-help groups, micro-credit societies, and so on (Mudingu, 2006).

The third category of NGOs concentrate on social action. They talk of strengthening people's capacities, releasing their inherent potentialities, enhancing the social awareness of the masses, overcoming the influence of pre-capitalist social systems, etc. These NGOs negotiate with the World Bank, IMF, WTO, and other UN agencies and suggest reforms, mobilize people peacefully and build pressure on these imperialist agencies and the governments to bring reforms and changes in policies (Mudingu, 2006).

NGOs are now able to get closer than ever to local communities and offer a voice to some of the most disenfranchised people on earth. Many of these NGOs operate in politically sensitive environments that are closed to more formal institutions. The world's leading NGOs advise the United Nations and help to shape its current reform efforts; they are also on hand whenever the UN High Commissioner for Refugees, the World Food

Program and other international donors need to feed thousands of refugees (Glasser, 2008).

Government will need to rely more on the private sector in its conduct of national security policy. Voluntary organizations often provide humanitarian relief more effectively than governments.

Governmental Organizations

There are many foreign government organizations committed with the United States to defeat the threat of international terrorism, military, diplomatic and intelligence organizations, as an example. Military, especially special operations forces, continually improve upon their capabilities in to combat terrorist in the asymmetric war we now face.

Intelligence Organizations and Cooperation

Intelligence is a critical element in homeland security, whether it is identifying international threats or assessing potential natural disasters. Intelligence drives all types of decisions, contingency planning as well as operational planning. The United States has committed significant resources to the intelligence community. Internationally, all nations have intelligence organizations and many nations also participate in multinational intelligence efforts.

As an example, INTERPOL is the world's largest international police organization, with 188 member countries. Created in 1923, it facilitates cross-border police co-operation, and supports and assists all organizations, authorities and services whose mission is to prevent or combat international crime (INTERPOL, n.d.).

The act also established the Central Intelligence Agency (CIA), which grew out of World War II era Office of Strategic Services and small post-war intelligence organizations. The CIA served as the primary civilian intelligence-gathering organization in the government. Later, the Defense Intelligence Agency became the main military intelligence body.

International Military Special Operations Forces

The Global War on Terror has increased the world's awareness of the role and mission of special operations forces. With the rare exception, all nations possess some military capability. For the majority of nations, the capabilities of their military are quite limited, for a few, the military capabilities are significant, with an extremely lethal arsenal of weapons and a highly trained military force. Many nations have developed within their military forces that are highly trained in what is termed as special operations capable. These forces can be called upon to perform non-traditional military operations that are not suited for traditional military forces. In the current efforts against the terrorist threat presented in diverse global areas, special operations forces play a key role.

While most Americans think of the United States Army Special Forces, Rangers, Delta Force, the United States Navy Seals or the United States Marine Corps Special Operations assets, the majority of the world's nations have special operations forces at their disposal. While the specific expertise of a special operations force many vary, generally special operations roles include capabilities in areas to include, but not limited to: Direct Action which includes short-duration, small-scale offensive actions such as raids, ambushes, hostage rescues, and "surgical strikes;"

Strategic (Special) Reconnaissance which are characterized by clandestine operations in hostile territory to gain significant information; Unconventional Warfare which includes advising and supporting indigenous insurgent and resistance groups operating in the territory of a common enemy such as the special operations work with the Northern Alliance in Afghanistan; Foreign Internal Defense which includes assisting host nation military capabilities to forestall or defeat insurgent activities; Civil Affairs which includes promoting civil-military cooperation between United States military forces and the foreign governments and populations within their area of operations; Psychological Operations which includes influencing the attitudes and behavior of relevant populations to assist in accomplishing security missions; Counterterrorism Operations conducted by Special Mission Units to resolve or preempt terrorist incidents abroad and activities to assist or work with other CT-designated agencies within the United States; Humanitarian Assistance in which the military is called upon to provide various rudimentary services to foreign populations in adverse circumstances; Theater Search and Rescue which includes finding and recovering pilots and air crews downed on land or sea outside the United

States, sometimes in combat or clandestine situations; Intelligence Support which includes clandestine direct-action operations, particularly those aimed at capturing or killing specific individuals or groups, depend for their success to a large degree on having timely, high-quality intelligence about the targets in question and Work with Resistance Forces to include efforts such as the assistance SOF units provided to the Northern Alliance and other indigenous resistance forces.

Though the more famous special operations forces include the British Special Air Squadron, the British Special Boat Service, the British Royal Marines and the German GSG9, most nations maintain some special operations capable forces. In Mexico, as an example, army and naval special operations forces, are involved in operations against the drug cartels in an effort to stem the violence that have moved Mexico to the edge of a failed State. In Colombia, the national hostage rescue/counterterrorist unit is the Fuerzas Especiales Anti-Terroristas Urbanas (AFEAU). It is made up of between 70 and 100 personnel from all branches of the Armed Forces as well as the National Police and is under the overall command of the Comandante de las Fuerzas Armadas (Commander of the Armed Forces) (Special Operations.Com. n.d.).

Private Contractors, Private Armies and International Mercenaries

Since the dawn of warfare, there have been soldiers of fortune, individuals who have been willing to sale their military skills to the highest bidder. By the end of the 20th century, private military recourses took a corporate form and companies of this type began to operate various parts of the world, to include Africa. Typically led by former military officers and soldiers, these organizations frequently maintained ties with diplomatic and intelligence services of major countries.

During the Persian Gulf War in 1991, one of every 50 people on the battlefield was an American civilian under contract; by the time of the peacekeeping effort in Bosnia in 1996, the figure was one in 10 (Wayne, 2002). Privatized corporate military operations now draw an estimated $100 billion in business worldwide each year -- much of it going to top United States corporations like Halliburton, DynCorp, Lockheed Martin, Grumman, and Raytheon. The military-industrial companies that once just created the guns and warplanes now provide personnel and expertise for "privately" carrying out the operations in countries to include Colombia where large numbers of "contractors" serve as agents and trainers for the United States government (Privatizing the Empire's Dirty Work, 2004).

United States operations in Iraq, as an example, have drawn heavily on military, security and support companies. Private contractors in Iraq are doing everything from rebuilding the education system and electrical grids to protecting fledgling democracy efforts. Unlike state military and police forces, these private companies operate beyond the realm of legal accountability and public oversight and the laws surrounding hired soldiers and civilian contractors is not clear and not well defined under international agreements.

By the 21st the military contractor for hire had evolved into a global business. As an example, MPRI is composed of former Pentagon officers, MPRI is under contract with the United States government. MPRI, formerly known as Military Professionals Resources Inc., may provide the best example of how skilled retired soldiers cash in on their military training. Its roster includes Gen. Carl E. Vuono, the former Army chief of staff who led the gulf war and the Panama invasion; Gen. Crosbie E. Saint, the former commander of the United States Army in Europe; and Gen. Ron Griffith, the former Army vice chief of staff. There are also dozens of retired top-ranked generals, an admiral and more than 10,000 former military personnel, including elite special forces, on call and ready for assignment. "We can have 20 qualified people on the Serbian border within 24 hours," said Lt. Gen. Harry E. Soyster, the company's spokesman and a former director of the Defense Intelligence Agency. "The Army can't do that. But contractors can (Wayne, 2002)." Though not a true mercenary force in the mold of Sandline or EO, MPRI trains the forces of governments in various military activities. Its list of operations includes teaching tactics to the Kosovo Liberation Army in the weeks before the North Atlantic Treaty Organization bombing campaign in 1999 (http://www.globalpolicy.org/security/peacekpg/reform/pmc.htm).

Kellogg Brown & Root, which was paid $2.2 billion to provide logistics support to American troops in the Balkans, was the subject of a General Accounting Office report entitled, "Army Should Do More to Control Contract Costs in the Balkans." The office found that the Army was not exercising enough oversight on Kellogg Brown & Root as contract costs rose, to the benefit of the company (Wayne, 2002).

The use of private contractors for service is a big business. At least 90 companies that provide services normally performed by national military forces but without the same degree of public oversight have operated in 110 countries worldwide (http://www.sourcewatch.org/index.php?title=Private_Military_Corporations). In fiscal year 2005 (the last year for which full data is available), the Pentagon spent more contracting for services with private companies than on supplies and equipment -- including major weapons systems. This figure has been steadily rising over the past 10 years. According to a recent Government Accountability Office report, in the last decade the amount the Pentagon has paid out to private companies for services has increased by 78% in real terms. In fiscal year 2006, those services contracts totaled more than $151 billion (Berrigan, 2008)).

Conclusion

Despite concerted worldwide efforts in the aftermath of September 11 that have disrupted terrorist plots and constrained al-Qaida's ability to strike the Homeland, the United States faces a persistent and evolving terrorist threat, primarily from violent Islamic terrorist groups and cells.

International crime, terrorism, mass migration, and environmental threats transcend national boundaries and often are not susceptible to traditional tools of statecraft designed for relations among sovereign states (Binnendijk, Winter 1995 - 1996).

We can destroy terrorist leadership, disrupt terrorist networks, and eliminate terrorist safe havens, but unless we prevent terrorists from recruiting new members, locally and expanding its reach globally, we will not be truly successful.

The war on terror will take many years. It will require patience, persistence, and a comprehensive approach. Military means alone will not be sufficient. Instead, the war will call for the concerted efforts of the entire interagency, international partners, and private sector. The public perspective should be that this is a national rather than a purely military problem and the world should see this war as an international rather than an American crisis.

References

About INTERPOL, n.d. retrieved on 11/30/2009 from
http://www.interpol.int/public/icpo/default.asp

Berrigan, Frida, The Pentagon's Cubicle Mercenaries, New America Foundation,
September 16, 2008 retrieved on 12/12/2009 from
http://www.newamerica.net/publications/articles/2008/pentagons_cubicle_mercenaries_7
923

Binnendijk, Hans and Patrick L. Clawson, Tuning the Instruments of National Power,
Joint Forces Quarterly, Winter 1995 – 1996

Colombia Special Operations and Counterterrorist Units. Special Operations.com
retrieved on 12/02/2009 from
http://www.specialoperations.com/Foreign/Colombia/Default.htm

Credibility and Legitimacy of NGOs, Global Policy Forum. n.d. retrieved on 12/15/2009
from http://www.globalpolicy.org/ngos/credibility-and-legitimacy-of-ngos.html

Drake, C.J.M. "Terrorists' Target Selection," New York N.Y.: St. Martin's Press, Inc.,
1998

European Cooperation With the United States in the Global War on Terrorism, William
P. Pope, Principal Deputy Coordinator for Counterterrorism, Remarks to the House
International Relations Committee, Subcommittee on Europe and on International
Terrorism, Nonproliferation and Human Rights, Washington, DC, September 14, 2004

Glasser, Robert, Why We Need to Look Hard at the NGOs' Flaws, Global Policy Forum
(Spring 2008), retrieved on 11/30/2009 from
http://www.globalpolicy.org/component/content/article/176/31435.html

Mudingu, Joseph. How Genuine Are NGOs? New Times. August 7, 2006. Retrieved
on 11/30/2009 from
http://www.globalpolicy.org/component/content/article/176/31491.html

Nunnenkamp, Peter, The Myth of NGO Superiority, Global Policy Forum, October 15,
2008. Retrieved on 12/15/2009 from
http://www.globalpolicy.org/component/content/article/176/31437.html

Private Military Corporations, n.d. retrieved on 11/15/2009 from
http://www.sourcewatch.org/index.php?title=Private_Military_Corporations

Privatizing the Empire's Dirty Work, (2004) Revolutionary Worker # 1236 retrieved on 12/16/2009 from http://revcom.us/a/1236/blackwater.htm

Special Warfare, The Professional Bulletin of the John F. Kennedy Special Warfare Center and School, PB 80-01-2, Spring 2001, Vol. 14, No. 2

Wayne, Leslie. America's For-Profit Secret Army. Global Policy Forum. New York Times October 13, 2002. Retrieved on 12/16/2009 from http://www.globalpolicy.org/component/content/article/199/41040.html

374

CHAPTER 14
THE FUTURE OF TERRORISM

The first issue that we have to determine is violent extremism in all of its forms. In Ankara, I made clear that America is not-at and never will be at war with Islam. We will, however, relentlessly confront violent extremism who poses a great threat to our security- because we reject the same thing that people of all faiths reject, the killing of innocent men, women and children. And it is my first duty as President to protect the American people.

President Barack Obama 4 June 2009

Introduction

Even though we cannot predict the future it is safe to say that terrorists and the use of tactics we call terrorism will continue to bring shock and surprises to the international community. The last decade has educated many of us on the subject of terrorism, but as we continue to learn, witness and experience terrorism and terrorist related events, we see we have much more to learn. Terrorism is a continually evolving tactic. It is predictable in that it is not predictable. With terrorism, the target, time and method of attack are in the hands of the attacker. The attack may be of extreme violence, designed to instill fear and shake confidence or it may be cyber in nature, designed to disrupt, interfere and inflict a different type of damage. It may be basic and almost primitive in its tactic or highly sophisticated. The attack may be local in nature or global in scope. What we do know is that terrorist and the use of terrorism will continue to challenge use and our allies well into the future.

Terrorism, Foundations for the Future

With the conclusion of the Cold War there has been a decline in state sponsored terrorism. This can be attributed to the success of international economic sanctions that have been imposed against those nations who sponsored terrorism. However, it is still strongly suspected that Iran is continuing to support terrorist groups like Hezbollah and Hammas.

Richard Clarke a former head our country's counterterrorism efforts under Presidents Bill Clinton and George Bush wrote a fictitious article for Atlantic Monthly magazine regarding the future of terrorism on the tenth anniversary of the September 11, 2001 attacks. In his article Tens Years Later, Clarke reveals how vulnerable the United States is to acts of terrorism. He depicted a female suicide terrorist detonating her suicide vest at a crowded roulette table within a Las Vegas casino. Simultaneously, terrorists brandishing automatic weapons were shooting shoppers at numerous shopping malls throughout the United States. Furthermore, Improvised Explosive Devices (IED's) manufactured from stockpiles of discarded explosives in Iraq, were used to blow-up our nation's surface transportation systems thus causing congestion and chaos on our highways and interstates. Clarke continued to illustrate a dismal state of affairs when he described how Al-Qaeda terrorists shot down several 767 commercial airliners with shoulder fired missiles. These attacks on our transportation system and critical infrastructure were designed not only to create a chaotic state but also to adversely affect our nation's economy. During the ten years following the 9-11 attacks, Clark describes the United States as a nation who has abandoned its constitution (civil liberties) in exchange for an unrealistic increase in security. The targets primarily mentioned in Clark's article can best be described as "soft targets" or those targets that have a minimum amount of security.

In the days and months following 9-11, the United States government has upgraded aviation security along with surface maritime transportation. In addition, subsequent to the bombings of our embassies in Tanzania and Kenya, the U.S. State Department has hardened our embassy security throughout the world. As a result of this increased security initiatives terrorists have opted to exploit "soft targets." A "soft target" is one which has little or no military protection or a minimum amount of security and is an easy option for a terrorist attack. Examples of a "soft target" would include venues such as shopping malls, sporting events, restaurants, night clubs, resorts or other locations where people would congregate. One should be mindful of the fact that terrorist target selection is not random. It is a very calculated decision.

This chapter will address the future of terrorism by identifying several problematic areas from around the world. Included in the text of this chapter will be a discussion on "homegrown" terrorism.

Southeast Asia

During the past several years various terrorist organizations have targeted "soft targets" throughout Southeast Asia. Most recently, many al-Qaeda affiliated terrorist organizations have targeted hotels and resorts owned by western hotel conglomerates. In 2002, the Jemaah Ishamiyah (JI) was responsible for bombing a resort in Bali Indonesia, which was frequented by Australians. The term *"Jemaah Islamiyah"* in Arabic means *"Islamic Organization."* This terrorist group is very active in Southeast Asia and especially in Indonesia and the Philippines. Like many other radical Islamic terrorist groups, their main mission is to establish an Islamic state in Southeast Asia specifically in Indonesia. Mobley (2004), claims that by attacking United States and other Western targets in Indonesia, Singapore, and the Philippines has been a key component of that mission.

"The group has its roots in Darul Islam, a violent radical movement that advocated the establishment of Islamic law in Indonesia, the world's most populous Muslim country" (Council on Foreign Relations, 2009, p.3). Moreover, Indonesia has an extremely diverse religious culture which includes Christians, Hindus, Buddhists, and Judaism.

IJ members are recruited from youth street gangs and placed in pesantrens which are Indonesian boarding schools where the recruits are indoctrinated in jihadist principles. Their modus operandi usually includes the use of car bombs however; most recently they have turned to suicide bombings as their primary terrorist tactic.

The leader has been identified as Azhari Hasin and Mohammed Noordin Top. Husin was an English educated engineer and explosives expert while Noordin a former accountant is believed to be responsible for numerous bombings in Indonesia (Council on Foreign Relations, 2009). Husin was killed in a police raid in 2005. Noordin was gunned down during an Indonesian Special Forces raid in September 2009. During the raid government authorities retrieved a laptop computer which allegedly contained documents indicating that Noordin was the leader of an al-Qaeda "spin-off" organization from the JI. According to Rosyd and Deutch (2009), reported that Noordin had a disagreement with leaders of the JI regarding the targeting of innocent civilians. Noordin desiring a more violent organization created the Tanzin Qaidat al-Jihad. His goal was to establish an

Islamic state in Indonesia, Malaysia, Brunei and the Philippines. Indonesian authorities claim that Noordin's death was a major blow to the JI's terrorist activities.

Mobley (2004) contends that the JI poses a moderate threat to the United States. This threat assessment is based upon evidence that JI planners in conjunction with al-Qaeda members were preparing to coordinate a September 11 "second strike" on U.S. West coast targets with commercial airliners hijacked from Southeast Asia (Mobley, 2004).

Pakistan

Pakistan has been described as an important player in the war on terrorism. However, their willingness to participate as an ally in the war on terrorism has been questionable to say the least. The Pakistani Inter-Services Intelligence (ISI) has been extremely controversial due to the fact that they have been accused of providing classified information to Osama bin Laden and al-Qaeda. Most recently they have been strongly suspected of providing financial support to the Afghan Taliban. Moreover, the British government has claimed that there has been a clear link between the ISI and three terrorist organizations operating in Kashmir a disputed region located between India and Pakistan. These allegations have been vehemently denied by the Pakistani government.

Former Pakistan Prime Minister Benazir Bhutto called the ISI a" state within a state" working without control and pursuing its own foreign policy" (Bajoria & Kaplan, 2009, p. 2). One of the major problems associated with the ISI is accountability. In 2008, the Pakistani government attempted to bring the ISI under control by mandating the intelligence organization report directly to the interior ministry but was shortly rebuffed by ISI officials.

Historically, Pakistan has been governed by primarily military rule with few periods of democracy. Since Pakistan became a republic in 1956, its government can best be described as being unstable. Currently, a majority of Pakistani nationals regard their government as a "puppet" of the American government. The United States presence in Afghanistan and Pakistan has been a motivating factor for an increase in the number of radical Islamic groups in the region. This is most evident in the Federally Administered Tribal Areas (FATA) which is located in the region between Afghanistan and Pakistan. The FATA is comprised of seven agencies (provinces) and is governed by the governor of the North West region. Moreover, this extremely harsh and mountainous area has served as a safe haven for members of the Afghan Taliban and as well as elements of al-Qaeda since they were initially driven out of Afghanistan by U.S. led Coalition forces.

In addition, Rashid (2009, p. 32) claims that the tribal area has become a "melting pot for jihadists from all over the world. He added "the Afghan and Pakistan Taliban, al-Qaeda, Chechens, and the Islamic Movement of Uzbekistan are among the militants who train in the tribal region." Since the Afghanistan War, Taliban members have made inroads into leadership positions within the tribal region especially in the agencies of North and SouthWaziristan and Bajaur (Rashid, 2009). The Taliban has made several power plays to gain political control of the tribal region. It has been reported that the Taliban have murdered tribal leaders for questioning their authority and for cooperating with the Pakistan government.

Another problem associated with the tribal region is the evolution of the Taliban Pakistan. The Taliban Pakistan or the *Tehrik-i-Taliban* (TTP) "is the largest organization of Pakistani militants operating in the country's North-West Frontier Province (NWFP), which includes the FATA (Yusufzai, 2009, p.1). The TTP's stronghold is primarily located in South Waziristan and North Waziristan. Valentine (2009) stated that the TTP is an umbrella group of various Taliban factions operating mainly in the South Waziristan agency of the FATA. The goal of the TTP is to oust foreigners especially Western non-Muslims from the country of Pakistan. Valentine (2009) adds the TTP desires to restore a Khilafat and establish a Shariah based homeland. Many of the TTP militants were former members of the Mujahedeen who were trained and funded by the CIA to fight the Soviet Union in Afghanistan and now they are taking the fight against the United States and its NATO allies. Furthermore, the TTP has launched a terrorist campaign against the Pakistani military and attempted to assassinate former President Musharraf on numerous occasions along with several other top government officials

As part of their campaign of terror against the secular government of Pakistan, the TTP has launched a campaign of suicide terrorism. "As of July 2009, Pakistan had suffered 36 suicide bombing incidents since January 2009, killing at least 465 and injuring more than 1120" (Lanche, 2009, p.1). At the time of writing, Pakistan has surpassed Afghanistan and Iraq in the number of suicide attacks between 2002 and 2008. Lanche (2009) claims that the suicide bombings in Pakistan have been directed against three targets:

1). the state
2). United States presence in Pakistan
3). Religious or sectarian opponents

Furthermore, these suicide bombings have been spreading throughout the entire country. However, the majority of the bombing incidents have occurred in the North West Frontier Province (NWFP).

Since the United States has contributed $4.75 billion in military aid to Pakistan to help support their counter terrorism campaign (Kronstadt, 2007). The sum of funding to Pakistan has brought about allegations of corruption and misuse of those funds that were designated to fight the Taliban and al-Qaeda insurgents. Many U.S. government officials are fearful that Pakistan has diverted many of the weapons provided by the West to the Pakistan-Indian border.

The British Broadcasting Corporation (BBC) reported on October 17, 2009, that the Pakistani army was conducting a military assault against the TTP in the TTP's stronghold of South Waziristan. The BBC added that the fighting was fierce and extremely intense. The objective of the military campaign is to remove the TTP from the area where they have taken the entire population hostage.

In January 2007, the outgoing Director of National Intelligence (DNI) John Negroponte testified before Congress claiming that Pakistan poses two problems to U.S. policy makers: "Pakistan is the frontline partner in the war on terror. Never the less, it remains a major source of Islamic extremism and the home of some top terrorist leaders" (Kronstadt, 2007, p.2). The DNI further commented by stating "that al-Qaeda is posing the single greatest threat to the United States and its interests.

In addition to being extremely concerned about the increase in the number of extremist groups located within Pakistan, U.S. government and military officials along with their allies are particularly interested in the security of Pakistan's nuclear weapon inventory. Islamic extremist groups would like nothing better than to obtain a nuclear weapon. This frightening scenario would have a major impact on the security and well-being of the entire free world.

Somalia

Somalia is an east African country located on the Gulf of Arden which is a major navigation route that links the Arabian Sea with the Mediterranean Ocean by the way of the Suez Canal. This maritime passageway has been the site of the numerous incidents of Somali piracy which has plagued this region for several years. This increase in piracy is partially due in part to the lack of a strong central government in Somalia.

Currently, there is an ongoing debate whether or not Somali piracy constitutes terrorism. According to the United Nations Convention, piracy is defined as "any illegal acts of violence or detention, or any act of depredation, committed for private ends by the crew or the passengers of a private ship or private aircraft" (Hanson, 2009, p.1). The main motive of a criminal organization is "monetary gain." They do not have a political agenda like terrorist organizations. However, the Somali pirates are non-state actors and target civilians (soft targets) very similar to terrorists.

The most compelling argument to be made that the Somali pirates are terrorists is that there is compelling intelligence that the Somali pirates have strong ties with al-Shabaab a Somali radical Islamic terrorist organization which means "the lads." This group was designated a terrorist organization by the United States Department of State in 2008 along with the Norwegian and Swedish Security Services. It is widely suspected that al-

Shabaab is closely associated with al-Qaeda. Al-Shabaab has been described as an extremely violent organization whose motivation is to establish an Islamic government in Somalia. Since 2008 al-Shabaab has controlled all of the territory from the Kenyan border to the outskirts of Mogadishu. Menkhaus (2009) claims that al-Shabaab is the strongest militia force in Southern Somalia. According to Hanson (2009), Somali pirates have been actively involved in training al-Shabaab members in terrorism tactics. The al-Shabaab has introduced new military technologies into Somalia especially the usage of Improvised Explosive Devices (IED'S) and suicide bombers (Menkhaus, 2009). Moreover, the usage of suicide bombers is considered "to be taboo in Somali culture, and its introduction into the country by al-Shabaab has come as a shock to Somalis" (Menkhaus, 2009, p.4).

A major concern for the United States and other Western powers is that Somalia will be used as a base of operations for international terrorist organizations. Furthermore, during this internal conflict thousands of Somali refugees have immigrated to many different countries throughout the world to include the United States. Gordon (2009a) claims approximately 200,000 have emigrated to the U.S. in communities such as Lewiston, Maine, Emporia, Kansas and Shelbyville, Tennessee. As a result of this massive emigration to the United States al-Shabaab members have been recruiting American-Somalis to return to their homeland to become Jihadist. In November 2008, an "American-Somali from Minneapolis was arrested in the Netherlands after allegedly recruiting and financing the travel of twenty émigré Somali youths who went to war torn Somalia to fight for al-Shabaab" (Gordon, 2009b, p.1). During the past year five Somali youths have mysteriously disappeared in Somalia and the FBI has initiated a criminal investigation to determine what happened to those individuals. However, it is feared that these individuals have been recruited to become suicide bombers.

Another concern of American homeland security officials is the possibility of these terrorist trained Somali émigrés might return to the U.S. and begin a campaign of terrorist activity within our nation.

Homegrown Terrorism

Subsequent to the tragic events surrounding 9-11, the United States has witnessed a major spike in "homegrown" terrorism. According to the "Violent Radicalization and Homegrown Terrorism Prevention Act of 2007" the term is defined as "the use, planned use, or threatened use, of force or violence by a group or individual born, raised, or based and operating primarily within the United States or any possession of the United States to intimidate or coerce the United States government, the civilian population of the United States, or any segment thereof, in furtherance of political or social objectives."

During an interview with CBS News (September 6, 2006), FBI Director Robert Mueller defined homegrown terrorists as "individuals who are inspired, motivated by al-Qaeda, but have not seen any direct connection with al-Qaeda."

Many noted counterterrorism officials claim that the next terrorist attacks in the United States will be perpetrated by an American citizen. Mitchell Silber and Arvin Bhatt, Senior Intelligence Analysts of the New York City Police Department (NYPD) claim that the "Islamic radical threat to New York City have been planned and conceptualized by unremarkable local residents/citizens who sought to attack their country of residence, utilizing al-Qaeda as their inspiration and ideological reference point" (2009, p.5).

The student of terrorism should be mindful of the fact that homegrown terrorists perpetrated the Madrid train bombing in 2004 along with the attack on London's transportation system in 2005. Both terrorist attacks inflicted considerable amount of death and carnage

As a result of this risk assessment, U.S. law enforcement and intelligence officials have begun to pool their resources in an effort to detect and identify any/all possible homegrown terrorists. An example of this cooperative effort is the FBI Joint Terrorism Task Force. This task force is a compilation of federal, state and local law enforcement agencies working in concert to identify and neutralize any/all domestic terrorism threat. The New York City JTTF was successful in arresting those responsible for the 1993 bombing of the New York City World Trade Center. Omar Abdel Rahman, the *"Blind Sheikh"* was the mastermind behind the WTC bombing who had espoused Islamic radical extremism in a mosque located across the river from the WTC in New Jersey. Rahman was convicted of crimes against the United States and is currently serving a life sentence at the Butner Federal Correctional Institution located in North Carolina.

In the study Homegrown Terrorists in the U.S. and U.K. authored by Daveed Garenstein-Ross and Laura Grossman indicated that many homegrown terrorists undergo a *"radicalization"* process for either religious or political reasons. The authors noted "Terrorists do not fall from the sky. They emerge from a set of strongly held beliefs. They are radicalized. Then they become terrorists" (Garenstein-Ross & Grossman, 2009, p.7). Brian Jenkins a renowned terrorism expert claims that the term radical "applies to one who carries his/her theories or convictions to their furthest application. It implies not only an extreme belief, but extreme action" (Jenkins, 2009).

In their study *Radicalization in the West: The Homegrown Threat,* Silber and Bhatt (2009, pgs.6-7) state that the radicalization process consists of four stages:

- Stage 1: Pre-Radicalization
- Stage 2: Self-Identification
- Stage 3: Indoctrination
- Stage 4: Jihadization

The Pre-Radicalization stage is the point of origin for individuals before they begin this progression. It is their life situation before they were exposed to and adopted jihad-Salafi Islam as their own ideology. Silber and Bhatt add that the majority of the individuals involved in these plots began as "unremarkable" they had ordinary jobs, had ordinary lives and had little, if any criminal history.

Self-Identification is the stage where individuals, influenced by both internal and external factors, begin to associate themselves with like-minded individuals and adopt this ideology as their own. The catalyst for this "religious seeking" is a cognitive opening, or crisis which shakes one's certitude in previously held beliefs and opens an individual to be receptive to new worldviews. Silber and Bhatt stated that there can be many types of triggers that can serve as the catalyst including:

- Economic (losing a job)

- Social (alienation, discrimination, racism-real or perceived

- Political (international conflicts involving Muslims)

- Personal (death in the close family)

Indoctrination is the stage, in which an individual progressively intensifies his /her beliefs, wholly adopts jihad-Salafi ideology and concludes, without question, that the conditions and circumstances exist where action is required to support and further the cause. That action is militant jihad. This stage is typically facilitated and driven by a "spiritual sanctioner." The authors contend that association with like minded people is a very important component of the indoctrination process.

Jihadization is the stage in which members of the cluster accept their individual duty to participate in jihad and self-designate themselves as holy warriors or mujahedeen. Ultimately, the group will begin operational planning for the jihad or a terrorist attack. These "acts in furtherance" will include planning, preparation and execution. Silber and Bhatt believe that the other phases of radicalization might take place gradually, over two to three years but the jihadization stage can be a rapid process taking anywhere from several months to several weeks to complete.

Unfortunately, the United States has had it share of homegrown terrorists. In 2001, John Walker Lindh, a California native was captured by Afghan Northern Alliance forces and was interrogated by the Central Intelligence Agency (CIA) during the invasion of Afghanistan. Lindh was charged and convicted for providing material support for the Taliban.

Adam Gadahn a U.S. citizen who was born in Oregon and raised in California is currently serving as an interpreter and public relations specialists for al-Qaeda. At the age of seventeen he began to study Islam at the Islamic Society of Orange County and became radicalized by several of the Islamic extremist mentors. In 1995, Gadahn moved to Pakistan to be join al-Qaeda. Since leaving the United States he has appeared in numerous video clips in which he advocated the overthrow of the U.S. government and applauded the killing of U.S. citizens during the attacks on September 11, 2001.

According to Sauer (2008), Gadahn is wanted by the FBI (FBI'S most Wanted List) for treason and is believed to be hiding out in Afghanistan. The U.S. State Department's Diplomatic Security Division has offered a $1 million reward for his capture as part of the Rewards Program. If Gadahn is captured and convicted he will be the first American to be tried for treason since World War II (Sauer, 2009).

On November 5, 2009, Major Nidal Hasan, an American born Muslim, went on a shooting rampage at Fort Hood, Texas, killing thirteen and wounding numerous other individuals. Major Hasan was a thirty-nine year old U.S. Army psychiatrist who had recently been transferred to Fort Hood from Walter Reed Army hospital located in Washington D.C. According to Gibbs (2009), Hasan jumped on a desk yelled "God is great" and began firing a handgun inside Fort Hood's processing center. This is the location where Army personnel update their personnel files prior to shipping out to Iraq or Afghanistan. There have been numerous reports that Hasan had become troubled because he had received orders to Afghanistan. He was troubled due to the fact he did not want to fight against other Muslims and he was vehemently against the Afghanistan war.

Moreover, it has been reported that while he was stationed at Walter Reed hospital he attended the mosque of controversial Yemeni cleric Anwar al-Awalaki who has been accused of having ties to al-Qaeda (Ghosh, 2009). A federal surveillance of al-Awalaki revealed that Hasan had sent approximately ten to twenty e-mail messages to al-Awalaki and that he made several attempts to meet members of al-Qaeda. President Obama along with members of the United States Congress and United States Senate has called for an intensive investigation of the incident. At the time of this writing, it appears that Hasan had been radicalized and adopted the ideology of Islamic extremism. However, it is not clear if Hasan acted as a "terrorist" or a psychopathic mass murderer.

Cyber terrorism

The next generation of terrorists will grow up in a digital world, with ever more powerful and easy-to-use hacking tools at their disposal. They might see greater potential for cyber terrorism than the terrorists of today, and their level of knowledge and skill relating to hacking will be greater. Hackers and insiders might be recruited by terrorists or become self-recruiting cyber terrorists, the Timothy McVeighs of cyberspace. Some might be moved to action by cyber policy issues, making cyberspace an attractive venue for carrying out an attack. Cyber terrorism could also become more attractive as the real and virtual worlds become more closely coupled, with a greater number of physical devices attached to the Internet (Denning, 2000).

The current state of cyberspace is such that information is seriously at risk. The impact of this risk to the physical health of mankind is, at present, indirect. Computers do not, at present, control sufficient physical processes, without human intervention, to pose a significant risk of terrorism in the classic sense (Pollitt, nd).

Future of Terrorism

As this text has indicated, it has been widely reported that the main threat to the national security of the United States emanates from al-Qaeda and radical Islamic extremism. According to the latest intelligence accounts the Taliban has started to reassert themselves in Afghanistan and Pakistan. As previously stated, we cannot predict the future but one thing is certain terrorism is here to stay.

Al-Qaeda has extended its organizational tentacles to countries throughout the world. The United States has been working tirelessly to counter the aggression of al-Qaeda by training the law enforcement and security forces of our allies. American intelligence officials strongly believe that Osama bin Laden is hiding out in the treacherous mountain region located on the Pakistan-Afghanistan border. The Pakistan government has initiated a military campaign against the Taliban and al-Qaeda members residing in this region in an attempt to flush them out. As long as people are politically and economically deprived there will be acts of terrorism. Until the free world can eliminate the root causes of terrorism, people will continue to turn to terrorism to achieve their goal.

References

Denning, D. (2000). Cyberterrorism. Retrieved November 25, 2009,
    From www.cs.georgetown.edu/~denning/infosec/cyberterror-GD.doc

Pollitt, M. (nd). Cyberterrorism, Fact or Fancy? Retrieved November 25, 2009,
    From www.cs.georgetown.edu/~denning/infosec/pollitt.html